O9-BTI-521

ROCKHURST COLLEGE LIBRARY
0 0006 0088049 6

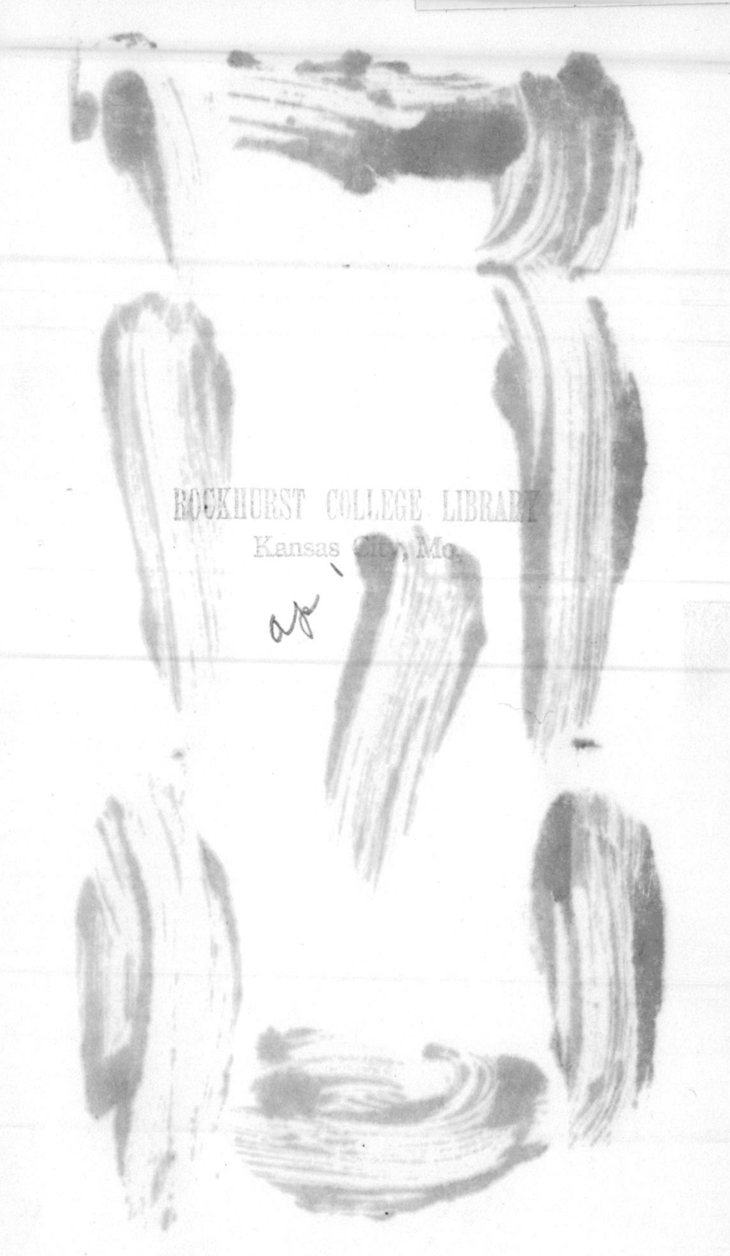

Principles of

Economic Policy

KENNETH E. BOULDING
Professor of Economics
University of Michigan

Principles of Economic Policy

Englewood Cliffs, N. J. • PRENTICE-HALL, INC. • *1958*

Library of Congress
Catalog Card No.: 58-7320

PRINTED IN THE UNITED STATES OF AMERICA

70902

Preface

Principles is a well-worn word; nevertheless, I could not have written this book if I had not believed that there are statable principles of economic policy, the understanding of which enables both the policy maker and the public to form wiser judgments in these matters. A study of economic policy is an introduction to economic principles. Policy is not one thing and principles another; the principles of economic policy are the principles of economics.

These principles do not provide quick answers for every occasion. They are a rather small-scale map of the great world of economic policy, and they do not give guidance in detail. A map is not a substitute for the land itself and should not be mistaken for reality. Without a map, however, it is easy to get lost in territory as wild and unfamiliar as this is. The development of better maps of economic policy has been one of the major achievements of the twentieth century. Reading this volume is not enough to make the reader an economist, but it will give him some notion of the "lay of the land," which he might not otherwise have.

Both the general reader and the student will find this an introduction to the principles of economics rather than to its techniques. Techniques have their place and are essential to the more advanced study of the subject. They appear in abundance in my *Economic Analysis,* the first part of which, at least, may be used as a supplement to the present volume. Principles, however, are more fundamental than techniques and can be understood without mastering the techniques in great detail.

Burdensome detail has been avoided as far as possible in this book. Factual material illustrates principles. This is neither an attempt at an encyclopedic coverage nor a discussion at a high level of abstraction. The volume began as a revision of *The Economics of Peace,* published in 1945. It soon became clear, as I began the revision, that the enterprise was going to turn into a completely new book. A small amount of material from the earlier book is included in chapters 2 and 4; but apart from that, the present volume is entirely new material. In the first part, the general objectives of economic policy are outlined. In the second part, application is made to the major specific areas of policy: fiscal, financial, income maintenance and social security, commercial and trade policies, and, finally, policies towards business, labor, and agriculture, with a chapter on the special problems of war and peace and another on the world economic perspective. The final chapter ties the work together with ethics, for at the policy level, economics without ethics is a lever without a fulcrum.

KENNETH E. BOULDING

Contents

1

What is economic policy?

Our policy, to be effective,
Must chase a suitable objective,
So, our economy should be
Both Growing, Stable, Just, and Free.
The Dog would surely be a Dunce
Who tried to chase four things at once,
Yet this is just the way we plan
The task of Economic Man!

The definition of policy. The word "policy" generally refers to the principles that govern action directed towards given ends. Any study of policy therefore should concern itself with three things—what we want (the ends), how we get it (the means), and who are "we," that is, what is the nature of the organization or group concerned.

Science is concerned with means rather than with ends. The study of "what we want" (objectives) extends beyond the boundaries of the social sciences into the field of ethics. It is not the business of the social sciences to evaluate the ultimate ends of human activity. The social sciences, therefore, cannot give a final answer to the question whether any given policy is "right." The social scientist can study what people say they want, what they think they want, and may even infer from their behavior what they "really" want, but it is not the business of science to say whether people want the right things. The critique of ends—that is, the discussion of what are the right things to want—is more in the province of the philosopher or the theologian than of the scientist.

Nevertheless, the social scientist can make important contributions to the discussion of objectives. He can point out, for instance, that many things that people think are ends are in fact means to some further end, and that a discussion that seems to be about ends may be more easily resolved if it can be stated in terms of a choice of means to some further end. He may also usefully point out that human activity seldom has but one objective, and that there are many ends, some of which may not be compatible. We want peace, but we do not want the things that make for peace; we want health, but we do not want the things that make for health; we want riches, but we also want things that make for poverty.

The search for regularities. The scientist is a good deal happier with the study of "how we get it" than with the study of "what we want." Means are his peculiar province. Scientific knowledge is almost equivalent to "know how," or skill. The greatest test of its validity is the ability to predict—that is, to devise forms of action with known consequences. What all science is looking for—and social science is no exception to this rule—is *regularities* in the universe. Where there is chaos there can be no science.

Unfortunately there is a good deal of chaos in the social universe. Many of the difficulties of the social sciences arise not from the difficulties of finding out the truth, but from the absence of any clear "truth" to be found out. Neither individual nor social behavior is always regular, and insofar as it is not regular its regularities cannot be discovered. We are often looking in the dark room for the black cat that isn't there.

Regularity commoner in mass than in individual behavior. Nevertheless, the situation is not all chaos. There are important regularities both in individual and social behavior. Indeed, the study of social behavior—*i.e.,* the behavior of aggregate quantities that are the summation of large numbers of individual events or characteristics—is more likely to lead to the detection of regularities than is the study of individual behavior. This is because of the principle of statistical law—that random variations in individuals become of secondary importance when the behavior of a mass of individuals is studied. Thus the behavior of the individual molecules of a gas is almost impossible to predict, whereas the behavior of a large aggregate of molecules is both regular and predictable. Similarly we may be much more sure about the response of a whole market to a change in a price than we are about the response of a single individual. The analogy must not be pressed too far—movements of infection and fashion exist in human populations that do not exist among molecules, and we cannot assume that all nonpredictable variations are random.

Identities. Beside the study of observable regularities (empirical law) the social scientist is also concerned with certain necessary and inescapable relationships called *identities.* In economics especially, identities have an important part to play. An identity is a relationship among various quantities that is true by definition. Most identities ultimately are derived from the proposition that any whole is equal to the sum of its parts. Any population can be broken down into two or more parts, and the total number of individuals in the whole population must be equal to the sum of the numbers in the various parts. Thus if the number of people in a room is A, and there are X people in the room with red hair and Y people whose hair is not red, then we know that $A \equiv X + Y$.[1] Identities can also be constructed by identifying two different breakdowns of a given whole. Thus if there are X people with red hair and Y people with "not-red" hair, H people with blue eyes and K people with not-blue eyes in a room, then, $X + Y \equiv H + K$. Both the sides of this identity are identical with the total number of people in the room. Identities can also be expressed in the multiplicative form—multiplying being only a shorthand form of adding. Thus the area of a rectangle is identically equal to the product of two adjacent sides. The total amount of steel used in a given period in automobiles is equal to the average amount of steel per automobile multiplied by the number of automobiles.

Identities are interesting if they coordinate decisions. An identity, once stated, is obviously true, and for this very reason many people have thought that identities could not be interesting. Not all identities, of course, are interesting—it is difficult to see any great significance in the one about red-haired people. Nevertheless some identities are very interesting, because the quantities in them may reflect independent decisions by unrelated groups of people. Suppose, for instance, that one committee decided how much steel was going to be allotted to automobiles, another committee decided how much steel the average automobile was going to contain, and still another decided how many automobiles should be produced. It is evident that though these decisions might be made independently, the results of these decisions would, willy-nilly, be coordinated by the existence of the identity mentioned above. If the first committee allocated a million tons of steel for automobiles, the second committee decided to put half a ton of steel into each automobile, and the third committee decided to produce three million automobiles, it is evident that at least one of these decisions would not be carried through! Either more steel would have to be allocated, or less steel would have to be put into each automobile, or fewer automobiles would have to be produced,

[1] Identities are usually distinguished by the sign $\equiv$ from *equations* which have the sign $=$. Identities are true for all values of the variables concerned; equations are true only for some value or values of the variables.

or some combination of these adjustments would have to be made. Exactly what adjustments would be made would depend on the dynamics of the decision-making process—generally it is the decisions that are adjustable that get adjusted! It is the basic identity, however, that imposes upon the system the eventual correlation and coordination of decisions.

Economic identities: the "bathtub theorem." Many of the basic identities of society are not immediately obvious, and it is one of the principal tasks of economic and social analysis to detect and state them. The interesting identities are those related in some way to the decision-making processes, for it is the potential incompatibility between the sum of decisions and the basic identities (as in the above example) that creates disappointments and dynamic readjustments. Some of the basic identities of economics may be mentioned here, and will be elaborated later. The first I have elsewhere, somewhat frivolously, called the "bathtub theorem." It is that the total addition to the stock of any item in a given period must be equal to the number of items produced (created), less the number of items consumed (destroyed). The stock of any item may be compared to the water in a bathtub. Production is like water running from the faucet, adding to the total stock. Consumption is like water running out of the drain, subtracting from the total stock. If production exceeds consumption, the excess must be equal to the rate of accumulation. If consumption exceeds production, the excess must be equal to the rate of decumulation, or negative accumulation.

The "material balances" identity. Closely related to the above identity is the *material balances* identity, which states that the sum of all the amounts of any given item consumed must be equal to the amount produced, less the amount accumulated (added to stocks). If the amount of materials of various kinds that go into the production of a given product is fixed, this identity imposes limitations on the amounts of all the various products of society that can be produced at the same time. Thus the production of all the various products that are made of steel is limited by the amount of steel production, plus the subtractions from, or minus the additions to, the stockpile of steel. An essentially similar identity is that the total number of people employed must equal the number of people available for employment, minus the number of people not employed. This holds for any particular form of labor as well as for labor as a whole. A similar identity holds for land—that the total number of acres devoted to all the various uses must be equal to the total area of land available for use or withdrawn from use.

The monetary identities. The above identities might be called the "real commodity" identities, as they relate quantities of production and consumption of goods. There are also important identities in the monetary system. The first is that the total stock of money must be equal to the sum of the money holdings in all particular accounts. This identity may seem very obvious, but the failure to understand it has caused a great deal of confusion in economic thinking. Another is that the total amount of money paid for anything is equal to the value of what is bought, which in turn is equal to the price multiplied by the quantity bought. There are also "balance sheet" identities, based on the necessary equality between net worth and the sum of all assets less the sum of all liabilities.

The basic identities define the limits of possibility. These identities serve to limit the social and economic universe to a certain area of possibility—they serve, that is to say, to define the impossible. The economic universe is described by listing all the economic quantities in a society—all prices, wages, interest rates, incomes, assets, property rights, taxes, expenditures, quantities of all commodities or securities consumed, produced, and accumulated, and so on. Any combination of these innumerable quantities, or any "position" of the economic universe that violates any of the basic identities, is clearly impossible. We cannot consume and accumulate more or less than we produce. Net worths cannot increase by more than net assets increase. We cannot currently produce more than our resources in labor, land, and capital permit. We cannot add to capital, and hence cannot increase future production, if production plus imports does not exceed consumption plus exports. We cannot have positive balances of payments in all accounts or for all countries at the same time. Average per-capita income cannot exceed total income divided by the total population. If the income going to one segment of society is increased, then either the national income must be raised, or the income going to other sections must be decreased. These are the great platitudes of economics, and they are no less important for being platitudes. A platitude, indeed, is a proposition that is so obvious that most people forget that it is true. It is an important service to the policymaker to fence off the impossible, for effort directed towards the impossible is apt to be wasted.

Empirical relationships define the *probable*. The possible, however, is a very big field, and it is easy to get lost in it. Analysis can do something more than to delimit the possible; it can draw a smaller, though vaguer, fence around the probable. Great areas of the possible are not probable. Thus is it possible that a sharp increase in taxes (other things equal) might have an inflationary effect, but it is much more probable that the effect would be deflationary. It is possible that a rise in the price of a commodity might increase its consumption, but it is more probable that consumption would be decreased. Just as the basic identities separate the possible from the impossible, so the basic empirical relationships or the observed regularities of the system separate the probable from the improbable. This separation is not as clear nor as certain as the separation between the possible and the impossible, but it exists, and the more accurately the regularities of the system can be observed, the narrower can be drawn the circle of the probable. Here again economic analysis, and especially quantitative empirical research, should be an important aid to the policymaker. We should think twice before attempting to attain the highly improbable. Insofar as economics can help in assessing the degree of probability of various consequences of proposed lines of policy, it helps in assessing the proposals' value.

Can we define the "optimum"? Even when we have delimited the most probable part of the economic universe we have still not solved the problem of what is the best policy, for within the probable area there remain a very large number of possible combinations of policies with all the various variables of the system. The question whether the area of reasonable choice of policies can be delimited even further has occupied a good deal of attention in recent years. The area of economic analysis known as "welfare economics" is largely occupied with this question. This subject is highly technical. A very rough idea of its methods and conclusions should, however, be given here.

The welfare function: astrology as "welfare astronomy." The central problem of welfare economics is the definition of an "optimum" or "best" position or set of positions of the economic universe. Curiously enough the problem is almost identical with that of astrology. The astrologer regards certain positions of the heavenly bodies as more "favorable" than others for certain individuals or groups, or even for mankind as a whole. That is, he regards certain positions of the astronomical universe as "better" or "worse" than others. He is postulating, in other words, what economists call a "welfare function" related to the astronomical universe, so that each position of the universe can be tagged with some measure or index of "goodness" for some purpose or another. The astronomer, on the other hand, either denies that such an astronomical welfare function exists, or at least is not interested in it—he is merely interested in the interrelationships and movements of the heavenly bodies, and as far as he is concerned one position is just as good as another.

The economic welfare function. Similarly the pure economist studies a universe, consisting not of the positions, masses, movements and so on of heavenly bodies, but of prices, quantities, exchanges, outputs, and so on of those things that can be classified as commodities. This universe, like the astronomer's universe, can be studied without any thought of a welfare function —the student simply observing what are, or predicting what might be, the magnitudes of all these quantities without any reference to the question whether one set of magnitudes is better or worse than another set. In the case of the economic universe, however, most of us have a strong conviction that welfare functions of some sort exist, a conviction which we do not generally have about the astronomical universe. The difference between an income of $1,000 a year and one of $10,000 is not merely of intellectual interest. Most of us feel that certain levels of income, certain distributions of income, certain rates of economic development, certain sets of economic institutions, are not merely different from, but are better or worse than others.

Policy implies control for welfare. Indeed, if this were not so the concept of policy would be meaningless. We do not have a policy towards the planets, not only because we are powerless to affect their motions, but because even if we had power over them, one set of motions is just as good as another set, so why bother. This situation might be changed, of course, if some wandering asteroid threatened to crash into the earth, or if it were discovered that certain heavenly bodies gave off hitherto unsuspected radiations that had a profound effect on human conduct and welfare. We do have policies in regard to the economic universe, not only because we believe we have a degree of control over this universe, but also because prices, incomes, wages, and so on are affected with human welfare, so that we regard one set of these quantities as better than another.

The "Paretian optimum." The problem of welfare economics, then, is how far can we go by means of "scientific" analysis towards defining the "best" position of any given economic universe. There have been two main schools of thought. One, associated mainly with the names of Pareto and Hicks,[2] has attempted to define a set of conditions according to the principle that any change that makes somebody better off, but nobody worse off, is desirable. The other school, represented by Bergson and Samuelson, contents itself with postulating the existence of any number of welfare functions related to the preferences or interests of various individuals and groups, and drawing certain rather formal conclusions regarding the advice that economists

[2] For further discussion of this problem (and a bibliography) see K. E. Boulding, "Welfare Economics," in *A Survey of Contemporary Economics, Vol. II,* ed. B. F. Haley (Homewood, Ill.: Richard D. Irwin, Inc., 1952).

might give to the various "clients." The first school seems to assume too much. It involves a number of ethical judgments that might not be shared by everyone—it attaches a high value to "trading," for instance, as opposed to "conflict," it assumes that people not only know what they want but should get it, and it assumes that there is never any positive value in somebody being made worse off. Nevertheless it is useful in that it shows that certain not implausible hypotheses regarding what we want can be used to narrow the field of possible choice of desirable policies, and it has served to clarify the nature of the value judgments that underlie policy recommendations.

The general welfare function. The second school perhaps assumes too little, and ends up with practically no conclusions at all. Nevertheless, the concept of a welfare function is a very valuable one, and it should be possible to explore the welfare function of various individuals by a judicious process of questioning and discussion in such a way as to clarify its general form and reveal any inconsistencies. It is evident that in any fairly homogeneous society something like a general consensus emerges out of political and economic discussion, and it is not therefore unreasonable to assume that over certain ranges of possible positions of the economic universe, the welfare functions—that is, the value systems—of most individuals are rather similar. If this were not so, no political process would be possible. We have cases, indeed, like the conflict between the communist and the capitalist worlds, in which the divergence in basic value judgments seems to be so strong that no political consensus is possible. One of the deepest roots of war, whether civil or international, is the breakdown of the political process as a result of divergences in welfare functions—divergences too great for the existing political machinery to handle.

Who are "we"?—the power state. We have seen that the discussion of policy of any kind, and of economic policy in particular, involves the questions "what do we want?" and "how do we get it?" Perhaps the most difficult question of all is the third—"who are *we*?" In the days of the mercantilists the answer was a fairly simple one—the "we" in the interests of whom economic policy was devised was the ruling class of the state. Government regulation of economic life was conceived to be aimed at increasing the power, and especially the military power, of the state, the state being conceived not as an aggregate of all its citizens but as an instrument of the men of power who controlled it. Thus an important objective of mercantilist policy was to keep wages low, in order to force the workers to work hard, produce much, and consume little, and so leave a large surplus of product for export or for the other uses of the state. The workers were thus thought of as instruments, much as cattle and machines were instruments, in producing economic goods for the ruling group. The very concept of a "subject" as opposed to that of a "citizen" had implicit in its early meaning the idea that the bulk of the human population of a state were mere instruments of the will of the king.

The "general welfare" state. With the rise in the concept of the "citizen" and the growth of democratic institutions the concept of the "power state" has been challenged by that of the "general welfare state"—a state that exists to promote the general welfare of *all* its inhabitants. The northwest European countries, the United States, and the British dominions have all felt the impact of this concept. It is, of course, a concept that has not remained unchallenged. Fascism is a very clear return to a mercantilist view of the state as an end rather than as a means. Communism is a more subtle and hence even more dangerous version of the same doctrine, in which a small group claims the right to administer the whole apparatus of society ostensibly on behalf of the whole population (once dissident elements have been exterminated!) but in fact without any adequate check on the power or even the whim of the controlling group.

Whose welfare?—the distribution problem. The concept of the general welfare, however, is not a clear or an easy one. The question "whose welfare?" is only dodged when we say "everybody's." It is almost impossible to carry out any policy, for instance, without affecting in some degree the distribution of income. Even if—according to the standards of the Pareto-Hicks brand of welfare economics—our policy makes some people richer and nobody poorer, there will still be complaints: "Why should he get richer and not I?" It does not seem to be possible, therefore, either in theory or in practice, to concentrate simply on increasing aggregate income or welfare without committing ourselves as to how it should be distributed. Even if the result of our policy is to increase everybody's economic welfare by an equal amount, or an equal percentage, there will still be objections, and fingers will still point at "happy, undeserving *A*" and "wretched, meritorious *B*."

Solution by ignorance: the impact of deflation and inflation on distribution. In American society we try to solve this problem partly by sheer ignorance, partly by a curious process of pressure, propaganda, and compromise. One suspects sometimes that ignorance plays such an important part in achieving practical policies that one wonders about the virtues of too great an increase in knowledge. Thus inflation and deflation are by far the most important agencies in changing the distribution of income, and this has been especially so in the past three or four decades. Indeed, all the other forces affecting the distribution of income—the rise of the labor movement, the development of agricultural policy, the tariff, even the progressive income tax itself, all taken together have not achieved half the revolution in the distribution of both income and wealth that decades of successive inflation, deflation, and inflation have achieved. Nevertheless there is remarkably little awareness of this fact. Political agitation continues to be concentrated on such relatively minor issues (in this connection) as labor unionism or agricultural subsidies; such matters as the enormous decline of interest as a share in the national income from 1933 to 1955, or the elimination of corporate profit in 1931-1932, pass almost unnoticed.

Policy as "justice." Where there is not enough ignorance to be bliss, however, policy is hammered out between the hammer of organized pressure groups and the anvil of electoral opinion. People have in their private welfare functions certain elementary notions of what constitutes economic justice, and policy results partly from the ability of organized groups to capture on behalf of their own group part of this desire for justice, and partly, it must also be admitted, by a process of log rolling and mutual back-scratching. We are all, or nearly all, uneasy if people starve, if children are hungry or are not being educated, if farmers are depressed, if private interests seem to be getting too powerful, or if there is large-scale unemployment, even if we are not personally affected by these evils. Consequently we are willing to vote for—or our congressmen or state and local authorities think we are willing to vote for—relief, public education, aid to agriculture, anti-trust and labor relations acts, public works and deficit financing, and so on.

Policy as an outcome of political processes. Nobody pretends that the political process, even in the most democratic of societies, produces perfect policies. Nevertheless it is the process by which policies are produced, and economists cannot afford to neglect it. Economists have a certain rather lofty tendency to frame policies without regard to their political feasibility, and then to denounce the political process, with suitable sneers, for not producing what the economist regards as desirable. There is some case for trying to develop an analysis of "ideal" economic policy, without regard to the political process, in order to set up a rough standard by which the results of the political process can be evaluated. Such a standard, however, can be no more than very rough, for in the very definition of an ideal policy certain elements of political process must be included. Statements to the effect that certain policies are "economically desirable but politically impossible" should be treated with the greatest reserve, for economic analysis does not produce a clear and unequivocal standard by which policies can be judged "economically desirable." It delimits an area of the impossible, as we have seen. It can also indicate an area of more or less probable consequences. It can indicate areas of greater or less probable wisdom. What it cannot do is to point its finger at a specific "best spot" in the economic universe.

The extension of the "we." The ethical problem involved in the question "who are we?" is not completely solved even by the institutions of the general-welfare state. Should economic policy be directed only towards the welfare of the inhabitants of a particular country, or should it be directed towards the welfare of all mankind? Are "we" merely the people who happen to be fortunate enough to live between the Atlantic and Pacific oceans, and the Canadian and Mexican boundaries, or are "we" all western peoples, or all the human race, or all living creatures, or what? The question is not an easy one to answer, either in terms of what people actually believe or of what people ought to believe. A rational ethic would certainly suggest that it is unreasonable to narrow the bounds of our concern to any particular group—why should folks in Maine be concerned about the welfare of Californians three thousand miles away, and not about the welfare of New Brunswickers next door to them? In a day when the choice before us may well be one world or none the narrowing of the scope of national policy to the national interest can be attacked on the grounds of plain dollars-and-cents economics as well as on the level of high ethical principles. The attempts on the part of each nation to maximize the welfare of its own citizens, without regard to the welfare of those outside the national group, can easily result in the beggarment of all, just as the attempt of each nation to provide for its own security can result in the insecurity of all.

The ecological approach: ecological equilibrium. The problem of the meaning of economic policy can be made more clear if we look at human society somewhat as the biologists look at the "society" of all living things. This is known as the "ecological approach." It is one of the basic ideas of almost all science. In any community of living things, such as a pond, a prairie, or a forest, we find large numbers of different species, in varying numbers, all acting and interacting upon each other. Some species compete with one another, so that an increase in each leads to a decrease of the other. Some species are mutually complementary, so that an increase of each leads to an increase of the other. Some exist in a parasitic or predatory relationship—the more of the host, the more of the parasite, but the more of the parasite, the less of the host. There are complex food chains—*A* is eaten by *B*, which is eaten by *C*, and so on. There are nutritive cycles, the essential food elements passing continuously through the bodies of many different species in a system of "trade"; thus animals take in (import) oxygen and give out (export) carbon dioxide; plants take in carbon dioxide and give out oxygen.

All these complex relationships, however, generally result in something like an equilibrium, at least in the short run. Remove 10 per cent of the fish from a pond, and in a relatively short while the fish population will be back to where it was before. If new species are introduced into a previously stable environment, either they will disappear in a relatively short time or they will find a "niche" somewhere in the system and create a universal readjustment of the various populations, displacing some and perhaps encouraging others.

Society as an ecosystem. In a rather similar way human society can be regarded as an ecological system, or "ecosystem," something like a great pond, filled not with fish and frogs, plants and bacteria, but with workers and employers, gas stations and power companies, counties, states, and nations, churches and lodges, automobiles and refrigerators, wheat and steel and uranium, and all the innumerable "species" of social life, organizations, households, businesses and commodities of all kinds. These populations of social species act and interact on each other in a great variety of ways. Some are mutually competitive—the more television sets, the fewer movie houses, both competing for "nutrition" in the form of the consumers' dollar. Some are mutually cooperative or complementary, like automobiles and gas stations. Some have parasitic relationships—the more cops, the fewer robbers, but the more robbers, the more cops! It is not unreasonable, however, in any given set of conditions to postulate a short-run equilibrium, in the sense of a set of populations the numbers of which are mutually consistent one with another. If this equilibrium is stable, then a small disturbance of any one population will set forces in motion tending to restore the original condition.

The irreversible processes. The equilibrium of society is constantly being disturbed. It may be disturbed by forces operating from outside the society itself. Thus the introduction of European man into the American continent has profoundly altered its whole structure of life, both human and nonhuman, and is still in the process of altering it. Equilibrium positions can also be changed by forces operating within the system itself. These are the nonreversible or cumulative changes that occur as a result of the processes and interactions of the system. Thus a pond gradually fills up, not only because soil is washed into it from "outside," but because plants in their processes of life and death absorb elements from the air and so gradually deposit a layer of solid matter on the bottom of the pond. In the processes of human society capital accumulates, both in the form of buildings, roads, and equipment and also in the form of knowledge and skill. Each year therefore society starts its operations from a new level, and it never returns to the old.

Ecological succession. The process by which the cumulative changes in a system gradually revolutionize its character is known as "ecological succession." It is convenient to think of this process as a succession of short-run equilibrium positions, each of which passes into the next, even though in fact the change may be continuous and no "equilibrium" ever stays put for very long. The process of ecological succession clearly takes place in human society. History, indeed, is largely the record of how one type of society is transformed into another, sometimes by invasions from without, sometimes by transformations from within. This process is fairly continuous, especially the latter, though occasionally changes take place so rapidly that they are given the name of "revolutions." Any division of history into epochs or stages, such as the "tribal economy," the "manorial system," the "domestic system," "industrial capitalism" and the like is bound to be arbitrary, though it is convenient for purposes of discourse.

Stationary states. Some conditions of society, both human and nonhuman, have reproduced themselves without perceptible change for such long periods that they deserve to be called "stationary states"—*i.e.*, a *realized* equilibrium in which each generation exactly reproduces its forebears, in which each year is exactly like the last, and in which there is birth, death, and reproduction of individuals but no history to the society. Paleolithic man is supposed to have remained in an essentially stationary condition for about half a million years. It seems almost inconceivable to modern man, that generation should succeed generation for about twenty thousand generations with sons and daughters virtual replicas of their fathers and mothers in habits, customs, and artifacts. Since the dawn of civilization man has been subject to—and has introduced—rates of change in the whole ecosystem of the earth that seem to be unique in the earth's history. So accustomed are we to rapid change and development that it is well to remember that in the long perspective of geological time the period of the last six thousand years is probably unique, and that periods of practically stationary equilibrium have been the almost universal rule.

Policy as ecological distortion. We are now in a position to get an ecological perspective on the meaning of economic policy. "Policy" is the deliberate distortion of the ecosystem in favor of the objectives of the policymaker. Thus agriculture is the process by which man distorts the ecosystem of a piece of land away from those species and populations that it would "naturally" contain in his absence, towards a quite different set of populations and species that he regards as more "favorable," that is, that are closer to his objectives. Land that in the absence of man bears forests, bears, deer, and beavers is thus forced to yield oats, corn, cows and sheep. This "distortion" of the natural system is achieved by action directed at diminishing the unwanted species (cutting down trees, hoeing weeds, shooting predators) and at increasing the wanted species—planting oats and corn, breeding cattle, and so on. The particular crops that the farmer encourages depend on his objectives. Insofar as financial reward is his objective, he will encourage the "profitable" at the expense of the "unprofitable" species, and the profit-and-loss account will determine whether he will raise trees, grains, or grass; corn or oats; cattle or sheep; cotton or tobacco. Nonfinancial objectives may also enter in. Plants and animals that are not profitable in the accountant's book may be encouraged because of aesthetic, cultural, or other values.

Economic policy as "social agriculture." In a rather similar way we can regard social or economic policy on a broader scale as a kind of "social agriculture," a deliberate distortion of the "natural" organization of society in favor of the objectives of the policymaker—raising up honest artisans instead of robbers, happy families instead of broken homes, productive and progressive enterprises instead of exploitative monopolies, city dwellers instead of rural folk (or the reverse), collective farms instead of peasant proprietors (or the reverse), milk instead of whiskey, and so on through the whole gamut of social organizations, ideas, ideals, characters and commodities.

Ecology and ethics. Looked at in this way the threefold nature of the problem of policy becomes even clearer—the what, the how, and the who! Policy obviously must always include a "what," even if the "what" is only a direction rather than a goal. We must know something about what direction of possible change is desired or desirable. Policy must also include the "how"—that is, the laws and relationships that define the possible positions of the social ecosystem, and the relations between the actions of the policymaker and the results of these actions. If we want figs we must not sow thistles. The ecological approach is especially valuable here in that it points up the complexity of these interrelationships, and warns against the possibility of getting some quite unexpected results. Rabbits introduced into Australia became a major pest and drove out the more valuable sheep. Prohibition suppressed saloons but encouraged the growth of speakeasies and gangsters. Organizations for peace may result in the promotion of wars. The more variables we can take into account in framing policy, the less likely we are to be surprised by some unexpected twist that our actions produce. Finally the question of "who" (in whose interests are policies made?) also has ecological overtones. Are we to regard the world of nature simply as a storehouse to be robbed for the immediate benefit of man? Is there such a thing as a "land ethic"—that is, does man have any responsibility for the preservation of a decent balance in nature, for the preservation of rare species, or even for the indefinite continuance of his race? These questions, difficult as they are, are implicit in the discussion of economic policy. It may not be possible to answer them, but it is always important to ask them.

The many dimensions of policy. The chapters that follow are concerned with the major objectives of economic policy. It must be emphasized again that it is impossible to postulate any *single* objective of policy. The various objectives cannot be reduced to one. We may have to sacrifice some of one in order to get more of another; some of them we may be able to pursue concurrently. In any event choices must be made, and what is more difficult, social choices must be made. It is not, perhaps, the business of the economist to say *how* these choices are to be made. He can, however, throw some light on *what* choices are to be made, and what are the real alternatives open.

The four objectives—progress, stabilization, justice, freedom. In the four chapters that follow I have collected the major objectives of economic policy under four heads—economic progress, economic stabilization, economic justice, and economic freedom. These goals are all interrelated, and have complex relations among themselves. Furthermore any set of boxes is bound to be a little arbitrary, and it must not be thought that all the objectives of economic policy fit neatly into one or another of these four categories. Nevertheless, this is a useful system of classification which leaves surprisingly few loose ends, and which gives us an analytical tool for the tentative evaluation of particular policies. The first two—progress and stabilization—are fairly clear, and enjoy the advantage of being roughly measurable by statistical indices. The latter two—justice and freedom—are vague and difficult to measure; nevertheless, they cannot be excluded on that account. Their intrinsic importance in moving the minds of men outweighs their vagueness and difficulty of definition. Indeed, their very vagueness contributes to their importance insofar as it contributes to conflicts and disagreements about them. I have considered whether a fifth objective should not be added which might be called "peace" or "integration." This is not quite the same thing as justice; nevertheless it is so closely related that it can be discussed under the same head. With this possible exception I have not found any objective of economic policy that does not fall easily under one or more of the four headings.

2

Economic progress

The wise economist is loath
To give up anything for Growth,
Though very rapid growth is able
To make a country quite unstable.
Poor countries can't afford to be
Both equal, just, controlled, and free,
So there are many virtues which
Are practiced only by the Rich.

Definition of "objective." An "objective" of economic policy is one of the variables descriptive of the economic system that is "significant," in the sense that either more or less of this quantity is felt to make the system better or worse.

Meaning of economic progress. One of the most important and significant variables in an economic system is its rate of economic progress, or economic development. Economic progress is not altogether easy to define and is even more difficult to measure. Nevertheless, the phrase clearly corresponds to a meaningful idea. We have only to contrast a savage society with our own. In a savage society, the same customs, the same techniques, the same ways of doing everything, from ploughing to praying, are maintained generation after generation, son following exactly in the footsteps of his father and daughter in the footsteps of her mother, without deviating an inch from the well-trodden way. In modern civilized society, on the other hand, there is constant change and flux; we are constantly improving on the methods of our ancestors, and indeed one of the surest ways to discredit anything is to call it "old-fashioned!" There are, indeed, cynical souls who see in this turmoil and bustle only change and not progress and who, perhaps, even sigh for the charm of a vanished day. But most of us, in spite of the terrors of modern warfare, would not readily change places with the past; we look from our day of electric light and automobiles to the days even a century ago of candles and coaches with a sense of great technical superiority, touched only with a twinge of sentimental regret. Probably not even the staunchest medievalist, were he really to be plunged into the smells and filth and inconvenience of a medieval household, would willingly exchange it for the cleanliness and sanitation of the twentieth century. In spite of an uneasy feeling that spiritually and intellectually we may not cut a remarkably good figure beside our ancestors, we have a certain confidence that we excel them in economic matters; that economic progress is not a vague and unreal thing, but a real experience of humankind which can be experienced even within the lifetime of a single individual.

Economic progress consists of improved means and does not concern ends. There is good reason for this belief. Economic progress consists in an improvement in the efficiency of the use of means to attain ends. Whenever we discard an old method of doing something in favor of a new method that has proved its worth without doubt, then economic progress is taking place. Economic progress, therefore, means the discovery and application of better ways of doing things to satisfy our wants. The piping of water to a household that previously dragged it from a well, the growing of two blades of grass where one grew before, the development of a power loom that enables one man to weave ten times as much as he could before, the use of steam power and electric power instead of horse or human power—all these things clearly represent economic progress.

This definition also enables us to account for our uneasy feeling that economic progress is not always progress in the noblest sense of the word. Economic progress is concerned solely with means, not with ends. It enables us to get what we want more easily than before, but it says nothing about the propriety of what we want. If we want the wrong things, then economic progress may enable us to damn ourselves all the more quickly and allow us to travel to hell at a hundred miles an hour instead of at ten. Indeed, economic progress makes a critique of wants all the more necessary, for the better we are able to satisfy our wants the more important it is that our wants should be "good" wants. We can see this clearly in the life of an individual. Increasing wealth is economic progress to an individual—for it gives him greater power to satisfy his wants. But the records are full of people who have been damned by a sudden increase in riches; whose wants were of such an undesirable character that while they did not have the power to satisfy them, they got along fairly well, but as soon as the power to satisfy these undesirable wants was granted, licentiousness, debauchery, and ruin followed.

Does progress debauch ends? The same may even be true of nations and societies. Indeed, one may question whether it is not true of our own society; whether the tremendous increase in riches that has occurred in the last hundred years or so has not actually perverted our taste, debauched our cultural life, and permitted us to indulge in wars of a scale and extravagance that poorer ages never dreamed of. It is sobering to reflect that we seem to be turning our surplus wealth and energies to destruction rather than to building up a nobler life for all, and one may be forgiven for wondering whether our boasted economic progress has not merely enabled us to destroy one another rather more expeditiously than our grandfathers were able to do.

It can be argued, therefore, by the more pessimistic, that economic progress is an undesirable quantity, and that the less of it the better. Many societies, indeed, have so argued, and argue to this day. It is an essential characteristic of a tradition-centered society that any movement away from the traditions is regarded as undesirable. In spite of the case against economic progress, however, it is a counsel of despair to advocate its suppression. Rather should we be concerned to see that moral and spiritual progress go hand-in-hand with economic progress—that our ability to want the right things improves along with our ability to satisfy our wants. Otherwise, there is nothing to do but to sulk in our tents. There is something in the world that drives us forward, and in spite of all the cynics and the standpats, the faith in progress is a persistent part of our spiritual equipment. Even though progress in the fullest sense of the word must include progress in the character of our wants as well as in the ability to satisfy them, economic progress is an essential part of this process and should not be despised simply because it is not the whole story.

Economic progress is important because our means are limited. If economic progress, then, signifies an increase in the efficiency of the use of means to satisfy our wants, we must know what those means are and why they are *limited*. It is the fact that our means are limited that makes economic progress significant—obviously, if we had unlimited means at our disposal, the efficiency of their use would be unimportant, as we could satisfy our wants completely no matter how inefficiently the resources were used. We must ask, therefore, what is the most fundamental limitation on our ability to satisfy our wants? The answer clearly lies in the fact that we each have only twenty-four hours a day to spend, and can never under any circumstances have any more time to spend than we have. The limitation of our natural resources—the "niggardliness of the soil" or of the sea or of mines—is also an important factor in preventing us from getting all that we want, but even this is secondary to the fundamental limitation of *time*. The scarcity or abundance of natural resources, or even of capital equipment, affects our wealth chiefly through its effect on the efficiency of the expenditure of man-time. When natural resources and capital equipment are plentiful, then we can do a great deal in an hour and produce a large quantity of satisfactions; when natural resources and capital equipment are scarce, we can only do a little in an hour, and can therefore produce only a small quantity of satisfactions. The fundamental quantity, however, is the "efficiency of the expenditure of man-time"—that is, the "output per man-hour"—output ultimately, of course, of want-satisfactions.

The measurement of economic progress. The measurement of economic progress is a difficult matter, owing to the difficulty of measuring want-satisfactions. Over relatively short periods, a fair measure could be obtained by an index of output of commodities per man-hour. Where comparisons have to be made over decades or centuries, however, the fact that the physical form of output changes makes it almost impossible to obtain a quantitative measure of economic progress. How, for instance, can we measure the change in want-satisfactions occasioned by the displacement of the horse and buggy by the automobile? Or how can we compare the output per man-hour of togas, chariots, and fibulas with the output of trousers, bicycles, and zipper fasteners? Even though an exact quantitative measure may be impossible, however, it may still be possible to define economic progress in a qualitative sense. Whenever one method of doing something displaces another, in the free operation of human choice, we may say after an interval of time long enough to ensure that the new method has had a proper trial, that economic progress has taken place. Thus the fact that the railroad displaced the stagecoach and the automobile displaced the horse and buggy indicates that these changes represent economic progress, assuming that the stagecoach and the railroad, or the horse and buggy and the automobile, represent alternative ways of doing the same thing. This broad definition avoids the difficulty that arises because most techniques do not have single ends in view, but are rather methods of satisfying a bundle of wants. Thus steam-trawling may be a much more efficient way of catching fish than the rod-and-line method, measured simply in the weight of fish caught per man-hour spent. Nevertheless, steam-trawling does not entirely displace rod-and-line fishing, because the latter method possesses a certain attractiveness in itself as a sport and thereby contributes to the satisfaction of wants other than the desire for fish. The fisherman with the rod catches not merely fish, but also the glints from the water, the excitement of the fight, the breath of the wind, and the freshness of the sunshine.

Progress measured by output per man-hour. In spite of the difficulties that are inherent in the measurement of economic progress, we can say with some confidence that it usually takes place whenever there is a rise in the amount of any commodity that can be produced with one man-hour of labor time. In counting the labor time necessary to produce a commodity, of course, we must include the labor necessary to replace the equipment that is used up in the process of production. A machine, for instance, may increase the speed of an operation, but this is not all a net gain in the efficiency of the expenditure of time, for the maintenance and replacement of the machine itself must be counted. A farmer with a combine harvester may be able to harvest four times as much wheat as he could with less elaborate implements, but this does not mean that the efficiency of the expenditure of man-time in wheat production is increased fourfold. A deduction must be made for the man-time necessary to replace the combines as they wear out, and a smaller deduction for the man-time necessary to replace the machines and equipment that make the combine, and so on.

The "significance" of commodities: the order of necessity. Even though it is practically impossible, therefore, to devise any *single* quantitative measure of economic progress, because of the complexity and noncomparability of the output of society at different times, it is possible to give a qualitative definition. Any change that results in the increased output of any valuable thing per man-hour of time expended is economic progress, if the complications resulting from the differing inherent satisfactions derived from different "hours" are neglected. It is possible to go further than this, however, and to assert that there are certain commodities that are more significant than others from the point of view of economic progress. A technical improvement in the production of wheat or bread might reasonably be expected to be more significant than a similar improvement in the production of caviar or lace.

Commodities can be ranged roughly on a scale of "necessity" —necessities being those commodities that are enjoyed at low levels of income, luxuries being those that are enjoyed only at high levels. If commodities are ranged in the order in which they enter the budgets of consumers as income rises, they stand roughly in the order of necessities. Such necessity may be culturally rather than physically determined—many people have died rather than eat unaccustomed food, for instance, but the physical necessities of life will normally be found in the first part of such a scale.

"Importance" and "necessity." We can say, then, that an improvement in the technique of production of a commodity is more significant for economic progress, the more *important* and the more *necessitous* it is. Importance in this connection is measured by the proportion of total resources devoted to the commodity. Clearly a technical improvement in wheat is more significant than a similar improvement in, say, buckwheat. The second part of the proposition is perhaps not quite so clear, and there may be exceptions to this rule. It is almost certain to be true, however, for poor societies. An improvement in the production of necessities *releases* resources for other things, and especially releases them for further economic development. Thus even apart from the relative importance of the commodities, an improvement in agricultural production may be of much greater significance to an underdeveloped area than an improvement in the production methods of luxury articles, for it will enable the country to produce its food needs with fewer people and hence will release labor for industrial development.

The conditions of economic progress. Our measures of economic progress are crude, but they are good enough to show that societies can be classified roughly according to their rate of economic progress. Some societies progress rapidly, some slowly, some not at all, some actually retrogress. One of the most important questions that can be asked of social science is what determines this rate of progress—*why* are some societies progressive, some stagnant, some retrogressive, and what is it in the make-up of societies that accounts for the differences between them?

This is a question that cannot be answered completely within the framework of economics, for the rate of economic progress in a society depends not merely on its economic institutions, but on all its institutions and its whole culture—its religion, its philosophy, its family patterns, its legal system, its customs and habits of daily life, the whole gamut of man's life and environment. Much more work needs to be done on this question before we can be sure of our answers. Nevertheless, we are not wholly ignorant, and certain principles that govern economic progress are fairly clear.

The accumulation of capital and skill. It is clear, for instance, that the two wheels on which economic progress rolls are the accumulation of physical capital, and the development of skilled, educated, and progressive people. The increase in the productivity of man-time, which we have seen is the principal measure of economic progress, is achieved mainly by having better equipment to work with and "better" men to work it—better in that they are more skilled, more adaptable, more educable. These wheels must roll together. It is no use popping a highly complex modern factory into a tribe of simple people and expecting them to be able to run it, or even work in it. Likewise it is no use having a skilled labor force if there is nothing for them to work with.

Investment in goods. To continue the metaphor, the two wheels are in a sense one, or at least have a common axle. This is *investment*—the devoting of resources to *accumulation* rather than to the satisfaction of current needs. Physical capital can only be accumulated if more things are produced than are consumed. A society that lives entirely from hand to mouth, that uses all its resources each day merely to provide enough food and shelter for that day, is caught in a trap of stagnation. It cannot progress, because it cannot accumulate. Consumption wolfs up all that is produced, and there is never any to store up. If, however, a little store of necessities can be accumulated it can be turned into durable equipment of some kind by devoting it to maintaining the makers of durable things—of tools, houses, and so on.

Investment in skill. It may be less obvious that the development of better skills is investment, in almost exactly the same sense in which the accumulation of tools, machines, and stocks of materials is investment. People can become skilled only by withdrawing themselves from the immediate productive activities of society. The student and the apprentice generally consume more than they are immediately producing. The excess of consumption (they hope) is being reflected in an increase in the capital value of their persons, an increase that reflects the improvement in their future productive capacity as a result of the present process of education or training.

If a society, therefore, is to educate and train its people, it must be able to support them during the period of schooling, either by using up previously accumulated stocks of goods or by withdrawing part of what the working members of the society are producing. In the first case the education represents a transformation of capital from the form of consumables to the form of skill. In the second case the education represents an act of saving on the part of the working members of society, who are consuming *less* than they currently produce in order to enable the students to consume *more* than they currently produce.

Motivations for investment. The intimate relationship between economic progress and investment, or the accumulation of capital, either in material or in mental forms, is the guideline to the understanding of the effects on economic progress of institutions, laws, customs, methods of organization, and so on. Foremost among the characteristics of a progressive society must be adequate concepts of property, and institutions that will establish reasonable security of property. Investment will not take place unless someone, somewhere in the society, is motivated to accumulate capital. The institution of property is perhaps the most widespread social arrangement by which people are motivated to accumulate. It operates by giving the accumulator, himself, certain rights in the things that he has managed to accumulate.

The concept of property. The concept of property needs some elaboration in this connection, for it is complex and easily misunderstood. By "property" we do not, of course, mean physical goods themselves, although often in common speech we speak of "property" where the economist would speak of "physical capital." That is to say, we speak of land, or houses, or machines, as "property," meaning the physical things themselves. Actually, however, "property" means a certain *relationship* among men (as owners) concerning physical things; a relationship implying that the owners have certain rights over the use of these physical things, or over the benefits to be derived from their use. These rights are in some sense *exclusive* —that is, the fact that a thing belongs to Mr. *A* implies that he has certain rights in it that other people do not. If I own an automobile, I have the right to drive it whenever I please, subject to certain important limitations, and as a necessary consequence, the right to prevent other people from driving it should I so desire. These "rights" are never absolute, but are always limited in some way by society and by law in the interest of general welfare. My ownership of an automobile does not entitle me to drive it down the wrong side of the street, or park it in front of a fire hydrant, or drive it at 60 miles an hour in a speed zone. Thus, property in any object consists of a "bundle" of rights concerning the object, a bundle that never includes all the possible rights associated with the object, and that may be broadened or narrowed to include more or less of the possible rights as law or custom may decide.

Security of property. It is not enough to have a good legal concept of property; the bundles of rights that constitute property must be *secure* if economic progress is to take place. For as economic progress always, or almost always, involves the accumulation of physical capital, unless the people who accumulate capital are reasonably secure in its possession and administration, it will not be accumulated. Even in the unusual event of "capital-saving inventions," where progress does not involve an increase in the total of capital, it always involves a change in the form of capital, and the new forms will not be created if their owners are not secure in their possession.

Thus, one of the great technical advances was the domestication of the horse. Horsepower could not be used extensively in agriculture, however, unless the farmer was secure in the possession of the horse. If the peasant's horse was likely to be stolen by any marauding band of robbers, or requisitioned by an invading army, the peasant would prefer to dig his land with the less efficient but more protectable spade rather than with a horse and plow. Theft is the worst enemy of economic progress —a fact which is enough to explain why war is so destructive to economic progress, for war is theft on a large and organized scale. Nothing renders property so insecure in the possession of its user than war, and especially civil war. It is no exaggeration to say that war, and not merely defeat in war, has been the cause of the downfall of all past civilizations.

The study of the relationship of property concepts and institutions to economic progress could easily occupy a book in itself. We may notice briefly two important problems: one, the nature of the owner, and the other, not unrelated, the nature of investment in skill and education.

Collective ownership. Property is not necessarily held by individuals. It may also be held by some collective organization —a corporation, a church, a monastery, a cooperative, a collective farm, a city, or a state. The question as to what kind of social organization shall be the property owner is perhaps today's most acute source of controversy, for it is the basis of the ideological dispute between capitalism and communism. The basic concept of property as a bundle of rights applies in all societies, but societies differ sharply in regard to what organization "owns" these rights. The idea of individual property is a fairly late development; in most primitive or even feudal societies property is for the most part owned and administered by a group—a family or tribe. In modern capitalist society a complex mixture of property rights and institutions is to be found. Property may belong to individuals, to families, to organizations of all kinds.

Security in administration of property. From the point of view of the theory of economic progress, security in the administration of property is even more important than security of ownership. A good example is the problem of tenancy. In America and some other countries owner-occupancy is often considered to be the ideal form of land ownership. If the man who operates the farm also owns it he is supposed to be motivated strongly to improve it. A tenant, on the other hand, is traditionally supposed to be careless with the land and equipment which does not belong to him, and unwilling to make improvements the benefits of which flow to the landlord. It is quite possible, however, to devise tenancy laws that give the tenant a great deal of security in administering the property that he does not own, and gives him property rights in improvements that he makes. Under these circumstances tenancy seems no less well adapted, and perhaps even more conducive to economic progress than owner-occupancy.

The organization of investment in skill. The encouragement of investment in personal skill and ability often requires rather special institutions, mainly because the persons in whom the investment is made (for example, students) are not generally capable of financing their own education or training. The investment therefore must be financed either by loans or by gifts. The risks involved in loans of this nature are apt to prevent any large-scale development of them. Gifts, therefore, must generally be relied on, either by the family, by the state or other political body, or by charitable foundations, in order to encourage an adequate investment in skill. In virtually all modern societies the state has had to step in to subsidize education, this being considered too vital a form of investment to leave wholly to private hands.

Frugality as a condition of accumulation. If capital is to be accumulated, as we have seen, production must exceed consumption. Another trait of a society, therefore, that is of importance in determining the rate of economic progress is *frugality*, or the propensity to hold consumption down in order to accumulate. In getting accumulation started in poor societies a frugal disposition of the people is almost essential, otherwise consumption will always press close on the heels of the meager production. Frugality also frequently goes along with a disposition towards hard work. A society of puritans, therefore, practicing simple standards of consumption, working hard, setting little store on leisure, and taking pride in accumulation, can hardly avoid a rapid rate of economic progress—progress, incidentally, which may easily undermine the puritanism that gave rise to it. On the other hand, an idle, pleasure-loving society, setting a high value on activities that are consumptive both of time and of goods, is unlikely to progress rapidly, and may even decline.

Dangers of frugality. The praises of frugality must not, however, be sung too loudly. Frugality is important in societies where there is great need for accumulation, and where the meagerness of the stockpile is the main limiting factor on production. Even in this case collective frugality, whether by the state, as in Russia, or by private corporations, as in the United States, may be more important than individual frugality, though the willingness of the individual to be frugal, that is, his willingness to accept present sacrifices for the sake of accumulation, limits the accumulative power of even the most absolute state. But when accumulation has proceeded to the point where further accumulation become less and less necessary, frugality may become a positive vice. Under certain circumstances, it will result in unemployment, and may even lead to actual retrogression, as in the depression of the 1930's. There are few more dangerous confusions of thought, in the present era, than between frugality and economy. These are frequently identified in the popular mind, and frugality is therefore crowned with all the virtues that belong to economy. Economy is the efficient *use* of resources, of which accumulated wealth forms a part. Frugality is the *accumulation* of wealth through the restriction of consumption. Economy is always desirable; frugality is only a virtue when accumulation is needed—that is, when the stockpile is low, relative to existing techniques.

Competition as a condition of progress. The third condition of progress is *competition,* in the restricted sense of the ability of the superior processes to displace the inferior. The opposite of competition in this sense is *protection* of the inferior methods, that is, the creation of institutions that will prevent the inferior methods from being displaced. It is clear that unless the superior methods are allowed to displace the inferior, the fruits of economic progress cannot be enjoyed. The coming of the railroads inevitably led to the disappearance of the stage coach, the rise of electric light led to the virtual disappearance of illumination by gas or oil, the automobile drove out the buggy, and so on.

The free market as a source of competition. One of the characteristics of a free market economy is a high degree of competition in the above sense. Inferior processes are driven out of existence because all their customers go to the superior ones, or they can only attract customers at prices that are too low for the inferior processes to be profitable. Interferences with the free market also frequently take the form of "protection" in the wide sense used above. It is no accident, therefore, that cultures with relatively free market economies have also frequently been characterized by rapid economic progress. The nineteenth century in England and America is perhaps the best example of this free market economy and economic progress.

It should not be concluded, however, that the free market is the *only* institution by which competition can be introduced into society. At the other end of the scale a ruthless totalitarianism can also suppress, by police action, processes, industries, and populations that it regards as "inferior." The displacement of the peasants by the collective farms in Russia, whether it is economic progress or not, was certainly "competition."

The costs of competition. It should not be inferred that because competition is essential to economic progress that it should of necessity be unregulated. Displaced resources generally present a real social problem, one that can ultimately be solved only by a transfer of these resources into other occupations. The sad story of the handloom weavers [1] is a weighty argument against the unrestricted and impersonal competition of the market. The even sadder story of the Kulaks is a still weightier argument against the unrestricted exercise of police power. There is a legitimate objective of policy in minimizing the *cost,* especially the human cost, of economic progress. The cost is minimized, however, not by protecting those who are threatened with displacement in their old occupations, but by assisting them to move into new ones.

The fallacy of "equalizing competitive advantage." Unfortunately, much present-day thinking on economic matters is based on the attempt to *prevent* the displacement of the inferior processes rather than on the attempt to lower the cost of displacement. The taxation of chain stores, for instance, is often defended on the grounds that they can perform the retailing function more cheaply than the independent stores, and should therefore be taxed to equalize the competitive advantage! The so-called "scientific tariff," which is supposed to equalize competitive advantages between domestic and foreign producers, is an example of the same fallacy. If it were applied rigidly a nation could never benefit from any improvement in techniques that took place outside its boundaries, for its domestic producers would be relieved of the necessity of conforming to improvements that originated abroad!

The fallacy of "parity price." The same fallacy also underlies the "parity price" formula for agricultural commodities.[2] This formula sets up as an ideal of agricultural policy the principle that the purchasing power of agricultural commodities should

[1] See p. 362.
[2] See p. 325.

be constant. If this policy were carried out strictly, the benefits from improvements in agricultural techniques could never be diffused through society in the form of cheaper food. Normally, when there is a technical improvement in the process of production of a commodity, the production costs fall and its price relative to other commodities—that is, its purchasing power per unit—also falls. In this situation, there is no injustice to the producer, for although one unit of his product buys less than before, because of the technical improvement, he can produce more than before; hence, his real income will be no less and may even be greater. Suppose, for instance, that because of a technical improvement, the average production cost of wheat fell from $1 to 50 cents. In the normal competitive process, the price of wheat would fall to somewhere around 50 cents, and everyone in society would benefit from the improvement. If the "parity" party had its way, however, and other prices did not change, the price would be held up at $1 no matter what improvements were made in the methods of production and nobody would benefit from improvements but the farmer.

Competition must not be too perfect. There is, however, another point of great importance in connection with the effects of competition on progress. If competition is too "perfect"—that is, if innovations are very easily imitated—it may not pay anyone to introduce them. Take again the example of wheat. Suppose that a new machine were invented that just about halved the cost of production of wheat. Those who first took advantage of this invention would reap large rewards, for while only a few used the new methods the output of wheat would not be greatly affected, and the price of wheat would therefore not be much changed. If, however, the new methods were easily imitated, more and more farmers would employ them, and it would become profitable to grow wheat by the new methods on land that previously had not been used for wheat. The output of wheat would increase and as it increased, the price would fall. The output would go on increasing until the price fell to about half what it was before, or perhaps a little more than half. Then all farmers would be producing with the new methods, for none could afford to produce by the old methods at such a low price. On the other hand, none of the farmers—not even those who had first introduced the new methods—would be making exceptional profits, for the new, low price would just about cover the new, low cost of production. If this process of imitation of new methods is too rapid, it will not pay anyone to introduce them, since the price of the product will fall almost immediately to the level at which, even with the new methods, production is just about normally profitable.

So we find ourselves in something of a dilemma: unless a new method can be imitated widely, it will not bear much fruit for society, but if it is imitated too rapidly it will not bear much fruit for the innovator, and hence may never come into being. History seems to show, however, that it is a very rare situation where the imitation of new methods is too rapid to make it worth while introducing them. Almost universally, an innovator of a successful new method can make profits sufficient to justify the special risk he has taken in the few years that elapse before the rise of competitors eats away his special position. Particularly is this the case, of course, where patent and copyright laws protect the innovator from imitators for a certain period.

Occupational groups may be organized in opposition to progress. Nevertheless, there is a real danger from the other side: that where occupational groups are politically organized, they may use their organization to prevent technical improvements that might upset their established ways. It may easily be to the interests of the mass of wheat farmers, for instance, to prevent the more progressive and adventurous of their number from introducing improved methods. Labor unions also are guilty of practices that prevent the introduction of improved methods, where these improvements will upset old established privileges. There is an alarming tendency in modern society for occupational groups to be organized in opposition to economic progress. The growth of agricultural protectionism and of the political power of the agricultural interest, is one sign of the attack on economic progress. In some phases of its activity, the labor movement also is more interested in the preservation of special privileges against the attacks of innovators than it is in improving techniques. Indeed, it might be said that the whole trend of governmental intervention today in the direction of more equal distribution of incomes may have a disturbing effect on the rate of economic progress. Even Social Security legislation may make people more unwilling to branch out on new lines of endeavor. It is indeed true, as one writer has said,[3] that there is a clash between security and progress. The price of progress is a certain amount of instability and insecurity, and while we are interested in obtaining progress at the lowest possible price, nevertheless we must beware lest our efforts to obtain security are purchased at the price of stagnation. It is often true that "security is mortals' chiefest enemy."

Religious origins of the "spirit of enterprise." Neither security, nor frugality, nor competition is in itself sufficient to insure economic progress, though insecurity, profligacy, and protection can suppress it. The *drive* for progress in a society comes from the spirit of curiosity, invention, and innovation. Unless there is a desire for change and improvement, an itch to experiment, a willingness to take risks—in other words, a spirit of enterprise, economic progress will not take place no matter how favorable the other conditions.

Very little work has been done on the causes of the growth of a spirit of enterprise in society. It is clearly connected with the whole nature of the culture. It probably has a good deal to do with the nature of the prevailing religion. Thus a religion that is ritualistic and tradition-centered, that lays stress on the performance of certain learned acts, and in which children are expected to grow up into the pattern of their parents without any particular emotional crisis of their own, is less likely to stimulate economic progress than a religion of immediate experience in which the individual is encouraged to form his own patterns, to make his own peace with God, and perhaps to pass through an emotional crisis of conversion. In other words, a religion of "confirmation" is more likely to produce tradition-

[3] A. G. B. Fisher, *The Clash of Progress and Security* (New York: The Macmillan Co., 1935).

centered behavior and is less likely to produce daring innovations than a religion of "conversion."

Illustrations: Islam and Protestant nonconformity. Evidence for this hypothesis can be found in many periods of history. Islam in its early years was a religion of "conversion"—often forcible, but also often genuine. It produced a period of rapid economic and cultural development in most of the countries that it affected. The legendary splendors of the Arabian Nights are a reflection of the impression made by this development! Yet in little more than two hundred years after Mohammed Islam had become a religion of hide-bound tradition, and in the past few centuries the Islamic countries for the most part have been sunk in economic stagnation and even retrogression.

Another example can be found in the Industrial Revolution of the eighteenth century, in which the British nonconformists played a part quite out of proportion to their numbers, not only in the development of new industrial techniques but in the development of the basic science on which the new techniques rested. The importance of evangelical religion in American history may also be related to the rapid rate of American economic progress. Religion is not, of course, the only element in society that is a significant determinant of progress, but it is likely to be one of the most important elements in determining the general atmosphere of a culture.

Progress and class structure. One last characteristic of the general social structure that is likely to be important in determining the rate of economic progress is the class structure, and especially the mobility among classes in the society. The society must not only produce innovators, it must have some machinery whereby these innovators can obtain the resources with which to pursue their innovations. If the people who have the will to innovate do not have the power, and the people who have the power do not have the will, the society will stagnate no matter how many potential innovators it may have. A rigid class or caste system, then, makes for stagnation, and a fluid class system makes for progress. If a small class is entrenched in control of the resources of a society it is likely to become complacent and conservative, and the would-be innovators in the lower classes get no chance to display their talents. If, on the other hand, there is a rapid "circulation of elites" as Pareto calls it, with energetic and enterprising individuals constantly rising in the scale of wealth and power, displacing the idle and profligate possessors of inherited wealth and position, progress is likely to be rapid.

Unstable free markets as a source of class mobility. To this process of class mobility the rise of the free market, and especially of the financial markets, made an important contribution. In a primitive economy, or even in a feudal society where economic relationships are governed closely by custom and precedent, there are few opportunities for talent to rise or for the established to fall. With the development of an exchange economy all classes become subject to valuations set on their persons and properties by the market, and the market is notoriously fickle! The growth of financial institutions—borrowing and lending, the stock market, banking, and so on—makes it much easier for the talented poor to lay their hands on resources that they do not themselves own, and for the untalented rich to relinquish the control of their property to others. This is not the only way to speed up the circulation of elites, but it is an important way.

Inflation and deflation also play a great part in circulating the property and power in a society. Inflation on the whole shifts the net worth of society towards the entrepreneurs who are actually administering the capital of society, and away from the bondholders and creditors who merely own it. Deflation has the opposite effect. It is not surprising, therefore, to find that a mild inflation has frequently been a stimulus to economic progress, whereas deflation is nearly always a deterrent.

Class *immobility* as a source of progress. The history of the Industrial Revolution of the eighteenth century suggests that under some circumstances certain *immobilities* in the class structure may be favorable to economic progress. The predominant part played by the British nonconformists in science and industry noted above may have been in part due not only to the enterprising nature of their particular subculture, but also to the existence of certain disabilities that prevented nonconformists from entering the universities, and hence the professions. The talent, thus diverted from the more respectable but also more conventional occupations, was forced into industry and trade. Thus, if the class structure of society is so fluid that there is equal opportunity for all to enter the easier-going professions, there may not be sufficient talent diverted into industry and trade to ensure a proper rate of economic progress. This is also likely to be the case where the prestige attached to political and bureaucratic occupations is great, and commercial occupations are despised. One of the things that has hampered the economic progress of countries as diverse as Rumania and India is that the educational system has drawn the best brains into politics, teaching, and the civil service, and consequently there is a lack of personnel in the various fields of industrial and commercial enterprises.

Political revolutions as a source of progress. The importance of class mobility in explaining economic progress also explains why political revolutions frequently have led to outbursts of economic progress, even though the turmoil and insecurity created by revolution in itself is an unfavorable factor. Thus in Russian society before 1917, as in French society before 1789, power and property were concentrated in the hands of a small, pleasure-loving and irresponsible aristocracy. Consequently the creative abilities of the masses found few opportunities for expression, while those that had the opportunities usually had no creative abilities. In both cases, the revolution produced a social ferment in which much of the hitherto unutilized ability came to the fore, and in which the older, conservative classes lost property and power. Not only did the revolution tap reservoirs of unused ability, but also it created a frame of mind in which old things were suspected and new things welcomed, and in which, therefore, the masses were willing to follow the innovators. It will not be surprising if Communist China follows the same pattern of technical development—not because of its communism, but because of its revolution.

"Continuous revolution" as a source of progress. It must not be thought, however, that violent revolution is of itself a cause of economic progress. A violent revolution is like an explosion that blows up a dam—the parched lands downstream do indeed get water, but they get floods as well that rob the water of much of its value. Where a revolution can be accomplished gradually and without serious violence, the results are greatly to be preferred. Thus the relatively bloodless revolution in England that began in 1688, and its American counterpart of 1776, led to an outburst of economic progress that has scarcely any parallel in history. In this case, the class structure of society was flexible enough to permit of a gradual replacement of an aristocracy by a commercial middle class. The relatively classless structure of American society in the nineteenth century was undoubtedly a major factor in America's astounding economic progress. The fact that there was little or no long-established "ruling class" meant that the new society could draw on practically its whole human resources for leadership. This was not true, however, in the ante-bellum South, and much of the economic backwardness of this part of the country may be attributed to its class structure. Even in old countries such as England and the Scandinavian countries, which inherited a fairly rigid class structure from feudal times, institutions have developed that permit the rise of able people in the working class to positions of leadership. The co-operative movement, for instance, is a good example of a form of enterprise that has thrived by tapping hitherto unused sources of managerial ability in the working class.[4]

Dissipation of the fruits of progress. Up to this point in the argument we have regarded economic progress as consisting essentially in an improvement in techniques of economic activity. It is now important to notice that an improvement in techniques does not necessarily result in an improved standard of life for the people as a whole. There are three principal ways in which the fruits of economic progress can be wasted—in which,

[4] See p. 155.

that is, improvement in techniques can fail to result in improvement in the lot of the people. Improvements can be wasted

1. In luxury.
2. In war.
3. In the increase of population.

1. *Luxury*

In some cases all the benefit from improved methods of production is seized by a small ruling class, which uses the resources that it commands for luxury and display. Ancient Egypt provides one of the best examples of such waste. The resources liberated by the invention of settled agriculture and the utilization of the Nile marshes were expended in the building of monstrous pyramids to gratify the vanity and the superstitions of kings rather than to improve the lot of the people.

2. *War*

In many more cases the benefits of economic progress are wasted in war, which is doubly destructive of wealth. Not only do the operations of war itself destroy wealth, but the withdrawal of the resources used in this destruction means that much potential wealth never comes into existence. The loss is not only what armies burn and destroy; it is what the armies might have produced in the way of useful goods and services had they not been engaged in destruction. Because of an instability that is inherent in the concept of defense,[5] there is a tendency for war to absorb a larger and larger proportion of

[5] The instability in any system of "national" defense arises from the circumstance that the security of one nation involves the insecurity of its enemy. Hence the attempt to achieve security implies that everybody has to be stronger than everybody else, which is usually impossible. The system therefore has no "solution"; national defense usually leads to competition in armaments, which in turn almost always leads to war. Competition in military strength therefore means that every nation must continually put more and more of its resources into defense, for no nation can afford to be weaker than its enemies. The only conceivable equilibrium of defense is one in which each nation is so far away from every other that it is stronger *at home* than any other, but weaker abroad. The United States in the nineteenth century came close to this situation, which accounts for the remarkably small proportion of resources absorbed by foreign wars in that period. In the twentieth century, alas, we are all so close to each other, thanks again to economic progress, that this solution is no longer possible!

resources as the wealth and power of nations increases. We see this clearly in our own day, where the proportion of national resources absorbed by war and war preparations has risen from something under 5 per cent in the eighteenth century to between 25 and 50 per cent today. War, indeed, threatens to absorb all the benefits of the technical revolution, and may leave us even worse off than we were before.

3. *Population*

The third method by which the fruits of economic progress can be—and all too often have been—wasted is by unrestricted increase in population. There are sharp limits to the amount of agricultural produce that can be obtained per acre of land, no matter how much labor is applied. No matter how good any given level of techniques, therefore, beyond a certain point an increase in population must result in a decline in income per capita. This is a consequence of the famous "law of diminishing returns." Suppose, for instance, we imagine the United States with seventeen hundred million people in it, instead of a hundred and seventy million. It is clear that we could not possibly expand our food supply ten times on our own land. It may be doubted whether even by the most intensive cultivation and the farming of every possible acre we could more than double, or perhaps treble, our food production. With ten times the present population, then, and our present techniques, most of us would live very badly, and perhaps even be constantly on the edge of starvation. With any given level of techniques there is some "optimum" population on any area which will give the highest income per head. After that point, the more people there are, the more difficult it is to feed, clothe, and house them.

The "dismal science." The population problem is the basis of the "dismal science" of Ricardo and Malthus—dismal not because it is dull, but because its conclusions are so depressing. The "dismal theorem" is that if nothing can check the growth of population but starvation and misery, then population will grow until it is miserable and starves. Technical progress therefore does us no good in the long run. It may enable us to live better for a while, but if the fact that we live better necessarily involves the growth of population, it will not be long before we are down at the starvation level again, where the sickle of death keeps pace with the harvest of the womb. Worse still, technical progress not only does no good; it actually increases the sum of human misery, because it enables a larger number of people to live in precisely the same state of misery in which people lived before. This is the "utterly dismal theorem"!

Fertility and progress. The logic of the proposition is flawless. Fortunately the dismal theorem can be recast into a cheerful form—that if there are other checks to population beside starvation and misery, there is no need for the population to rise until it is checked by these grim forces. Fortunately the technical revolution may create these other checks to population which are so necessary to its long-run success. There seems to be a clear positive relationship between fertility and the standard of life. Up to a point, the higher the standard of life, the lower the fertility. The causes of this phenomenon are not well understood—many factors from cleanliness to contraceptives have been suggested as reasons. A recent writer suggests that the type of food eaten is an important factor in fertility—the fertility of the poor being due to the large carbohydrate intake, the infertility of the rich to their large consumption of proteins. Probably the most important single reason is the growth of economic (that is, calculated as opposed to traditional) behavior, as the standard of life and education rises. Economy, paradoxically enough, seems to be a luxury that is not available to the very poor! With increasing riches, families become more sensitive to the economic cost of having children, and hence come to limit their numbers as they come to limit expenditure on any expensive good. The mechanics of this limitation, whether by late marriages or by the use of contraceptives, is probably much less important than the motivation: if there's a will, man (or woman) will find a way!

The need for *rapid* improvement: the jump from the Malthusian trap. Whatever the reasons for this connection between riches and family limitation, the empirical fact is well established. It is a fact of momentous significance, for it means that if a society can improve its techniques and its standards of consumption *fast enough*, the rise in the standard of life will be permanent, for the rising standard of life will inhibit the growth of population. If, however, a society improves its techniques too slowly, the traditional habits will persist and the rise in population will keep pace with the improved production, thus preventing any improvements in the average level of living.

There have been many examples in history of these tragic situations. The introduction of the potato into Ireland resulted in a quadrupling of its population, with disastrous results in the famine of 1846. The introduction of American standards of public health into Puerto Rico likewise has resulted in a population expansion that helps to keep ever-larger numbers of people in semistarvation. Many areas in the East are undergoing population explosions which may lead in another generation or two to famines on a scale never before known by man. The Malthusian trap can be escaped only by a big leap; if the initial jump is too small the society will fall back into the trap, even worse off than before.

Geographical expansion. The possibilities for escaping the Malthusian trap depend also on whether a society has room to expand geographically. In this respect European-American society has been in an extraordinarily favored position for the past two hundred years, and has availed itself of an opportunity that is unlikely to avail itself to the human race again for a very long time—barring the colonization of new planets! The European peoples had great and almost empty areas into which to expand—America to the west, Australia to the south, and Siberia to the east. The technical revolution, therefore, which brought an enormous population expansion to the European peoples, also enabled them to utilize this expansion to populate the empty spaces, so that English is spoken in Alaska and Tasmania, Russian in Kamchatka, and Spanish in Patagonia.

The Malthusian problem in the rich nations. This expansion gave the European peoples a breathing spell sufficient to allow the economic checks on population to become operative. In the

1930's, indeed, it looked as if the economic checks to population were too effective, and the Western populations were threatened with race suicide. Hardly any Western nation in those years was producing enough children to maintain its population indefinitely, much less to increase it. In 1957 the position was much less clear. Birth and reproduction rates had increased strikingly, and a new phenomenon had been making itself apparent—a rise in the number of children per family with *increase* in incomes in those groups that had adopted the "economic" attitude towards children. Even though families in our era count the cost of children, as they grow richer they feel they can afford to have more. A level of national income now seems to have been reached in the United States at which the average family feels able to afford three to four children, and in consequence the population is increasing rapidly. It still remains to be seen, therefore, whether even the advanced nations will avoid the Malthusian trap in the very long run. In this case, however, it is a much larger and more agreeable trap, for the level of income at which people voluntarily limit births because they cannot afford more children is a different order of magnitude from the level of income at which families do not limit births at all, but at which enough children starve and perish to keep the population constant.

The overcrowded areas. The whole situation in regard to economic progress is much more difficult for the already overpopulated regions of Asia and Africa. These societies have very little room to expand geographically. A little waste land can be reclaimed, a few underpopulated areas can be filled up, but on the whole these opportunities are very sharply limited compared with the enormous increase in population that seems to be just over the horizon. Consequently there is grave danger that the technical revolution, as it comes to these areas, will be too slow to bring them over the "hump." The benefits of the improvements will be almost immediately swallowed up in the avalanche of new mouths.

"Social space" and progress. Even if these areas were not faced with rapidly increasing population, the problem of reorganization of the society along modern technical lines would still be difficult, because of the enormous shifts of occupations involved, and especially the shift from rural to urban occupations. It is not difficult to construct a "model" of a reconstructed India or China, even with their present populations, in which much higher standards of life would be possible. If, for instance, some two hundred million people could be taken off the land in either country, the tiny farms consolidated, and modern methods of agriculture introduced, the displaced millions could produce all the tractors and machines needed by the remaining farmers, and much more in the way of conveniences and luxuries beside. It is probable that with a reorganization of this kind India and China, and countries like them, could produce more food in toto with a third or less of the present number of food producers. It is easy to see the goal. What is difficult is to find a road that goes there, especially when the society has no place to expand geographically and when it is bound by an ancient and rigid social system.

The problem is something like the puzzle in which fifteen square pieces are moved about on a sixteen-square board. As long as there is one empty space, all the pieces can be moved. Sixteen pieces on a sixteen-piece board, however, can never be rearranged. The problem of development sometimes therefore may involve the creation of a social space into which some of the pieces of a complex society can be moved while the other pieces are being rearranged with as little disorganization as possible.

The costs of progress. How to accomplish a reorganization of this magnitude painlessly is a problem that no country has yet been able to solve. England had her enclosures and "sturdy beggars," her factory children and handloom weavers. Russia had her dispossessed Kulaks and starving peasantry. America, with her mobile populations and abundant land, probably achieved the transition with the least social cost of any country. For the thickly populated and underdeveloped countries, however, the cost of the new technical society may be high in terms of present misery and social disorganization.

Migration and progress. Migration is sometimes advocated as a method by which the immediate pressures of the overpopulated areas can be relieved and a cycle of economic development started. The present opportunities for migration, however, are very limited. It should also be realized that migration, like technical development, is no solution for the problem of overpopulation if it is on too small a scale.[6] If a country is really limiting its population by starvation, migration does very little to alleviate the population pressure. Every emigrant releases food supplies that will support another child. For every emigrant that leaves, therefore, one—or perhaps even two—children who might otherwise have died in infancy will grow up to take his place, and the population pressure may even be made more acute. Only a dramatic and very large-scale migration would be sufficient in such a case to create a permanent improvement.

If, for instance, we suppose that two hundred million Asians were to be settled in the Amazon valley in the next twenty-five years, the resources released in Asia might be sufficient to raise standards of life and nutrition drastically enough to produce the desired curtailment in fertility. Migration on such a scale, however, is inconceivable in the present world situation, and if the Asian countries, and others like them, are to achieve a high-level technical society it must be done by methods very different from those that have produced this society in Europe and America. In the West the technical changes came first, and the cultural adaptation followed. In the East it may well be that the cultural adaptations must be made first, in the way of changes in religion, in family patterns, in the status of women and children, in political ideas, and so on, before the technical revolution can be successful. Exactly what these cultural adaptations must be a mere economist like the author cannot be expected to know. It is not unreasonable, however, to surmise that they must be large and far-reaching. The mere *economics* of development—of plans such as Point Four and the Columbo plan—must be a relatively small part of the total picture if these

[6] See p. 260.

schemes are not to be self-defeating, for economic progress involves changes in *all* aspects of life, not only in those that are more usually regarded as "economic." Economic development, therefore, must always be placed in a setting of over-all cultural change.

3

Economic stability

Our system is depressive-manic;
Its runs to boom, or else to panic.
In view of this it would be wise
For Government to Stabilize—
Remembering the need for both
Stability and steady growth,
And that inflation dulls the enjoyment
Even of constant full employment.

The concern for stability. At the time of writing (1957) the economy of the Western world is experiencing a period of relative stability, and the problems of economic instability lie somewhat in the background. In the recent history of the Western economies, however, instability is the problem that has perhaps been most prominent in the minds of those concerned about economic policy. Especially is this true of the twentieth century, which has witnessed a great depression of unprecedented depth and several inflations of astronomical magnitude.

What do we want to stabilize? Let us examine first what it is that fluctuates, and what we want to stabilize. Stabilization does not, of course, imply stagnation. We have already seen the paramount importance of economic progress as a goal of economic policy, and economic stability clearly does not mean staying at the same economic level. When we think of economic stability what we are really thinking of is *steady* progress. It is precisely in the progressive societies that economic stability becomes an important problem. Stationary societies are not bothered much by instability, except those due to the random and unpredictable effects of the weather. It is only as a society leaves the stationary condition, and begins the long climb of economic development, that it begins to exhibit alternations of rapid and slow progress, or of high and low prices, which constitute what are called "economic fluctuations" or "business cycles."

These fluctuations occur in a great many different economic variables—in fact, hardly any variable that interests the economist, whether prices, wages, interest rates, incomes, or outputs, fails to show fluctuations of some kind. The fluctuations are not always, or even usually, very regular. Indeed, the irregularity of most economic fluctuations is so great that there is some question whether it is proper to apply the term "cycle" to them, for "cycle" implies a certain pendulumlike regularity of swing. Economic fluctuations are more like those of an elevator than those of a pendulum—periods of rising, falling, or stable quantities alternate, often almost at random, subject to certain limitations of "floors" and "ceilings."

Output and price fluctuations. Fluctuations may be classified into those related to *outputs* (or *inputs*), those related to *prices*, and those related to *incomes*. Fluctuations in inputs and outputs are very closely related, especially over short periods, as the ratio of inputs to outputs changes slowly. Consequently fluctuations in employment (labor input)—and inversely, in unemployment—correspond very closely with fluctuations in output. For short periods they may be regarded as practically the same thing, though of course over longer periods economic development continually raises the amount of output per man, and so output rises faster than employment.

Fluctuations in employment and output tend to run into a "ceiling" of "full employment" or "capacity output." This is a somewhat flexible ceiling, especially under conditions of stress. During a war, for instance, many people enter the labor force who would not normally do so, but even here there is a fairly sharp upper limit at any one time to the volume of both employment and output. There are no such physical limitations on the rise—or even on the fall—of prices, but there may be sharp limitations imposed by inflexibility in the total stock of money. If the stock of money can be indefinitely increased, however, there is no clear upper limit to the rise in prices, and in the great "hyperinflations" as they are called—for instance in Germany in 1923, or in Hungary after the second World War—prices have risen by billions. The world has never experienced a "hyperdeflation"—in which, for instance, prices would go down and down without apparent limit—mainly because there is a certain indestructible core of the money stock which gives a floor to the price level. But if the stock of money could be contracted without limit as it can be expanded without limit there is no theoretical reason why a hyperdeflation should not be possible.

Income fluctuations. Fluctuations in incomes are closely related to *both* output and price fluctuations, because of the fact that every income can be derived by multiplying outputs by their prices. Thus if a farmer produces 10,000 bushels of wheat at a price of $2 per bushel, his gross income is $10,000 × $2, or $20,000, all of which is distributed either to himself or to the various factors of production or other inputs that he has bought to produce the wheat. If prices double while outputs remain the same, or if outputs double while prices remain the same, the incomes associated with these outputs will double. There are difficult—indeed in a sense insoluble—problems involved in the measurement of large heterogeneous aggregates of outputs and prices, problems that need not detain us now. It is generally possible to devise index numbers of output and price levels that are meaningful at least over periods of decades, and it is generally possible to define these index numbers in such a way that the national income, for instance, is the product of an index of output and an index of the price level of that output.

Payments fluctuations. Closely related to, though not identical with, fluctuations in income are fluctuations in *payments* —that is, in receipts and expenditures of money. Every payment, or transfer of money, from one person or account to another, is simultaneously a receipt to the person who gets the money and an expenditure to the person who gives it up. Payments are not the same things as income—many goods, for instance, are bought and sold several times before coming to rest in the hands of the final user, so that the volume of payments exceeds by several times the national income. If payments decrease or increase, however, income is likely to do the same, because of the impact of payments either on prices, or on outputs, or on both.

Stock fluctuations. Finally we should mention fluctuations in stocks of commodities, of money, and of securities as perhaps the most important single element in the dynamics of the whole system. If stocks of commodities, for instance, are rising faster than the stock of money, there is a strong tendency for prices, outputs, and incomes to decline, unless there is a compensating increase in the willingness to hold larger stocks of goods. It is through fluctuations in the stocks of money, and of securities, that the main instruments of control of economic fluctuations operate. By increasing or decreasing the stock of money, for instance, the government can produce inflationary or deflationary forces operating on the whole system.

Why control fluctuations? Now let us ask why the control of fluctuations should be an objective of economic policy. In other words, what is the matter with fluctuations: why should we not tolerate them, or even enjoy them? We actually pay to go on roller coasters; most people prefer a rolling or even mountainous landscape to a flat uniform plain. Why then should we worry about the ups and downs of economic quantities? Is not a fluctuating system actually to be preferred, as more interesting and exciting than a dull level of monotonous prosperity?

Price fluctuations redistribute wealth and income. The case both for and against fluctuations depends very much on what variables we are contemplating, and also of course on the magnitude of the fluctuations themselves: small fluctuations may be tolerable in a way that large fluctuations are not. Let us for the moment consider separately fluctuations in prices and fluctuations in outputs, even though in practice these generally go hand in hand. Suppose to begin with we had a system in which outputs were fairly stable, or steadily increasing on the whole, with some perhaps displacing others, but in which there were sharp fluctuations in the general level of prices. What objections could be raised against such a system, and why might it be regarded as a legitimate objective of economic policy to diminish these fluctuations?

The main objection in this case would be that fluctuations in the general level of prices produce random, meaningless, and essentially unjust changes in the distribution of both income and wealth. When prices rise there is a redistribution of total wealth away from those whose holdings are mainly in the form of money or contractual obligations (bonds), towards those whose holdings are mainly in the form of commodities or equity securities. A rise in the price level is exactly the same thing as a fall in the value of money: the "dollar" buys less and less "bushels," the "bushel" buys more and more dollars. Hence the holders of dollars lose and of "bushels" gain. If holdings of various types of assets, both of money and "not-money," were equally distributed over the persons of the society, there would be no redistribution, as what each person lost in the value of his money and bonds he would gain in the value of his goods and shares. However, holdings are never so distributed, so that in fact fluctuations in the price level always cause sharp redistributions: rising prices shift both income and wealth towards holders of goods and profit-makers, and away from bondholders and receivers of relatively fixed money incomes, such as salaried and government workers, pensioners, and even perhaps wage earners, if money wages lag behind the rise in the prices of the things that workers buy. Similarly falling prices redistribute income and wealth towards creditors and holders of money and towards fixed-income recipients, and away from profit-makers and holders of real goods and equity capital.

—but why shouldn't they? It is at least worth asking, why should we worry about these redistributions? Is not the chance of gain or loss through inflation or deflation one that everyone has to take? If people are foolish enough, or unlucky enough, to come out on the wrong side, why should they have anybody but themselves to blame? We do not generally regard protecting people against mistakes in investment as an objective of economic policy; it is indeed one of the principal justifications of a system of private property that the ownership of property entails risk, and profit is frequently justified as a reward for risk-bearing. If then there is a reward for risk-bearing, people have no right to complain when the gamble does not come off and they lose their capital. Inflations and deflations are just additional risks; the bondholder and the moneyholder in effect gamble on deflation, the commodityholder on inflation. If their gambles do not succeed, they should have no more right to complain than the man who bets on a losing horse.

Because of unnecessary risk. Unfortunately, the matter is not quite so simple. The risks involved in committing resources to a particular industry or form of investment are in a sense necessary and inevitable. There is no way in which we can be sure in advance that a new product is going to sell, or a new enterprise be successful. The risks of inflation and deflation, however, are not necessary nor are they inevitable in quite the same sense, insofar as both inflation and deflation are the result of government policy, or at least of government inaction. Consequently if a government that is able to prevent these fluctuations permits them to occur, it is introducing unnecessary risk into the holding of assets and the conduct of enterprise. We must recognize, of course, that sometimes governments get themselves into situations—for example, during a great war or the aftermath of a war—in which inflation seems to be the only answer to their problems, and that also they may be prevented even from attacking a deflation by their own ignorance and the ignorance of their people. Nevertheless, insofar as inflation and deflation are controllable by government action, the question as to what is the practicable ideal in this matter and how is it to be attained cannot be evaded. It is literally impossible for a government to "do nothing" in regard to this situation, for even doing nothing has some effect on the movements of the price level.

The ideal rate of price change. On the question of the ideal rate of inflation or deflation there is room for a certain range of opinion, and also room for the pull of different political pressures. Creditor classes naturally favor deflation, debtor classes inflation. The case against deflation, however, is a strong one. For reasons which we shall examine in greater detail later, deflation is almost always associated with a fall in output and employment as well as a fall in prices. This is partly because of the redistributive effects of deflations; the decline in profits especially discourages investment and enterprise, and the benefits to rentiers and pensioners do not compensate sufficiently in increased consumption. It is partly also because of certain rigidities in the price structure. Whatever the reasons, the facts are clear: deflation has always been accompanied by unemployment, slack markets, a high rate of business failure, a low rate of investment—in one word, by depression.

While there may be some doubt as to whether a simple redistribution of income is good or bad—the gain to the gainers *may* be greater than the loss to the losers—there is little doubt that a diminution in the income to be distributed is bad, for then the losses are almost sure to be greater than the gains. There are some, however, who argue that if prices and wages were sufficiently flexible a fall in prices would not result in lower output and employment, and they suggest as an ideal the situation in which per-capita money *income* is held constant, and increases in productivity result in lower prices. It is clear that the rise in real income which should—and which must—accompany rising productivity can come about in many ways, and that if money incomes are held constant while prices fall this is equivalent to a rise in real incomes, just as if prices were constant and money incomes rose, or prices rose and money incomes rose faster. The case for the "constant money income" ideal as we may call it rests on the belief that the creation of new money (which is almost certainly necessary if the price level is to be kept stable in the face of rising productivity and rising money incomes) cannot be accomplished without causing serious distortions in relative prices and relative outputs. Although the possibility of such distortions cannot be ruled out, there is not much evidence that they are important quantitatively.

The case for a stable price level. There seems to be a stronger case, therefore, for the constant price level with money incomes rising with productivity as an ideal of policy. The case for the constant price level is that this would create the least interference with long-term contracts and would permit the accounting system to operate without distortion of information. Money is a measure of value, and it is a general rule of all measures that they should be constant and should always measure the same quantity. If the foot were to be 10 inches one year and 14 the next it would clearly be a very inefficient measure of length; at least we should always have to specify "1957 feet" or "1958 feet" in recording length. This, however, is just what happens to the dollar: the 1958 dollar buys only about half as much as a 1940 dollar, and it is the purchasing power of the dollar that constitutes its real significance. When the dollar fluctuates in value a highly speculative element is introduced into long-term contracts when these involve undertakings to pay or receive sums of dollars. What is perhaps even more serious, most standard accounting procedures are based on the assumption that the dollar is a constant measure of value. If inventories and fixed capital are valued in the accounts at cost, for instance, less whatever adjustments may be made for depreciation, this means in effect that they are measured in dollars as of the year of purchase. If in the meantime there has been a change in the value of money these dollars do not have the same significance as current dollars. Thus the balance sheet is really a sum of dollars of different "years": an old piece of equipment may be measured in 1930 dollars, a recently purchased item in 1956 dollars. This is like adding a sum of "feet" when some of the feet are 6 inches, some are 12, and some are 20! Such a sum would not be very meaningful, and if we tried to act on it would be positively misleading. On this ground alone, therefore, there is a strong case for the ideal of the stable price level.

The case for a rising price level. There is also a case, however, especially under the conditions of modern American society, for a slowly rising price level as an ideal, with incomes rising somewhat faster than prices. The main argument for this ideal comes from the observation that labor-management relations are more apt to be peaceful under a slowly rising price level than they are if the price level is stationary, for with a slowly rising price level it is always possible for management to give wage concessions which are then quietly eroded away through rising prices.[1] This is largely a matter of the nature of the perceptions involved: a rise in money wages is perceived by the worker either as an act of management or as a "gain" won by his union: a rise in prices, which is equivalent to a fall in real wages, is perceived as an "act of God"—something for which neither management nor the union is responsible. Consequently, when prices are rising, industrial peace can be bought easily with small apparent gains; when prices are falling, or even when they are stationary, management is more resistant to a rise in money wages, and it is more difficult for a union to obtain the gains that it needs to maintain morale among its members. If the price level is stationary, gains in money wages must be confined roughly to what is allowed by increasing productivity, and this may not be enough to keep union-management relations on an even keel.

Doubts about a rising price level. It may further be argued that the difficulties mentioned previously that are associated

[1] See p. 154.

with a long-run rising trend of prices—the injustice to creditors, pensioners, and so on, and the distortion of accounting information—can be corrected by appropriate adjustments in our institutions. Long-term contracts can be safeguarded by "purchasing power clauses" which fix the obligations in terms of dollars of constant purchasing power; the distortions in accounting can be corrected by modifications in accounting procedure; provisions for old age can be made through Social Security, with payments adjusted to current purchasing power, and any injustice to bondholders can be adjusted through higher nominal rates of interest. The arguments are plausible: nevertheless one is a little uneasy with them. The argument from industrial relations seems to rest on a kind of fraud or at least an illusion, and one wonders how long the illusion will last. Many of the benefits of mild inflation, indeed, follow from the fact that it is unexpected. It can be argued that most of the redistributive effects of inflation (and deflation also) arise because these movements of the price level are not generally anticipated. If they were anticipated people would protect themselves against them. Thus if everyone were sure that the price level would rise at 5 per cent per annum for the next fifty years, nobody would lend money—at least on long term at less than say 8 or 10 per cent—because at 5 per cent the real rate of interest would be zero. People would not accumulate money or bonds for their old age, but would rather invest in real property; they would, indeed, hold on to money as little as possible. Many of these phenomena are to be observed in a country like Brazil, which has had a fairly steady inflation for about a hundred years, and in which therefore almost everybody anticipates a continuance of the rise in the price level.

Rising prices tax money holdings. There is one result of inflation (or deflation), however, that does not depend on expectations. Whether expected or not, inflation acts as a tax on the holdings of money, deflation acts as a subsidy. To put the same thing in other words, when the price level is rising holdings of money bear a negative real rate of interest—they are declining all the time in purchasing power. If the price level rises 5 per cent in a year, $100 held in a hoard would only buy on December 31st what $95 would have bought the previous January 1st. Similarly, when the price level is falling, holdings of money bear a positive real rate of interest. This fact again points up the conclusion that deflation is a disaster, while inflation is an inconvenience to a market society. The way to get rich in a deflation is to sell one's goods, abandon one's enterprises, lay off one's employees, and hold as much of one's capital as possible in the form of "idle money." The way to get rich in an inflation is to buy as much as possible, employ as many people as possible, hold as little money as possible, and devote one's capital and talents to the administration of real capital. It is little wonder that the deflation of 1929-32 rocked capitalism almost to its foundations, whereas countries have been known to advance even in the acute disorganization of hyperinflation.

One may perhaps venture a tentative conclusion that price stability is a useful ideal, but that errors in the direction of inflation are much less serious than errors in the direction of deflation.

Output stability: the capacity ideal. Turning now to the other great aspect of economic stability, that of output or of what is almost the same thing, real income, we find probably less disagreement about the nature of the ideal, for almost everyone agrees that full employment, or operation at full capacity, is the ideal, and that unemployment, or undercapacity operation, is undesirable. This agreement, however, conceals a very substantial disagreement in practice as to how full is full! Capacity, as we have seen, is a flexible concept. We could have a much larger product if we gave up vacations, worked more hours a day, and drew more people into the labor force. It is more than doubtful whether this would be desirable. The whole notion of "capacity" therefore is itself an ideal, rather than a sheer physical limit.

The "peak load" theory. There are also two views of output fluctuation that seem to deny that steady full employment is a realizable ideal—views that are at least worthy of serious examination. The first of these might be called the "peak load" theory of undercapacity operation. A power station operates "under capacity" at 4 A.M., because it must have capacity to handle the peak load at, say, 5 P.M. The whole economic system similarly exhibits seasonal "peak loads," and we would not regard a failure to reach full capacity in the off seasons as a departure from the ideal. This is not to say, of course, that fluctuations of a peak-load character cannot be lessened by judicious planning. There comes a point, however, at which fluctuations of this type cannot be reduced except at a cost that is more than the gains. It is an interesting question whether there are longer fluctuations of this type. Certainly in a society that is subject to recurrent wars war represents a "peak load" and results in a distortion of the industrial structure that may result in unemployment during peace, especially in the war-related industries. Another possible source of a peak-load phenomenon is the tendency of major improvements and developments to "bunch," so that periods of rapid growth may alternate with periods of slower growth. The economy adapts itself to the rapid growth, then finds itself with too large a proportion of its resources devoted to investment industries when the rate of growth slackens.

The seriousness of the peak-load problem for the economy as a whole depends on the *specificity* of its resources—that is, on the degree to which they are adapted to only one use, or at most a few uses. The power station operates much under capacity in the off hours because it is adapted for one purpose only, and if there is not sufficient demand for electricity to utilize its capacity at one particular time, it cannot be devoted to other things for which there might be a demand. Over a large, complex, and especially a growing economy, however, the specificity of resources is much less than in the case of a single power station. Furthermore, there is reason to believe that the specificity of resources has been decreasing. The automobile has greatly increased the geographical mobility of labor; the ever-increasing range of substitute materials and the continued expansion in the possible uses of materials, and the versatility and standardization of modern machinery, have made it easier to change the composition of output. We see this dramatically exemplified in the conversions of modern economies from peace to war and back to peace again. The American economy especially seems to be capable of changing the composition of its output by almost 50 per cent in a year if necessary. We must conclude therefore that depressions, at least serious depressions, do not represent a true peak-load problem, although we cannot altogether rule out the possibility of a small necessary fluctuation owing to this cause.

The "hangover theory." The other view that might deny validity to the ideal of stable full employment is what has rather irreverently been called the "hangover" school of business-cycle theorists.[2] This view is that a depression is the result of certain structural maladjustments that developed as a result of the previous boom, and that therefore the only way to get rid of depressions is to get rid of booms. In a boom, it is argued, there is excessive creation of money and credit. As a result profits are inflated beyond the level that can be maintained in the long run, and investments are started in this flush of optimism that cannot be carried through to completion, either because of the increasing scarcity of the resources that they require, or because when all the investment plans become visible and known there are drastic downward revisions of expected profits. Thus, suppose there is room for two new office buildings in a city, both of which might be profitable. In the heat and excitement of the boom, and in the false expectations of profit that inflation creates, perhaps four such buildings might be started by different groups of builders and financiers. Each project is started without full knowledge of the others: as the projects approach completion, however, the knowledge about them spreads, and it becomes apparent that the city is overbuilt. Building ceases for a while, no new buildings are planned, and work may even be abandoned on existing projects. In 1932, for instance, Detroit was studded with half-finished skyscrapers on which work had been virtually abandoned. The boom then can be regarded as

[2] J. P. Wernette, *The Control of Business Cycles* (New York: Farrar, Straus, & Cudahy, Inc., 1941).

the time when mistakes are made; the depression is when they are found out.

Structural vs. aggregate fluctuations. It is a real virtue of this school that it calls attention to structural problems in the economy that the smooth aggregates of the Keynesian economics are apt to pass over. The assumption, however, that these structural adjustments necessarily involve a fluctuation in the general level of output, remains to be proved. It may well be that a fluctuation in the *composition* of output is necessary or even desirable, with more skyscrapers at one time, more vacations at another, more hospitals at another, and so on. It may be also that it is practically impossible to achieve the appropriate fluctuations in the composition of output without some fluctuation in the over-all volume. We cannot always insure that the expansion of one component will always just offset the contraction in another, if only because the decisions that eventually bring about these contractions or expansions must be made in advance of them, and often well in advance, and we can never be sure just what will be required or how these independent decisions will add up. Just as in the case of the "peak load" problem—which is itself essentially a problem in the timing of structural adjustments—there may be an irreducible amplitude of fluctuations in aggregate real output under any system, simply because of the knowledge-and-information problem involved in coordinating the necessary adjustments in composition and structure.

Unnecessary fluctuations and the Keynesian Revolution. What is also certain, however, is that depressions of the amplitude of the 1930's or 1870's go far beyond any "necessary fluctuation," and that it is this problem of "unnecessary fluctuations" that we generally think about when we talk of the "unemployment problem" or the "instability of a market economy." When aggregate output falls by more than a third in three years, as it did from 1929 to 1932 in the United States, the fluctuation has clearly gone far beyond anything that might be necessitated by adjustments in the structure or composition of output. It is precisely because of its success in explaining—and in prescribing for—these large, obviously unnecessary fluctuations in aggregate output and employment that the Keynesian economics has proved so popular. There has been a change both in theoretical outlook and in the available information in this area in the past twenty-five or thirty years which is sometimes called the "Keynesian Revolution." This revolution, like any other, has been the work of many men, both before and after Keynes. Nevertheless it justly goes by his name, for the major change in theoretical outlook must be attributed to him.

The change would not perhaps have come about so quickly, nor would it have been so well founded, had it not been for an important change in the collection and presentation of economic information represented by the development of national-income accounting, pioneered by the National Bureau of Economic Research in the 1920's, and flowering in the Department of Commerce National Income Statistics from 1929 on. One is reminded of another occasion in human history when a change in the image of reality and an improvement in the techniques of collecting information went hand in hand—the Copernican Revolution in the view of the solar system, and the improved means of celestial observation—the telescope—that ensured its victory. The Keynesian Revolution is not perhaps so deep or so far-reaching a change in the "view of the universe" as the Copernican. Nevertheless, there are similarities between the two; both involve the abandonment of an "observer-centered" view of the universe, and require a certain leap of the imagination to see the system *as a whole* as something apart from the direct experience of the individual observer.

The Bathtub Theorem. What, then, is the Keynesian "view" of the economic universe? It has two aspects—a "real" aspect, which considers the stocks and flows of real goods and services, and a "monetary" aspect, which considers the creation, destruction, and circulation of money. In its real aspect—perhaps its most important contribution—we visualize the economic system as consisting of a vast stockpile of goods—buildings, machines, houses, clothing, furniture, and even perhaps certain nonmaterial goods such as skills and feelings of satisfaction. *Production* is the act of adding to the stockpile—wheat is added to it as it grows on the farms, flour as it is ground in the mill, bread as it is baked in the bakery. *Consumption* consists of subtraction from the stockpile—bread is eaten, clothes are worn out. *Accumulation* or *physical investment* consists in *net* additions to the total stockpile. For any particular item the "Bathtub Theorem" identity is necessarily true:

$$\text{Accumulation} = \text{Production} - \text{Consumption}$$

If 100 units of something have been added to the stockpile and 90 units taken away, there must have been a net increase of 10 units in the total stockpile in that period.[3]

The principle of the overflowing tub. The "Bathtub Theorem" provides several keys to the problem of economic instability. The first might be called the "principle of the overflowing bathtub." In a normally progressing society we would expect the total stockpile to grow. Suppose, however, that it grows faster than the society is able and willing to "take." Then we are likely to run into trouble. The trouble may take two forms.

First, there may be a decline in *prices*. Suppose, for instance, that there are large stocks of many kinds of commodities—wheat, tin, steel, and the like. It is a fundamental principle, at least of a capitalist economy, that these stocks must be owned by somebody. Suppose, however, that most of the owners feel they are holding too much in the way of goods, and want to unload. Each individual owner does this by trying to sell some of his stocks. If everyone tries to sell, and nobody wants to buy, there must be a fall in prices, unless the government stands willing to support prices by taking stocks off the hands of the private owners. Once prices start to fall, however, the private owners' motivation to unload stocks becomes intensified. When prices are falling the value of money is rising, and it pays the individual to hold money rather than commodities. If a fall in prices leads to expectations of a further fall, owners become

[3] We may note here that we face a problem of "netness" in the definition of production and consumption, which is considered in the Appendix to this chapter.

still more anxious to sell, still less willing to buy, and prices fall still further.

The second possible response to the "overflowing bathtub" is a cutback in output and a consequent decline in employment. If a manufacturer finds his warehouses or storage lots crammed to overflowing—with a corresponding decline in his liquid assets—a common reaction, though not the only one possible, is to cut back output, reduce his labor force, and hope that by getting production below sales his customers will empty his warehouses at a rate faster than he is filling them. If he does this, however, income declines, unless there is an offsetting expansion somewhere else in the system. The people who suffer this decline in income—the workers, for instance, who have lost their jobs—will restrict their own consumption, and this may cause unwanted accumulations of consumer goods elsewhere in the system. This may cause further cutbacks, and a "vicious spiral" of declining output and increasing unemployment sets in.

Thus, suppose an automobile manufacturer finds that his stocks of unsold cars have increased—because sales have lagged behind production—to the point where no further increase in these stocks can be tolerated. To deal with this situation he shuts down the assembly line and lays off men, in the hope that sales will now be greater than production and his stocks of unsold cars will diminish. Because of the decline in income this layoff represents, however, fewer houses, vacuum cleaners, shoes, and so on are sold. Producers of these things find as a result that their stocks also are piling up; they may also react by cutting down output and employment, which will lead to still further unwanted stocks, and still further cutbacks, and so the process goes on. We might picture Production as a young lady pursued by a laggard lover, Consumption. The distance between them is Accumulation—the rate at which stockpiles are growing. If this gap is too great, Production may slow down, hoping that Consumption will catch up with her: when she slows down, however, he slows down too, so that the gap is not reduced by as much as she expects—she slows down further, and so does he, until finally both are crawling along at a pace so slow that he cannot help catching up a little!

Four ways of disposal of product. It may be useful to look at the same matter in a slightly different way. The total volume of production—the flow of shoes and ships and sealing wax that streams continually out of our factories and farms—must be *disposed of* in some way. There are five broad ways of disposing of the product of any particular country. We think first of production as originating in the possession of *businesses.* Then (1) some of it will be taken off the hands of businesses by households. (2) Some of it will be taken off the hands of businesses by government. (3) Some of it will be exported—taken off the hands of businesses by foreign purchasers. Imports, however, represent goods that come into the hands of domestic businesses from abroad, and have the same effect on stocks as production, so that strictly only *net* exports (exports minus imports) represents aggregate disposal of domestic production. (4) Some of it will be consumed or depreciated by businesses in the course of the productive process—for example, in the wear and tear of machines, buildings, and so on. (5) Anything that has not been disposed of through the four previous channels must still be left in the hands of businesses as an addition to stocks, or as business accumulations.

Aggregate effective demand. Suppose now that we define the "willing accumulations" of businesses as that increase in stocks that is neither so large that it motivates businessmen to contract output, nor so small that it motivates them to expand output. Then the sum of the first four items of disposal plus the total of willing accumulations is known as "aggregate effective demand." If now the Gross National Product is greater than the aggregate effective demand there will be "unwanted accumulations" in the hands of businesses, and as we have seen this is likely to motivate a decline in outputs, and therefore a decline in GNP. Similarly if the GNP is less than the aggregate effective demand there will be "unwanted decumulations," or, at least, accumulations in the hands of businesses will be less than desired. This creates a motivation towards a rise in outputs.

Whether this rise can in fact be accomplished depends on whether there are unemployed or underemployed resources available; that is, on the degree to which the system is operating at "capacity."

The notion of capacity, as we have seen, is not wholly clear. As output increases from any given level it becomes more and more difficult to bring about further increases. With a given population and resources some level of output may be regarded as "normal" or "ideal." Output can of course be increased beyond this point by working longer hours or expanding the labor force to include those not normally in it, so that no notion of "capacity" is absolute. When we speak of "capacity" output, then, we really imply some ideal level, at which further increase in output would not be considered worth the sacrifice in non-earning assets involved.[4]

The "sub-Keynesian" system. Let us now examine the simplest possible system that yields an equilibrium level for output or income as a whole. The system is simpler than any of Keynes' models, and might almost be called the "sub-Keynesian" system, as it underlies all the more complicated systems. We take the basic identity in its simplest form,

$$\text{Accumulation } (A) = \text{Production } (P) - \text{Consumption } (C).$$

Then we suppose that for each level of production (output) there is a corresponding level of consumption. This is what is meant by a "consumption function." Given the level of consumption that corresponds to each level of production, then we can calculate the actual accumulation that would result from each level of production. We then find the level of desired accumulation (investment), and find the level of production that is consistent with this amount of actual accumulation.

This model is illustrated in Table 1.

The first row represents some hypothetical figures for total production, the second line shows the corresponding amount of

[4] There are difficult problems involved in the measurement of heterogeneous aggregates: these, however, are postponed to the Appendix concluding this chapter.

consumption, and the third line shows the difference between the two, which must be the actual accumulation. Lines 3 and 1 together then show us what volume of output will be consistent with any given level of *desired* accumulation: this is the investment-output function. If, for instance, desired accumulation is 50, production will reach an equilibrium at 360. If production is less than this, say 340, actual accumulation will only be 40, there will be a deficiency in accumulation and a motive for expanding output. If production is greater than the equilibrium value, say 380, actual accumulation will be 60, there will be unwanted accumulations amounting to 10, and there will be strong motives to cut back output to get rid of the unwanted accumulations.

TABLE 1

1. Production (GNP)	300	320	340	360	380	400	420
2. Consumption	280	290	300	310	320	330	340
3. Accumulation (Actual)	20	30	40	50	60	70	80

Equilibrium at undercapacity. The important point now is that nothing in this model requires that the *equilibrium* output, at which desired and actual accumulation are equal, should be "ideal" or "full employment" output. In the above case, for instance, it might well be that the "ideal" output of the society is 400. At an output of 360 there will be unemployed resources; idle men, idle machines, unused factories. As long as consumption remains at 310, however, and as long as the desired rate of accumulation remains at 50, there are no forces operating in the society to increase output and employment. Indeed, any increase in output will result immediately in unwanted accumulations, which will depress the output back again to 360.

Possible solutions. Now let us look for various ways out of this situation. Let us suppose first that we can add 20 of government expenditure (or purchases) to the situation in Table 1, without affecting either consumption or desired accumulation. The situation will now be as in Table 2.

Accumulation is now equal to production less what is taken by consumption, less what is taken by government. We see that actual accumulation is smaller at each level of production, and that it is equal to 50 at the full-employment output of 400. Therefore, we now have an equilibrium at the ideal output, which is the main objective of full-employment policy.

TABLE 2

1. Production (GNP)	300	320	340	360	380	400	420
2. Consumption	280	290	300	310	320	330	340
3. Government	20	20	20	20	20	20	20
4. Accumulation (Actual)	0	10	20	30	40	50	60

The reader may, and indeed should, now object that it is most unlikely that government would take its 20 without diminishing consumption. Let us suppose, then, that for each dollar of government purchases, two-thirds of a dollar is taken from consumption. Government purchases will now have to be expanded to 60 to give us an equilbrium output of 400, as we see in Table 3; as taxes, and the like, force a reduction in consumption of 40.

TABLE 3

1. Production (GNP)	300	320	340	360	380	400	420
2. Consumption	240	250	260	270	280	290	300
3. Government	60	60	60	60	60	60	60
4. Accumulation (Actual)	0	10	20	30	40	50	60

If an expansion of government expenditures causes an equal contraction in consumption, or in consumption plus desired accumulation, the expansion will of course contribute nothing towards increasing the equilibrium output. As we shall see more clearly later, however, this result is most unlikely, even if the expansion in government expenditure is wholly financed by increased taxes.

The main lines of full-employment policy. In spite of the extreme simplicity of this model it does reveal at least the main lines along which full-employment policy may be directed. With any proposed policy we can ask four questions: at a given level of GNP, what does the policy do (1) to consumption? (2) to the amount the system is willing to accumulate? (3) to net exports? (4) to government purchases? If the net effect is to raise the total of these four components, then the policy is a good one for raising employment in an undercapacity situation.

To give a complete answer to the question of the effect of a given policy on the level of output and employment, of course, we must know *how much* it affects each of the four items. This is often difficult to predict. Consequently it is especially difficult to predict the effect of policies that affect the various components in opposite directions, unless we know more about the "how much" than we generally do.

Consider, for instance, the impact of a program of public works financed by increased taxes. The public works increase the government purchases. The increased taxes of themselves diminish household purchases, but as the government expenditure ends up as household income, the increased income may offset the increased taxes, and income after taxes (disposable income) may not be much changed. Government gives with one hand, as it were, in its expenditures what it takes with the other in taxes. If, however, the government purchases include a lot of consumer goods, prices may rise and consumption be restricted on that account. The government purchases may also have an effect on the willingness of private persons to accumulate, though what direction this effect will take is not always easy to predict. If the government purchases again result in a rise in the price of investment goods, or if such behavior on the part of government scares the wits out of capitalists so that they diminish their willingness to increase their holdings of real assets, the results will be unfavorable; if, on the other hand, the government purchases create facilities such as roads, harbors, cheap power, and so on, which are complementary to private investment, there may be an increase in the willingness of capitalists to add to their real assets. The effects on the foreign balance are even more difficult to predict; fortunately for a country as large as the United States this is a small item. The great virtue of the above type of analysis is not that it necessarily leads to definite answers in the form of sharp predictions, but that it leads to the asking of important questions, and to discovering important deficiencies in our economic information system.

Relation between price and output movements. We must now go on to consider the relation between the price movements described in the first part of this chapter and the output movements described in the second part. The main key to this relationship, and perhaps even to the understanding of both types of movements, is the system of money and finance. The first key to the understanding of the monetary system is the simple proposition that every purchase or sale involves an exchange of money for an equal value of goods or services, and that the value of a given quantity of goods or services is equal to the unit price multiplied by the quantity. Every purchase of course is a sale from the point of view of the seller, every sale a purchase from the point of view of the buyer, so that we can speak either of sales or purchases and mean the same thing. Suppose then that *A* sells 100 bushels of wheat to *B* at $2 per bushel. The value of the wheat sold (or purchased) is $200; the amount of money that changes hands is also $200. These facts can be expressed in a simple identity:

Money paid = Value of wheat sold = Price of wheat multiplied by the quantity of wheat,

or

$$E = L = P \times Q.$$

If the flow of money that is directed towards the purchase of goods increases, therefore, either the price of goods (P) or the quantity of goods purchased (Q) must increase, or, of course, both may increase in suitable proportions. Thus if, in the above example, the amount of money directed towards the purchase of wheat rises from $200 to $300, then if the quantity sold remains unchanged at 100 bushels, the price must rise to $3 per bushel; if the price remains unchanged at $2 per bushel, the quantity sold will rise to 150 bushels; and if, say, the price rises to $2.50, the quantity will rise to 120 bushels.

National money income depends on money flows. It is only a slight oversimplification to say that what happens to the *dollar value* of national product, roughly, the National Money Income) depends on what happens to money flows, but that the effect of a change in the dollar value of the national product may be divided between a change in prices and a change in outputs. Thus, if there is a rise in the dollar value of the national product, this may take the form of a rise in prices, with outputs remaining the same, or a rise in outputs, with prices remaining the same, or of some combination of a rise in outputs and prices. The more prices rise, the less outputs rise; the more outputs rise, the less prices rise. The importance of this proposition may be seen in the diverse experience of agriculture and industry in the course of a severe depression. Both sectors of the economy suffer a decline in the total value of their product—that is, in the dollar income that the sale of their product brings in. In agriculture, however, there is little or no decline in output. Almost all the decline in income, therefore, is reflected in a decline in prices. In industry, prices and money wages are less flexible, and do not fall as much as the total income. There is, therefore, a compensating fall in output and employment.

Velocity of circulation. From 1929 to 1932 the dollar value of the American national income just about halved. In order to understand a movement of this magnitude we must look to the monetary system for an explanation. Let us make first a very simple "model" of a monetary system in which there is only one kind of money, and the amount or stock of money is fixed at M dollars. Every time a dollar changes hands the transaction is both a receipt and an expenditure—an expenditure to the person giving out the money, and a receipt to the person taking it in. Every expenditure is a receipt to some other person; every receipt an expenditure from some other person. In our personal experience, of course, receipts and expenditures are not the same thing, and it is quite possible for an individual to spend more or less money than he gets and so run down or build up his stock of money. In a closed society, however, expenditure and receipts are exactly the same thing, being merely two different ways of recording a single set of transactions.

Now let us suppose that all the people—or even most people—in the society decide that they are holding too much money, and decide to spend more than they are getting. Remembering our initial assumption that the stock of money is fixed, we can see that the result of this cannot be a decline in the stock of money: one person may be able to diminish his money stock, but only if others increase theirs. The money stock is a shifting cargo, which shifts around among the pockets of the people, but does not change in quantity. If everyone increases his expenditures, therefore, the result is that everyone finds his receipts are also increased, and his money stock will probably be about the same as before.

A movement of the kind described above is what is known as a rise in the *velocity of circulation*. The velocity of circulation (V) is measured by the following ratio:

$$\frac{\text{total expenditures (or receipts)}}{\text{total stock of money}} \text{ or } \frac{E}{M}.$$

That is,

$$V = \frac{E}{M}, \text{ or } E = MV.$$

In the absence of a change in the money stock a rise in velocity must raise (and a fall must lower) total receipts. What the velocity measures is the psychological attitude of people towards their stock of money in relation to their flow or "throughput" of money. If velocity rises, this means that people wish to hold less money in relation to their flow of receipts or expenditures. It thus measures a fundamental psychological magnitude which has a certain stability, but which is also subject to long-term drift and to important short-term fluctuations. It is closely related to "liquidity preference," which is measured by the preferred proportion of money to *assets:* a rise in liquidity preference usually implies a fall in velocity. A diminished desire to hold money will raise velocity, whether because of a change in habits of payment (more frequent paychecks), a diminution in the general uncertainty about the future, or a fear that the value of money will fall because of an inflation of prices.

The instability of velocity and money flows. Even if there were no changes in the quantity of money, we can now see how the dynamics of velocity might generate instability in the total volume of expenditures. Let us suppose that there is a random increase in velocity: people as a whole suddenly decide that they have been holding too much money, and everyone increases his expenditures. This raises total receipts, and unless there is a corresponding increase in outputs, this will raise prices. If the rise in prices leads to a feeling that money is going to drop further in value, this may lead to a further increase in velocity, and a further rise in prices. Eventually, however, prices will become "high" relative to some standard in the minds of people, generated by their past experience. When people begin to perceive prices as "high" they begin to expect a fall: this means they become more eager to hold on to money, and anxious to try to increase their money stocks. This in turn means a fall in velocity, a fall in expenditures, and—unless offset by a fall in outputs—a fall in prices. When prices begin to fall, however, people tend to expect a further fall: this decreases velocity still more, and the more people try to hang on to or to increase their money stocks, the more receipts and prices fall. Prices cannot fall without getting "low": at this point people begin to expect a rise, velocities start to increase, people start trying to unload their money stocks, and prices rise again.

Even if velocities, expenditures, and prices and outputs have been fairly stable for a period, this stability may not last, because of the dependence of velocity on uncertainty. In a period of relative stability uncertainty declines, hence people become less willing to hold money simply as a "precautionary" measure. Velocity therefore may increase, and an upward drift in expenditures sets in. This may be sufficient to set off a cycle of the kind outlined above.

For stability, money-stock fluctuations must offset velocity changes. It is clear that if a velocity cycle is to be smoothed out, there must be an increase in the stock of money to offset a decline in velocity, and a decrease in the stock of money to offset an increase in velocity. Suppose we start from a position where the stock of money is 100 and the velocity is 20 times a year:

total expenditures (or receipts) will be 2,000. If the velocity now rises to 25 times a year, and there is no change in the stock of money, total expenditures (receipts) will be 2,500. If we wish to stabilize expenditures at 2,000 we must diminish the money stock to 80. Similarly, if velocity falls to, say, 10 times a year, this can be offset by an increase in the money stock to 200.

Unfortunately, under a system like the present American economy where by far the larger part of the money stock consists of commercial bank deposits, changes in the stock of money are more likely to intensify rather than to smooth out the velocity cycle. When velocities are rising, the total volume of bank deposits is also likely to expand, thus accentuating the rise in expenditures, receipts, incomes, and prices; when velocities are falling, the reverse process takes place. Explanation of the exact reasons for this and of the mechanisms by which the process operates must wait till a later chapter.[5]

Government as the governor. It is clear, however, that the "private" money system is likely to be destabilizing rather than stabilizing, and that if we are to find a stabilizer in the system it almost has to be government. Government, that is to say, has an inescapable obligation to act as a "governor." The analogy of the governor or thermostat (a class of operations known generally as "cybernetic mechanisms," from the Greek word meaning "steersman") is fairly exact. A governor on an engine is a device that speeds the engine up when it is going "too slow" and slows it down when it is going "too fast." A thermostat turns on the heat when the room is too cold and turns it off when the room is too hot. Similarly a monetary stabilizing mechanism would "slow down" the expansion of the money stock when the economy got "too fast" and would speed it up when the economy got "too slow." What this means roughly is that government must act in an inflationary manner when the private sector is being deflationary, and vice versa.

[5] See pp. 217-219.

Difficulty of stabilizing *both* prices and outputs. The ways in which a government can act in an inflationary or deflationary manner will be discussed in more detail in Chapters 8 and 9. Here we may note briefly that budget deficits are inflationary, surpluses are deflationary; big budgets, even if balanced, are inflationary, small budgets may be deflationary. In addition to the more direct impact of expenditures and taxation there are many regulatory policies that may be either inflationary or deflationary. All in all, it is not difficult for a government to act in a *generally* inflationary or deflationary manner. The problem of economic stabilization, however, is greatly complicated by the fact that we want to control not one variable but at least two—both prices and outputs. If the stabilization problem merely involved the control of aggregate money income it would not be too difficult, though even here there may be some unsolved problems of timing and information—of knowing just *when* to act. Even if we succeeded in stabilizing aggregate money income, however, there might still be fluctuations, in opposite directions, in output and prices. Thus with an aggregate money income of 400, one year the output index might be 400 and the price index 100, another year output might be 300 and the price index 133. Conversely, if we succeeded in stabilizing prices there could be fluctuations in output and money income; if we stabilized output there could be fluctuations in prices and money income.

The dilemma of stabilization. It is this twofold nature of the stabilization problem that gives rise to what may be the greatest dilemma of economic policy: can we stabilize both outputs and prices?—and if not, which do we abandon, or how do we divide our efforts between them? It is clear that if we have to choose between the two evils of unstable outputs and unstable prices —more exactly, in the way this dilemma is actually posed, between unemployment and inflation—we would choose inflation, for our values are profoundly colored by the shock of the Great Depression. On the other hand a people who have gone through the experience of hyperinflation, like the Germans, may well feel that a little unemployment is a small price to pay for the blessings of continued price stability.

The problem resolves itself into two. The first is, how far can we *avoid* the dilemma—how far can we manage to stabilize both output and prices within reasonable limits? All the institutions and policies of society can be scrutinized with this aim in view. The second problem is posed if, after all our efforts to avoid the dilemma, we still find that the desired level of output can only be achieved by continued inflation, or that the desired degree of price stability can only be achieved by allowing output sometimes to fall below what we desire. For how, then, do we choose among the various alternatives? We may note that this is the way economic problems generally pose themselves—if we cannot have enough of both *A* and *B*, we first ask how can we get more of both (this is economic progress); then, when we have pushed as far along this line as we can, we are compelled to ask "is it worth giving up what must be given up of *B* in order to get an additional quantity of *A*?" or vice versa. The problem is "solved" when we feel that any sacrifice of *B* for *A* or *A* for *B* will not be worth while—that is, what is gained is worth less to us than what is given up.

APPENDIX TO CHAPTER 3

Definition and measurement of economic aggregates

In this chapter we have made a great deal of use of economic aggregates like National Money Income, Gross National Product, aggregate consumption (or output or accumulation), and so on. We should not leave the subject without noting certain difficulties in both the definition and the measurement of these concepts.

The problem of "netness." There is first the problem of "netness" in the definition of the aggregate output (product), consumption, and accumulation concepts. Every item of production involves some item of consumption as a "cost." Thus, when wheat is ground into flour, the stock of flour increases but the stock of wheat diminishes. We wish to define the "net production" involved in the grinding of wheat into flour, therefore, as the flour *less* the wheat. But the grinding process has also involved the payment of wages and the wear and tear of machines, which are also in a sense "costs." How shall we treat these? Ricardo, for instance, in defining the net product, subtracted the consumption of the laborers, just as we subtract the feed of a cow in calculating its net production of milk. For most purposes this seems altogether too "net"—there is surely a difference between the food a cow consumes and the food a workman consumes! There are further difficulties involved in estimating wear and tear, or depreciation of fixed equipment. The equipment might have depreciated even if it had not been used: hence in calculating the net production involved in grinding the flour we should only count as consumption the difference between the actual wear and tear of the machines and what would have happened to them even if they had not been used —this Keynes called "User Cost."

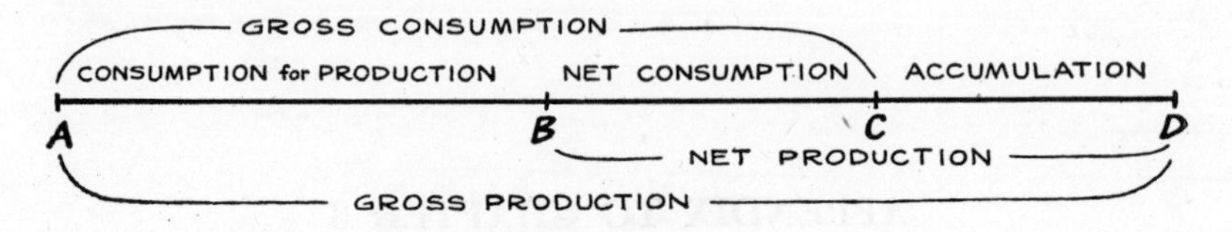

Figure 3-1.

Whatever our concept of "netness," however, it is always possible, by making our definitions of production and consumption consistent—that is, of the same degree of netness—to insure that the "basic identity" of the bathtub theorem remains true. This is illustrated in Figure 3-1. *AD* is gross production, and *AB* is the consumption necessitated by this production, so that *BD* is net production. *AC* is gross consumption, so that *CD* is accumulation, and *BC* is net consumption. We can see readily that no matter where we put the point *B*—*i.e.*, no matter how broadly or narrowly we define "consumption involved in production"—provided we stick to the definition it is always true that accumulation is equal to either gross production less gross consumption, or net production less net consumption.

In National Income Accounting the most "gross" concept usually employed is that of the Gross National Product, or GNP, which is defined as total production net of all obvious raw materials or intermediate products, but not net of depreciation of fixed capital, nor, of course, of the consumption of wage earners. Subtracting the depreciation of fixed capital from the GNP we get the Net National Product, or NNP. In the United States accounts various other deductions are made from the NNP (mainly indirect taxes) to get what is called the National Income. There are various other refinements of these concepts making allowance for taxes, government transfers, and so on, which need not detain us now. The reader who wishes to go into these details will find them in the National Income supplement of the Survey of Current Business, issued by the Department of Commerce.

The measurement of heterogeneous aggregates. Even when we have defined the aggregates we wish to measure, we have still not solved the problem of measuring them. The problem arises because the aggregates of production, consumption, and accumulation are "heterogeneous"—that is, they consist not of a single number or of a collection of similar items but of a *list* of different items—so many bushels of wheat, ounces of gold, barrels of oil, Thunderbird cars, this house and that picture and the other custom-built hi-fi set. No matter how complex the list, something like the "bathtub theorem" holds, for the change in the list of the stock of goods (accumulation) is equal to the items added to the list (production) minus the items taken away from the list (consumption). For most purposes, however, we want to represent these long lists of items by single numbers, and the only way in which this can be done is through a system of valuation by which each item on the list is replaced by an equivalent number of units of the "measure of value." The commonest measure of value is, of course, money—say, dollars—and it is in dollar terms that aggregate production, consumption, and accumulation are usually measured. Thus when we say that the GNP in 1956 was 412 billion dollars, we mean that every item in the long list of products has been valued in dollar terms and these sums added up. Thus instead of having something like, say, x tons of wheat and y ounces of gold and z Thunderbirds, we have $\$X$ worth of wheat, $\$Y$ worth of gold, and $\$Z$ worth of Thunderbirds, or $\$(X + Y + Z)$ worth of all three together.

In order to reduce tons or ounces to dollars worth we have to multiply the physical quantity by a ratio of "dollars worth per unit," which looks very much like a price but is better called a "valuation coefficient." Thus 100 bushels of wheat at $2 per bushel is 200 dollars worth of wheat; the $2 per bushel is the valuation coefficient. If the valuation coefficients are current prices we get the *current* value of output, of the GNP, of consumption, of national income, or of whatever aggregate we arc considering. If, however, we wish to obtain a measure of the "real" volume of these physical aggregates that will hold from year to year we must value the items at *constant* valuation coefficients. The usual practice is to select some year—1939 in the U. S. Department of Commerce figures—and take the prices of that year as the valuation coefficients. Then we calculate *what would have been* the value of the various aggregates at 1939 prices. Real difficulties arise with this procedure when the commodities themselves change in quality and in kind—we cannot, for instance, compare directly the output of television sets with radios, or automobiles with horse carriages. There are great difficulties also in estimating the output of government, especially in such matters as defense expenditure. In spite of these difficulties, however, the figures obtained by the various procedures have some meaning, provided that we do not take them as an exact measure of something that by its very nature can only be roughly quantitative.

4

Economic justice

Democracies can not afford
To let injustice be ignored,
Though it might cause them some surprise
To find just where injustice lies.
We know less clearly what is meant
By Justice than by Discontent,
And so the search for Justice leads
To balancing Desert with Needs.

Justice as political discontent. The concept of justice has always been an elusive one, and has concerned man from the earliest times. For all its elusiveness it has been of enormous importance in the dynamics of human life and society, at least in a negative sense, for it is the sense of injustice that more than anything else drives men to political action of all kinds.

The sense of injustice is the feeling that something is wrong not merely with our personal condition but with the world at large. It is this sense of something needing amendment in the *world at large* that makes the feeling of injustice so important for *political* action. A merely personal discontent leads to merely personal policies and activities, within the existing framework of laws, customs, and institutions. If we don't like our job we look for another, if we don't like our house we look for another, if we don't like the town where we live we move to another. Political discontent, however, leads towards organization to change the framework of the society within which we move, by voting in a new party, by lobbying for new laws, or by fomenting a new revolution.

A "discontent" as a divergence of "real" from "ideal." If, then, we are to understand the dynamics of the movement towards economic justice, we must look for the economic sources of political discontents. We must ask ourselves what aspects of the over-all economic system are perceived as "wrong." In order to answer this question we must ask what would be perceived as "right"—that is, what are the ideals by which existing situations are judged? A "discontent" is a perceived *difference* between an imagined ideal state of affairs and a perceived reality. The source of discontent, therefore, is found in the nature of the image of the ideal on the one hand, and of the perception of the real on the other.

"Commutative" justice as ideal distribution. Stated in this way, economic justice seems to include all the goals and ideals of economic life. There is, however, a more restricted use of the term in the sense of "justice in distribution"—sometimes called "commutative justice," to which we shall devote particular attention in this chapter.

The particular discontent that gives rise to political activity directed towards redistribution also depends, of course, on a comparison of a perceived "real" state of affairs with some image of the ideal. In this case, however, the image of the ideal is hard to establish clearly and firmly. There seem to be several conflicting ideals among which some compromise must be made.

This makes the problem of ideal distribution much more difficult than, say, the problem of progress or of stability. Not that the problem of conflicting ideals is absent in these other cases. Economic progress, for instance, frequently has a high cost, and we certainly cannot say that any increase in the rate of economic development is always desirable. But we do have a feeling that the answer lies in a fairly simple balancing of advantage against social cost, and that in economic development we are at least proceeding down a single street. In considering the ideal distribution, however, this "linear" aspect of the problem is absent: we wander all over the map in a maze of conflicting objectives.

Conflicting ideals of distribution: "merit" *vs.* "need." Let us consider, for instance, two conflicting, and yet plausible ideals of distribution. One, which goes back to an ancient notion of justice as a situation in which everybody gets what he deserves, may be called the *merit standard.* The other, which goes back to another ancient notion of justice as the situation in which everybody gets what he needs, may be called the *need standard.*

The "contributive standard" substitutes for the "merit standard." The singleminded pursuit of either of these standards alone leads us into impossible contradictions. In both cases we find ourselves at the outset faced with the problem of an objective *measure*—of desert in the one case and of need in the other. This is a problem of agreement as to what constitutes information: how can we know, for instance, in a way that will be agreeable to all, what each deserves? "Use every man after his desert and who should 'scape whipping." Most of us probably have a somewhat inflated notion of our own merits, and the device of simply asking everyone what he thought he deserved would probably not result in a solution acceptable to all. Consequently the ideal of the merit standard inevitably gets pushed towards a somewhat different ideal, that of the *contributive standard*—to each according to his contribution. It would be a dangerous ethical fallacy to equate desert with contribution. Yet this identification seems to offer the only hope of solid ground in the midst of a bog of tentative opinion and private judgments. Otherwise, who is to judge between "Happy, undeserving *A*" and "wretched, meritorious *B*"?

Reward as the measure of contribution. Even the contributive standard presents the gravest difficulties of measurement. The most objective measure would seem to be obtained through the impersonal dictates of a free market. In such a market an equilibrium set of prices tends to be established for factors of production. The contribution to the total product made by any factor can then be estimated by multiplying the price of its services by the quantity rendered. Thus, if the market price of the services of my person is $2 per hour, and if I work 2,500 hours a year, the contribution I make to the total product and the value of the reward I receive are both equal to $5,000. Stated in this crude way it is clear that contribution has simply been measured by actual reward, and we have really said little more than "everybody gets what he gets."

Physical and value products. Attempts have been made to avoid the apparent tautology involved in measuring contribution by reward by supposing that contribution is measured by the marginal product, and that reward is only equal to marginal product under some circumstances, so that the possibility emerges that reward may not be according to contribution. The problems that emerge here are of a rather technical nature. The difficulty, however, can be grasped more easily than the solution. In a simple case of a workman producing with his own hands and tools a single product the concept of "contribution" is fairly clear: the cobbler has contributed the shoes on his shelves, the farmer the wheat in his barn. The "take" of the cobbler, however, is not shoes, nor that of the farmer wheat, except in small part, and if the shoes and the wheat and the million other products of economic activity are to be added up into a single measure of output or income, they must be priced or valued in terms of some common unit, say the dollar. Thus the value of any physical product depends on the whole price system, and for each set of prices there is a corresponding set of incomes of different contributors. We feel a little uneasy, however, in supposing that there is always *one* price system that is "right" from all points of view. But if there is not a single, unequivocal price system at which the various contributions and rewards are valued, physical product does not unambiguously determine either contribution or reward. Even if the physical productivity of the shoemaker does not change, a change in the price of shoes will change both his contribution and his reward.

The measurement of need. The problem of the measurement of "need" is also a great obstacle to the establishment of a "need standard" as an ideal of distribution. Just as it is impossible to judge the deserts of another in a way that will command general acceptance, so it is impossible to judge his need. On these grounds alone the need standard as a single ideal breaks down. Nevertheless, there are situations in which distribution according to rough estimates of needs is possible. Such a situation is found generally within the confines of the family, where the total family income is spent according to some rough criterion of the needs of the members. In emergency situations, as among a group of castaways, or in time of war or famine in larger societies, rationing is used as an attempt to apportion according to need.

Rationing. Nothing illustrates the difficulties of the need standard as clearly as the problems encountered in rationing. The simplest method of apportionment is, of course, to give everyone an equal share. This has been done—in wartime, for instance—in the case of sugar and coffee. Equal distribution, however, is clearly inequitable, for needs are not equal. Some like sugar, some do not; some bake cakes, some do not; some are diabetic, some are not. Hence, rationing means no hardship for some, and considerable hardship for others. The equal rationing of coffee is even more inequitable—a household where only one member drinks coffee feels no pinch, whereas a household of heavy coffee drinkers is sharply restricted. Gasoline rationing is even more difficult. With the same ration, *A* is happy, *B* is not; for *A* the car is a luxury, for *B* it is a necessity.

Even for the simplest needs, therefore, equal rationing is hopelessly unjust. Hence, there must be graduated rationing; special food rations for heavy workers, special gasoline rations for heavy drivers, and so on. The attempt to ration for individual needs, however, results in a piling of board on board and application on application until red tape engulfs everybody. Even in the case of such a basic "need" as food, rationing cannot be applied as a universal principle. If all food were rationed, no matter how carefully the ration were to be graduated according to age, sex, and occupation, some would starve and some would be relatively comfortable, for nutritional requirements differ markedly from person to person. It is a basic principle of food rationing in wartime, therefore, that some important source of calories must be left unrationed—such as bread in England or potatoes in Germany.

The "point price" system. It is significant that as the technique of rationing develops it tends to approximate more and more to a price system, using the criterion of effective demand rather than of need. Point rationing is a partial return to a price system; what is, in effect, a supplementary money is issued (the ration tickets), and demand is equated to supply by adjusting "point prices" rather than the regular money prices. But whereas money prices can adjust to every local situation, rising to accommodate a temporary scarcity and falling to relieve a temporary glut, "point prices" have to be fixed by the rationing authority at regular intervals. Errors in the setting of point prices therefore lead to large wastages of perishable products before they are adjusted. Any "administered" price system is bound to run into these difficulties, and as the control of distribution necessarily involves control of prices, controlled distribution likewise runs into a similar administrative impasse.

Difficulty of estimating "needs." If the criterion of need is so difficult to apply even in the case of basic necessities, how much more difficult would it be to apply it to the luxuries and conveniences of life! The thought of distributing phonograph records, books, travel, and the like according to individual need by some rationing authority is one before which the stoutest communist might quail. It may be objected that we can still permit goods to be allocated through the price system, so that there is a certain amount of consumers' choice, and yet ration *incomes* according to need. But what standards could we follow in such a case? Should we give all university graduates double the income of high school graduates, because presumably a college education breeds expensive tastes? There is simply no administrative solution to the problem of allocation according to need, once we get away from the barest necessities, and even there the administrative problem is almost insuperably difficult and can only be solved by rule-of-thumb methods.

The "merit standard" denies *community*. Even if the measurement problems could be solved, there are more fundamental reasons why neither the merit standard nor the need standard is satisfactory as a single criterion of ideal distribution. The merit standard, at least in the form of a contributive standard, breaks down because we are forced to recognize that society has certain obligations towards nonproducers, particularly towards children, old people, the sick, the insane, and the involuntarily unemployed. We must break down the criterion of "reward according to contribution" in some cases; hence, it loses its validity as a general formula. The reason for this seems to be that there is a certain sense of kinship that binds us all together and makes us feel in a measure responsible for the welfare of all. We must support the unproductive elements of society because in some sense they "belong" to us, just as a limb belongs to us. A craftsman does not deny his feet shoes because he earns his living with his hands. We cannot be pure individualists because we are not pure individuals; we are bound together in a social web that permits none of us to be either completely independent of others or completely nonresponsible for others. We have seen that the contributive standard breaks down in the case of the family. It is because society in some measure shares this family feeling that the standard breaks down for society as a whole.

The "need standard" denies "scarcity." Even if there were no difficulties in the measurement of needs, the need standard would still face certain fundamental difficulties of application. The main difficulty here is that there is no particular reason to suppose that distribution according to needs would just exhaust the product: the sum of needs may be either less than or greater than the total product. We are less likely to encounter this difficulty in the case of the contributive standard. If everybody gets what he puts into the pot there is a certain presumption that this rule of distribution will just exhaust what is in the pot to be distributed. If everyone gets what he "needs," however, either there may be something left over in the pot, or the pot may prove to be not quite large enough to supply all the needs of those who are to be served from its contents.

The "pure communist" criterion. The difficulties in the application of the need standard are brought out clearly when we examine the possible application of what might be called the "pure communist" criterion—"From each according to his abilities, to each according to his needs." There is much that is appealing about this standard, and a good deal of the ethical appeal of communism rests on it. Nevertheless, the attempt to apply it is tragically self-defeating, simply because abilities and needs do not usually correspond. The things we most want to do, and are best able to do—those activities miscalled "leisure" —do not in general produce a sufficient quantity of the commodities that we need. This is the fact that makes necessary the whole system of economic values and institutions. Suppose, for instance, that we had a sociey in which everybody liked fishing and had great ability in the art, but in which nobody liked fish, and in which, to make the case even stronger, fish did not agree with the people so that they had to live mainly on bread. It would require a remarkable act of chemical magic to transform the fish that the abilities produced into the bread that the needs demanded! Such a society would be forced to do something to make fishing unattractive relative to breadmaking. The price of fish and the wages of fishers would have to be low, and the price of bread and the wages of breadmakers high, even though the needs of the two groups might be identical. The logic of valuation would force the authorities to abandon any attempt to distribute solely according to need; they would have to distribute in order to encourage some lines of production and discourage others. This is what has happened in Communist Russia, where the desire for increased production continually thwarts the desire for equalitarian distribution.

The "equality standard": equalization of marginal utility. A special, and more sophisticated, case of the need standard is the "equality standard"—the claim that the ideal mode of distribution is to have all incomes equal. The theoretical foundations of this standard are worth examination, not only because of its historical importance as an element in political dynamics and as a mover of both men and nations, but also because some of the basic problems involved in a critique of standards emerge clearly.

Let us suppose first that it is possible to assign to any individual a number that measures his state of well-being or welfare. This is his "total utility." Suppose further that for each level of a person's income we can assign such a utility number. We then define the marginal utility of income as the change in total utility that results from a unit change in income. Now suppose that it is possible to add the total utilities of different individuals to get a total social utility for the whole society. On these assumptions we could say that total social utility was at a maximum when the marginal utility of income of all individuals was equal. Suppose, for instance, that for individual *A* the marginal utility of income was 5 "utils per dollar" and that for individual *B* it was 3 utils per dollar. Then if a dollar were taken from *B* and given to *A*, *B* would lose 3 utils and *A* would gain 5 utils, there being a total social gain of 2 utils. If now we suppose a law of diminishing marginal utility of income with increase of income, as we go on transferring income from *B* to *A*, *A*'s marginal utility of income falls as he gets richer and *B*'s marginal utility of income rises as he gets poorer until finally both are equal, say at 4 utils per dollar. At this point it no longer increases social utility to transfer income from one to the other, for the gain of one would be just equal to the loss of the other.

Equality of marginal utility does *not* imply equal incomes. It should be observed that the equality for all individuals of their marginal utility of income does not in itself imply that social utility is at a maximum when all incomes are equal. Thus in

Fig. 4-1 we draw the marginal utility of income curves for two individuals. Individual I cares very little for riches, and his marginal utility of income diminishes rapidly as his income increases. Individual II enjoys riches a great deal: his marginal utility of income declines very slowly. If now both have the same marginal utility of income, O_1A_1 ($= O_2A_2$), individual I will have a much smaller income (A_1B_1) than individual II (A_2B_2).

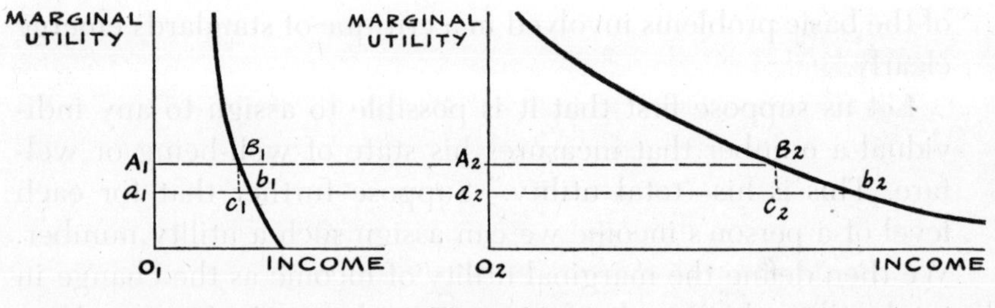

Figure 4-1.

An even more striking conclusion follows from this figure. If income increases, the marginal utility of income will fall, say to O_1a_1. The increase in the income of the second individual (c_2b_2) then should be greater than the increase in the income of the first (c_1b_1). Not quite "to him that hath shall be given," but "to him that enjoyeth most what he hath, to him should be given more." In a society where individuals are unlike in regard to the slopes of their marginal utility curves, assuming that the marginal utilities of different individuals are roughly the same for subsistence levels of income, then an increase in the total income of the society should result in more unequal distribution as the increase in income should go mainly to those who will enjoy it most.

Incomes should be equal only if all men are alike. The conclusion that incomes should be equal, therefore, follows from the principle of equality of marginal utility of income only if the further assumption is made that all men are alike, at least in regard to their utility of income curves. Lerner has tried to argue that although we do not know this, in the absence of knowledge this is the most probable assumption.[1] This argument from ignorance is not very convincing: to say that something either will or will not happen is not the same as to say that there is a 50-50 chance of its happening. Nevertheless, the assumption that men are all very much alike is the foundation of democratic institutions ("We hold these truths to be self-evident . . .") and we certainly do not attempt in politics to give the voter a number of votes in proportion to his intelligence and his ability to use them. The one-man-one-vote principle is forced upon us by the recognition of the practical impossibility of any other. So, the equalitarians argue, there is no good reason why one man should have more "dollar votes" (income) than another.

The case for inequality—the "peak" as ideal. On the other side, however, it must be admitted that there is a case for inequality. The most convincing argument is that it is not the average level of achievement that measures the value of a culture, but the peak levels that it reaches. On this standard a society of mud huts and a great cathedral is better than a society of equal resources having stone huts and no cathedral. One perfect lyric is worth a million tons of trashy Sunday Supplements. It is by the quality of its saints and heroes, not its common men, and by its masterpieces and not by its domestic utensils, that a culture should be judged. This point of view is not to be dismissed lightly, even though it is capable of absurdity and perversion, and though it does not fit comfortably into the ideals and prejudices of a predominantly democratic society. Like any other standard it becomes absurd when it is pushed to its logical conclusion, which would be that in economic terms anything that made the richest man in a society richer would be an improvement! It is an idea that is also capable of being put to very base uses in the support of fascism and other authoritarian and antidemocratic ideologies.

The optimum degree of inequality. Nevertheless the notion that there is some "ideal" degree of inequality is a useful one.

[1] A. P. Lerner, *The Economics of Control* (New York: The Macmillan Co., 1944), Chapter 3.

As we move away from this towards greater equality we lose "peakedness," interest, color, excitement, drama: the perfectly equal is the perfectly dull. As we move away from this imaginary ideal in the other direction, towards greater inequality, we lose democracy, brotherhood, the concern and responsibility of all for all which is what makes organization tolerable. Somewhere in the middle, at the blessed Aristotelian mean, is an optimum point from which any movement one way or the other costs us more than we gain. It is easy, of course, to postulate the existence of such a point—it is quite another matter to find it, or to agree on where it is. There is likely to be a constant tension in society between the democratic forces pulling towards greater equality and the aristocratic forces pulling towards greater "peakedness." Where the balance lies depends on the general nature of the society.

Rich societies can afford to be equalitarian. In this connection we might venture one hypothesis. It is that the richer the society —that is, the greater its per-capita income—the more likely it is to move its ideal distribution towards the equalitarian end of the scale. Equality, in other words, is a luxury of rich societies. If a poor society is to achieve anything at all it must develop a high degree of inequality—the small economic surplus must be concentrated in a few hands if *any* high-level achievements are to be made. Thus, all ancient civilizations rested on a high degree of inequality: the achievements of Egypt, Babylon, Greece, and Rome rested on slavery, which is about the most unequal state possible. Yet an equalitarian society with the limited techniques and resources that ancient civilizations had at their disposal could never have produced art and architecture, philosophy and science. It is only with the rise of modern science and technology that we have perceived the possibility of a society that is *both* equalitarian and rich in high achievements.

Exploitation and discrimination. Just as the need-standard, coupled with a belief in the basic similarity of all men, leads to a demand for equality, so the merit-standard, coupled with a belief in the worth of all men, leads to a demand for a society free from exploitation and discrimination. It is not easy to frame exact definitions for these concepts. Nevertheless, they correspond to an important source of the feeling of injustice, and these subjective feelings of being exploited or discriminated against frequently are derived from the observation of objective realities.

In the broadest sense, exploitation may be said to occur whenever one receives less than his contribution and another receives more. As we have seen, however, the contributive standard cannot be applied rigidly because of the universally acknowledged necessity of supporting many noncontributors—children, old people, the sick, and so on. The definition of exploitation must therefore be narrowed, and yet at the same time it becomes more difficult to apply: we are thrown back in a sense on the vagueness of the merit-standard itself, and we have to say that there is exploitation when some get less than they "deserve" and some get more. Still another implication of the concept of exploitation is that of the relationship between the exploiter and the exploited—the exploiter "exploits" the exploited by taking away from them what they have produced. We see that the concept of exploitation runs into all the difficulties that we have previously observed in the contributive standard. Nevertheless, we cannot cast the concept aside. We can neither deny the possibility—indeed, the actuality—of exploitation, nor claim any very good way of recognizing it when we see it!

Exploitation and monopoly. The economist has attempted to solve this problem by relating exploitation to the presence of monopoly, and this is at least a guide line. The monopolist gets more than he "deserves" because, if it were not for monopoly, what he supplies would be supplied cheaper. Because the monopolist is in a position to restrict output below what it would be if there were not a monopoly he can thereby obtain a higher price for what he sells. Monopoly, that is, represents an obstacle to the free flow of resources among occupations. On the monopolist's side of the obstacle there are fewer resources and therefore higher rewards than there would be if the obstacle were not present.

It is easy to see that a monopolist is an exploiter: it is more difficult to identify those whom he exploits. The question of the distribution of the losses of monopoly among those who are adversely affected by it is by no means easy to answer. On the one hand there is something lost by the purchasers of the monopolist's product, who have to pay a higher price than they otherwise would. Then there is something lost by those who would *like* to be making the monopolist's product at prices between the monopoly price and the competitive price, but who are excluded from this occupation because of the obstacle that is the source of the monopoly power. Finally, we may have a situation known in economics as "monopsony," where resources receive a return less than they should, not because they are prevented from getting into some other occupation, but because there are obstacles to their leaving the occupation that they are now in.

"Natural" and "artificial" monopoly. One of the difficulties in dealing with monopoly is that it is not always easy to tell when the "obstacles" to the movement of resources, the obstacles that are the source of the *differences* of remuneration, are "natural" and when they are "artificial." Where the obstacles are natural we would not generally regard the difference in rewards as a sign of exploitation. The high incomes of the movie star, of the author of best-sellers, of top executives, may well be a result of a natural and inevitable scarcity of the peculiar talents—or luck—required by these positions, and not a result of any artificial obstacles to the performance of these tasks. What prevents the ordinary person from earning these high incomes is not that he is excluded from these occupations by law, custom, or the political and economic power of the incumbents, but that he does not possess the rare degree of ability required.

Monopolies of knowledge. When the obstacle to movement is not some innate and unalterable ability but ignorance—a lack of knowledge that may conceivably be remedied—then the situation looks more like exploitation, especially if the dominant class (the one on the favorable or high-income side of the obstacle) has control over the sources of knowledge. A monopoly of education is probably the most dangerous of all monopolies, because it is the most stable. Indeed, were it not for the fact that formal education is by no means the only way to acquire knowledge, a monopoly of formal education would be almost unshakable. It may happen also that the knowledge that is transmitted in formal education becomes in part useless or obsolete with the gradual change in the circumstances of the time. When this happens a revolutionary situation is in the making: a new class rises, possessing and transmitting the knowledge requisite to the times, and if the old governing class does not adapt itself it will eventually be displaced by the possessers of the more appropriate knowledge. Thus with the rise of commerce from the fourteenth century on in the Western world, the knightly and churchly knowledge on which the governing class of the Middle Ages based its dominance gradually lost much of its relevance, and the mercantile and commercial classes, whose knowledge was not for the most part gained from schools but from informal oral teaching and experience, became the key centers of relevant knowledge and so gradually—or sometimes violently—displaced the older.

Exploitation by artificial immobility. When the obstacle to movement consists of statutory regulations or prohibitions sanctioned by law or even by custom, the presence of exploitation may almost be taken for granted. By immigration restrictions a country may "exploit" those who otherwise might wish to emigrate to it, though this problem, as we shall see, becomes much more complicated when long-run dynamic considerations are taken into account.[2] A craft union that sets up artificial barriers to entry and that can prevent non-union members from working at the trade "exploits" both those who would like to enter the craft but are prevented by the restrictions, and those who purchase the ultimate product of the craft. An employer who can "tie" his labor force to him, whether by reason of geographical isolation as in some isolated manufacturing or mining town, or even by quasi-benevolent schemes such as pension plans, may be in a position to exploit his workers

[2] See p. 49.

"monopsonistically"—they may be paid less than the prevailing wage because they cannot leave the occupation.

Discrimination. An important aspect of the problem of exploitation is *discrimination.* This is the term given to the situation where certain *groups* or classes of individuals receive less than they "should" because of certain obstacles to movement into or out of occupations that they face as a group. Wherever, that is to say, an individual is exploited because of his membership in a group, we have discrimination.

There are many kinds of groups that suffer discrimination. Racial discrimination results in Negroes, Mexicans, Chinese, and certain immigrant groups receiving lower wages for a given job than native white Americans. Sex discrimination results in women receiving lower wages for a given job than men. Age discrimination results in the exploitation of children and old people. Caste discrimination results in lower wages for people with "inferior" language and manners.

It is a general economic principle that discrimination exists only in the presence of monopoly. If two different prices exist for the same commodity in a competitive market, all the buyers will rush to buy from the venders selling at the lower price, so that their price will rise, while the lack of buyers forces the high-price sellers to lower *their* prices, until everyone is selling at the same price. If the labor market were perfectly competitive, with large numbers of both workers and employers, and open knowledge of the wages and abilities offered, there could not be different wages for the same work, for employers would all rush to employ the low-wage workers, thus bidding up their wage, and would not employ the high-wage workers until their wage had come down to the general level. If the labor market were perfectly competitive, for instance, it would be impossible to maintain a higher wage rate for whites than for Negroes of equal ability in identical jobs, for in that case employers would rush to employ Negroes, and any employer who employed whites only would be forced out of business.

Monopoly may be on the side of employer or workers. Discrimination can exist only where there are elements of monopoly, either on the side of the employer, or on the side of organized labor. If, for instance, we have a situation in which a single employer is faced by two groups of employees, one of which is prepared to work for a lower wage than the other, he may be able to make greater profits by paying the less-favored group a lower wage, provided that he is in something of a position of monopoly. Or, on the other side, an organized labor group may be able to get higher wages for its members by the process of shutting out certain groups, classes, or races from its ranks. This again is really an exercise of monopoly power, and the story of trade unions is full of examples of it. The discrimination of a few unions against Negroes and against women, is a good example. If a union can keep Negroes or women out of a particular employment, a higher wage can thereby usually be ensured for the members. This is simply an example of the general method of exercising monopoly power—through the restriction of supply of the monopolized commodity by the ability to prevent "outside" resources from entering the occupation.

"Unearned" income. One further aspect of the problem of exploitation should be mentioned here, though fuller treatment must wait to a later chapter. This is the problem of "unearned" rewards. The attitude towards "unearned income" varies greatly. At one extreme we have the Marxist view that *all* income that is not derived from labor is unearned; this view would condemn all profit, interest, and rent as the result of the exploitation of the working class. At the other extreme we have the view that all property income is justified, or even the very extreme mercantilist view, which is hard to find expressed nowadays, that any income to labor above minimum subsistence is "unearned," labor merely being a passive resource which would produce nothing unless organized by the property owners.

Economic rent. The view held by economists will fall somewhere between these two extremes. Economists have held almost without exception from the time of Adam Smith that there are some incomes that are "unearned" in the sense that they are greater than what is necessary to call forth the activity or contribution of the income receiver. This is what is known in economics as "economic rent." Ricardo, and for that matter Adam Smith, tended to identify economic rent with income from land, and this tradition found later expression in the proposals of Henry George for the taxation of rent and of any rise in land values. The modern view is that the situation is more complicated than either Ricardo or Henry George thought, and that though economic rent unquestionably exists in almost any society, it runs through all forms of income and is by no means easy to identify.

Thus, suppose we have a situation in which in equilibrium there are 1,000 people employed in a particular occupation. The "equilibrium" means that the wage of these people is just enough to persuade exactly 1,000 people to engage in this particular occupation. If we wanted 1,100 people, we might have to offer a somewhat higher wage; if we wanted only 900 people we might get them for a somewhat lower wage. The people who are only just attracted to the occupation at the going wage are said to be "marginal" to that occupation. If, however, we have to pay a wage high enough to attract the marginal men, this implies that unless *all* the people who work at this occupation are marginal, in the sense that they would leave the occupation if the wage were lowered even slightly, there will be some people who would actually be willing to work in this occupation for *less* than the equilibrium wage. The difference between the least wage for which they would be willing to work and the actual (equilibrium) wage is economic rent. This assumes, of course, that the same wage is paid to all workers.

Discrimination to eliminate economic rent. The only way to eliminate economic rent is to discriminate—to pay each worker the least he would be willing to work for. This is impossible in a competitive market, and is probably sociologically impossible even under monopoly, because of the effect such a practice would have on the morale of the organization. It is only in institutions such as universities where the conventions of polite society prevent the discussion of sordid matters like income, that employers are able to discriminate effectively among individuals in the extraction of economic rent. Where the individidual's income is a dirty little secret between his employer and himself, discrimination may be practiced without danger to morale. A man who has to be paid well to keep him from seeking greener pastures elsewhere, is paid well; a man who may be of equal value and service to the organization, but who is willing to serve for less, is paid less.

It is clear that there is a real conflict here between the ideal of no discrimination ("equal pay for equal work") and the ideal of the elimination of private income that is economic surplus ("nobody should be paid more than is necessary"). In practice some compromise must be worked out among these various ideals, leaning to one side or the other according to the importance of the ideal in the value systems of the society.

The dynamics of distribution. On the whole our discussion of distributional justice up to this point has been conducted in a static framework. We have conceived the problem in terms of the "best" distribution of a *fixed* total income among the various individuals and groups in society. We know, however, that total income is not fixed, and that in a developing society it grows and in a declining society it shrinks. In a dynamic theory of distributive justice, therefore, we must liberate ourselves from the narrow view of the problem that conceived it in terms of sharing a fixed "pie," and think of it in terms of sharing an expanding or possibly a contracting pie. We must, that is to say, try to bring together the ideals of distribution with the objectives of economic progress. This, however, is a surprisingly difficult task, and one that has not yet adequately been worked out even on the theoretical level.

We face, for instance, the problem of *who* are the sharers in the pie—how do we reconcile the claims of one generation against another, or of posterity against the present? This raises the whole problem of the conservation of resources as an ideal. We face also the problem of how present changes in distribution among present claimants may affect the future size of the pie that is distributed. Suppose, for instance, that we achieved what we thought was an ideal distribution of *current* income among the various claimants. Suppose further, however, that some other distribution would result in a higher rate of growth of total income. We would be in effect redistributing income from our children and descendants towards ourselves, or even from ourselves in old age towards ourselves now.

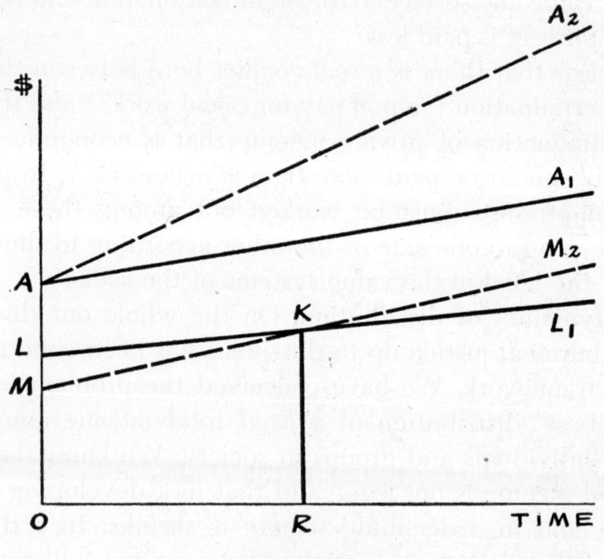

Figure 4-2.

Equality versus progress. The dilemma is pointed up in Fig. 4-2. Here we measure time along the horizontal axis, with the present at the origin, *O*. Income is measured along the vertical axis. *OA* is total present income. We suppose this divided into two parts, *OL* and *LA*. To fix ideas, suppose *OL* represents labor income and *LA* nonlabor income—interest, profit, and rent. Suppose now that total income grows along the line AA_1, and that the same proportional distribution is maintained, so that labor income grows along the line LL_1. Now let us suppose a redistribution in the present, resulting in a permanent shift in proportional distribution, so that labor now gets a smaller relative share than before, and so that this smaller share persists into the future, but suppose also that as a result of the redistribution the rate of growth is greater. Total income now grows following the line AA_2. Labor income is reduced from OL to OM in the present, but also follows a faster growth curve, MM_2. It is clear from the figure that MM_2 and LL_1 must intersect at some point, K, at the time OR. From the date R forward not only is total income greater than it would have been without the redistribution, but labor income in absolute terms is also greater: KM_2 lies above KL_1.

Even if we took an extreme Marxist position, therefore, that only labor income possesses social utility and that therefore any transfer to labor away from nonlabor income is always desirable, we might well prefer the distribution M to L in the present provided that we estimate the "loss" involved in the triangle LKM to be less than the "gain" involved in the open-ended triangle KL_1M_2. The situation is complicated also by the fact that future incomes and distributions are uncertain and distant, and may be discounted on both these scores. It has long been recognized that a bird in the present hand may rationally be preferred to two birds in some future bush. For this reason the "gain" triangle KM_2L cannot be regarded as infinite. If it were not for uncertainty and time preference, however, no matter what our preferences in regard to distribution, *any* reorganization that was favorable to income growth, no matter what its impact in the present, would be preferred over one that was less favorable to growth. The sum total of income, no matter how weighted by our preferences as among different recipients, would always be greater with greater rates of growth. Uncertainty and time discounting, however, destroy the delightful simplicity of this proposition and make the problem of choice between the ideals of distribution and of progress both real and difficult.

Relation between distribution and growth is little known. The problem of what in fact is the relationship between distribution and economic progress is one of the least known relationships in all of economics. In the illustration of Fig. 4-2 I supposed, purely for the sake of illustration, that a reduction in the proportion of income going to labor would increase the rate of income growth. This is certainly not always true, and under many circumstances the reverse might well be the case, and a shift in distribution towards labor income might increase the rate of income growth. The most general and most reasonable hypothesis would be that there is some distribution at which income growth is at a maximum, and therefore on the one side of this an increase in the proportion going to labor raises the rate of income growth, and on the other side of it the reverse is true. Where, however, in any actual society this maximum point is to be found, is almost impossible to discover. The difficulty is more fundamental than merely that of collecting information. Both the distribution system and the rate of economic growth are themselves determined by the whole complex of forces operating in society, and until we understand better the details of this complex, it is dangerous to assume any simple and stable relationship between distribution and growth. The same redistribution, achieved in different ways, might have profoundly different effects on growth.

Monopoly and growth. In the light of this dynamic analysis, many of the propositions and prescriptions of the economist that are based on essentially static considerations become exposed to serious doubt. We may take as an example the general and almost universal condemnation of monopoly by economists. As long as we stick to static considerations, these condemnations are very securely founded. Monopoly results in both restriction of output and exploitation of society by the monopolist. The monopolist is like a greedy boy at the table who not only grabs more cake than he should, but in the process actually spills cake on the floor, so that there is less altogether. When, however, we take the dynamic viewpoint, the case against monopoly is much weaker. It may be, indeed, that economic growth tends to proceed outward from little shelters of monopoly in society, and that without these shelters growth would not take place. We give this hypothesis official recognition of sorts in the patent and copyright laws, the object of which is to reward the innovator by granting him a temporary monopoly. We do not really know, however, whether some other method of rewarding innovation, such as direct payments, would not be even more effective.

Monopoly may stimulate growth by reducing uncertainty. There is a good deal of evidence that *uncertainty* is itself an important element in preventing change, and especially in preventing investment. The investor who commits his resources in specific and definite forms—such as specialized equipment—is a hostage of the future; and the less certain that future, the less likely he is to commit himself. From this point of view, then, it can be argued that stability of prices encourages economic development, and that therefore monopoly, by contributing to stability of prices, eventually results in a cheapening of the monopolized commodity even though at first the price may be higher than it would be in a competitive market. Thus by an argument akin to that of Fig. 4-2 we might balance the period from some point in the future when monopoly would give us lower prices against the period before this critical point when monopoly would give us higher prices. The questions we have just raised are extremely difficult to answer. They must be raised, however, if we are not to have illusions about the simplicity of the problem.

Interpersonal comparisons of utility. We should not omit from this discussion a very basic objection that has been raised against any attempt to give theoretical solutions to the problem of distribution. It is argued by the purists among the welfare economists [3] that any discussion of ideal distribution must involve what is called "interpersonal comparisons of utility," which are held to be illegitimate. An individual, it is argued, can judge fairly accurately whether one state of affairs is better or worse *for him,* because in this case he is comparing two things in his own mind. Nobody, however, can compare a state in his mind with a state in some other mind, and hence we can never make comparisons of utility from one individual to another.

[3] See, for instance, Lionel Robbins, *Essay on the Nature and Significance of Economic Science,* 2d ed. (Toronto: The Macmillan Co., 1935). Marshall and Pigou had no particular qualms on this score—see A. C. Pigou, *The Economics of Welfare,* 4th ed. (London: Macmillan & Co., Ltd., 1938)—but what is called the "Paretian" welfare economics carefully eschews interpersonal comparisons. See Melvin Reder, *Studies in the Theory of Welfare Economics* (New York: Columbia Univ. Press, 1947).

This means that a total social utility cannot be derived from adding up the individual utilities of the people composing the society, and that hence it is illegitimate to compare the marginal utilities of income of different individuals.

Responsible decisions necessitate interpersonal comparisons. The trouble with the above argument is that it seems to prove too much. Any responsible decisions—that is, any decisions that are made on behalf of others, whether by a parent, a businessman, a trade union leader, or a politician—do in fact involve interpersonal comparisons. On the fundamental principle, therefore, that anything that exists must be possible, interpersonal comparisons in some sense must be possible. The criticism that has been leveled against the simple summation of arithmetical utilities is justified—we cannot strap a galvanometer to the seat of the emotions and simply add up the figures obtained for different people. In throwing out a too simple and mechanical interpretation of the process of making interpersonal comparisons, however, economists have cut themselves off from the study of responsible decisions, which means they have really cut themselves off from any study of economic policy.

The dilemma can be resolved when we realize that comparisons between the welfares of different individuals are in fact made in the mind of a single individual—the responsible decision-maker—and do not, therefore, involve comparing things in one mind with things in another. The parent decides that one child needs a new coat worse than the other, the union leader sacrifices the younger men for the older in a contract for seniority, the businessman decides to expand one department at the expense of another, the politician votes for a progressive income tax or for subsidies to agriculture.

The control of responsible decision-makers. A theory of responsible decision-making would carry us far beyond the usual confines of economics—it is, indeed, perhaps the most basic question of political science. In what way, for instance, is the responsible decision-maker made *responsive* to the wishes and opinions of those for whom he is responsible—those, that is, who are affected by his decisions? How, in other words, are the decisions of the responsible decision-maker fed back to him from those whom his decisions affect?

There are, of course, a great many different answers to this question. The bad king may eventually get dethroned. The incompetent dynasty eventually is replaced by a more vigorous successor. The bad dictator may be eventually deposed, or even assassinated. In democratic societies the politician whose actions arouse discontent may fail to be reelected. In a free market economy the businessman who fails to satisfy his customers and his suppliers may eventually go bankrupt; the unsuccessful executive may be forced out by his superiors, or by a stockholders' revolt. In all societies there are *some* mechanisms for dealing with "unsuccessful" or irresponsible decision-making where these decisions affect the welfare of others. Some of these mechanisms, however, as in authoritarian societies, are slow, crude, clumsy, and may be almost as damaging in their consequences as the evils that they eventually try to correct. It is the great virtue of the invention of representative democracy, that it has permitted more rapid and exact feedbacks to the politician from those who are affected by his decisions. It is a great virtue also of a free market economy that the power of businessmen is sharply limited by the ability of their customers not to buy from them if they don't like the product, or if it is too expensive, and is limited also by the abilities of their suppliers of labor or materials to turn to other purchasers if the terms are not satisfactory. The feedbacks to the businessman in a competitive society are sharp, rapid, and frequently painful. Only when he has established a position of monopoly can he afford to be insensitive in some degree to the responses of those who are affected by his decisions.

Conflict of ideals resolved by responsible decision-making. To return now to the question of the ideal distribution of income. It is clear that no simple mechanical definition of ideal distribution can be given. Nevertheless, there are responsible decisions to be made in this area, and these decisions are not reached wholly in the dark. There are notions of what constitutes ideal distribution abroad, and where a divergence is felt between the ideal and actual distribution in the minds of responsible decision-makers and of those who are influential in affecting their behavior, action will be directed towards eliminating the divergence. There may be, as we have noticed, a certain conflict of ideals. Like all conflicts of ideals, these are usually resolved by compromise, each ideal being carried to the point where a further realization of it would not be judged worth the sacrifice of some other ideal.

The limits of tolerance—the basic minimum. We can, however, be more specific than this. Even though the exact compromise between these various ideals cannot be worked out in advance, but must depend on the nature of the political process by which it is achieved, nevertheless each of the ideals may be used to prescribe certain *negative* limits which give minimum standards of performance for the system. Thus, although the need standard is not, as we have seen, capable of being erected into a complete system of distribution, it does lead to the proposition that there should be in every society a basic minimum standard of life below which no one should be allowed to fall. This notion of a basic minimum level is an old principle—it is involved, for instance, in any "poor law." The practical problem—and the one that is likely to cause most controversy—is that of deciding where this minimum level should lie. The English Poor Law of 1834 decreed that it should be at the barest minimum necessary to sustain life. As society becomes richer, however, the basic minimum it can afford can be raised. The level of the basic minimum that a society can afford depends, of course, on economic surplus; the larger the surplus, the higher the basic minimum can be. We have good reason to suppose that, in the Western world at least, we can now afford to set a basic minimum much higher than we have been accustomed to in the past, because of the rise in productivity and in the economic surplus. A flat basic minimum could only apply, of course, to a fairly homogeneous region. Over a large and heterogeneous area, it would be necessary to set lower basic minima in those areas less technically advanced and more accustomed to poverty.

The control of monopoly. The merit standard likewise is not capable of universal application. Here also, however, it is possible to spell out certain gross violations as constituting a lower limit of tolerance. Monopolistic privileges should not be tolerated unless a strong case can be made for them on the grounds of their contribution to economic progress. Artificial restrictions on the entry of capital and labor into (or their exit out of) any occupation should be discouraged. There is a strong case for having some agency in society to keep a watchful eye on monopoly (like the anti-trust division of the Department of Justice) even if the rules by which it operates are obscure and its policies not always consistent. In the movement towards equality, however, we must beware of attempting to redistribute more than the economic surplus: if taxation, for instance, cuts below the supply price of some essential factor, that is, the minimum "reward" which is necessary to keep it functioning, the supply of this factor will be curtailed to the loss of the whole society.

We have by no means exhausted the subject of this chapter, which is perhaps the most difficult of all economic policy questions. We will return to it, however, in considering some of the practical policies that may be employed in actually trying to move towards an ideal distribution.

5

Economic freedom

Freedom is what's inside the fence
Of Morals, Money, Law, and Sense,
And we are free, if this is wide
(Or nothing's on the other side).
We come to Politics (and Sin)
When Your fine freedoms fence Me in,
And so through Law we come to be
Curtailing Freedom—to be free.

Ambiguity of "freedom." Freedom is a fighting word. It arouses deep emotions and desires and clearly evokes something that is very precious to the human heart. Its very power, however, depends in part on its vagueness. It means many different things to different people. When Americans speak of the "free world," when Hitler used "Freiheit" as one of his slogans, when St. Paul wrote that "in His service is perfect freedom," when Roosevelt and Churchill promulgated the "four freedoms," and when communists claim that theirs is the only free society, it is obvious that the one word covers a multitude of meanings. This is a source both of confusion and conflict. The fact that a term is vague does not imply that it is meaningless—indeed, the difficulty with a word like freedom is that it has too much meaning, not too little. Without forgetting the richness and significance of the word, however, it may help to reduce both the confusion and the conflict that surround it by trying to analyze it somewhat into its components.

Freedom as an aspect of power: the "possibility boundary." For the individual, freedom is simply an aspect of his power, and his power is measured by the area within which choice is possible. If you have no choice, you have no power. Power, in other words, is measured by all the things you *could* do if you desired. From where he stands, each individual looks out into a universe, parts of which are accessible to him and parts of which are inaccessible. In terms of space and time, for instance, I might ask myself where I *could* be this time tomorrow. I could, of course, be right here in Michigan: I could be in New York, or San Francisco, or perhaps even in London or Paris. I certainly could not be in Australia or Tibet. I could draw a rough map with a boundary dividing the world into those places to which I *could* go and those to which I could not. This is a "possibility boundary": within it I am free to choose where I shall be, outside it I cannot go. The wider this boundary, the greater my power and the more extensive the area of my freedom.

The possibility boundary may be defined—and freedom may be circumscribed—by many different circumstances.

Physical limitations. There is first the *physical* limitation. I cannot get to Australia within the next twenty-four hours simply because planes do not fly fast enough to get me there. I cannot go to the moon within any immediate period because rocket ships have not yet been invented that will take me there. If

I am seriously ill I probably cannot go beyond the confines of my house or the hospital. One of the most striking results of technical progress is the pushing back of these physical limitations on the field of individual choice. In this way we have enormously increased at least the potential area of individual freedom. Even thirty years ago I could not have reached London or San Francisco in twenty-four hours. Two hundred years ago I could have gone hardly more than a few miles.

Other limitations. The physical limitation is the widest boundary of freedom; beyond that we cannot possibly go. The boundaries that most of us face, however, are much smaller and closer to us than the physical boundary. We are hemmed in by psychological, social, legal, and economic boundaries far inside the physical limit. Thus, even in the field of space and time, although it may be physically possible for me to fly to London within the next twenty-four hours, it is not *legally* possible because my passport has expired and it would take a week or two to renew it. An American may not legally visit certain countries because the State Department will not permit such a trip. It is not legally—or morally—possible to break into my neighbor's house or to drive my car at seventy miles an hour through a crowded street. If I have a morbid fear of flying, it may not be psychologically possible for me to get to San Francisco by tomorrow morning, even though it is physically and legally possible.

Economic limitation. For most people, however, the most stringent limitation on freedom is the economic limitation. I may be able to go to New York tomorrow physically, legally, and morally, but I still may not be able to afford the fare. This is a curious kind of limitation, rather different from the others. I may actually have the fare in my pocket and still feel I cannot afford to go because of the other claims on the money. Physical and legal limitations, even psychological limitations, are apt to be in the nature of well-marked boundary lines, dividing the universe sharply into things I can do and things I cannot. The economic limitation is more like a limitation on the *general area* within which I can operate. If I go to New York I cannot go to

Florida; if I go to Florida I cannot go to New York. Suppose, for instance, that I am limited in my ability to travel simply by the fact that I have only $100 to spend. If I spend it all on going east, I cannot go west; if I spend it all on going west, I cannot go east; if I want to go both east and west, I can spend only $50 going either way. The richer I am, of course, the less stringent is this economic limitation. If I have $200 to spend on travel, I can obviously go farther in any direction, or any combination of directions, than I can if I have only $100. An increase in income, therefore, has the effect of pushing back the boundary of the economic limitation, just as technical improvement pushes back the boundary of the physical limitation. The economic limitation can be pictured as a kind of rubber band surrounding the individual: he can push it out in any direction, but only at the cost of pulling it in elsewhere. He may even stretch it a little by working harder and devoting himself more assiduously to economic pursuits, though there are limits on its stretchability. The poor are hemmed in by very small bands, the rich have large bands, the very rich perhaps escape the economic limitation altogether and are restricted only by physical, legal, or psychological limitations.

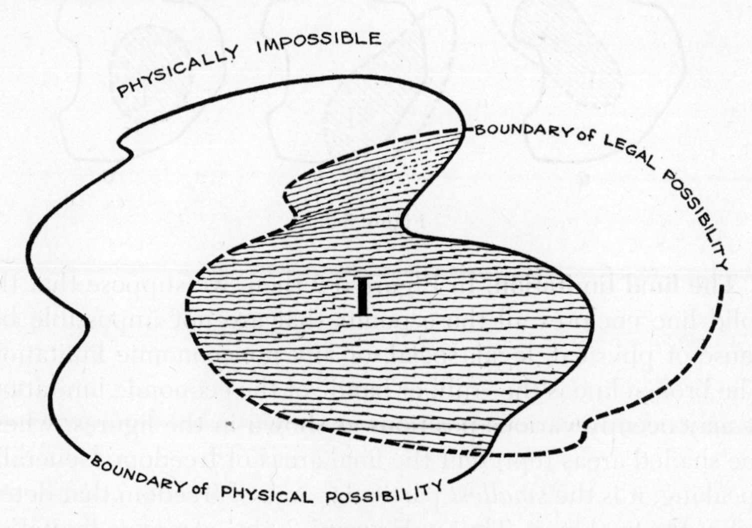

Figure 5-1.

The "field" of possible action. Figure 5-1 may make these distinctions more vivid. We imagine an individual, *I*, in the middle of his universe or "field." The field consists not only of times and places, but of anything that concerns him: emotions, friendships, goods and services, interests, activities. The heavy black line denotes the physical limitation. Anything beyond this is physically impossible: going to the moon, living to be 200, jumping 50 feet into the air, and so on. Anything inside the line is physically possible. Similarly, the broken line is the boundary of, say, legal possibility: things beyond it are illegal, things inside it are legal. The shaded area where these overlap (called the "union" of the two "sets" of the legally possible and the physically possible) delimits that part of the field that is *both* physically and legally possible: anything outside this is either physically or legally impossible, or both. Similarly, we might add boundaries for the psychologically possible, the morally possible, and the socially possible, the politically possible, and so on. Each boundary that we add is likely to restrict the "overlap" or union where *all* possibility conditions are met.

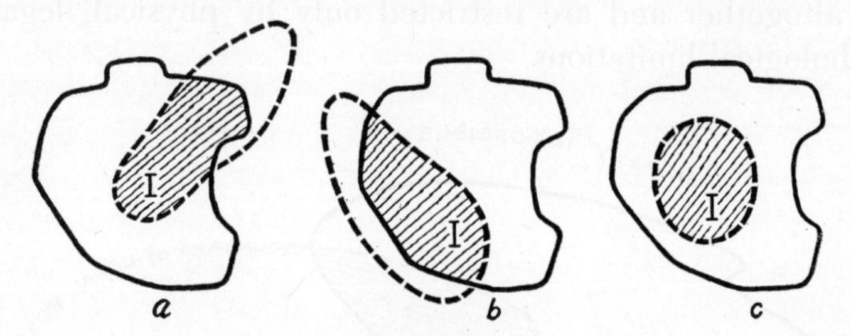

Figure 5-2.

The final limitation. In Figure 5-2 then, we suppose that the solid line encloses all those points that are not impossible because of physical, legal, social, or any noneconomic limitation. The broken line is the "rubber band" of the economic limitation. It may occupy various positions as shown in the figures, where the shaded areas represent the final areas of freedom. Generally speaking, it is the *smallest* particular area of freedom that determines the final limit. Thus in Figure 5-3, the economic limitation lies completely outside the others. In this case, the noneconomic limitations are dominant and determine the ultimate limits of the individual's choice. The miser, starving and freezing to death over his hoarded money, is a good example of a psychological limitation so severe that it dominates the economic limitation. The prisoner in his cell is an example of a physical–legal limitation overriding the economic, especially if he has a hoard of cash somewhere outside!

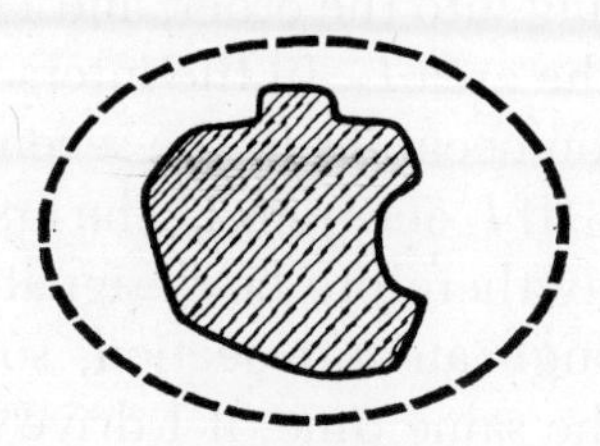

Figure 5-3.

The principle of exclusion creates *conflict*. Up to this point we have considered freedom simply as an attribute of a single individual in relation to his environment. If this were the whole problem it would be fairly simple. The freedom of an individual can be increased simply by making him richer, which pushes back the economic boundary; by repealing all laws, which pushes back the legal boundary; by denying all morality, which pushes back the moral boundary; and by science and technology, which push back the physical boundary! Merely stating the matter in this way, however, brings us sharply against the *political* and *social* problem of freedom, which is the question of what happens when one person's exercise of freedom impairs the freedom of another. This happens, for example, when two people cannot occupy the same "position" at the same time. In a sheer physical sense this means simply that two people cannot be in *exactly* the same place at the same time. We might call this the *principle of exclusion*.

In social relations, of course, the principle of exclusion goes far beyond the mere physical limitation of space and time: two people cannot occupy the same job, or the same house, or have the same wife or husband, or sit in the same seat at the theater. When we have two people, therefore, the area of freedom around them divides into three parts: each has a part of the field into which he can move without regard to what the other does, but then there is a third region into which each can only go if it is not already occupied by the other. This principle is illustrated in Fig. 5-4. The two circles represent the areas of freedom of two people, I_1 and I_2. I_1 can move anywhere in the area I_1 without running into the other, and I_2 similarly has absolute dominion over the area I_2. In the intersecting area U, however, if the first person occupies it, the second cannot, and he is reduced to the area I_2. If I_2 occupies U, the first person is confined to I_1. The area U may therefore be designated the area of *conflict.* If I drive through an intersection, someone else cannot drive through it at the same time; if I drive a car, someone else cannot drive it at the same time. If I build a house, someone else cannot build it on the same lot. If a piece of land belongs to one nation, it cannot belong to another, except in the rare case of condominium. If one union claims to organize a particular group of workers, another cannot organize them without contesting the claim. If a man is converted to one point of view, it usually means that he has to relinquish another.

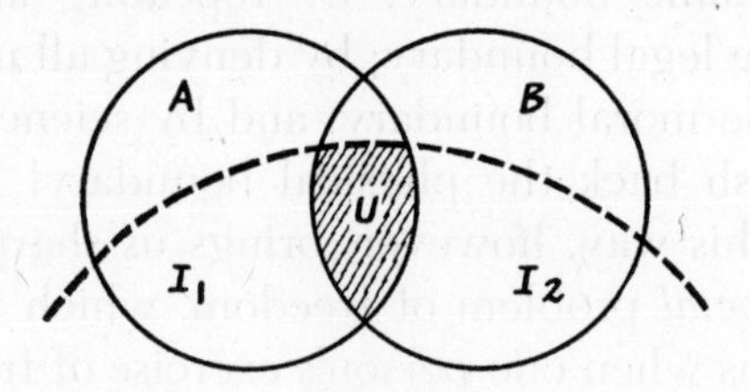

Figure 5-4.

The cost of conflict. If both parties try to occupy an area of conflict, the result may be a conflict that will, itself, limit the freedom even of the victorious party much more than the limitation involved by letting the other get away with the area of conflict. What any one loses by the conflict, itself, is more than he could hope to gain from the other party by victory in the conflict area. Thus in Fig. 5-4, we suppose that if there is an overt conflict between the parties in regard to the area U, this will limit the freedom of both of them within the boundary of the broken line. If party I_1 wins the conflict, he gains the shaded part of U, but loses the area A because of the conflict itself. If party I_2 wins, he likewise gains the shaded area U, but loses B. If now the area gained by the conflict is less than either A or B, both parties have a strong incentive to avoid this *form* of conflict, and if another form can be substituted in which the costs of conflict are less, both parties will have an incentive to make the substitution.

Solutions to conflict: diminishing *cost* or *area* of conflict. The incentive to substitute less costly forms of conflict diminishes as the cost of conflict diminishes, and at some point one party will feel that his chance of gain through winning the conflict is worth more than the chance of loss through conflict, and the incentive to diminish the cost of conflict ceases. One can interpret the rise and development of a great many social institutions according to this principle of diminishing the cost of conflict. The substitution of law for war or personal combat, and the substitution of arbitration for the costlier processes of law, are good examples of the principle.

One can indeed distinguish two broad avenues of solution to the problem: one is the diminution of the cost of conflict through some agreement among the parties, the development of some custom, convention, or law governing the conflict, to which both parties subscribe. The other is the diminution of the *gains* from conflict by the reduction of the *area* of conflict. If the potential gains from conflict to any party are very small, or if they are nonexistent, the chance of the parties getting into costly conflicts is correspondingly reduced. In Fig. 5-5(a) we have the same situation as in Fig. 5-4, except that the cost of conflict has been lessened: A and B are now substantially smaller than U. In Fig. 5-5(b) we have removed the areas of freedom of the two parties so that they no longer overlap: conflict has been eliminated altogether. The same result might be achieved by building a barrier down the middle of the area of conflict, as in Fig. 5-5(c), and restricting each party to his own side of the barrier, so that again the areas of freedom do not overlap.

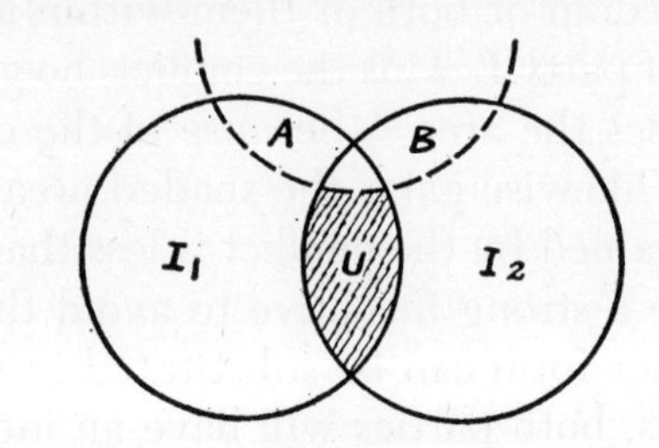

Figure 5-5(a).

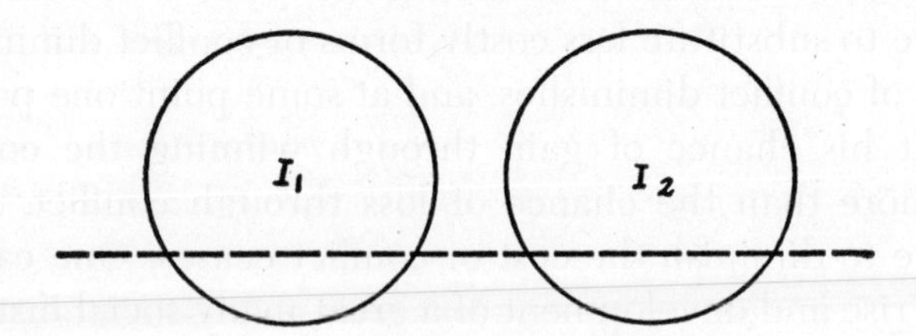

Figure 5-5(b).

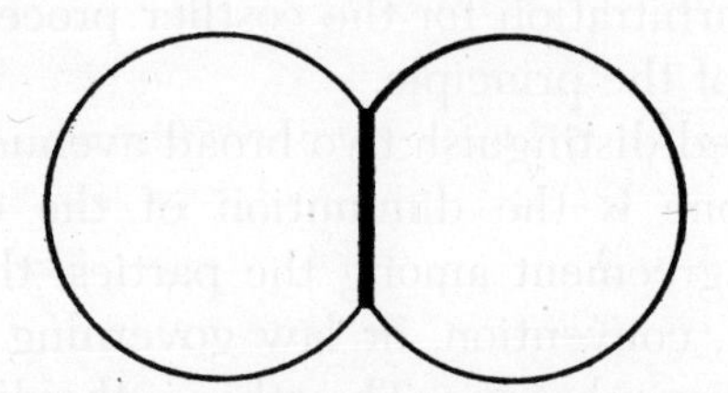

Figure 5-5(c).

Property as a solution of the problem of conflict. There are innumerable examples of these various methods of solving the problem of "inconsistent freedoms" or conflict. The problem created by the fact that two cars cannot cross an intersection at the same time is solved by putting in a stoplight: this corresponds to the solution of Fig. 5-5(c). Instead of both lines of traffic having the right to cross the intersection at all times (which would result in dangerous conflict and even impact!)

each line of traffic is given certain specific times at which it has the sole right of way. The whole notion of "property" is really an example of this type of solution. In the case of the stoplight the "green" means that at that moment one line of traffic has "property" in the right of way, in the sense that the other line is excluded from it. Property involves the *right to exclude.* Property in my house implies that I can prevent anyone from living there except by my consent; property in anything, whether a house, car, land, stocks, bonds or money, or even in slaves and wives in some societies, means that the owner can exclude others from the use, sale, usufruct or enjoyment of these things.

At first glance the whole concept of property seems like a shocking infringement on liberty—one recalls the famous dictum of Proudhon that "property is theft." It is, however, an institution that has emerged in the course of human development mainly as an attempt to solve the problem of the loss of liberty involved in conflict. In theory, property eliminates conflict by separating each of us from those others whose areas of freedom might impinge on ours by a high wall of legal or generally accepted rights and obligations. The virtues of property are extolled in the homely wisdom of "good fences make good neighbors," and "everybody's property is nobody's property." The "magic of property" which makes the desert blossom as the rose is noticed—by the Western observer, at least—even in Soviet Russia, where it is reported that the carefully tended and intensively cultivated little private plots of the peasants contrast sharply with the slovenly fields of the collective farms.

There are objections to the whole notion of "privacy" which we shall examine in the next chapter. For the moment, however, we shall accept the machinery of property as neutral, and note that the justification, in terms of the broadening of freedom, for any particular form or institution of property must be argued in terms of whether the losses caused by the restrictions imposed are greater or less than the gains derived from the elimination of costly conflict. This is always a very difficult question to answer; there are no nice market places of freedom in which it can be measured by the measuring rod of money. Nevertheless, in one form or another this question lies behind most of the great policy matters of our day.

Segregation as a solution of conflict. Let me take for an example the problem of segregation. This is an attempt to solve a problem of conflict between groups partly by increasing the "distance" between them, as in Fig. 5-5(b), partly by a delineation of their respective areas of freedom, as in Fig. 5-5(c). This is an old solution; men always seem to have associated themselves in some sort of exclusive groups. The family itself is an example of segregation—nonmembers of the family group are not admitted to certain places, acts, and rituals of the family. The caste system is an early example of segregation according to descent, race, color, or occupation within a larger society, and it exists in greater or lesser degree in all societies. Prisons, mental hospitals, and concentration camps are examples of enforced segregation of the criminals, the mentally sick, and the politically unacceptable, the theory being presumably that the loss of freedom involved is justified by the conflict and disorganization that would be introduced into society if these elements were not segregated. Every society faces the question of whether it has too much, too little, or the wrong kinds of segregation, and the pattern is continually modified as dissatisfactions arise with existing arrangements.

Racial segregation as an unacceptable solution. In the United States we are in the midst of a profound change in the patterns of racial segregation, mainly because it has become widely felt that the loss of freedom involved in existing patterns no longer can be justified by any possible gains in terms of social peace. Racial discrimination has always been incompatible with the view of the rights of man held by the founders of the United States and enshrined in its classic documents. A nation that declares its independence in the ringing phrase, "We hold these truths to be self evident, that all men are created equal, that they are endowed by their Creator with certain unalienable Rights . . ." cannot live comfortably with slavery or second-class citizenship: the replacement of the splendid words "all men" with the "some men" implied by historic practice puts a big crack in the Liberty Bell. In the light of the Declaration of Independence not only rank but race, color, shape, or any other politically irrelevant quality are but the guinea stamp, and a man's a man for a' that. When these ideas become widespread, segregation on racial lines becomes irrelevant, simply because it does not correspond to the real lines of conflict. It is like putting stoplights where there are no crossroads.

In South Africa, by contrast, we see a country dominated by a wholly different ideology, where the dominant group does not accept equality as an ideal, and where the sense of racial conflict is so acute that segregation is constantly made more and more rigid in an attempt to stave conflict off. Against modern technology, however, segregation everywhere is fighting a losing battle. In the face of the machine, as in the face of the doctrine of Human Rights, there is a strong tendency for men to become equal, whether they are created so or not. Modern technology breaks down old cultures, old crafts, old skills, transmitted through the family circle, and replaces them by skills that can be acquired in a short period of training. By increasing geographical mobility through improved means of transport it breaks down the old local, isolated communities and so promotes the mingling of cultures. As a defense against the diminishing physical distance we may find an attempt to increase "social distance" through prejudice and segregation. The forces of technology constantly are at work, however, to create "individuals" who can find a home for themselves anywhere in the world, and are not confined to a small cultural niche.

Property as a bundle of rights. As a society becomes more and more complex, so does the concept of property. In a simple society property may simply be defined as easily identifiable physical objects, and ownership is the physical control of these objects; theft is the removal of these objects from the physical presence and control of the owner. This concept, of course, persists. The theft of a car is the same sort of thing as the theft of a horse, or a chariot, or a flint axe. As society develops, however, the concept of property shifts from that of simple physical control of an object to that of a bundle of rights associated with it. If I own a car the law will try to protect me and recover it if it is stolen, but the law will not protect me if I injure someone else through my poor driving, or if I drive above the speed limit, or through a red light, or if I park where parking is prohibited. The ownership of a car is not a right to do anything I like with it, but only to use it within a carefully demarcated set of rights. A man's house may be his castle, but his car certainly is not!

From the notion of property as a bundle of rights connected with an object, it is not hard to move to the notion of a bundle of rights not connected with any object. The tenure of a professor, the seniority rights of a union member, the civic and political rights of a citizen, are all in a sense "property." Some of these may be regarded as "inalienable" and so do not enter the market—one cannot usually sell one's citizenship to another, or one's right to tenure. Some of these abstract rights, however, are freely alienable and become "assets," bought and sold in a market. A good example is a "quota": under certain agricultural legislation, for instance, the sale of specified products is allowed only if the seller possesses a "quota"—a purely abstract right to sell. In some cases these quotas are freely salable: people who want to start producing or selling the commodity have to buy a quota from someone who is just giving up the business. Sometimes the quota goes with some other item of property. Thus in the United States Tobacco Marketing scheme the quotas go with the farm, and as a consequence a farm with a large quota sells for much more than one with a small one, and for very much more than one with no quota at all.

The protection of property by law and custom. The definition and protection of property and abstract rights is the prime business of law and the legal system. We must not suppose, of course, that the formal apparatus of legislatures, courts, and lawyers is the *only* agency in society concerned with these matters. There is a large body of custom and informal procedures and pressures that is concerned with these matters. Thus there may be no legal obstacle to turning my front lawn into a hayfield, but the social pressures against my so doing are so strong that hardly a householder in any suburb has the fortitude to let his front lawn go to wilderness, however great his passion for the wild or his dislike of lawn mowing. The most effective punishment that society can impose is the disapproval of one's peers—that is, of the people in one's own "gang." The very persistence of premeditated crime in the face of fines and jails and even capital punishment is clear proof that all these supposed deterrents are weak compared with the almost invisible but unrelenting force of social disapproval from one's own group. Social disapproval from outside one's group may even reinforce the disapproved conduct. Thus, for one who belongs to and identifies himself with the "criminal" subculture, all the disapproval and punishments imposed by the rest of society are chaff in the wind compared with the massive penalties involved in breaking with his group, turning sissy and going straight. Nevertheless, the legal and punitive system does have some effect on the culture of the groups against which it is directed. The criminal subculture may persist, but it is at least stunted by the majesty of the Law. Businessmen and union leaders may sail close to the wind, they may seek loopholes and evasions in anti-trust or labor or tax laws, but their basic identification with the need for law and order makes the law a very real limitation on their freedom of action.

The "theft of values." As society gets more complex, so does the law. If the property concept were confined to the simple possession of physical objects, the law could protect property simply by preventing theft. Suppose, however, that a man leaves me in full possession and control of some physical object, but does something that destroys its *value*. He may, for instance, build a smelly factory next to my house, or he may invent a machine that takes away my job, or he may open a supermarket that destroys the value of my store. Is this theft? Is it a violation of my "rights"?

This is a very difficult question to answer. In the United States, at any rate, we believe in "competition" but we do not believe in theft—yet the distinction is by no means always easy to draw. What is the difference between a man who steals my physical goods and the man who makes them worthless? This line of argument, if we are not careful, drives us towards the position that all existing values are sacred, and that all interests should be permanently vested: the people have a right to enjoy in perpetuity whatever situation they now happen to be in. Carried to an extreme, of course, this position would block all economic progress, for as we have seen, progress implies competition, at least in the sense of the ability of "superior" processes to displace inferior ones. The logic of conserving all existing rights would lead us to tax any improved process to the point where the existing, less efficient processes could compete with it. We would have taxed railroads so that stage coaches could compete with them, and taxed automobiles so that horses could compete with them, and so on.

Equalizing competitive advantage. In spite of the absurdity of this principle when pushed to its logical conclusion, it nevertheless has had, and still has, considerable influence in determining economic policy under the notion of "equalizing competitive advantage." Thus one finds legislation against chain stores defended on the ground that they have a competitive advantage over the independent stores and so should be taxed to permit the independents to survive. Even more important is the argument that the function of tariffs should be to equalize competitive advantage as between foreign and domestic producers, an argument that has had, and probably continues to have, great political weight. Yet this principle, too, carried to its logical extreme, would eliminate all the advantages of international trade, and indeed would largely eliminate trade itself!

Limitation of rights of possession. On the other hand, we cannot quite put ourselves in the opposite position of saying that property should be defined and protected only as physical possession, without regard to abstract rights or values, and that there should be no limitations of the right to exchange, transform, or do what we will with our own physical possessions. Custom itself is a powerful limitation on what we can do with our physical possessions, and law cannot evade the task of limiting the right involved in physical possession when there is a clear social demand for such limitation. However, the line between regulations and limitations that limit freedom in the ultimate interests of freedom, and those that are unnecessary, meaningless, and arbitrary limitations on individual freedom, is very hard to draw, and the intensity of much political argument is a testimony to the difficulty of finding agreement in these matters.

Hierarchy and organization as limits on freedom. The problem is made still more complicated because of the rise of large-scale organization and the consequent development of *hierarchy*. There is an obvious difference between the situation of an independent craftsman—say a shoe repairer working in his own shop and serving a large group of customers—and that of an employee of a large corporation or of a government. The first is "independent" in a sense in which the latter is not—like the jolly miller, he is free to "care for nobody, no not I, for nobody cares for me," because he has many customers and therefore many masters, and if he offends one he may be able to get another. He can set his own times of working, within limits; he can work as fast or as slow as he pleases; and he does not have to adjust his work habits to an assembly line or a group spirit. The employee, on the other hand, no matter how highly placed, is a member of a hierarchy—a line of subordinates and superiors. Unless he is at the top of the ladder he has a "boss," and unless he is on the bottom rung of the ladder, he is a boss: there are those above him and those below him. He receives instructions from those above him, and transmits instructions to those below him. The existence of hierarchy therefore always imposes limits on freedom: it draws tighter, in certain directions, the boundaries of choice. An employee in an organization usually has to work at specified hours, in specified ways, and within his work hours he is strictly confined by the needs of the organization. This is true even of those at the top of the hierarchy. The president of an organization may not have a superior in the hierarchy, but the needs and demands of the whole organization press down on him so strongly that he is frequently much less free than those down the line. The employee sacrifices his freedom eight hours a day—the president carries his burden home with him and frequently works himself to death.

The "Organizational Revolution." We have seen in the past hundred years a rise in the scale of organizations so striking that I have elsewhere dubbed the whole movement the "Organizational Revolution." [1] The movement manifests itself in almost all fields of life: we see it in the rise of large corporations, large labor unions, farm organizations, professional and scientific societies, great governmental and administrative organizations, and so on. In a sense the movement culminates in the totalitarian communist state, where almost all economic life is organized in the gigantic corporation of the State, and where hierarchy becomes almost universal.

The growth in the scale of organizations, and the consequent growth of hierarchy, has not come about without good reasons. The main reason is a very simple one: many of the technical changes of the past hundred years have operated to remove certain obstacles to the growth of large-scale organizations, and have pushed back the point at which organizations run into "diseconomies of scale"—the inefficiency, poor communications, red tape, and so on which increasingly beset large organizations as they get larger. Some of these changes are mechanical—the typewriter, the telegraph and telephone, the duplicator, and so on. Some are "social inventions" like the professional organizer, the vice president, the business school. Whatever the reasons, large organizations have been able to offer sufficient inducements in the way of income and other benefits to overcome the loss of freedom of personal act that is involved in the transfer from the status of independent craftsman or farmer to that of a wage worker or a salaried employee. In terms of Fig. 5-2, although submission to hierarchy may—indeed, must—involve a contraction of the boundaries of noneconomic limitations on the individual's freedom of action (the solid line), it may permit an expansion of the economic limitation (the broken

[1] K. E. Boulding, *The Organizational Revolution* (New York: Harper & Brothers, 1953).

line) through the increased personal real income that more extensive organization permits. Especially in the case of the very poor, Fig. 5-2(c) where the economic-limitation boundary lies wholly within the noneconomic, a restriction of the noneconomic is hardly felt at all, whereas an expansion of the economic boundary (increased income) is felt strongly and immediately.

Checks on hierarchy: (1) the market. The restrictions imposed by hierarchical organization are, however, felt strongly if there is no escape from them, either through counterorganization or through flight to alternative occupations or organizations. In practice the limitations on freedom that are imposed by hierarchy are attacked in both these ways, which to a considerable extent are mutual substitutes. If, for instance, there is a very active labor market, so that an employee who does not like the organization he happens to be working for can easily find a job elsewhere, the power of the employer over the employee is strictly limited and the employee's freedom is correspondingly greater. The freedom to quit is perhaps a more fundamental freedom than is generally recognized. The freedom to quit, however, is intimately bound up with the ability to find another job or another relationship elsewhere that can replace the old. Especially in a time of unemployment the freedom to quit is an empty freedom. When there is not an active labor market, then, it is not surprising to find that workers who find themselves under the pressure of a "boss" organize into labor unions, and try to set up by collective bargaining a system of "industrial government" that will protect the worker against the arbitrary exercise of power by his bosses.

(2) Countervailing power. The principle of protecting freedom by counterorganization is an example of a still larger principle which has been called by Galbraith the principle of Countervailing Power.[2] Any organization gives those who control it power over others, whether this is the king of a feudal state, the president of a corporation, a labor union, or a democratic republic, or the dictator of a totalitarian society. If this

[2] J. K. Galbraith, *American Capitalism; The Concept of Countervailing Power* (Boston: Houghton Mifflin Co., 1952).

power over others is felt by them as a loss of freedom, they too may organize as a "countervailing power." The nobles organize against the king, the merchants against the nobles, the farmers against the towns, the workers against the employers, protestants against the Church, parties against each other, tax lawyers against tax collectors, and so on almost ad infinitum. Society is thus conceived as an immense system of pressures and counterpressures, checks and balances, pulling and hauling.

There is much to be said for this view. In stressing the importance of counterorganization, however, we must not forget what is perhaps the even more important check on power—the defense of freedom provided by the market, and especially by the labor market. The power of a tyrant may be undermined more by quiet desertion from his cause than by organization against him. The power of a "boss" is sharply limited if his workers can find other bosses. The power of a husband over his wife is limited by the ability of women to find jobs, and by the right of divorce.

The balanced solution. There is a real problem in society of finding the right balance between these two solutions to the problem of freedom in hierarchy. A "pure market" solution, in which the only check on an unsatisfactory relationship is the ability to change partners, is not acceptable because it does not lay enough stress on the problem of working out good relationships within an existing connection. It is generally felt that "quitting" a relationship is at least a sign of failure, and that effort spent in forming new combinations might be better employed in improving an existing relationship. On the other hand, if we rely entirely on the ability of parties to work out a satisfactory power-and-freedom structure within a permanent and inescapable relationship, this may result in permanent subjugation of the weaker parties, or in a perpetual failure to work out a satisfactory relationship. Thus in the domestic relationship in marriage a solution that involved a perpetual shopping around for new partners at the slightest signs of a rift would not be regarded as generally acceptable, and there is a strong feeling in most societies that once a marriage relationship has been entered, most of the efforts of the parties should be devoted to making it work rather than to trying other combinations. On the other hand, a situation where divorce is impossible and women have no alternative means of support can lead to abominable domestic tyranny. Similarly in the industrial relationship, although there is greater tolerance for the "shopping around" or market solution, and workers are not supposed to feel wedded to their jobs, still there is a strong sense that the parties should be able to work out good "labor-management relations," and a high labor turnover is regarded as a sign of weakness. Here again, however, a system of slavery or serfdom where there is no labor market and the workers are tied to their employers is regarded as an intolerable infringement on basic human freedom, no matter how great incentive this provides to work out a satisfactory human relationship within the system.

Complexity of the ideal of economic freedom. We can now see at least why the ideal of economic freedom is such a complex one, and why it is difficult to construct any measure of economic freedom by which to compare the success or failure of various policies. It is very hard even to say whether one society has more or less economic freedom than another. The best we can hope to do with our present intellectual tools is to put the various controversies regarding economic freedom in a broad setting of the *total* limitations on the power of the individual.

The closest we have come to quantification of the economic-freedom notion is the idea of the "area of choice" or the "area of power" within the boundaries formed by the most restricting limitations on the power of the individual. This is a many-dimensioned "area" or "space," and it cannot easily be reduced to a single number or measure. The concept, however, forces us to consider *all* the limitations on choice, not merely the legal or physical or financial limitations. Attempts to define economic freedom in terms of any single limitation are bound to be misleading: freedom in general is not *always* lessened by an increase in legal restrictions or even by a fall in income, for a tightening of one boundary may result in a loosening of others. On the other hand, there is a strong presumption that any tightening of one boundary—provided that it is a real limitation on action—must be justified by a loosening of others. In particular the imposition of legal restrictions on action must be justified by pointing to other kinds of limitations that are loosened as a result.

Even if we could show, however, that the limitation on the freedom of one person led to a greater expansion of freedom of another, we would still be faced with the problem of interpersonal comparisons that plagued us in Chapter 4. Suppose *A* does not care for freedom and prefers a restricted life, hemmed in by secure but narrow boundaries, whereas *B* is an unconfinable spirit, demanding an enormous room for his creative gyrations: should we confine *A*, that *B* may be free? These are the questions, as we have seen, that can only be answered in the pull and pressure of political and responsible action. There are no readymade solutions arising out of *a priori* theory.

6

Means, ends, and the conflict of objectives

> Human nature always tends
> To worship Means instead of Ends,
> And so we often miss the bus
> By lingering in the Terminus:
> And yet he loses all his friends
> Whose Means he justifies by Ends,
> Because it cannot be denied,
> There's much enjoyment in the ride.

The four primary objectives. We have now defined four broad objectives of economic policy, which can be summarized by the four great words Progress, Stability, Justice, and Freedom. In greater or less degree, in open or in disguised form, these objectives are present in any society. Even in a completely tradition-bound and static society, progress is conceived in terms of more perfect conformity to the wisdom of the past; retrogression, in terms of deviation from this wisdom; justice, in terms of everyone performing his traditional duties and receiving his traditional rights; injustice, in terms of deviation from this norm. Perhaps even the problems of stability and freedom are found in embryo in primitive societies, although the static character of these societies seems almost to preclude the first, and their poverty the second.

Merely stating these objectives, however, is not enough to equip us as judges of policy. There are difficult problems of measurement, as we have seen. We may be able to agree on fairly simple and calculable measures of progress and stability —for instance, the growth and fluctuations of per-capita real income, though even here there are rival measures. But justice and freedom cannot be reduced to a single, one-dimensional measure: they are complexly structured, many-sided concepts that can neither be reduced to simple index numbers nor dismissed as unimportant.

Conflict of objectives. Even if we could measure all these objectives separately, and even if we knew the exact effect on each of any particular policy, we would still be faced with the problem of possible conflict among them. Suppose, for instance, that a certain policy increases the rate of progress, but that in our estimation it both makes distribution more unjust and reduces the present freedom of most individuals. Is the gain in progress worth the loss of freedom and justice? Our answer to this question depends, of course, on our relative marginal estimation of the various objectives. If progress is extremely important to us, and losses of freedom and justice are not felt too keenly, we are more likely to choose those policies that favor progress even at considerable costs in other objectives. If we are deeply sensitive to the problem of freedom and justice in the present generation, we may prefer to sacrifice some progress to the attainment of these goals.

Complementary and competitive objectives. We do not have to assume, of course, that the various objectives are always competitive. It is probable, indeed, that for low levels of success in achieving these objectives they are all complements, in the sense that an improvement in one leads to, or makes easier, an improvement in others. In a stagnant, feudal society with very unequal incomes, a low or even zero rate of progress, and almost complete absence of personal freedom except for the privileged few, increasing freedom (*e.g.*, by abolishing feudal obligations) is almost certain to increase the rate of progress, and is quite likely to improve the distribution of income. As we move towards higher levels of achievement of any of these objectives, however, we are more likely to run into competitive relations among them. Doing away with large depressions seems almost certain to increase the over-all rate of progress. There may come a point in the quest for stability, however, when further reduction in the amplitude of fluctuations can only be achieved at the cost of a slowing down of economic growth. There may be an inevitable "lumpiness" in the growth process; there may even be a stimulus to growth in the recurrence of small depressions. Similarly, the quest for justice may at first stimulate growth, but if it leads eventually to a penalizing of the efficient and the innovating members of society to support the idle and unproductive, it can easily reduce the rate of growth.

Time perspective in judging objectives. Our relative judgments as to the importance of the various objectives will depend a good deal on our time perspective. All policy problems envisage some kind of time horizon and time perspective, insofar as they involve possible present sacrifices for future gains. Generally speaking, the further off is our time horizon and the less we discount future events simply because they are future, the more we are prepared to sacrifice for progress. We must not fall into the fallacy of supposing that all growth or progress involves present sacrifice. Growth may be "built in" to some organizations, just as it is in the youth of all biological organisms —a child does not have the option of stopping growth and devoting the resources released to increasing present activity. Nevertheless, beyond a certain point increased rates of growth always involve some kind of present sacrifice. Education involves loss of present earnings, capital accumulation involves sacrifice of current consumption, even invention requires time and resources that might otherwise have been devoted to immediate pleasures.

How ideologies widen time perspectives. These choices become grimmer when we face the problem of poor societies. Here, in effect, communism offers them a high rate of economic growth at the cost of loss of many personal and political freedoms, coercion, conformity, ruthless suppression of opponents, rigid restrictions on consumption, and so on. The bargain, of course, may not be a true one, and I shall argue later that the communists, at least in Russia, have actually hampered their economic growth by their suppression of freedom. Still, the question remains in some form or other: how much present sacrifice is future bliss worth?

The answer to this question depends almost wholly on our time perspective. On the whole, faiths and ideologies, by liberating man from his bondage to his immediate environment, extend his time perspective and make him more willing to endure sacrifices in the present because of the prospect of good things to come, either for himself or for the larger society with which he identifies himself. Thus, in the Christian system, identification with Christ leads to the hope of sharing in his resurrection, so that St. Paul wrote, "I reckon that the sufferings of this present time are not worthy to be compared with the glory which shall be revealed in us" (Romans 8,18). In Marxism there is likewise a vision of future "glory" (the classless society) in the light of which not only present suffering but even present wickedness is justified. Societies that are dominated by ideologies stressing the reality of the historical process and the interpretation of history in terms of some kind of dramatic process are likely to have longer time perspectives and to be more willing to sacrifice the present for the future than those societies that do not have strong and complex historical ideologies and that are centered in the enjoyment of the present.

Means come to be regarded as ends. The choice among competing objectives is greatly complicated in practice because the *means* by which these objectives are achieved come in part to be regarded as ends in themselves, perhaps because they are more visible than the more ultimate objectives. The confusion of means and ends is so common a human experience that we may almost regard it as being natural and inevitable; and we may suppose that all means come to be regarded in part as ends in themselves, and that this "endiness" of them must be respected, even where it costs something in terms of ends that can be regarded as more ultimate. Perhaps the most extreme example of this confusion is to be seen in the instances where people have starved to death rather than eat unfamiliar food. The familiar becomes the end in itself; and something else that could accomplish the ostensible end is rejected simply because it is unfamiliar. Rice-eating people have starved in the midst of supplies of wheat; and grain-eating people have starved in the midst of a plague of edible and nutritious locusts, which they could not bring themselves to regard as food.

Institutions come to be treated as ends. When we come to the more complex problems of attitudes towards institutions and organizations, the tendency for means to become ends in themselves grows very pronounced. The nation is a means towards the orderly development of mankind, yet there are people who would be willing to condemn mankind to extinction rather than to suffer even the slightest diminution of power of their particular nation. The labor union is a means towards the elevation of the status of the workers, yet there are people who would rather have the workers languish with a union than prosper without one. The church is an instrument for the salvation of souls, yet there are people who would rather have souls damned inside their church than saved outside it. At a more subtle level there are people who believe so passionately in the free market that they resist all efforts to remove its imperfections, and there are people who believe so passionately in socialism that they would rather have the most grotesque inefficiencies in collectivized industry rather than permit private enterprise where this is demonstrably more efficient and appropriate.

Example: the socialist controversy. Much of the "socialist controversy," which has occupied so much attention in the past century, and which is still a vital controversy in many parts of the world, can be shown to be the result of erecting relative means into absolute ends. At one end of the scale we have those who deny all right of private property in the means of production, who regard all nonwage income as derived from exploitation, and who therefore believe that all enterprise should be conducted by political, or at least nonprivate agencies. The communists, of course, are the most extreme representatives of this view. At the other end of the scale we have the right-wing "libertarians" who make an almost absolute value of the right of private property, freedom of contract, unregulated markets, and consumers' sovereignty, and who therefore deny almost any economic function to government beyond that of defending the right of property and the enforcement of contracts. These issues are so important that we must examine them in some detail. The problem here is not which of these systems is most "efficient" in the sense of most effectively satisfying the four basic objectives—progress, justice, stability, and freedom. Rather it is the question of what is it about these systems that impels people to value them highly or otherwise, quite apart from their effects. That is, even if the two systems were equally effective in satisfying the basic objectives, there would still be some people who would take a socialist position, some a libertarian.

The socialist value orientation: labor as the source of value. Let us examine the socialist system first. The problem is, what is it in a man's value system that would give him a prejudice towards socialism? There are many answers to this question; indeed, even a casual study of the psychology of socialists, still more that of communists, would carry us far beyond the scope of this volume. We can, however, distinguish some broad value orientations that impel people towards socialism.

There is first a high valuation of income derived from work as contrasted with income derived from the ownership of material property. In Marx, for instance, the labor theory of value, which in Adam Smith and Ricardo had been mainly an instrument for explaining the relative prices of goods, became an instrument of moral disapproval of nonlabor income. The argument is simple: labor, directly or indirectly through its embodiment in material equipment, makes everything—that is, it is solely responsible for the product of economic life. Labor, however, does not get the whole product, but only part of it. Part goes in one form or another to the owners of capital, who, on this doctrine, have not contributed anything to its production and who therefore do not deserve to receive any. This is the Marxist doctrine of exploitation: that all income is ultimately produced by labor and that therefore any income that does not ultimately revert to labor is stolen from labor. The theory is based ultimately on a mechanical view of the economic process (a view which, it must be confessed, goes back mainly to Ricardo) in which commodities are envisioned as "jellies of embodied labor." The typewriter at which I am working, for instance, sits on my desk today because of innumerable pieces of human activity—by transport workers, salesmen, factory workers, engineers, steelworkers, miners, and so on—that have contributed to making it and bringing it here. If all capital can thus be reduced to labor, it would seem that there is no real function for the capitalist—that is, the owner as such—and that therefore his income is "exploitation." He is taking from others what they have produced.

The "capital theory of value." What is missing from this account of the economic process is the element of organization. Let me for a moment stand Marx on his head and produce a "capital theory of value." According to this view, labor is an amorphous mass that never produces anything in the absence of someone to direct and organize its activity. Labor "goes into" the process of production, it is true, but so do raw materials, and labor is no more than a raw material, lying inert in the mine of the human personality until it is extracted by an organizer. Who, however, is the organizer? It must be the *controller* of the capital—that is, of the material equipment of society. Only he who has yarn and a loom can organize the process of cloth production. The ultimate controller of capital, however, is the owner: this is the essential meaning of property. It is the capitalist, therefore, who by making decisions about the form and use of his capital really organizes the process of production. The worker is a passive agent who would produce nothing, just as ore in the mine or fertility in the field produces nothing, without the organization that is provided by the capitalist.

On this view, therefore, it is labor that exploits capital. Capital produces everything, but insofar as labor obtains more than a subsistence wage, capital does not get what it produces, but has some of its product taken away from it by labor! This view will quite properly strike the reader as absurd. It is no more absurd, however, than the Marxist view, which attributes all product to labor. The truth is that the process of production, as it extends through time, is a complex interaction of activities and institutions, and any attempt to identify any single element in it as "the" productive factor is doomed to failure.

What the socialists generally fail to recognize is that property and the price system are a form of social organization, just as much as a hierarchical socialist state is a form of organization, and that lack of hierarchy does not necessarily mean anarchy. The libertarians, on the other hand, equally fail to recognize that the price-property system is not the only system of organization, and that other systems and forms of organization may legitimately compete with it.

"Publicness" *vs.* "privateness." Another element in the socialist controversy that has played an important part is the valuations that have been placed on the "public" as opposed to the "private" character of institutions. "Publicness" has tended to become an end in itself among the socialists, "privateness" among the libertarians. There is a real tension here which cannot be resolved easily. The ethical teaching of all great religions lays stress on the subordination of individual desires and activity to the desires of others in a larger group. Selfishness is decried and unselfishness praised, and selfless devotion to a group beyond the self is regarded as the epitome of human greatness. Collective action, therefore, takes on a moral aura derived from our high valuation of unselfishness, and collective institutions attach to themselves something of the same aura. On the other hand, we also attribute moral worth to independence and individuality: man is not an ant or a bee; he does not exist to serve society; rather, society exists to serve him. Change and progress only come as individuals defy the existing collectivity, defy the pressures and conformities of the group around them, and strike out for themselves in new directions. The figure of the lonely prophet, the ridiculed inventor, the persecuted revolutionary, even the rugged individualist, is also among our heroes.

The profit motive and the profit system. It is not the business of this work to resolve the moral tension between selflessness and independence—perhaps, indeed, this is a tension that should not be resolved. Creative individuals and creative societies may be those in which these opposites are held in tension; it may be that when the tension fails to maintain itself the society—and the person—falls either into tyranny or anarchy. What we must point out, however, is that much confusion is caused by investing *institutions* with moral qualities, which are in no way inherent in them, and then setting up—or beating down—these institutions as ends in themselves. A good example of this confusion is found in attitudes towards the "profit system" which are based on disapproval of the "profit motive." It is argued that the profit motive is "selfish," and that men should be motivated not for their own interests but for the common good. This may be very true, and yet it is quite irrelevant to the question as to whether particular parts of economic life should be organized by governmental organizations, deriving their support ultimately from the coercive power of the state, or whether economic life should be organized by private organizations, such as the corporation or private businesses, deriving their support from their ability to sell their product and to buy their inputs of labor and materials in a market. This, however, is the question that is involved in the criticisms of the "profit system." The profit system is essentially a market system; its characteristic institution is an organization that obtains the resources it needs by giving something for them, and that is able to give something for these resources because it gets something by selling what it makes with them. The alternative system is that of governmental organization, which can employ not only market incentives and resources but coercive power, through, for instance, conscription or taxation.

Application to other institutions. This is a distinction that goes far beyond what are usually thought of as economic institutions. It is the difference, for instance, between a "free church" system in which the churches are private enterprises, supported not by the state but by the voluntary contributions of their adherents, and a "state church" system in which the church is supported by tax funds. It is the difference between a "private school" system in which schools are supported by fees and a "public school" system in which they are supported out of taxes. It is the difference between private insurance conducted by private companies and social insurance based on compulsory contributions. And, of course, it is the difference between private business, which can survive only if it can sell its product on the market for enough to cover its costs, and public business, which can, if necessary, cover out of tax revenues the excess of costs over receipts from sales.

Mixed systems. Merely stating the distinction is enough to show the futility of either damning or praising an institution *merely* because it happens to be public or private. In some areas of life we almost all agree that public institutions are more effective; in others, private institutions. What is more, in many cases public and private institutions can live together, and be useful one to another, even when they are serving the same end. In the United States there is a strong feeling that the church should be a private institution; this is the essential meaning of the "separation of church and state." In England we find a mixed system: the Church of England has some of the attributes of a public institution, but there are many "private" churches (the "free churches") and there is freedom for any group of people who wish to form a church to do so. In the Scandinavian countries and in Spain the church is a state church, supported by tax funds, and many difficulties are placed in the way of those who wish to organize a private church. In almost all countries today we find a mixture of public and private education. Few people would wish to deny the right of parents to send their children to a private school of their own choosing. On the other hand, few people would be wholly content to leave education entirely in private hands. Similarly, few people would deny the right of people to organize insurance companies and to sell or to buy private insurance, though there would probably also be wide agreement that private insurance companies should be inspected and governed by some regulations to protect the public against fraud or unwise policies. On the other hand, there is also a widespread feeling that private insurance cannot do *all* the job that needs to be done, and hence there is almost universal support for some kind of social insurance, even though this involves an element of compulsion. Similarly, some businesses are regarded as peculiarly suitable for government operation, such as the post office, though even here some might feel that a little competition from the private express companies is not undesirable. At the other end, businesses such as small retail operations are so clearly unsuitable to public operation that they are frequently left in private hands even in communist countries. In between there is disputed ground. In some countries, for instance, the railroads are publicly owned and operated; in others they are private. It does not seem to make a great deal of difference in this case which form of organization prevails.

Different "mixtures" appropriate to different cases. In any case, the argument should rest not on whether it is good in itself that any particular industry should be publicly or privately owned or operated, but whether in each special case public or private operation is most likely to be effective in furthering the ultimate objectives of economic life. Which will be the case depends on the peculiar circumstances, on the nature of the culture, and on the stage of development in which the society finds itself. Where there is a strong tradition of active, energetic and responsible private enterprise, as in the United States, the case for socialization is weak. Where private enterprise is inactive, weak, and irresponsible it may well be that extensive government enterprise is in order. In underdeveloped countries, for instance, which are exhibiting a vigorous national renaissance, it is neither surprising nor inappropriate to find in some areas extensive state enterprise that would be quite inappropriate in developed countries with a long tradition of competent private enterprise.

Consumers' sovereignty. One of the principal arguments against socialism, and indeed against state enterprise or regulation of almost any kind, is that it violates "consumers' sovereignty." Consumers' sovereignty thus becomes an end in itself by which systems are judged. We shall do well to examine the concept in some detail, especially as it is in many ways a subtle concept as well as an important one.

We can best explain it, perhaps, by contrasting a system of the freest possible private enterprise, where the functions of the state are strictly limited to maintaining order and the rights of property and contract, with a "liberal" socialist regime that allows the maximum possible freedom of consumer choice and that uses the monetary mechanism, but in which very large areas of economic activity and property are controlled by the state, and all economic life is subject to an over-all plan. In the first case, the choices of consumers determine both the prices and the quantities of goods produced and consumed. In the second case, an individual consumer may have considerable freedom of choice, but the price system is manipulated by those who control the system in order to make consumers as a whole take what these controllers have decided to produce.

In a "pure market" system. We may illustrate the first case by supposing that the system is in equilibrium, with all industries normally profitable and able to sell their whole output at a price that just covers their costs plus normal profit. Now let us suppose that there is a shift in consumer preferences, let us say from tea to coffee. Immediately the price of tea falls, for consumers are not willing to buy the existing output of tea at the old price; the price of coffee similarly rises. This makes tea production abnormally unprofitable, coffee production abnormally profitable. As a result, capital will leave the tea industry, and will enter the coffee industry; the production of tea will decline and of coffee will increase. As this happens, however, the price of tea will begin to rise again, and the price of coffee will begin to fall. This will go on until a new equilibrium is restored, with the output of tea less than before and of coffee greater, and with the prices of tea and coffee at a level that will make the industries at their new outputs just normally profitable again. If the industries are operating under "constant costs"—that is, if the average costs of production do not depend on how much is produced—the new equilibrium prices will be the same as the old, though of course the outputs will be different. If costs are not constant the new prices will not in general be the same as the old, because to be equilibrium prices they must just cover costs, including normal profit, and if costs have risen in tea because of its smaller output and fallen in coffee because of its larger output, the new equilibrium price of the tea will be somewhat greater and of coffee somewhat smaller than the old.

—Contrasted with "liberal" planned economy. Contrast this ideal picture with what would happen in a "liberal" planned economy. The first effect of such a change in tastes would be, of course, that stocks of tea would begin to pile up and stocks of coffee would tend to disappear. The pricing authorities might deal with this situation, as in the first case, by raising the price of coffee to discourage its consumption and by lowering the price of tea to get rid of the accumulating stocks. At the new prices consumers have as much *choice* as before. Their choices, however, do not necessarily have any direct impact on the outputs of these commodities. If the economic plan does not call for any shift of production as between tea and coffee, the only effect of the shift in taste will be that coffee will be taxed and tea will be subsidized. In the coffee industry the money coming in will be greater than that going out, and in tea the reverse will be the case, but this need produce no change in outputs unless there is a change in the over-all plan. The final result, then, is that in spite of the change in tastes people drink just about as much tea and coffee as before, but their consumption of tea has to be encouraged by a low price and of coffee has to be discouraged by a high price.

"Consumers' sovereignty" in occupational choice. We should observe that the concept of "consumers' sovereignty" goes far beyond choices in consumption. It applies equally well to choices in regard to the individual's output of services. Suppose, for instance, that the society is swept by a passion for technical education, so that there is a strong increase in the desire to become engineers, and a corresponding decrease in the desire to become, let us say, lawyers. This is a "change in tastes" just as the shift from tea to coffee was a change in tastes. If we follow through the consequences of this change in our "pure market" society we find, starting again from a position of equilibrium, that the first effect is that students throng into schools of engineering and that law schools have many empty places. In a few years the number of trained engineers increases and of lawyers diminishes. The result of this change is that engineers find it harder to get jobs, and are willing to accept jobs at lower pay. The average reward of engineers falls, and similarly, because of the scarcity of lawyers, the reward of lawyers rises. This will go on until the differential between the two professions is sufficient to overcome the repugnance to the law and the delight in engineering. A final equilibrium may be reached at which the financial rewards of engineers are somewhat smaller than before and of lawyers are somewhat larger than before, and at which engineering schools may be somewhat larger and law schools somewhat smaller, but there will be no further tendency to change. In our ideal planned economy, on the other hand, such a change in tastes could be countered simply by subsidizing or forcing people to go to law school or by simply excluding applicants from engineering school, if the change in tastes threatened the original plan.

Consumers' sovereignty in capital accumulation. An even more important point is that in the pure market economy the over-all rate of capital accumulation is determined by individual decisions to save or consume and not by the central planners. Suppose, for instance, that from a position of equilibrium again the society is swept by a general increase in the desire to save—that is, to increase net worths, or to accumulate personal capital. There will be a fall in purchases of consumers' goods, and people will try to purchase securities with what they save by restricting their consumption. This will lead to a rise in the price of securities, which is equivalent to a fall in the rate of interest. It leads also to a fall in the prices of consumers' goods, which makes it less profitable to produce consumers' goods. The fall in the rate of interest now makes it more profitable to produce "investment goods." Consequently there is a shift of resources from consumers' goods to investment goods. The society produces fewer personal services, for instance, and more steel mills, and so accumulates at a faster rate. Under a planned economy, on the other hand, the over-all rate of investment is determined by the planning bureau, and the rest of the people have little or no say in the matter. If they wish to consume more than is available under the plan, this can be countered by price increases, by tax increases, or by rationing. If there is an increase in the desire to accumulate, this will simply be reflected in a slight easing of the restrictions on consumption; it will not be reflected in any change in the rate of accumulation. Russia is an excellent example of a society in which central decision has maintained a rate of accumulation much larger than would have been maintained by the sum of individual decisions. The Russian people have been subjected to "forced saving" on a scale almost unparalleled in human history.

The critique of consumers' sovereignty. Again, merely stating these two extreme positions brings out the fact that the demand for consumers' sovereignty is not trivial and it cannot be ignored, and that failure to provide for it is a serious criticism, at least of the naive socialists who simply do not see the problem, and who assume that the benign providence of an all-wise mother-state will give every individual not only what he wants but what he ought to have. On the other hand, it also reveals clearly that the mere absence of government economic policy does not necessarily insure a system that will operate in the way described above to give the sovereignty of the individual full expression. In the first place, the free flow of resources among industries and occupations is obstructed by all sorts of difficulties—by natural costs of transfer of resources from one occupation to another, by artificial restrictions such as licensing laws and immigration laws, and by monopoly in all its many forms. Consequently, a real problem of the conflict of freedom arises. If consumers are perfectly free to switch from tea to coffee as the whim seizes them, this may involve high costs of transfer of resources, both human and nonhuman. Tea plantations cannot generally be turned into coffee plantations; indeed, in the short run practically nothing can be done with a tea plantation but to produce tea with it. A shift from tea to coffee therefore may involve a long, painful depression in the tea industry, with workers and landowners unable to make the shift into other occupations, and an equally long but quite fortuitous and undeserved prosperity in the coffee industry, as it takes a long time to plant coffee bushes and bring them to fruition. Under such circumstances it would not seem unreasonable to ask consumers to bear the costs of their freedom of choice, even if this takes the form of a tax on coffee and a subsidy to tea!

Neither price system nor planned system ensures optimum expression of consumers' sovereignty. We cannot honestly maintain, either, that the price system is the *only* method by which information in regard to changing individual tastes can be transmitted or can act upon the decisions of those who control the allocation of resources. Nonprice information is an important aspect of any system, and though it is true that in the planned economy the effect of consumer discontents is felt much less immediately and urgently by the planners than would be the case in a market economy, we cannot assume that planners would be totally incapable either of receiving this information or of acting upon it. If certain commodities prove difficult to sell, or have to be disposed of at prices that clearly do not cover their costs, this information will probably reach the planning authority and even may cause a change in the plan.

On the other hand, a hierarchical planning structure is peculiarly subject to distortions of information. Performance is judged by conformity to the plan as revealed in reports to superiors. It would be surprising if a good deal of effort did not go into the reports rather than into the performance. It is the great danger of any hierarchy that it tends to control its own information system. Hence the "boss" surrounds himself with "yes-men" who feed him the information that he desires to hear, and he may become increasingly cut off from the realities of the world outside. It is the great virtue of a market system that it provides many independent channels of information and many independent foci of decision-making. The weakness of a pure market system is that the exercise of rather unimportant freedoms on the part of some may seriously limit important freedoms in others, and also that the market system may be subject to essentially meaningless fluctuations, as we saw in Chapter 3.

Sovereignty may have to be sacrificed to freedom. Consequently, although consumers' sovereignty is by no means an unimportant element in judging a system, we cannot conclude either that consumers' sovereignty is an absolute ideal to be attained at all costs, nor even that a completely unfettered and unregulated market system is the best way to achieve that degree of consumers' sovereignty that we regard as desirable. Neither in economic nor in political life, is sovereignty identical with freedom. In the world of nations the exercise of the unlimited sovereignty of states leads to a diminution of the freedom of all, and in the interest of freedom it is clearly necessary to limit sovereignty. The same is true also of the sovereignty of individuals. Where the exercise of individual sovereignty limits the freedom of all, sovereignty must be sacrificed to freedom, for freedom is a much more fundamental ideal than sovereignty. This does not mean, however, that we must plunge headlong into the socialist state and the planned economy, for this may involve a sacrifice not only of sovereignty but of freedom.

Organizations as ends: the problem of loyalty. Another area in which means come to be regarded as ends is in *forms* of economic organization. There are people who believe that the way to economic salvation is *only* through cooperatives, or labor unions, or publicly owned and operated enterprises, or private corporations, or small business, or large businesses. All these organizations or forms of organization have their virtues—and their vices. There are circumstances in which each is appropriate, other circumstances in which it is not. It would seem appropriate to take a pragmatic view, judging each type of organization by how far it serves the more fundamental ends of economic organization in each particular circumstance. Nevertheless, we must recognize that there are loyalties to particular forms of organizations as such, and that these loyalties must be taken seriously and must enter in some degree into our final judgments.

Loyalty related to involvement. The problem of the "springs of loyalty"—what determines the affection and attachment that people have for various organizations—is a difficult one, and we certainly have not heard the final word on it. We may identify one major element in the creation of loyalty as *involvement.* The more deeply a person is involved in an organization, and the more he associates it with great experiences and deep needs, the greater will be his loyalty and attachment to it. We must be careful, however, of circularity in the argument: people involve themselves in an organization because they are loyal to it, and become loyal to it because they are involved in it. Hence neither loyalty nor involvement is a simple "cause" of the other; both participate in a complex dynamic process in which each, up to a point, encourages the other.

We have frequently observed the spectacle of a person who has not shown much interest in an organization, who, being asked to take some responsibility in it, then became increasingly both involved and loyal. On the other hand, it is also noticeable that too great a degree of involvement produces reactions in an opposite direction. Involvement may become so great as to become a burden, and then it destroys loyalty rather than creates it, and leads to its own self-destruction. We are here dealing with subtle and complex psychological processes about which it is hard to make secure generalizations. Yet it is these very processes that are at the heart of the dynamics of society.

What we must not do is to take loyalty for granted. Sometimes it grows and organizations become stronger internally, more meaningful, enjoy a greater inherent "life." Sometimes it dies away. Sometimes it collapses quite dramatically, and something that men have been willing to sacrifice their very lives for is suddenly perceived as futile and unworthy of support.

Why market institutions do not attract loyalty. One of the problems of the market relationship and market institutions is that the exchange relationship is one of the least "involved" and most abstract of all human relationships, and hence market institutions do not attract much loyalty. The main weakness of capitalism is that nobody loves it. Properly managed it is an efficient system, scoring high on all four main objectives of economic life. It is frequently politically unstable, however, because of its inability to attract loyalty. A purely market-oriented organization creates so little involvement, except at the center of decision-making, that it attracts little loyalty for itself among those who trade with it. Indeed, the very concept of pure competition implies a denial of loyalty to any particular buyer or seller. In the pure competition model, exchangers are supposed to be actuated solely by perceived price differences. Buyers always flock to the cheapest seller, sellers to the cheapest buyer, no matter how small the differentials. As soon as "loyalties" develop, pure competition is replaced by monopolistic competition, where each seller has a cohort of loyal buyers who will stick to him even if he is not the cheapest source, or each buyer has a cohort of loyal sellers who will sell to him even though they could get more elsewhere. The very overtones of moral disapproval in the word "cheap" (for instance, in the combination "cheapskate") indicate a need for at least a minimum of loyalty and involvement.

Loyalty to the national state: war involvement. To illustrate this principle, let us contrast four types of organization, all of which have important economic functions: the national state, the labor union, the cooperative society, and the ordinary "business."

The national state attracts very intense loyalties, perhaps the most intense of any present-day organization. It has not always done so, and it still does not do so in many parts of the world where family or religious loyalties frequently transcend those of the nation. The growth of loyalty towards the national state may not unreasonably be attributed mainly to an increasing degree of involvement in its activities. This involvement takes two forms, which might be summed up as war and welfare. It is one of the peculiar penalties of economic development that the very liberation of a society from the necessity of spending by far the greater proportion of its resources just keeping its people alive has also permitted a much greater degree of involvement of the whole population in war. In an underdeveloped country where, say, 80 to 90 per cent of activity must be devoted to the sheer business of keeping people alive, even if all available resources were devoted to war it could not involve directly more than a small fraction of the population. In a developed country, on the other hand, it is possible to devote a half or even more of the national product to war. Then, because of the probable instability of the balance of power in international relations in times of crisis, a nation may be expected to devote all or nearly all of its available resources, or economic surplus above the minimum necessary to keep it going, to war. In developed nations, therefore, war reaches very deep into the life of the people. Less than two hundred years ago Adam Smith could write, "Among the civilized nations of modern Europe, it is commonly computed that not more than one-hundredth part of the inhabitants of any country can be employed as soldiers without ruin to the country which pays the expense of their services." [1] Today conscription reaches into almost every family. The armed forces and their suppliers may approach 50 per cent of the labor force in time of war. Whereas in the eighteenth century and even later war was a peripheral activity of society, except in those unfortunate areas where battles were actually fought, today it has become central and dominant. This has created an involvement and commitment to the national state that never existed before. One wonders, however, whether the

[1] Adam Smith, *The Wealth of Nations,* Book V (Modern Library edition, pp. 657-58).

cost of this involvement is becoming so great that it may eventually destroy loyalty rather than maintain it.

Welfare involvement. The other, and more cheerful, side of the picture is that the national state has become increasingly an agency for protecting the individual against the vicissitudes and misfortunes of life. This is the welfare aspect of the state, as reflected in social insurance, income-maintenance programs, police protection, protection of civil rights, and so on. It is perhaps the greatest achievement of the modern democratic state that for the first time in history large societies have emerged that are internally integrated in the sense that few persons or groups within them are excluded or do not "belong." This in itself attracts loyalty to the national state that provides these benefits, though it may well be that loyalty is fired more by the demands made upon individuals than by the benefits conferred upon them.

Integrated nations and disintegrated world. It is perhaps the peculiar tragedy of the present period in man's history that the very success of the national state in attracting man's loyalty and creating an integrated society threatens to disrupt the international order, and perhaps threatens even the very existence of man. We see this not only in the threat of war, which has become more and more menacing as nations have become better integrated internally and more developed economically, but we see it also in the decay of the international economic order—the collapse of the gold standard, the decline in foreign investment, and the rise of trade restrictions. We shall pursue this theme further in later chapters. Meanwhile, it is sufficient to note that there is great danger today of the world "separating out" into rich countries that go on developing and increasing their per-capita incomes and economic power, and poor countries that are prevented from developing by their very poverty, and that are not adequately assisted by the rich countries because of the absence of foreign investment and the disintegration of the international economic order. A world in which the rich countries are continually getting richer and the poor countries are either getting poorer or at least merely staying where they are is not a world to which we can look forward with any satisfaction or confidence.

It is part of the ideological strength of socialism that it caters to the sense of loyalty to the state—to the loyalty that men have for "public" as opposed to "private" institutions. Nowhere, however, is the dilemma of loyalty more apparent than in the development of socialist—or at least "welfare"—nation-states. Internally there is much that is appealing in the notion of a society in which the welfare of each is the concern of all. As always, however, loyalty exacts a price, perhaps in terms of a certain slackening of the rate of economic progress, more certainly in terms of restrictions on personal liberty—on the liberty to travel, to migrate, to change one's occupation, to start new enterprises, and so on.

The dilemma of loyalty in the labor movement. The same dilemma of loyalty is found in a somewhat different form in the labor movement. One of the great motivations behind the rise of labor unions has been dissatisfaction with the impersonality of the labor market and a strong desire for status and job-security on the part of workers. As long as the relationship between employer and employed is a pure market relationship, to be broken at any time when it seems to the advantage of one of the parties, we cannot expect loyalties to be developed towards any of the institutions concerned. We cannot expect the worker to be loyal to an employer who may fire him at any time, or who regards his work simply as a "commodity" to be purchased like any other raw material and fabricated into a product at the will of the employer. Where the employee does not participate in any way—even vicariously—in the decisions of the firm, we cannot expect loyalty towards it. In consequence largely of the inability of the firm to attract loyalty, workers have developed their own organizations—the unions—by which they can satisfy in part their needs for status, for participation, for the absorption of self in a larger whole. There are important analogies between the union and the national state: both attract loyalty not merely because they offer benefits but because they demand sacrifices; both go through periods of crisis in which their existence may be at stake and in which great sacrifices may be expected from the members—war in the case of the state, strikes in the case of the union. Loyalty to the organization is fostered by the memory of these struggles and of the heroes and even martyrs who have carried them on, and by certain "myths" which attribute great importance and significance to these struggles.

Worker's loyalty to the firm. The firm frequently tries to counter the formation of unions by attempting to create loyalty towards itself—for instance, by means of company unions, welfare programs, sports teams, magazines, clubs, and so on. These efforts are apt to be successful only where the firm has a very stable labor force and hence does not really need a "labor market." Even then these efforts not infrequently backfire; the workers feel that there is something "phony" about loyalty of this kind which does not involve real *responsibility*. We require of our employer that he be just rather than lovable!

It will be interesting to see whether the experiments in "co-determination" (representation of workers on the board of directors of a firm) now taking place in Germany will have much impact on attitudes of workers either towards the unions or the employers. Profit-sharing schemes also in part represent an attempt to build responsibility and participation, and therefore loyalty, into the worker's relationship to the firm. Here again, however, the sense of participation is often tenuous, and is bought at the price of tying the worker to the firm. The basic dilemma here is that loyalty to the firm is incompatible with the existence of a mobile labor market where man can shift jobs easily from firm to firm, place to place, and industry to industry. Yet in a dynamic society mobility in the labor market is in itself highly desirable, because of the constant shifts in demand for labor brought about by changing tastes or technologies. If labor is immobile, we are apt to get "pockets" of depressed areas and industries—pools of stagnant and decaying communities left by the shifting tides of commerce.

Loyalty to the union. To some extent the dilemma is resolved by loyalty to the union. However, even this has its costs. It, too, may lead to immobilities, not so much between firms as between industries and occupations. It may lead to attempts to create little labor monopolies by restricting jobs to union members and restricting membership in the union—though quantitatively this is not very important, as it can only be effectively practiced by fairly small unions. Where pension plans and seniority provisions tie the worker to the firm, or even the plant where he works, they may substantially diminish the bargaining power of the individual, insofar as they limit his ability to quit, and may even diminish the bargaining power of the union. At its worst the union becomes a cloak for racketeers and an agency of sheer exploitation and extortion. In spite of these dangers and defects, however, the union is capable of attracting powerful loyalties and it stands high on the list of institutions that we wish to preserve, quite apart from its ultimate consequences. It gives its members a sense of status, of "belonging" to a community. It helps to overcome the sense of helplessness that an individual feels in the face of a great impersonal labor market or a great impersonal corporation. In both Britain and the United States the labor movement has performed the important function of integrating its members into the society of which they are a part—giving them a sense of participation in, and therefore loyalty to, the system within which they live and move. Quite contrary to Marx's expectations, the labor movement at least in these countries has become an important conservative force, loyal to the basic institutions of capitalism even when it proclaims itself socialist!

Inflation as a possible cost of "loyalty." The labor movement evokes loyalties to its own institutions that are much too strong to make their destruction, or even substantial modification, practical politics even were it theoretically desirable, which it is not. As always, however, there are costs of loyalty, and it may well be that the cost of the high degree of organization of society, not only in the labor movement but in many other aspects of life, is that the economy cannot run without continued inflation. Industrial relations are certainly much easier to manage in a period of gentle inflation, when money wages are rising. They are very difficult to handle in a period of deflation when money wages are falling. This may be because of an illusion—that changes in money wages are the consequences of action by the union or by the employer, whereas the changes in innumerable prices that change real wages are "acts of God," not attributable to any specific human agency. Nevertheless this is a powerful illusion, and indeed is something more than an illusion. The responsibility for change is much easier to identify when the change is in a single variable than when it is in many variables. In an inflation, therefore, the union—and the employer—get credit for rising money wages and do not get the blame for the rising prices that limit the rise in real wages. In a deflation the union and employer get the blame for falling money wages, and do not get the credit for any fall in prices that may raise real wages.

The cooperative movement. Another expression of dissatisfaction with the institutions of the market is found in the cooperative movement. A cooperative society may be defined very briefly as a business that is owned by its customers. There are two broad classes of such business—the consumers' cooperative, which is owned by the people who buy from it, and the marketing cooperative, which is owned by the people who sell to it. Some farm cooperatives combine both aspects. In either case the members are customers, the organization is financed partly by the sale of fixed-interest obligations (called "shares," but actually more like "bonds") to the members, and partly by the reinvesting of profits (or "earnings," as cooperators prefer to call them). Any residual earnings are distributed to members not in proportion to their capital stock, as would be the case in the capital-stock corporation, but in proportion to purchases from the organization (in the case of the consumers' cooperative) or sales to the organization (in the case of a marketing cooperative). The members elect the board of directors who in turn appoint managers. The election is usually on a basis of one vote per member, rather than according to the number of shares held as is customary in the case of a capital-stock corporation.

Conditions for success of cooperatives. There is nothing in the cooperative form of organization that guarantees business success. Nevertheless, the cooperative movement has attracted a good deal of loyalty, and in many special situations it has been highly successful, in other situations less so. It has been most successful where it has been able to open up opportunities for managerial ability that otherwise would have gone unused, because of the class or linguistic structure of the society or simply because of the inertia or the unwillingness of the existing managerial class to receive recruits. Thus in England and Scandinavia the cooperative movement is a "working class" movement drawing its resources and its managerial personnel largely from previously unused or underused abilities in the working class. In the United States the most successful cooperatives have been in agriculture, where again a certain social immobility may prevent the full utilization of human resources by "conventional" business. On the other hand, the consumers' cooperative movement in the United States has been on the whole a failure, mainly because it could not compete with the existing retail organizations, and could not find any source of managerial talent that was shut out from other opportunities. Nevertheless, it must be recognized that there are loyalties to the cooperative form of organization as such; this fact is reflected, for instance, in government support and encouragement and even subsidy of such organizations. It can be argued that the cooperative form of organization, because it involves greater participation on the part of the customers, evokes greater loyalties, has a greater value in character training and in the development of responsible attitudes, and has therefore a superior inherent ethical value. These are imponderables; there may be something in these claims. On the other hand, we know very little about the effect of various types of organization on character formation.

The critique of specialization. Most of the arguments on the inherent advantages and disadvantages of various forms and kinds of organization revolve around two points—*specialization* and *size*. Much of the protest against the market, whether this protest takes the form of the labor movement, the cooperative movement, or the socialist movement, is against specialization —specialization as between boss and bossed, capitalist and customer, capitalist and laborer. Even the protectionist movement can be regarded as a protest against specialization in international trade. This protest is not to be taken lightly. Even Adam Smith,[2] we may profitably recall, denounced the division of labor as a producer of narrow-minded specialists "as stupid and ignorant as it is possible for a human creature to become," and praised the unspecialized state of barbarous society in which "every man has a considerable degree of knowledge, ingenuity, and invention." Too-great specialization leads to a loss of "wholeness" of life, even if it does lead to greater productivity of goods. At some point we may want to discourage further specialization, even at the cost of smaller real incomes, in the interest of "character" or "quality of life." It is always well to remember that the ultimate business of economic, as of all human organization, is to produce the Good rather than goods, and that all commodities are intermediate goods in the production of the Good Life. Here, however, we are greatly hampered by ignorance—especially by ignorance of the ultimate sources of human character. It is easy to be led away by sentimentality into propositions that are not securely tested, or even testable, and it is not a foregone conclusion that the struggling peasant farmer becomes a finer character than the Detroit auto worker.

The critique of size. The problem of the inherent defects or virtues of *size* of organization is not unrelated to that of specialization, for large size permits great specialization, and the protest against "bigness" as such is not unrelated to the protest against excessive specialization. A good deal of ethical feeling is channeled into this form. We sympathize with the "little fellow" whether the small businessman, the family farmer, the independent craftsman, or even the small nation. The preservation both of "small business" and of the family farm is an explicit

[2] Adam Smith, *The Wealth of Nations*, Book V (Modern Library, p. 734).

objective of American economic policy, and there is a distinct political prejudice against "big business" as reflected, for instance, in the administration of the anti-trust laws.

On the other hand, there is also a certain ambivalence in our attitudes towards "bigness." We are proud of being a big country, we are proud of the great corporation, the Empire State Building, and the giant university. We have the paradox that whereas nobody approves of "bigness," everybody wants to grow! We may be uneasy about "big business," "big labor," "big government," but we also have a certain pride in the giant organization. This ambivalence is reflected in the constantly shifting tack of the anti-trust administration. It is reflected in an agricultural policy that ostensibly sets out to protect the family farm but actually subsidizes the large producer more effectively than the small. Here is a clear example of policies being uncertain and often contradictory because we are not sure of the ideal towards which we are striving.

7

The principles of action applied to government

It's wise to use the Public Purse
To Wheedle rather than Coerce,
And so the self-restraint exhibit
To Regulate and not Prohibit;
Because, when things are going slick,
The Carrot can supplant the Stick,
Till, in the glare of Fortune's Frown,
The Stick comes up, the Carrot down.

The principles of action. In the first part of this book we have discussed "policy"—the general "principles that govern action directed towards given ends"—mainly in regard to the ends, especially of economic activity and institutions. We now turn towards *action*, which we shall discuss in many specific instances and, examples.

What we shall be discussing is not so much individual acts, however, as *principles of action*—general formulae which govern whole sets of acts. Thus shaving is an individual act; the decision to grow a beard or to be clean-shaven is a principle of action. Once such a decision is made a whole set of acts is determined by it. If I decide to be clean-shaven, I shall have to shave every morning; if I decide to grow a beard I will not shave every morning, but will have to trim the beard once a week. No principle of action, however, can be framed in the absence of knowledge about the consequences of individual acts. I cannot decide to be clean-shaven if I do not know how to shave. Furthermore, no *decision* about a principle of action can be made in the absence of the power to perform individual acts. I cannot decide to be clean-shaven, even if I know how to shave, if I do not have a razor.

The act as a change of state. The attempt to clarify exactly what we mean by an "act" leads to a quite surprising entanglement of logical and philosophical difficulties which we shall not attempt to explore very far. It raises, for instance, the age-long dilemma of free will and predestination, and it raises the even more fundamental question of what is really involved in the concept of change. Let us start, however, with the notion of a *state* of the universe. This is simply a description of things as they exist at a moment of time—a glorified balance sheet, as it were, of the whole, or at least of the relevant universe, a flashlight photograph of "things" (whatever a thing is) as they exist at a moment of time. Every act changes the state of the universe: it is described by comparing the state before and the state after the act, assuming no other acts have taken place. At 7:50 A.M., there is an unshaven face in the universe; at 7:55 there is a shaven face. The act of shaving is described by the difference between these two universes. We can, of course, break up any act into smaller sub-acts. In the course of shaving, the blade sweeps an inch across my face. At 7:57 and 10 seconds there is a universe with a patch of whiskery skin; at 7:57 and 11 seconds there is a universe with a patch of shaven skin: this is the act of passing the blade across the face. If we were to break down a single act of shaving into its sub-acts volumes would have to be written describing them—the innumerable changes, psychological, physiological, chemical, physical, and so on, that take place in successive moments. All this mass of complexity is summed up in a single act of shaving, which in turn is described by its beginning and end states, rather than by what has gone between.

Action as transaction. When we look at an act as a change in the state of the universe, it becomes clear that we cannot change the state of one part of the universe without changing the state of the rest of it. That is to say, every action is also a *transaction.* This follows from the basic principle of conservation, according to which all changes in the state of the universe consist of rearrangements of its constituent "stuff"—matter, energy, or whatever the stuff may be.[1] Thus the act of shaving moves us from a state of the universe with whiskers on the chin to one with whiskers in the shaving water: it involves the rearrangement of whiskers rather than their annihilation. If I buy a watch there is a shift from a state with a watch in the store and money in my pocket to a state with a watch in my pocket and money in the store. If I write a check for a Community Chest there is a shift from a state with $\$x$ in my account and $\$y$ in the Community Chest account to a state with $\$(x - z)$ in my account and $\$(y + z)$ in the Community Chest account.

External and internal transactions. The acts of any organization (actor) can be divided into two kinds: external transactions and internal transactions. An external transaction involves some other actor; an internal transaction involves a reorganization of parts within the actor.

An *exchange* is a good example of an external transaction. It can only take place between two exchangers, and it involves a redistribution of at least two assets or exchangeables between

[1] It is an open question as to whether the principle of conservation is universal. According to Fred Hoyle it is violated even at the physical level. It is certainly violated at the level of organization and information: when a teacher teaches a class the class knows more but the teacher does not know any less. However, these infractions of the principle of conservation do not seem to upset the principle that every action is a transaction.

them. When I buy a watch I have one more watch, the store has one less watch; I have five less dollars, the store has five more dollars. Both watches and dollars have been redistributed between owners.

Production is an example of an internal transaction. When a miller grinds wheat into flour, the internal composition of his assets changes (less wheat, more flour) but the transaction does not involve outside organizations *directly*. Indirectly, of course, all production involves exchange—the miller must buy his wheat and perhaps labor and other things, and must sell his flour, but the simple isolated act of production is an essentially internal transaction.

Exchanges and transfers, destructions and creations. External transactions may be divided into *exchanges* and *transfers*. A transfer is a transaction like a gift or a tax in which something simply passes from one party to another; at the end of the transaction one party has *x* less of the transferred item than before, the other party has *x* more. An exchange consists of two transfers in opposite directions between two parties: *A* gives up *x* to *B*, *B* gives up *y* to *A*.

Similarly, internal transactions can be divided into *transformations* and a category of events for which there seems to be no generic name, but which must be described as *creations* or *destructions*. A transformation is the destruction of one thing and the simultaneous, or at least related, creation of another. When wheat is ground into flour, wheat is destroyed, flour is created. There are some acts of pure creation, however, in which something appears that was not there before, and acts of pure destruction or consumption, in which something that was there before disappears.

A transformation, then, is a combination of a destruction and a creation, just as exchange is a combination of two opposite transfers. We may say if we like, of course, that both creation and destruction are themselves kinds of transformation, if the law of conservation is to hold. Creation then is defined as a transformation from the nonsignificant to the significant—a "birth" into some population with which we are concerned.

Destruction similarly is a transformation from the significant to the nonsignificant—a "death" out of a population of importance to us. In a sense, therefore, all the acts that we have so far discussed can be thought of as *transactions.*

Simple acts. In addition to the various kinds of transactions, acts can also be classified as *simple* and *regulatory*. A simple act is one in which the consequences do not go beyond, or at least much beyond, the transactions that describe the act. The purchase of stamps at the post office is a good example of a simple act. As a result of the transaction the post office has more money, fewer stamps, the purchaser has less money, more stamps. The consequences of the act do not go much beyond this, though of course a number of such acts will eventually lead the post office to replenish its stock of stamps, and such acts cannot go on indefinitely unless the purchasers replenish their stocks of money. The simple act, that is, although it may lead to other acts of a "homeostatic" or restorative nature, does not in itself set the conditions for other acts.

Regulatory acts. A regulatory act, on the other hand, is one that sets conditions for other acts, and especially, eventually, for a whole set of simple acts. Thus, if the regulations of the United States Post Office are changed—for instance, if the first class postal rate is raised from 3 cents to 4 cents per ounce—this affects *all* transactions involving this rate in a like manner. The setting of any price is a regulatory act: it sets one of the conditions—the rate of exchange—under which transactions can be made involving the purchase and sale of the commodity in question.

For some purposes it may be important to distinguish between acts that are "spontaneous" and acts that are "responses" or "reactions." This distinction is not a sharp one, and for the determinist it may disappear altogether. Nevertheless, there is a qualitative difference between acts that in some sense "could have been otherwise" and acts that are "forced on" the actor by circumstances. Thus at Pearl Harbor the action of Japan was more spontaneous than the reaction of the United States; given the situation, Japan might have done something else, or might at least have postponed action. Once the Japanese attacked, however, given the habits and national psychology of the United States, the United States had very little "freedom of action." Certain conceivable modes of behavior (concessions to Japan, nonresistance, and so on) were not in the perceived field of possible action, and in fact most people, and all government people in the United States, felt that there was only one thing to do—the act was "forced on" us by circumstances—we had to make war on Japan.

The distinction between situations in which there is "only one thing to do" and situations in which there are many things to do and only one of them is done, is a real distinction. It is possible, of course, that the belief that there are many things to do is an illusion, and that we are irrevocably pushed towards one thing by our "nature" and the situation. However, the philosophical question of determinism or free will is not relevant to the distinction. If free will is an illusion, then the distinction *A* between cases where we have this illusion and cases where we do not is important. If free will is not an illusion, then the distinction *B* between cases where we have freedom and cases where we do not is likewise important, and for purposes of this analysis is identical with the distinction *A*.

Hierarchy and spontaneity of acts; action *vs.* reaction. In any organization there is a hierarchy of acts which corresponds roughly—though not necessarily exactly or formally—to the hierarchy of the actors. The acts of the "boss" are generally more spontaneous, and more regulatory, than those of the "bossed." The decision to declare war, for instance, may or may not be spontaneous, but it is highly regulatory—that is to say, it sets in motion a very extensive chain of subordinate acts, the function and purpose and content of which are determined largely by the initial act of declaring war. The decision to declare war, however, can be made only by the topmost authority of government—the President, or the Cabinet, or whatever is the authority from which in this matter there is no appeal. Once it is made, innumerable acts follow—mobilization of the armed forces, new taxes, government borrowing, price control, and so on—acts that reach down into the life of every inhabitant of the nation and change his condition.

The hierarchy of *regulation,* however, is not necessarily identical with the hierarchy of *spontaneity.* Thus in a certain situation of international tension a minor officer may precipitate a war by a spontaneous act of aggression. In any organizational structure there is a certain necessity for the higher-ups to "support" the lower-downs. Hence it is quite possible to find organizational structures in which the hierarchy of spontaneity is actually reversed—in which only those *low* in the scale of hierarchy and regulation have any spontaneity about their actions, and in which those high in the scale of hierarchy simply have to *react* to the actions of their formal subordinates, or even to the actions of those outside the organization. A depression, for instance, may be "caused" by the cumulative effects of innumerable actions of managers, investors, consumers, quite outside the hierarchy of government; nevertheless, it is likely to produce profound reactions in government behavior and policy.

The pure homeostasis model. This distinction between the spontaneous act and the response can be seen very clearly if we construct an extreme model of organizational behavior according to the principle of *pure homeostasis.* Homeostasis is a very useful word which comes originally from physiology [2] and describes the activity of the *maintenance of a state* in the face of circumstances that would otherwise change it. Thus in any living organism there are certain states—*e.g.,* blood temperature and pressure, water content—which the organization is set up to maintain. In the human body, for instance, if the outside temperature is so warm as to threaten to raise the blood temperature above the normal, 98.4°, sweat glands open, respiration increases, a desire for shady spots and leisurely activities arises, and the organism cools off. If the outside temperature is so cold as to threaten to lower the blood temperature below 98.4°, sweat glands close, teeth chatter, muscular heat-producing activity increases, and a desire arises for warm fires, hot-

[2] See W. B. Cannon, *The Wisdom of the Body* (New York: W. W. Norton & Co., Inc., 1932).

water bottles, and heavy clothing. Similarly we can think of a social organization, such as a firm, an army, or a government, as simply maintaining a given state: if anyone leaves the organization by death, retirement, or severance, someone just like him is hired or promoted to replace him; if someone is promoted, the place he leaves is filled by a similar person, and so on. There may be a constant throughput of people, but the structure of the organization personnel remains the same. Similarly, if the organization's physical assets are disturbed, by sale or by depreciation or consumption, they are simply replaced. If goods are sold, the money is used to replace the goods. Every time anything is used up in production, it is replaced. There may, of course, be certain time-lags between the event and the corresponding homeostatic act of replacement, so that there may be short-run fluctuations in the "state" that is maintained, just as there are small fluctuations in body temperature or in the temperature of a house governed by a thermostat. These do not violate—indeed, are strictly necessary to—the general principle of homeostasis or state-maintenance. Such an organization does not have any spontaneous acts: its acts are all reactions to what happens to it—that is, to "acts" of other organizations or parts of the universe that constitute its environment.

Policy as volitional changes in ideal states. No organization, of course, is completely "homeostatic" in its behavior. For one thing, every organization exhibits more or less progressive changes in state. A living organism, for instance, passes through its life cycle from the fertilized egg to its final dissolution. Social organizations—firms, churches, states—exhibit much more complex "life cycles," with periods of decay frequently alternating with periods of revival and rejuvenation. Further, there seems to be nothing inherent in the social organization, as apparently there is in a biological organism, that carries it relentlessly towards death and dissolution. Social organizations "die," of course—firms are bankrupted, states are conquered, churches die away. But there is nothing in the social organization as simple as the biological life cycle of conception, birth, growth, maturity, senescence and death, even though there may be analogues of all these successive states. More important in the social organization is the "volitional" change of state—the spontaneous act or decision leading to a change, even to progressive and irreversible changes, in the ideal that is being maintained or striven after through the reactions of homeostasis. It is these volitional changes of ideal states that best deserve the name of "policy." These may consist of changing the magnitude of variables of the state or condition that are regarded as ideal, as when, for instance, a government that has previously been content to stay within traditional boundaries finds these boundaries too narrow for its ambition or its concept of defense and decides to attempt a geographical extension of its territory and power. Or changes may consist of bringing altogether new variables into the ideal state, as, for instance, when a government that has previously not concerned itself about poverty undertakes to maintain the income of any citizen above a certain minimum.

Application to government: transactions *vs.* regulations. This brief sketch of a "theory of action"—or at least, a classification of action—may seem abstract and remote from the hurly-burly of government operations and policy. We shall find it a useful guide, however, in examining the behavior of government in all of its many branches, and the impact of this behavior on the economic life around it. It is clear, for instance, that there is an important distinction between the *transactions* of government with private persons and organizations, and the *regulations* or laws of government as they affect the transactions that private parties have one with another.

The transactions of government always involve some kind of redistribution of assets between government and private parties. A tax payment, for instance, is a transfer of money—usually a bank deposit—from a private party to government account. A subsidy, or relief payment, or a pension or unemployment insurance payment, is a "negative tax"—a transfer of money from government to a private account. Government sales or purchases, whether of labor or commodities, involve an exchange, which as we have seen consists of two transfers in opposite directions between two parties. Thus when government buys, let us say, wheat, money is transferred from a government account to the account of the seller of wheat, and wheat is transferred from the ownership of the seller to the ownership of government. Similarly when government sells, let us say, war surplus to the public, goods are transferred from government to private parties, and money is transferred from private parties to government. The purchase of labor by government is perhaps a somewhat special case: here there is a transfer of money (the wage or salary) from government to the employee, and it might look at first as if no commodity or asset passed from the employee to government. The government, however, is presumably in some way better off as a result of the work of the employee; and it is this "better-off-ness" that constitutes the gain on government account to offset the money paid out. In this way the purchase of labor by government differs from a mere subsidy or pension. A subsidy is a pure transfer of money: nothing passes the other way in exchange. When labor is purchased the purchaser acquires the "product of the work," whatever that is. The worker gives up the product that he might otherwise produce with the time he spends working. Although, therefore, the purchase of labor differs in many important respects from the purchase of commodities—and this is true whether the purchase is made by government or by private employers—nevertheless it can be brought under the general class of exchanges.

Transaction involves consent. Because both transfers and exchanges and transactions involve at least two parties, even government transfers and transactions involve the consent of the private party with whom the transaction is made. The government cannot even give money to those who are unwilling to receive it. Still less can it take money from those who are unwilling to give it up, though here the apparatus of coercion is usually available to increase the "willingness" of people to give up money—for instance, in taxes, by providing various unpleasant alternatives for those whose "willingness" is deficient. The ability of government to make free exchanges depends on its ability to find purchasers for what it has to sell or sellers of what it wants to buy. Occasionally we find coerced exchanges, as in conscription for military service or in forced loans. For most of their transactions, however, modern governments generally rely on free exchanges, and their ability to find partners for these exchanges depends generally on the terms on which the exchanges are offered. A government that cannot sell its bonds at one price may be able to sell them at a lower price (that is, at a higher rate of interest). A government that cannot find enough schoolteachers or civil servants at one wage will be able to find plenty at higher wages. Insofar as it depends on free exchanges to get the things it wants, government has to rely on prices to attract customers just as a private business does.

The "counterpart principle" in government transactions. The transactional nature of government action becomes clear when we reflect that all activities and many states of government have opposite counterparts in the private economy. Thus, every government expenditure is a receipt to the recipient; every government receipt is an expenditure to the payer; every government purchase is realized income to the seller; all government debt is assets to the holders. Much confusion in thinking about government comes from a failure to realize the two-sided nature of transactions and of debt, and from thinking as if the government side of the transaction were all that mattered.

Cash deficit of government = cash surplus of private sector. A very important proposition follows at once from the transactional view of government operations: it is that the *cash deficit* of government is a *cash surplus* or an addition to money stocks of the private economy. Similarly, a cash surplus of government is a cash deficit of the private economy. A cash deficit of government means that over all government transactions, both exchanges and transfers, more money has been paid out than has been paid in. Suppose this deficit were one billion dollars: this would mean that government expenditures of money exceeded government receipts of money by one billion dollars. This of necessity implies, however, as government expenditures to private parties are the same thing as private parties' receipts from government, and government receipts from private parties are the same thing as private parties' expenditures to government, that private parties have received from government one billion dollars more than they have paid out. This means that the money stock of private parties increases by the amount of the cash deficit of government. If government takes in 40 billion from all sources, and pays out 41 billion to all recipients, then simply on account of these transactions private balance sheets have one billion more cash in them than before.

The principle of reciprocal transactions. The above proposition is an example of a general principle of reciprocal transactions: that the excess of government output over government intake of *any* asset is equal to the increase in privately held stocks of this asset *directly* caused by the government transactions. Thus, if government sells more government securities than it redeems, the amount of such securities in the hands of private parties must increase by the exact excess of issue over redemption, as nobody but the government can create or (we suppose) destroy government securities. In the case of assets that can be both produced and consumed by private parties, the situation is a little more complicated. Private holdings of such assets can change not only because of government purchases and sales of them, but because of private consumption or production. In this case we have the following identity for any asset, say wheat:

Increase in private holdings ≡ Government sales − Government purchases + Private production − Private consumption.

In such a case, of course, an excess of government sales over purchases may not actually increase private stocks, as it might be offset by an excess of private consumption over private production. It is particularly difficult to assess the impact of government transactions where these have indirect effects on private decisions—that is, where the transactions have a regulatory as well as a simple exchange aspect. Thus, suppose government decided to diminish private stocks of wheat by a program of government purchases. As a result of these purchases the price of wheat would rise; this would encourage the production of wheat and discourage its consumption, which would have the effect of increasing private stocks. The diminution of private stocks resulting from government purchases would then be offset in part or even completely by the increase in private stocks resulting from the price change. If the offsetting movement is large, the result of government purchases of wheat may actually be to *increase* wheat stocks in private hands.

Government impact on GNP. Similar propositions can be developed in regard to income and national product. Government purchases of goods and labor, by the conventions of national accounting, contribute directly to the Gross National Product. Gross National Product, however, is the sum of three other components, as well as government purchases: household purchases, gross business accumulations (investment), and the foreign balance (the excess of exports over imports). Therefore, although an increase in government purchases will increase the GNP directly, it may cause changes in the other components that may either reinforce or offset the direct effect. Thus in a time of severe depression an increase in government purchases is likely to increase household incomes and therefore will increase household purchases; this is especially likely to be the case if the increase in government purchases results in a cash deficit so that the money stocks of private parties likewise increase. An increase in household purchases may also lead to an increased willingness of business to accumulate, which again reinforces the increase of GNP. On the other hand, especially if the economy is close to full employment, an increase in government purchases may produce *offsetting* reactions on the other components. Shortages of the purchased goods may compel a reduction of household purchases, either through the redistributive effects of inflation or through formal or informal rationing. There may also be a reduction in business accumulations for rather similar reasons.

Impact of national debt. An increase in the national debt again in itself increases the amount of bonds held by private parties. This effect again may be either reinforced or offset by secondary reactions on the creation or redemption of private debt, so that the total volume of privately held debt may not reflect the change in government debt. The problems here are quite complex and will be reserved for a later chapter.

Government regulation: coercion and consent. It is through its external transactions and their direct and indirect effects that government makes its most immediate and obvious impact on the economy. It also, however, makes a great impact, especially in the long run, by its laws and regulations setting the framework within which private persons make transactions with each other. Thus it protects—or does not protect—the rights of property; it sees to the enforcement of contracts; it outlaws certain types of production and consumption, certain types of transactions, certain types of organization. By differential taxation, subsidies, tariffs, import restrictions, and so on, it can encourage some industries or occupations or forms of organization and discourage others. Its instrument in all this is a curious mixture of the apparatus of coercion with both the expression and the manipulation of consent. To date, at any rate, no government—not even that of the mild and benevolent William Penn—has been able to operate without some apparatus of coercion—prisons, fines, and so on. On the other hand, no government has been able to operate without very widespread willingness to obey its laws, regulations, and prescriptions. When this basic consent disappears, no amount of coercion can compel compliance, if only because the instruments of coercion themselves—the police and the army—become disaffected, or cannot maintain their morale in the face of widespread popular disapproval of their acts.

The "government factor" in private transactions. What the "law," then, does to private transactions is to introduce an additional variable into them—the "government factor." If the transaction is legal and complete in itself, the government factor may be almost totally absent. If the transaction is legal but involves long-term obligations or undertakings, such as a debt contract, there may be a government factor in the background in the form of potential penalties for nonfulfillment of the contract. The governmental penalties for nonfulfillment may, of course, be quite unimportant compared with the "private" penalties—loss of reputation, loss of ability to make further contracts, loss of self-respect, and so forth—which might follow from nonfulfillment, and many contracts are in fact made in which governmental penalties are either altogether absent or not invoked by the mutual consent of the parties. When the transaction is illegal the government factor becomes of great importance; it may not prevent the transaction altogether, but it introduces a large element of *risk* of penalties, which at least discourages the transaction. In a law-abiding population, also, it is not merely the risk of externally imposed penalties that discourages illegal transactions. There are internal penalties in the form of an uneasy conscience that may actually be more effective than any fear of coercion. This is particularly apt to be the case if the legal proscription of the act merely registers a widespread moral disapproval. In the absence of such moral disapproval the threat of coercion may actually be quite ineffective—as it was, for instance, in suppressing liquor under prohibition, or in suppressing underground resistance to an occupying power, or even in preventing evasion of taxes where these are felt generally to be unjust or exorbitant.

The "compliance factor." In assessing the impact of any particular regulation, then, we must always take account of a "compliance factor." Only a certain proportion of the prohibited transactions will in fact disappear because of the prohibition. In the case of a government that has the full support of the bulk of its people this factor may be close to 100 per cent; in the case of a hated occupying power the factor may be quite small. In most of the discussion that follows we shall neglect the compliance factor and assume that for the most part the number of illegal transactions is small. In the case of a stable and prosperous country with a democratic government, like the United States, this assumption is on the whole justified. We must be careful, however, not to apply too hastily the conclusions that are appropriate in this fortunate situation to situations in which government is weak, or not respected, or even hated. A policy that may be appropriate if the compliance factor is large may be quite inappropriate if the factor is small. It may be better to have a "poor" policy that can be carried into effect than to have a theoretically "good" policy that cannot. This is particularly apt to be true of tax systems, where the sheer necessity of collection often forces governments into forms of tax which have practically no virtue but collectibility.

Government and the "laws of society." Even where there is a general willingness to comply with the law, government regulations can frequently be ineffective if they violate the "laws of society"—that nexus of necessary conditions and relationships that limits the possible set of social variables and imposes constraints on the coexistence of these variables. Government cannot, by simply passing a law, make a poor nation rich, or, if the per-capita income is small, make the poor rich by redistribution. There are certain inexorable social identities that no amount of coercive power can overcome—such as, for instance, that per-capita income cannot exceed the total product divided by the population, and that the total product is limited by the skills, equipment, culture, and organization of the people. There is even a certain inexorability about the price system, as governments have found to their sorrow at least from the time of Diocletian. If they attempt to create by fiat a set of prices that diverges from some loosely defined set of "normal" prices, they will run into trouble even if the legal prices are obeyed—that is, if no transactions take place at illegal prices. Some prices will be "too high" and the corresponding commodities will develop surpluses; some will be "too low" and there will be shortages; if prices are fixed very much below "normal" the commodities will disappear from the market altogether.

Government schizophrenia: British pig policy. Ignorance of the laws of society frequently results in the frustration of government policies. There is a kind of delicate irony about history which often leads to things turning out almost the opposite of what they were consciously intended to be. Just as the schizophrenic embroils himself further and further with an increasingly hostile universe because of his failure to interpret the messages he receives, so governments (the behavior of which frequently resembles that of schizophrenic patients) misinterpret the information they receive and behave in ways that do not advance them towards their avowed ends because they have a distorted view of the social universe. Some examples will illustrate the point.

In 1934 the British government was under strong pressure from the agricultural interests to "do something for pigs." The price of pigs was very low, pig producers were in trouble, and the producers were evidently influential enough politically to get action. The action took the form of a quota on imports of Danish bacon into Britain. It is considered legitimate for governments to be inconsiderate of those who are not their citizens, and the object of this policy presumably was to benefit the British pig producers at the expense of the Danes, who being foreigners and therefore not having a vote in the British Parliament, and being citizens of a small country, had a traditional right to be pushed around by citizens of a big Britain. The policy was based on the assumption that British and Danish bacon were good substitutes in the mind of the British housewife, so that British bacon would rush in to fill the gap left by the restriction of imports. Unfortunately for the British and fortunately for the Danes this assumption turned out not to be true. The British housewife evidently differentiated sharply between the lean, shapely rashers of the Danes and the greasy, slovenly product of the home producer. Demand for Danish bacon turned out to be quite inelastic; the British housewife much preferred it, and she was willing to pay a considerably higher price for it rather than substitute British bacon. The upshot was that the price of Danish bacon rose sharply—so much so that the British actually paid the Danes more money for less bacon than before, the Danes were able to eat some of their own bacon for a change and still were better off, the British pig producer was very little, if at all, assisted by this program, and a policy that was designed to help a selfish and inefficient British industry at the expense of the Danes actually helped the Danes and hurt the British.

Regulations *vs.* transactions as policy instruments. Not infrequently an objective of government policy that cannot be achieved, or can be achieved only at great cost and difficulty, by means of direct legal prohibitions can be achieved fairly easily by means of appropriate government transactions. Thus, suppose—to take a very simple example—that the government wished to maintain a fixed price for gold in terms of its own currency—say, $35 per ounce. It might try to do this by imposing harsh legal sanctions on anyone who bought or sold gold except at this price—all transactions in which dollars exchanged for gold at any other price than $35 per ounce being illegal. Such a prohibition would be very difficult to enforce, as transactions in gold can be carried on secretly. Unless the "normal" price of gold just happened to be $35 an ounce extensive black markets in gold would develop which in all probability no amount of legal repression could destroy. If gold were scarce, people would be found willing to risk the penalties and buy gold above $35 an ounce rather than go without it; if gold were plentiful, people would be found willing to risk the penalties and sell gold below $35 an ounce rather than not get rid of it. There is, however, a much more effective way of controlling the market price of gold than by legal prohibitions. If government, or some agency of government, stands ready to buy and sell gold in unlimited quantities at $35 per ounce, the market price cannot vary more than a very small amount from this price, and this without any legal prohibitions on sale at other prices. If the market price rises even a little above $35 per ounce it will pay buyers to buy from the government rather than pay the higher market price; this will remove buyers from the market and will soon bring down the market price. If the market price falls a fraction below $35 per ounce, it will pay sellers to sell their gold to the government rather than to private parties; sellers will withdraw from the market and the competition of buyers will soon force the price up. This is the principle of the traditional Gold Standard.

The government price can only be maintained as long as the government has stocks of both gold and dollars to exchange. If there is a very strong upward pressure on the market price of gold, owing, say, to continual increase in stocks of dollars, the price will be continually rising above the government price and the government will continually be selling gold. If this goes on for very long the government stock of gold will be exhausted. Even before that point, however, the government stock of gold may fall to a point where further declines cannot be tolerated. At this point the government offer to sell gold must be withdrawn (the government "goes off the Gold Standard") and the market price is then free to rise. Under these circumstances, however, legal prohibitions on transactions at high prices would be even more impossible to enforce.

Price maintenance of government securities. The principle of maintaining a price by government purchases and sales is a very important element in government price policy in all fields. Thus in managing the national debt a government—or an agent of government such as a central bank—can maintain the price of government securities by purchasing or selling as much as the market wants to sell or buy at the maintained price. This effectively fixes the rate of interest on this type of security, and through this has a profound effect on the whole structure of rates of interest. As we shall see in Chapter 9, the question as to how far the Federal Reserve System should control the price of government securities in this way has been an important source of controversy in the United States. When the Central Bank stands ready to buy or sell government bonds at a fixed price it is not unfair to say that there is a "government bond standard." The mechanism is similar to that of the Gold Standard.

Price supports for agricultural products. Another example of maintaining prices by government purchase and sale is found in price-support programs for agricultural commodities. Government can maintain the price of a storable commodity above what would otherwise be the market price by offering to purchase as much as is offered to it at the support price. The actual machinery of purchase may be quite complicated and will be discussed in Chapter 13; the principle involved, however, is precisely what is involved in the Gold Standard, except that in this case the objective of the policy is usually to raise prices rather than to stabilize them. Where the supported price is "above normal," however, this will result in a continual accumulation of stocks of the commodity in government hands. This will lead either to a breakdown of the policy, to the deliberate destruction of stocks, or to the attempted control of production.

Transactional *vs.* coercive powers of government. An interesting example of a case where the government's transactional powers and its coercive powers are clear alternatives is seen in the various policies used to get people into the armed forces. A "volunteer" army is raised by use of the transactional powers; a conscript army by use of the coercive powers. As long as a government sticks to its transactional powers, then if it cannot obtain enough people for its armed forces it must attract more by offering a higher price—in terms of some combination of wages, pensions, conditions of service, and the like. If it uses its coercive power directly through conscription it can get people cheaper because of the penalties for noncompliance. This is not to say, of course, that it is *only* the legal penalties that induce people to comply with conscription. Where conscription is generally accepted as just and equitable, the social and personal penalties may in most cases be much more important than the legal penalties. Nevertheless, the whole system rests ultimately on the legal penalties, and if these were removed it is highly probable that it would fall apart; what anyone can get away with everyone wants to get away with.

It may be argued, of course, that the transactional powers of government also depend indirectly on its coercive powers; that if, for instance, a government decides to raise an army by voluntary enlistment under highly attractive conditions rather than by conscription, this decision also involves higher taxes, which again invokes the coercive power. There is, however, a real difference between the use of the coercive power in a relatively abstract and impersonal way through the tax system, and the use of the coercive power directly on persons through conscription.

Coercive power grows in times of stress. It is a reasonable generalization that under conditions of strain the use of the direct coercive power tends to grow at the expense of the use of the transactional power. In a time of secure peace, for instance, governments are likely to abandon conscription and raise voluntary armies; they abandon price control in favor of various transactional devices, and encouragements tend to take the place of prohibitions. In times of war, stress, and crisis, however, the use of the direct coercive power increases, and conscription, price control, direct allocation of materials, forced loans, requisitions, become the order of the day. The reason for this seems to be that the use of the coercive power *in any one direction* runs into diminishing returns as the use expands. In a peaceful and orderly society the use of the coercive power may be confined almost entirely to the tax system and the system of "ordinary" criminal law in the protection of life, property, and contracts. All other controls imposed on the system by government can be carried out through the transactional system; the carrot, not the stick, is the dominant instrument of policy. As government tries to extend its powers, however, whether because of some political philosophy such as socialism, or simply because it faces some internal or external threat, the tax system fails to respond to the additional burdens put upon it. The supply of carrots is inadequate to the demand; government is therefore reduced either to the creation of money, which is itself—as we shall see—a crude form of taxation and which brings many other troubles in its train, or it is forced into more and more direct coercion—conscription, forced labor, forced loans, confiscation of property, price control, and so on. As each form of coercion runs into diminishing returns it is forced into a worse one.

Government as a complex of agencies. In all the preceding discussion we have assumed that "government" is first of all a homogeneous entity, and secondly is something separate from the people whom it governs. Neither of these assumptions is strictly true. In thinking about the impact of government on economic life we must be careful not to allow what is a useful abstraction—the notion of government as an entity distinct from the people—to blind us to the very complex reality. In fact "the government" is a complex maze of agencies, each of which possesses a certain life and autonomy of its own, and has policies of its own which may by no means be consistent with the policies of other agencies. The U. S. Army Corps of Engineers, for instance, is an agency with a considerable spirit of independence, its own friends in Congress, almost one might say its own sources of funds, and its own set of ideals and policy principles which may not be at all consistent with those of other agencies in related fields, such as the Bureau of Reclamation. In the Federal Government of the United States there are some 2,000 different agencies, and for some purposes "the government" must be thought of as a vast ecosystem in itself, where policy emerges as the result of a complex process of bargaining, argumentation and conversation among large number of bureaucratic agencies, Congressional committees, courts, and so on. When we add state and local governments, and the vast interlocking jigsaw of school districts, drainage districts, soil conservation districts, irrigation districts, and the like, it seems almost absurd to talk of "the" government, and one feels that government should always be a collective noun taking the plural form of the verb!

The "core of control." Nevertheless, there is a hierarchy of responsibility in government, and a real core of control, whether this be the President, a Cabinet, or a dictator. This is especially true of the executive branch, but even in a system as complex as that of the Federal Government of the United States, even though the locus of power may be continually shifting between the President, the Congressional leaders, and the Supreme Court, as the accident of personal skill or the shifting spotlight of Constitutional responsibility may direct, still there are loci of power, there are people who in virtue of their office have to make decisions that affect the lives of millions of others. When we talk of "the" government it is of these crucial decisions of which we are speaking, and it does not perhaps matter very much whether these decisions are made by a President, a Cabinet minister, a Congressional leader, or a Supreme Court Judge.

Responsibility in government. The question of the relation of the government to the people is an even more complex one. In our analytical scheme we think of government as one "sector" of society, of the "people" or "private parties" as another "sector." It is at least part of the mythos of democracy, however, to insist that the government *is* the people, and that this clear separation of the government from the people may be an accurate picture in a monarchical, tyrannical, or imperial government but it is not descriptive of a modern democracy. The mythos is much more than a myth. Governments in the Western democracies are extremely sensitive to popular opinion, at least as reflected in lobbyists. The politically active citizen of the United States is continually writing to his congressmen or to the President, and these messages are taken seriously by the recipients, especially on controversial issues.

This does not mean, however, that government is *identical with* the people. Government is an organization of decision-makers. They may be *responsible* decision-makers, and their decisions may be influenced by the people who elect them, but it is not unrealistic to assume that these decisions are separate from the decisions of the electors and citizens at large. The significance of *responsibility* in government lies in the extent of the feedback of information from the people to government, and in the response of government decision-makers to this information. A government that does not receive, or does not act upon, feedback information following its decisions, and that does not modify its decisions in the light of their presumed consequences to "the people," is not responsible. A responsible government is one with a sensitive feedback mechanism.

Government of, by, or for the people. These principles can be illustrated well by an analysis of Lincoln's famous phrase, "government *of* the people, *for* the people, and *by* the people."

When we speak of government *of* the people we are thinking

of the kind of model we have used for the most part in this chapter, where we are considering the effect of the decisions of governmental decision-makers on the nongovernmental sector of society.

When we speak of government *for* the people we are thinking of the principles that govern these decisions from the point of view of the decision-maker himself. Will he consider a policy "good" simply because it benefits him and his friends or his class, or will he consider it good only if in his opinion it benefits the mass of the people?

When we speak of government *by* the people we are thinking of the nature of the feedbacks from the people to the decision-maker, and the nature of the control that the people have over the occupier of the decision-making role. A government decision-maker may believe that he is acting "for" the people, but unless he is open to having his decisions modified by messages from the people who are affected by them, he cannot be said to be governed "by" the people.

In the next few chapters we shall go on to consider government economic policy under several classifications: fiscal policy, monetary policy, business policy, commercial and trade policy, labor policy, income maintenance policy, agricultural policy. The classifications do not, of course, reflect rigid or absolute distinctions. Almost every aspect of policy in one field will affect the economy in others. Labor and agriculture are profoundly affected by fiscal and monetary policy, monetary and fiscal policy are affected by wage or price-support policy, and so on. Nevertheless, it is convenient to consider policy by sections, either as it especially affects industrial sectors of the economy such as agriculture, banking and finance, transportation, retail trade, and so on, or as it affects class sectors such as industrial workers or farmers, or as it affects general aspects of government relations and transactions with most people, such as taxation. We will begin, therefore, with the most general aspects —fiscal policy, monetary policy, banking policy, trade policy— and then go on to consider policy affecting particular classes and industries—business, labor, agriculture, and so on.

8

Fiscal policy

Every action has two facets;
Public debt is private assets,
My receipt is your expense,
Your aggression, my defense.
It's just as true as it is funny,
That Deficits increase our money;
In understanding this there lies
The power of States to Stabilize.

Fiscal policy deals with money flows of government. The term "fiscal policy" refers to those aspects of government that are broadly concerned with the taking in and paying out of money. Acts of government in which money is taken in or paid out, however, are far from homogeneous, so that it is difficult, and indeed probably undesirable, to try to set up a general rule that will cover all of them. Thus money may be paid out or taken in, as we have seen, either in transfers or in exchanges. When the payment is a simple transfer, as it is, for instance, in the payment of a tax, subsidy, or "income payment," money passes either from a private account to government or from a government account to a private account, but nothing passes the other way. In an exchange, on the other hand, not only does money change hands, but "something else" changes hands also. The "something else" may be a commodity, as when government buys or sells gold or wheat, it may be a security, as when government buys or sells bonds, it may be some other kind of money, as when government buys or sells foreign exchange, or it may be labor or the immediate product of labor. In all these cases the transfer of money is only half the transaction; consequently we cannot treat such transactions without regard to the "other half"—the thing for which money is exchanged. A government receipt of money in exchange for a bond, for instance, has a different effect on the economy than a simple government receipt of money from taxation. In the first case the private sector has less money, but more bonds; in the second case it simply has less money.

Regulatory effects of money flows. Money payments may also have a regulatory aspect, as we have seen in the previous chapter, and may be a substitute for, or a reinforcement of, the regulation of private transactions. Thus a government offer to pay money or take money for a commodity at a fixed price effectively regulates the market price of that commodity in private transactions. The federal government may offer "matching funds" to the states to induce them to set up state regulations or state payments—for instance, in Social Security or relief payments. Furthermore, the way in which a specific money payment is assessed or calculated may have a profound effect on economic behavior. This applies especially to transfers such as taxes or subsidies. In the case of exchanges, the only problem in determining the amount of the payment is that of setting the price and the definition of what the money is paid for. In the case of a transfer, however, there must be some method of determining how much shall be transferred—the extent of a tax liability, or of a relief payment, or of a subsidy. These methods of determining "how much" shall be paid may have an important effect on the other transactions and general behavior of the individuals concerned. It is hardly too much to assert that any quantity that is used as an index to determine the extent of an individual's liability to tax or subsidy payments will be perverted simply because it is used for this purpose. Thus during the Napoleonic War the British Government laid a tax on the number of windows in a man's house, hoping that this would measure his ability to pay, on the grounds that the rich were likely to have more windows than the poor. This led immediately to the bricking up of windows, no doubt to the detriment of the convenience and health of the domiciled, as well as to the treasury. Similarly, a tax on profits will lead to padded expense accounts, a tax on one commodity will lead to the substitution of other commodities, a tax on income will lead to emphasis on capital gains, a tax on corporations will lead to a rise in unincorporated business. In the extreme, the power to tax becomes the power to destroy: a tax on private bank notes, for instance, drove them completely out of existence. Even in moderation, however, the necessity to tax is the necessity to distort. We cannot set up any tax system that simply takes money from people without in some degree changing their other activities and behavior.

The money-flows identity. In spite of the heterogeneity of money payments, there is also a quantitative homogeneity about them which justifies our speaking of "fiscal policy" as a whole. This follows from the identity noted in the previous chapter, that the total cash deficit (or surplus) of government is a net contribution (or withdrawal) from the cash balances of private accounts. More accurately, as we cannot assume, at least in a modern society, that money is not created or destroyed in private accounts, we may write the basic identity as follows:

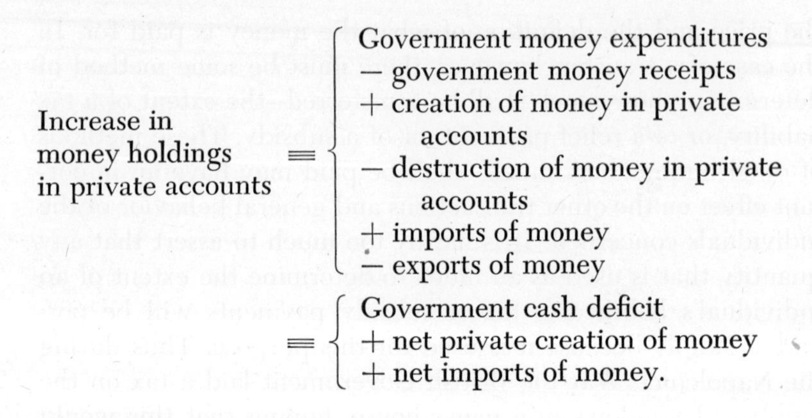

$$\text{Increase in money holdings in private accounts} \equiv \begin{cases} \text{Government money expenditures} \\ -\text{ government money receipts} \\ +\text{ creation of money in private accounts} \\ -\text{ destruction of money in private accounts} \\ +\text{ imports of money} \\ -\text{ exports of money} \end{cases}$$

$$\equiv \begin{cases} \text{Government cash deficit} \\ +\text{ net private creation of money} \\ +\text{ net imports of money.} \end{cases}$$

In its quantitative aspect it is clear from the above identity that one of the main consequences of the fiscal system, as reflected in the government cash deficit (or surplus) is the change in the total private money holdings that results from it. The main policy problem, therefore, on the quantitative side of the fiscal system is the *control* of the private money stock.

Private determinants of the money stock. If we were to assume that the net private creation and net imports of money were independent of the fiscal system and especially of the government cash deficit, then the problem of control of the private money stock would be fairly easy. If government wished to increase the private money stock by an amount *X*, it could do this by arranging its receipts and expenditures—*e.g.*, through changing tax rates—so that it had a cash deficit of *X*; if it wished to diminish the private money stock it could do so by having a cash surplus. The only problem here is that of estimating the change in government receipts or expenditures that results from a specific policy, such as a tax cut or increase, designed to effect such a change. This is essentially the problem of tax yield, to which we shall return. Unfortunately for the simplicity of the problem, however, we cannot assume, especially in a modern society, that net private creation or imports of money will be unaffected by policies designed to change the government cash deficit or surplus. Indeed, the method that is chosen to effect a change in the government cash deficit may affect these "private" determinants of the total money stock, so that, for instance, an increase in the cash deficit that is brought about by one method may be offset (and by another method may be reinforced) by induced changes in the private determinants.

Thus, suppose that—for whatever reason—it is decided to lower tax receipts in order to increase the private money stock. If this is done by reducing taxes that businessmen dislike, or feel injured by, there may be increased business optimism, increased borrowing from the banks, and therefore an increase in private money creation which will reinforce the effect of the increased government cash deficit. If, on the other hand, it is done by reducing consumption taxes, so that households feel better off and experience a wave of optimism, consumer purchases increase, inventories diminish, there may be even a decline in bank loans and deposits which will in part offset the tax reduction. This last effect is much less likely than the first, and in general the effects on the private determinants are more likely to reinforce than to offset the change in government cash deficit. Different policies, however, will involve different degrees of reinforcement, and the possibility of offsets is by no means to be left out of account.

Quantitative aspects of fiscal policy deal with economic stability. When we look at fiscal policy from the point of view of our four major objectives of economic policy—progress, stability, justice, and freedom—it is clear that the *quantitative* aspect—*how much* money should be collected and disbursed—is important mainly from the point of view of economic stability, though it has some implications from the point of view of progress and growth. The *qualitative* aspect—*what kinds* of taxes, subsidies, payments, should be made—is related more to the other three objectives. It is necessary to emphasize again the interdependence of the major objectives. The kind of solutions we find for the problem of economic stability, for instance, may profoundly affect the rate of progress and the sense of justice and freedom. Nevertheless, there are broad foci of interest, and we shall not go far wrong with the above distinctions as long as we do not take them too seriously.

Objective of preventing "unwanted" movements in the private money stock. In its quantitative aspect, then, the main objective of fiscal policy should be first, to prevent "unwanted" fluctuations in the private money stock, and second, to insure the growth of the private money stock at the desired rate. These objectives run counter to some very ancient and respectable canons of public finance, and we are under some obligation to explain just how these more sophisticated objectives differ from certain objectives that are still commonly held.

It is frequently believed, for instance, that the main object of fiscal policy is to "balance the budget"—that is, to raise a sufficient volume of government receipts through taxation and sales of services so that all government payments are covered, and no government securities or additional money are issued. This policy states in effect that there should be no government contribution to or withdrawals from the private money stock or private holdings of bonds. All changes in the private stock of money would then be the result of private creation or destruction of money, or of net imports or exports of money. On the whole this would represent the views of the "orthodox" classical economists such as Adam Smith and Ricardo, though not of the more heretical Malthus. It is a view that deserves to be taken seriously, not only because of the authority of its advocates, but also because it is grounded on certain views of governmental behavior that may not be wholly inappropriate to certain states of society. It rests on the assumption that if there is a deficiency or excess in the private money stocks of society, each condition will set off movements in the private economy to correct itself, either through increased or diminished production of the monetary commodity, or through the increased or diminished production of money substitutes.

The classical view: Ricardo's model. Thus let us suppose with Ricardo that either we have a system of pure metallic money, so that the money stock is the same as the gold stock, or that even if there is paper money and a banking system, the volume of nonmetallic money is firmly linked to the gold stock so that both must rise and fall together. In such a system let us suppose a deficiency in the gold stock, leading to a fall in prices and money incomes. Under these circumstances the purchasing power of money, and therefore of gold, rises. This makes gold mining unusually profitable relative to other occupations, and increases the likelihood that prospecting for new mines will be profitable. Under these circumstances gold production increases, because it pays to work old mines more intensively and pays also to find new mines. The monetary stock therefore increases, and as it increases, prices rise again. If, on the other hand, this movement goes too far and there is an excessive rise of prices and incomes, this will make gold production unprofitable. The price of gold will be low relative to other things, and wages and other costs in gold producing will rise. The production of gold will shrink and the stocks of gold will eventually shrink also, and prices and incomes will fall again.

Adam Smith's model. Adam Smith took an even more optimistic view of the self-regulating powers of the private money stock, for he believed that in the absence of government deficits not even the growth of bank notes and deposits would disturb the stability of prices and incomes. He visualized the monetary circulation as a fixed channel, requiring a fixed money stock under given conditions of trade, and believed that if the banks created money in excess of this fixed requirement the excess would simply flow back to them in purchases of gold. In both Adam Smith and Ricardo the belief in the self-regulatory character of the private monetary stock was reinforced by a profound disbelief in the ability of government to behave sensibly or moderately in this area, a view for which history affords some evidence. Here again we see the operation of a principle suggested in the previous chapter—that the degree of confidence that can be placed either in the wisdom or in the authority of government decision-makers plays an important role in determining the policy to be advocated. If government action *could* do good but is more likely to take forms that would do harm, it may be better to advocate inaction than to advocate a type of action that is ideal but action that one knows is unlikely to be followed.

Objections to the classical view. The dissatisfaction with the classical economists' views on fiscal policy arises from two main sources, (1) the belief that the self-regulatory mechanisms of the private monetary stock are inadequate, and (2) an increasing confidence in the ability of government to use wisdom and discretion in stabilization policy.

The difficulty with Ricardo's mechanism is that it is too slow and insensitive, even though there is a good deal of historical evidence as to its operation. Thus the long inflation in Europe that followed the introduction into European circulation of the gold looted from America led to a marked drop in gold production. In the nineteenth century the long deflation after 1815 certainly had something to do with the gold discoveries of 1849 and 1850 in California and Australia. The inflation that followed led again to a decline in gold production, leading to the deflation of 1870-90, which in turn led to new gold discoveries in South Africa and improved methods of gold production. The action of chance and autonomous technical change, of course, cannot be ruled out, but the evidence at least strongly suggests the operation of the Ricardian mechanism. It operates, however, with about a thirty-year lag, which is longer than the period for which most politicians get elected, and the demand for a more sensitive control mechanism seems hardly unreasonable.

Adam Smith's optimism seems even more ill-founded. As we shall see more clearly in the following chapter, inflationary or deflationary movements in bank money may be self-justified up to a point. An increase in bank money leads to a rise in prices, which leads to higher values for collateral and hence higher bank loans and more bank money, at least to the point where there is pressure on reserves. Here, again, the idea of a self-regulating private mechanism is not absurd. It is true that historically the rise in bank credit went hand in hand with a great rise in the volume of trade; it is true that *if* the price level is stable, bank credit will tend to rise and fall with the volume of trade. Here, however, the mechanism is perhaps too sensitive, and tends to accentuate fluctuations rather than to control them.

The problem of confidence in government regulation. It is not surprising, therefore, that faith in the self-regulating stability of the private monetary system has been thoroughly shattered, especially by the Great Depression of the 1930's, and that there is an almost universal demand for government policy directed towards monetary stabilization. Some of this policy may be "indirect," being concerned with affecting the private creation or destruction or circulation of money, either through legal regulations or through government sales and purchases—for instance, of securities. But the most powerful instrument of stabilization policy is the direct impact of cash surpluses or deficits.

Now, however, we run into the problem that the ability of governments to maintain a system of public finance that will make for economic stability has very little support from the historical record. The record of governments in this area, especially where they have not been checked by strong "conservative" taboos such as the taboo against unbalanced budgets or against breaking with the Gold Standard, is a record of ineptitude in the face of deflation and a chronic tendency to initiate inflation. It is an almost universal rule that over the long pull all currencies depreciate and all price levels rise. This was true even before the invention of paper money and banking. Kings who got into financial difficulties frequently resorted to the device of "debasing the currency"—calling in the existing metallic money and minting it into a larger number of debased coins, thus creating a "cash deficit." With the invention of paper money and banking, of course, the operation became even easier; paper money can simply be printed, bank deposits can be created by printing government securities and selling these to the banks. By whatever means, the creation of money and the development of a cash deficit has frequently been the easiest way out of financial difficulties for almost all governments. It is not surprising, therefore, that war has almost universally brought inflation, for war always brings large government expenditures in excess of the amount that the tax system is able to cover.

The middle ground of cautious regulation: the search for rules of action. There are no guarantees that government action will never be stupid, ill-advised, or inappropriate. Nevertheless, somewhere between the counsel of despair (no government policy is better than the foolish policies we are likely to get if we permit any) and the counsel of naïveté (government should be trusted at all times and places to do the right thing) there is surely a middle ground which recognizes that there are inescapable responsibilities of government in this area, but which also attempts to chain these responsibilities to a firm base in constitutional or conventional taboos and in prescribed rules of action. It is the search for the appropriate *rule* of action here that is so important—a rule that will not be rigid, but that will set clearly visible limits to discretionary action. It was a great virtue of the Gold Standard that it provided such a rule, inadequate though the rule might be. The abandonment of this rule as inadequate does not mean necessarily the abandonment of all rules, but the search for better ones.

The adjustable tax rule. One such rule that has been proposed is the *adjustable tax rule*. On this rule some index of inflation or deflation is agreed upon—let us call this the "signal." The rule would then be set up so that a one-point rise (or fall) in the signal automatically establishes an x per cent rise (or fall) in tax rates. Inflation originating in the private sector would then automatically set off a deflationary force in the fiscal system, for the rise in tax rates would diminish the cash deficit (or increase the cash surplus) of government, assuming no change in government outlays. Similarly, deflation originating in the private sector would automatically set off an inflationary force in government, through the fall in tax rates and therefore in tax collections.

The problem of the "signal." Two problems in the application of an adjustable tax rule present some difficulty. The first is the definition of the "signal." No single index—either of prices, outputs, incomes, or employment—is entirely satisfactory for this purpose. If the price level alone is taken as the index, a deflationary force that reflected itself solely in declining employment and output would not be reflected in the signal, and would not give rise to compensatory action. Similarly, if the employment or output level is taken as the signal, an inflationary force that reflected itself solely in rising prices would not give rise to compensatory action. An index that followed prices up and employment down might be an acceptable compromise. Even here, however, we might get into difficulties; in 1936, for example, prices began to rise even at very low levels of employment. Another possible compromise is to use per-capita disposable income, following a curve of estimated normal growth. Thus, if the estimated normal growth is 3 per cent per annum, a growth of per-capita disposable income at a slower rate would call for tax reductions, at a larger rate for tax increases. This would be satisfactory only if the proportion of the national product going to government were fairly stable. A substantial rise in government purchases, for instance, would always necessitate a decline in per-capita private disposable incomes in real terms, and if these incomes were kept stable in money terms this would necessitate a rise of price levels. It would not be impossible, however, to prepare for each year an estimate of "available" per-capita disposable income, at constant prices and full employment, and to use this as a standard of comparison. A "range of tolerance" should then be established on each side of this standard to allow for errors of estimation and to prevent the compensatory apparatus from being too sensitive. A decline in the actual per-capita disposable income below the lower limit of tolerance would then be a signal for automatic tax reduction; a rise above the upper limit of tolerance would be a signal for an automatic tax increase.

The problem of uncertain taxes. Another objection to such a plan is that the additional calculations and uncertainties involved in frequent tax adjustments would be onerous and unsettling. The mere mechanical problem could be solved very easily by setting up a special kind of money for paying taxes and establishing a variable rate of exchange between ordinary money and tax money. Then if the situation required a rise in tax payments there need be no change in assessments at all, but merely a rise in the price of tax money, say to $105 of ordinary money for $100 of tax money, and similarly for a fall. The argument that this would add to the uncertainty of the economic future and so discourage investment is more apparent than real. The really crushing uncertainty is uncertainty about the future of the general level of income. If this level were stabilized the slight uncertainty introduced into tax payments would be small by comparison with the great diminution of uncertainty over income and markets.

Built-in flexibility: a progressive tax system. Even without any plan for adjusting tax rates, existing tax systems frequently exhibit automatic adjustment to deflationary or inflationary movements. This is known as "built-in flexibility." It arises from two sources: the tendency for government tax receipts to decline more (and to rise more) than income declines (or rises), and the tendency for government expenditures to decline less (or rise less) than incomes. Several factors contribute to both these phenomena. Where the progressive income tax is an important source of revenue this in itself acts as an effective compensating mechanism. An inflation automatically carries more people into the upper income brackets, and the proportion of income paid in taxes increases; similarly a deflation carries more people into lower brackets, or out of the taxable range altogether, and the proportion of income paid diminishes. An effective and steeply progressive income tax is an almost foolproof safeguard against hyperinflation, for it becomes almost impossible for government to avoid substantial cash surpluses if inflation proceeds far enough, and this will drain money from the public and check the inflation. A system of excise taxes on luxuries will have a similar effect. As income declines, people will buy less of these commodities and tax collections will fall; as income rises, they will buy more and tax collections will rise. In general we may say that as long as the whole tax system is progressive—or even somewhat regressive—it will be compensatory. If, however, it is highly regressive, it may be anticompensatory: a fall in income will increase tax collections; a rise will diminish them.

Compensatory expenditures. On the expenditures side, such devices as unemployment insurance, parity payments to farmers, and most income-support measures, are compensatory in their effect. If a deflationary movement causes a rise in unemployment, payments in unemployment compensation increase; if farm prices fall, payments to farmers increase. Even in the absence of tax changes this will tend to produce cash deficits of government which will tend to offset the deflationary movement. Similarly in inflation unemployment compensation payments are low, farm-support payments are low, and so on.

The problem of the lag. The important question here is a quantitative one: whether these built-in compensatory systems are large enough (or perhaps too large) to insure a reasonable stability. There is also a very important question in regard to the *timing* of these effects. If there is a long lag in them the action may actually be anticompensatory. In connection with this latter point the wartime invention of the deductible-at-source, currently liable income tax is of great importance. This may go down, indeed, as one of the great social inventions of the present century. Where tax collections in one year are based essentially on the income of the previous year, the compensatory effect even of a progressive tax system is largely lost. It is as if, for instance, a thermostat always instructed the furnace to act on what the temperature was an hour ago. In inflation, tax collections, being based on the lower incomes of the year before, actually may fall as a percentage of income; in deflation, being based on the high incomes of the year before, they may actually rise. However, where tax collections are based on current income, even on estimates of current income, the tax system becomes an extremely sensitive compensatory mechanism. Every little decline in income results in an almost immediate fall in tax collections, and if government expenditure is more stable than tax receipts—which is almost certain to be the case—a decline in income will immediately result in an increased cash deficit; a rise, in an immediate decrease.

Quantitative impact of the *size* of the "fisc." The problem of the quantitative impact of the "fisc" on the economic system is not confined to the impact of the various surpluses and deficits—especially, of course, of the cash surplus or deficit—but also involves the impact of the over-all size of the government operation. Even if there is no change in the cash deficit, a rise in the over-all level of government operations—involving therefore an equal rise in both government expenditures and receipts—will have an inflationary effect on the private economy. If the economy is already operating at or near capacity, a rise in the level of government operations must reduce private consumption and investment. If there is no cash deficit, or surplus, there will be no change (from this cause) in the private money stock, which now circulates against a smaller volume of goods. There will be a tendency, therefore, for prices to rise. If, however, the expansion of government operations starts from a position of less than full employment it may simply result in an increase in total output, and if this is sufficient there will be no decline in private consumption and investment, and no change in the price level.

Qualitative aspects: the problem of incidence. We now turn to consider the qualitative aspects of the fiscal system. The total of government receipts and expenditures must be distributed over the various individuals and organizations of a society. The way in which the tax liability of an individual is calculated is bound to affect his behavior, and through his behavior the fortunes of other persons. The effect of the distribution of tax payments on society is not, therefore, to be discovered merely by looking at the accounts out of which these payments come. This problem of tracing the ultimate effects of tax payments is what is known as the "incidence" of taxation. An exactly similar problem arises for subsidies, which are, as we have seen, only negative taxes. This is one of the most difficult fields in economics, and there are many unsolved problems in it. The difficulty arises because of the complexity of the interactions involved; it is essentially a problem in the general dynamics of the whole system, and it cannot be solved satisfactorily by means of "partial" analysis. We can hardly ever assume that the person or institution out of whose account the tax is paid "really" pays the tax, simply because the tax may affect his revenues as well as his expenditures. Thus the corporation tax is "paid" by the corporation in the sense that it represents a transfer of cash from the corporation to government account. If, however, because of the tax the corporation is able to increase its selling prices, or diminish its buying prices, the tax will increase the receipts, or will diminish the nontax expenses, of the corporation, and the net "incidence" of the tax on the corporation—that is, the loss in net income as a result of the tax—is less than the actual payment. In this case we say that the tax is "passed on" to customers or to suppliers.

Effects on composition of output. The qualitative effects of taxation resolve themselves into two broad areas—the effect on the distribution of income among persons or groups, and the effect on the composition of output by products or by major types. The effects on the composition of output (the "product mix") are fairly easy to specify in a rather rough, qualitative fashion. The effects on the distribution of income are extremely difficult to specify because of their very great complexity. Even here, however, certain rather general propositions can be formulated in which we can have a degree of confidence.

Tax-distortion of product mix depends on elasticity of supply. Let us begin with the effects on the composition of output by products. It is clear that a tax the total amount of which varies directly with the production, or sale, or consumption, of a particular product will distort the product mix away from the taxed product and towards others. These taxes usually take the form of excise taxes, which are transfers from the producer of a product in proportion either to the quantity or to the value of the product that he produces. When the tax is proportionate to the physical quantity of the commodity it is called a *specific* tax; when it is proportionate to the value it is called an *ad valorem* tax. Processing taxes are generally transfers from the purchaser of a raw material. Or there may be sales taxes, which are transfers from retailers or wholesalers.

The general principle of incidence of taxes on the product mix is that where the total amount of tax transfer is directly dependent on a certain activity, whether production, processing, or sales, that activity will be discouraged relative to others, unless there is something very peculiar about the conditions of demand and supply. *How much* it will be discouraged depends on a very complex set of circumstances which are summed up roughly in the concepts of elasticity of demand and supply, but which also include such matters as the degree of monopoly or competitiveness in the market. If the activity that is taxed is very *price-inelastic*—that is, if the quantity of the activity does not depend much on how much people get for it—it is clear that though the tax makes the *price* of the activity somewhat more adverse, this does not affect the *amount* of the activity very much. Under these circumstances the purchasers of the activity will not find the quantity much curtailed, and they will not, therefore, have to offer much more for it. The performers or suppliers of the activity will have to take less for it; most of the burden of the tax therefore falls on them. If the supply of the activity is perfectly inelastic—that is, if the quantity of the activity performed is quite independent of the price received—the whole burden of the tax will fall on the performers (suppliers) of the activity, and none on the purchasers or users of it. This is an important principle, as we shall see, in determining the ultimate effect of the tax structure on the distribution of income as well as the product mix.

—and demand. Similarly it is easy to show that if the demand for the taxed product or activity is price-inelastic—that is, if the purchasers of the activity will buy just about the same amount, within limits, no matter what the price—the quantity of the activity will again not be much changed by the tax, but this time the price to the purchaser will rise, as his purchases are not much affected by this rise, and the purchaser will bear most of the burden of the tax. The division of the burden of the tax thus depends on the *relative* elasticities of supply and demand; the burden is shifted towards the more inelastic, because inelasticity in this connection *means* an ability and willingness to continue an activity, whether of producing, selling, or buying, in spite of an unfavorable movement in its price or "terms of trade." The burden goes to those most willing to shoulder it!

Modifications owing to monopoly. These conclusions may be modified somewhat, though not perhaps very greatly, by the existence of monopoly or imperfect competition in various forms. Here the problem is made more complicated by the almost necessary introduction of dynamic and informational factors. Thus a tax on the profits of a monopolist is not supposed to affect his output, according to the elementary theory of the firm, because if he is already maximizing his profits he maximizes them at the same output after the tax, so provided the tax does not drive him out of business altogether it will simply result in a diminution of his profits, and cannot be passed on to his customers or back to his suppliers. It still pays him best to sell as much as before and to buy as much as before: if his markets are not affected by the tax (a big "if," as a matter of fact) he will still therefore have to charge the same price to his customers and pay the same price to his suppliers in order to sell (or buy) the same quantities.

In fact, however, monopolists are often so ignorant of their markets that their price policies may be very far from maximizing their profits, and under these circumstances a tax may very easily cause a shake-up in their policies and a readjustment of conventional or traditional price structures. This is particularly apt to be the case if prices are determined initially on some rule-of-thumb basis, such as "cost-plus," or what is sometimes called the "markup" system—that is, by making a rough calculation of the average cost of the product and adding a traditional markup of, say, 15 or 25 per cent for profit.

—or oligopoly. Under conditions of oligopoly, where we have a few sellers selling a fairly uniform product, there is great danger of "price wars." Under these circumstances once a price has been established for a time it comes to have a certain stability, simply because each firm is afraid to change it—especially to lower it—for fear of setting off a price war. Under these circumstances the removal or lowering of a tax may not cause any change in the price. In this case prices are usually less adjustable downwards than they are upwards: the imposition or raising of a tax may result in higher prices while the removal or lowering of a tax may not result in a fall. All these peculiar cases, however, can be brought under the general concept of elasticity of demand and supply, for the general principle still holds that whatever makes for lack of adjustment in quantity makes for adjustment in price, and vice versa. The great principle of adjustment is that what adjusts is the adjustable! We can think of a tax as a *strain* laid on a highly complex interrelated system; the stiff ("inelastic") parts do not "give," the flexible ("elastic") parts bear the burden of the adjustment.

Yield depends on tax-elasticity. These considerations are important in considering the *yield* of a tax. If the payment depends directly on the amount of the activity or commodity taxed, the yield—that is, the total amount paid in tax—depends on the effect of the tax on the amount of the activity. If the activity is tax-elastic—that is, if the tax results in a large decline in the activity taxed, the yield will be lower for a given tax than if the activity is tax-inelastic. Where the activity is tax-elastic, a lowering of the tax per unit can result in a rise in the total yield. Thus, suppose a commodity is taxed at 25 cents per unit produced, and under these circumstances 1,000,000 units are produced; the yield of the tax is $250,000. Now suppose a reduction of the tax to 20 cents per unit so encourages the production of the commodity that 1,500,000 units are produced. The yield of the tax is now $300,000. Something like this has happened often enough in the long history of taxation to show that these are not just idle theories! Both from the point of view of revenue and from the point of view of creating the least distortion of the economic system, therefore, there is everything to be said for laying taxes on tax-inelastic activities.

The concept of "desirable distortions." This raises the awkward question, however, as to whether we *wish* to avoid distorting the system, in regard both to the product mix and its distribution among persons or classes. The answer is clearly that virtually all tax systems envisage a *desirable* distortion of the system. The system that would arise in the absence of taxation is in no sense regarded as the most desirable, and the tax system is used as an instrument of social policy to distort the economic system in a direction that is felt, by those who frame and legislate tax systems, to be socially desirable.

In the first place, there are some activities that are recognized as individually desired but socially undesirable; this is perhaps the best definition of "vice." There is a lot to be said, therefore, for the taxation of vice. This is the usual justification for the high taxes on liquor and cigarettes. Oddly enough, this principle is often violated, because in some sense the imposition of a tax gives a certain aura of social approval to the thing taxed—we cannot tax anything without making it at least slightly respectable. It is only the respectable vices, therefore, that can be taxed; the more disreputable ones, like gambling and prostitution, frequently escape taxation because of the fear of giving them a stamp of social approval. The ideal system of taxation from the point of view of an individual, of course, is that all vices should be taxed in which he does not indulge! This is a principle that is hard to apply universally and still get any revenue.

Taxation to correct for hidden social costs. A ground for distortion of the system through taxation that is related to, though not quite the same as, social disapproval is that of social cost. There may be some activities that have consequences that cannot be easily identified or charged for. If they are not curtailed by some social means, therefore, these activities tend to expand beyond the socially most desirable level. Thus, quite apart from the question whether cigarette smoking is a "vice," there is no doubt that it causes fires and little doubt that it causes poor health and earlier death. These effects, however, are not in the price system; fire insurance companies cannot recover from the tobacco industry, neither can medical and life insurance companies. There is much to be said, therefore, for raising the price of cigarettes to the point where the revenue from them would cover not only the costs of the tobacco industry but the additional costs in fire, sickness, and earlier death that are the by-products of this industry. This can be done—and as a matter of fact probably is done, though for the wrong reasons—through the taxation of cigarettes. We might extend the principle a little further and use the proceeds of the tax to subsidize fire, health, and life insurance, to the further benefit of the nonsmoker. Similarly, the liquor industry might be charged with a certain proportion of the costs of alcoholism, delinquency, automobile insurance, and so on.

—or hidden social benefits. The same principle applies in reverse to those activities that have social benefits that cannot be charged for directly. The tax concessions given to churches and educational and charitable institutions are generally justified on these grounds. The case for social support of education is particularly strong, as the costs of education must be borne for the most part by persons other than those who are receiving it, whether parents, graduate students' wives, endowments, or the state, whereas the benefits are received largely in the next generation, not only by those receiving the education but by society at large. If education is left purely in private hands, therefore, there are strong reasons to suppose that there will be far too little of it, for the people who will ultimately receive the benefits are not currently in a position to pay the cost, and there are no financial institutions that can bridge the gap.

Application to tariffs. Many of the principles we have outlined above are applicable to taxes on imports (tariffs) or on exports. Whereas an excise tax on the production of a commodity, or a sales tax on its purchase, is applied at all points where it is produced or consumed within the taxing country or district, a tariff is a tax on *transportation* across a national boundary. In assessing its impact, therefore, we cannot avoid getting involved with the problem of the *location* of economic activity—a difficult and still not fully explored field. It is to be expected, however, that a tariff will diminish trade, will increase domestic production, and will diminish foreign production of the commodity taxed. Paradoxically enough it is by no means impossible for a tariff to increase the world volume of production of the commodity taxed—if the foreign supply is rather inelastic it may not shrink much, and if the domestic supply is elastic it may expand more than the foreign supply shrinks. The incidence of a tariff again depends on the relative elasticities of demand and supply in the two countries. If domestic demand and supply are inelastic and foreign demand and supply are elastic, the price will rise domestically (as this neither cuts off much domestic consumption nor encourages much domestic production) and will not fall much abroad, as a slight fall suffices to cut off enough foreign production and consumption to adjust to the reduced trade. In this case the main burden falls on the domestic consumer; the domestic price rises by almost as much as the tariff, the price received by the foreign producer does not fall much. If, however, foreign demand and supply are inelastic and domestic demand and supply are elastic, the domestic price cannot rise much, for if it does, domestic consumption will be much reduced and production expanded. In this situation, the main price burden falls upon the foreigner.

Infant industries and balanced growth. The problem of "desirable distortion" applies also to tariff policy. The "infant industry" argument for tariffs rests on the assumption that there are certain industries that cannot survive foreign competition when they are small, but that are subject to declining costs as they expand, so that if they are allowed to grow behind the shelter of a tariff they will eventually get to the point of self-sufficiency. The "balanced growth" argument, especially in the case of underdeveloped nations, is a modern and more general application of the same principle. It is argued that certain industries create opportunities for growth in others, and that a national economy will grow faster if it has many related industries than if it specializes to the full in, say, a one-crop economy, even though there may be temporary advantages in this extreme specialization. It is difficult to assess the value of this argument in each special case, and one suspects it can be too easily used for rationalizing support of powerful special interests. It cannot, however, be disproved by simple appeal to "classical" static economics; the laws of growth are too subtle for that.

Ad valorem and specific taxes. A word should be added on the subject of ad valorem and specific taxes (or tariffs). In times of stable price levels the difference between these two forms of assessment is not very great—it does not matter much whether we lay 20 cents tax or a 20 per cent tax on a dollar article. In times of changing price levels, however, specific taxes do not of themselves keep pace with the changes, whereas ad valorem taxes tend to adjust themselves automatically. Thus, if the price of the above-mentioned article went to $2, the specific tax of 20 cents would be only 10 per cent of the price, the ad valorem tax of 20 per cent would be 40 cents. As it is a long and cumbersome procedure to adjust specific rates, an inflation inevitably lowers the yield of specific taxes, whereas a deflation raises it. A specific tax structure is thus "anticompensatory." Tax receipts dry up in inflation, just when they are needed, and expand relative to income in deflation when they are not needed. On these grounds ad valorem taxes are to be preferred as being at least neutral in regard to compensation for inflations or deflations.

The broader the tax, the less the distortion. From the above considerations a simple general principle emerges: that the broader the coverage of a tax system, the less likely it is to have distorting effects. We do not assume, of course, that no distortion is desirable. We do want to avoid unintentional distortion. Like Oscar Wilde's gentleman, who never insulted anybody unintentionally, a tax system should only distort the system in ways in which we want it to be distorted. Unperceived distortions are dangerous.

From the point of view of avoiding distortion, a general sales tax is probably better than a tax confined to a few commodities, and an income tax probably better than a sales tax. It is virtually impossible, however, to devise a tax that does not distort the economy to some degree. Thus, suppose we had a proportional income tax on all income, so that all incomes were reduced by an equal percentage by the tax. Even this tax would distort the relative product mix somewhat, as there are some commodities that are purchased more at high incomes than at low, and these "superior" goods would suffer relative to "inferior" goods. It might be argued that this is not really a "distortion" as this is what we mean in real terms by a reduction of income. If the production of all commodities were reduced in the same proportion, this itself would be a distortion. It would be absurd, for instance, if we had to halve our income, to cut our food consumption as well as our cosmetic consumption in half; with a fall in income the proportion spent on food should rise. Even apart from this rather dubious type of distortion, however, an income tax of any kind produces a distortion as between work (income-producing activities) and leisure. Even a proportional income tax lowers the marginal return to work. Unless, therefore, the supply of work is completely inelastic with respect to its marginal return—which is unlikely—the proportion of time devoted to work will change. If incomes are perceived as fairly adequate to maintain existing standards of achievement, an income tax will discourage work; if incomes are felt as inadequate the tax may actually encourage work, as people now have to work harder to maintain the desired standard of life.

Lump-sum taxes minimize marginal distortions. The tax that produces the least distortion is the "lump-sum tax" that is imposed on income-earning *capacity* but that does not depend on the amount of income earned. The local property tax is an example. The owner of a house pays the same tax whether he derives income from his house or not. Hence the tax does not act as a discouragement to the earning of income—for example, by renting rooms. The lump-sum tax, however, suffers from the serious disadvantage that it is difficult to assess; assessments constantly get obsolete and inequitable even in the case of property taxes. The problem of assessment in the case of a lump-sum tax on individual earning capacity seems to be quite insoluble if we are to preserve the "capacity to pay" principle, and still more if we are to establish the principle of progressive taxation.

The effect of taxes on the distribution of income. This brings us to the problem of the effect of the fiscal system on the distribution of income. More equal distribution of income has become an accepted objective of tax policy in virtually all free-market countries, and in the attainment of this greater equality the tax system is perhaps the most important instrument. Two main devices work towards this end. The first is a system of commodity taxes in which "superior"—"rich-man's"—goods are taxed more than "poor man's" goods—heavy taxes on furs, jewelry, and other luxuries; light taxes or no taxes, or even subsidies, for basic foodstuffs, low-cost housing, and so on. The second is a progressive income tax—that is, an income tax in which the proportion of income paid as tax is larger, the larger the income.

Several attempts have been made to estimate the over-all impact of various fiscal systems on the distribution of income—that is, to compare what would be the distribution of income without the fiscal system with the distribution with it. These estimates usually come out with the answer that most modern tax systems are regressive at the lowest extremity, neutral in some middle range, and progressive at the upper levels of income. The very poor seem to pay a somewhat larger proportion of their income than the middle groups; the rich pay a much larger proportion of their income than the average. The regressive character of the tax structure at the lowest levels is caused for the most part by commodity and sales taxes, and the progressive character at higher levels is due to the income tax. Recent studies have indicated, however, that even in countries like the United States and Great Britain where marginal tax rates on high incomes are very high indeed (above 90 per cent), the loopholes in the system at high levels (for example, through converting income into capital gains) are so great that in fact few incomes are taxed at rates exceeding 50 per cent. At very high levels, therefore, it is quite possible that these tax systems become regressive again, or at least proportional.

Incidence of profits taxes—in the short run. It must be emphasized, however, that these estimates are all based on assumptions about the real incidence of the fiscal system that are subject to a good deal of error. The great conundrum here is the incidence of the corporate profits tax: is this passed on to consumers, is it passed back to workers, or is it absorbed by the shareholders? If it is absorbed by shareholders this will be a more progressive tax than if it is passed on to consumers, especially if the corporation makes articles of low-income consumption, for on the whole shares are a "superior" asset—that is, rich people are likely to have a larger proportion of their assets in this form than poor people. The evidence indicates that in the short run the tax is passed on mainly to consumers, and that profits rise by just about the amount of the tax. Suppose, say, that a billion dollars in tax that previously has been paid out of personal income is now moved to corporate incomes. If wages, salaries, and dividend payments do not change, householders will find themselves with a billion dollars more to spend per year. Businesses will therefore be able to raise their selling prices so that their total gross revenues will be about a billion dollars more. Their costs are still the same, however, so that profits before taxes are a billion dollars more; the tax is a billion dollars, so that profits after taxes will be much the same as before. This seems to have been what happened when corporation taxes were increased during the second World War: profits-after-taxes remained pretty stable, and profits-before-taxes rose by about the amount of the increased tax.

—and the long run. In the long run, however, there is more chance that business taxes may be absorbed by the profit-receiver. Certainly the fact that unincorporated businesses escape the corporation profits tax has operated to distort the distribution of business organizations towards the unincorporated form. A case can be made that this is a desirable distortion. It is not, however, a completely clear case. On the larger question whether business taxes as a whole are passed on in the long run, we must await further research, both theoretical and empirical.

The incidence of progressive income taxes. A question even more difficult to answer is whether the progressive income tax is frustrated in the long run by raising high-level incomes before tax in order to compensate for the high taxes. If the demand for the kind of scarce abilities that command high salaries is very inelastic, the fortunate possessors of these abilities may be able to push a lot of the tax on to the purchasers of their services—which is, ultimately, on society at large. There is some evidence that this is so, at least in part. It is more difficult for the owners of material property to escape income taxes in this way, simply because high incomes from property are usually the result of having a lot of property, not the result of having exceptionally *scarce* property as is the case with high salary incomes. This whole problem is extremely complex, however, and requires more refined methods of analysis for its solution than we now have available.

Effect of taxes on the distribution of property: inheritance taxes. A very important long-run impact of the fiscal system on the distribution of income is its effect on the course of the distribution of property (net worths) among the individuals of a society. By and large, the more the ownership of property is concentrated in the hands of the few, the more will income be so concentrated. A society with widely distributed property will also tend to have a fairly equal distribution of income. The distribution of property, however, is the result of a long process through time in which inheritance and the saving habits of the various groups play the major role. The fiscal system can greatly affect this process, both directly through inheritance taxes and death duties and indirectly through current redistributions of income. The inheritance laws and customs themselves also have an important effect on the long-run course of the distribution of property. Thus, where primogeniture is the rule, the estate of the father passing unbroken to the eldest son, there is a tendency for property to remain concentrated in few hands; where equal distribution of estate among children is the rule, property tends to become more and more diffuse. Heavy inheritance taxes tend to break up large concentrations of property; progressive income taxes make it harder for the rich to save, and so also prevent the concentration of property. Low interest rates and easy finance—*e.g.*, of homes—create conditions in which it is easier for lower income groups to acquire property. All these movements, however, are complex in their effects. Societies may presumably be divided into those in which the dynamic processes lead to greater concentration and those in which they lead to greater diffusion. It is not easy to identify these societies merely on the basis of the observation of their institutions.

9

Monetary and financial policy

The Fruits of the Financial System
Are quite impressive, once you list 'em,
Although the system has the power
To turn its fruits extremely sour.

So let us sing the praise of Debt—
Provided that we don't forget,
The Debt can scourge the foolish nation
That can't prevent a sharp deflation.

Financial policy defined. Money is only one among a large number of "financial instruments." Its operation cannot be understood, or controlled, save in the setting of the "financial system." Fiscal policy, therefore, must always be supplemented by financial policy, or, as it is often called, "monetary policy." The nomenclature here is confusing, for it is fiscal policy that is primarily concerned, in its quantitative aspects, with the money stock, whereas the so-called monetary policy is mainly concerned with the regulation of certain financial instruments, such as bank loans, which are not usually regarded as money. For this reason it is perhaps better to use the term "financial policy" to cover all government concern for financial instruments, both public and private. Financial policy thus covers such matters as the regulation of banking and insurance, the creation and management of the national debt, the operation of central banks, the control of the stock and bond markets, and so on.

The financial instrument. The basic concept in this area is that of the *financial instrument*. This is a *promise* or undertaking of some kind on the part of the issuer, an *expectation* of some kind on the part of the owner. The promise or expectation usually takes the form of promises to pay, or expectations of receiving sums of money in the future. We can broaden the concept of a financial instrument, however, to include the futures contract, which is a promise to pay certain stated amounts of *commodity* (*e.g.*, wheat) at some date in the future, or a "short sale," which is a promise to deliver certain other financial instruments, such as stocks, at some date in the future.

Financial instruments may be divided into *debts* and *equities*. The characteristic of debts is that the promise is to pay certain definite sums, either of money or of other things. Equities (for example, corporate stocks) consist of promises to pay contingent sums—sums that are, for instance, dependent on the profitability of the enterprise. Equities also usually involve certain rights of control—for example, voting rights in the election of corporation management. There are, however, many different kinds of financial instruments—*e.g.*, nonvoting stock, preference shares, and so on—with varying degrees of rights, privileges, and obligations. There are also many different kinds of debt. A commercial bank *demand deposit* is a promise by a bank to pay the owner of the deposit or any person or institution designated by him in a check, *any* sum up to the amount of his deposit at *any* time when the depositor asks for it. A time deposit is a promise to pay the owner himself any sum up to the amount of the deposit a certain short period after he asks for it. The bank loan is a promise on the part of the *borrower* to pay the bank a certain sum on a certain date, or a series of sums on a series of specified dates. An installment contract is a promise by a householder to pay the finance company certain sums on certain dates. A bond is a promise on the part of the issuer—whether a government or a private corporation—to pay the holder certain sums on certain dates. Debts may vary in the penalties provided for nonperformance. For example, a mortgage is a debt "secured" by a piece of real estate. If the borrower, or issuer of the promise to pay, does not perform, then the lender, or purchaser of the promise, has the right to "foreclose"—that is, become the owner of—the particular piece of property by which the debt is secured.

Money as a financial instrument. Money may be regarded also as a financial instrument. In the case of demand deposits, which are usually regarded as money, their nature as a financial instrument—a peculiar kind of debt—is obvious. Even "hard money," however, can be regarded as a promise on the part of the society that accepts it to pay the owner goods, or anything that is offered for sale for money, in return for his money up to the value of it. A thousand dollars, even in gold, is a kind of certificate giving the owner the right to purchase a thousand dollars worth of anything that is being offered for sale for dollars! It is this "acceptability" that constitutes the essential "moneyness" of money. This acceptability, however, is what justifies us when we place money in the classification of a financial instrument.

The financial system: (1) the stock and interdependencies of financial instruments. The financial system then consists first in the inventory or stock of all financial instruments, including money, as they exist at a moment of time. This description would include the quantities of various instruments, their distribution among various owners, and also their relationships of dependence one on another. This dependence rests on the contingent rights that the possession of one instrument may imply in regard to others, or on the effects that the failure to fulfil one "promise" may have on others.

Thus, suppose one firm holds the bonds of a second, which fails. The value of the financial instruments issued by the first firm will be adversely affected by the loss of value of the instruments of the second. The value of the stock of a holding company or of an investment trust depends on the value of the stocks of other companies that it holds as assets. Even the value of bank deposits depends ultimately on the value of the bank's assets. This system of dependence is expressed through the system of balance sheets; if we are given the balance sheets of all persons and organizations, and if we can identify the holders of all financial instruments, it would be possible to trace the effect of the change of value of any one instrument on all the others. This is because every financial instrument appears in at least two balance sheets—in one as an asset and in the other, or others, as a liability or equity. Thus a bank deposit is an asset to the holder, a liability to the bank; a bank loan is an asset to the bank, a liability to the borrower; a bond is an asset to the holder, a liability to the issuer; a share of stock is an asset to the owner, a liability or "equity" to the issuing firm. In any balance sheet liabilities and equities must equal assets, by definition; a decline in assets must cause a decline in liabilities, and there are fairly good rules to determine *which* liabilities should decline—equities (stocks) first, then private debts, then obligations to government. As these liabilities decline (or grow) the assets in other balance sheets that represent these same financial instruments also decline or grow, with consequent decline or growth in still other liabilities. So the whole structure of "book values" of financial instruments is held together in a complex pattern of interrelated balance sheets.

(2) **The exchange of financial instruments and their prices.** The next aspect of the financial system is the *exchange* of financial instruments one for another. These instruments constantly circulate among various owners, and an exchange pure and simple is merely a mutual transfer of ownership. When a man buys a bond with a bank deposit, the bond passes from the

seller to him, a bank deposit of equal value from him to the seller. These exchanges take place, however, at a system of *prices;* these prices are determined in the financial markets by the general principles of demand and supply which govern all price determination. Where there is an increased desire, for instance, to hold bonds rather than money, the price of bonds will rise—at the old price there will be unsatisfied would-be buyers who cannot find sellers, and who will therefore bid the price up. The price structure of financial instruments therefore represents the relative willingness of people to hold the existing stocks of the various instruments. An increased desire to hold a certain kind will raise its relative price. Relative to people's preferences for different kinds of assets and to the existing stocks of them, there is some set of prices that will just persuade people to hold what is there to be held! It must be recalled, however, that a government, or a semigovernmental agency like a Central Bank, can fix the price of any asset simply by offering to buy and sell it in unlimited quantities at the fixed price. In this case an increased desire to hold the asset in the private market simply results in enough being sold by the governmental agency to satisfy the increased demand at the fixed price. Similarly a decreased desire to hold it will result in enough being bought by the agency to diminish the quantity in private hands to what people are willing to hold at the fixed price.

And consequent interest rates. The set of prices of financial instruments determines the set of interest rates on currently purchased or created assets. The higher the price of any given instrument, the less will be the rate of interest earned on it, assuming of course that the expected benefits from the instrument remain unchanged. Thus, suppose I am buying a promissory note that is a promise to pay $100 one year from the present. If I buy this for $100 now there is no interest at all; if I pay $95 for it the rate of interest is a little over 5 per cent $\left(\frac{5}{95}\right)$; if I pay $90 for it the rate of interest is a little over 11 per cent $\left(\frac{10}{90}\right)$. If all assets were exactly similar from the point of view of safety, respectability, and nonfinancial benefits, we would expect the preferences for different kinds of assets to adjust themselves to the point where the rates of interest of all assets, as determined by their current prices, were equal. Thus, if the prices of assets were such that one of them carried an expected yield of 10 per cent whereas all the others yielded only 5 per cent, the preference for this asset would rise, and its price would also rise until its yield had fallen to the general level. In fact there are wide differences among assets in regard to their "general" desirability. The less generally desirable an asset, the lower will be its price, and the higher its nominal yield. Risky assets, inconvenient assets, disreputable assets, and so on will be priced low, so that their nominal yield is high; safe, convenient, and respectable assets, and assets that have peculiar legal or customary attractions, will be priced high, and their nominal yield will be low.

(3) **The creation and destruction of financial instruments.** The third aspect of the financial system is the creation and destruction of financial instruments. When a loan is made, a financial instrument (*e.g.*, a promissory note) is created by the borrower and sold to the lender. The fact that the creation and sale (exchange) of the instrument occur in the same transaction has frequently caused confusion between the two acts of creation and exchange. It is important, however, to separate these two phenomena conceptually, even if they are frequently combined in practice, because once created a financial instrument may be bought and sold many times, and participates in the general melee of exchanges—provided, of course, that it is a negotiable (*i.e.*, exchangeable) instrument. The price structure of these assets depends on the quantity of them existing in the market, as well as on the preferences for them. The quantity existing in the market at any one time is equal to the quantity that has been created in times past, minus the quantity destroyed. If, therefore, a large quantity of some instrument (*e.g.*, government bonds) is created, this will increase the stock of these in the market, and will depress their price—other things being equal. The creation of a large quantity of money, on the

other hand, will tend to raise the prices of the other assets, as the holders of money will be anxious to exchange some of it for other assets and will bid up the prices of these assets. Financial instruments are destroyed when loans are repaid or when stock is retired or becomes worthless. Whether the total stock of any particular instrument—*e.g.*, bank loans—is increasing or decreasing, depends on whether new creations exceed or fall short of repayments. This depends in considerable degree on the price of these instruments, as determining their yield, relative to the yield on those other asset-combinations that loans permit the borrower to control.

Debt creation related to expected profit minus interest. This point is so important in determining the rate of debt creation that we must examine it further, and ask *why* do people borrow and get into debt. Borrowing increases the *total* on both sides of the balance sheet of the borrower. If a man borrows $10,000 his liabilities are increased by $10,000, represented by the promissory note that he has created, and his assets are increased by the proceeds of the sale of this note. These proceeds may be in the first instance in the form of money—say a bank deposit. He can exchange this money for other things, however, and the net result is that he now has a larger asset total to manipulate. In the course of these manipulations—which may include buying, selling, producing, or simply holding earning assets—the asset total may be expected to grow. The rate of growth of the asset total may be called the rate of profit. In considering whether or not to borrow a man weighs the chance of additional profit on his asset total against the certainty of additional interest payments on his liabilities. If we ask, therefore, what limits the amount that people borrow—that is, why does a man not borrow more—one answer is that the chance of profit on the increased assets is judged to be not worth the certain cost of interest and repayment of the loan. Another answer is that the *lender* may be unwilling to lend, because of his unfavorable estimate of the chances of the borrower's making profit, for if the borrower takes losses he may not even be able to repay the loan. In both cases, however, the more favorable and the more certain the expectation of profit, relative to the rate of interest, the greater the willingness of both borrower and lender to expand the volume of loans. With a *given* expectation of profit, however, a higher interest rate on loans may be expected to diminish the amount of loans created.

The peculiarity of banks. The peculiar position of banks, especially commercial banks, in the financial system requires special attention. The peculiarity arises from the fact that most of the liabilities of banks, whether deposits or notes, are liquid assets to the holder, and are therefore virtually indistinguishable from money. An over-all expansion of bank *assets,* therefore, by the purchase either of promissory notes (loans) or of other securities (investments) of necessity leads to a general expansion in bank liabilities, and therefore to an expansion of the money stock. When a private person makes a loan a financial instrument is created by the borrower (the promissory note), and money passes from the lender to the borrower in return for the promissory note. When a bank makes a loan, however, *two* financial instruments are created—the promissory note, created by the borrower and transferred to the bank, and a bank deposit, created by the bank and transferred to the borrower. When a bank buys an already existing security—say a government bond—it creates a deposit and transfers this deposit to the seller of the security. When government creates a security (issues a bond) and sells this to a bank, the bank creates a deposit which it transfers to the government. In general, then, when a security, whether a promissory note or a bond, is created and sold to a bank, a deposit is also created, and the volume of both securities and money increases.

Limits on bank-loan expansion. The net effect, of course, may not be an *equal* increase in securities and deposits, for as a result of purchasing one security a bank may limit its freedom to purchase others. Thus, suppose a single bank makes a loan of, say, $10,000. The borrower receives a deposit—rather less than $10,000, to allow for interest, but for simplicity let us neglect this—and the bank receives a $10,000 "security"—the promissory note. The borrower now, we suppose, spends his deposit—that is, pays it out to other people in return for other assets. If these other people bank at the same bank and redeposit the checks received from our borrower, all that happens from the bank's point of view is a shift of deposits among depositors, but no change in the total. If, however, as is likely to be the case, some of these checks are paid in at other banks, or are cashed, the bank will have to pay out its own liquid assets (reserves) in settlement of these checks. The loan results, let us say, in a $2,000 increase in its deposits, and an $8,000 decline in its reserves. If it does not wish to allow its reserves to fall in this way it must replenish them by borrowing from a reserve bank (*i.e.*, creating a promissory note of its own and selling this to a reserve bank) or by selling securities on the open market, or by "rediscounting"—*i.e.*, selling some of its promissory-note assets ("bills") to other banks—or by not renewing a note as it falls due. The complex technical details and ramifications of possible reactions would lead us far afield; here it is sufficient to note that while a single bank acting in isolation is greatly limited in its power to create deposits by the fear of loss of reserves to other banks, if *all* banks expand their loans in rough proportion they will all "lose reserves to each other" and each will gain from other banks as much as it loses. There may then be some loss of reserves to the system as a whole, as the public demands a larger amount of cash in proportion to its enlarged holdings of deposits, and there will certainly be a fall in the "reserve ratio"—that is, the ratio reserves ÷ deposits—as deposits increase, unless reserves are increased proportionally. If now the banks are checked in their expansion of loans only by the fear of a decline in their reserve ratio below some legal or customary limit, an authority that can control both the total volume of reserves and the reserve ratio can control the total volume of bank deposits. This is generally regarded as the function of a *central bank.*

Central banks' roles. A central bank is primarily a "bankers' bank"—a bank whose deposits are owned mainly by other banks. Even where there is no official central bank certain banks in strategic positions in the system tend to become central banks;

thus the Bank of England grew almost imperceptibly into a central bank, and before the establishment of the Federal Reserve System in the United States—and to some extent even today—some of the larger city banks, especially in New York, came to be "bankers' banks." In almost all countries today, however, central banks are set up under governmental or semigovernmental auspices, and central bank policy must therefore be regarded as an integral part of over-all economic policy.

(4) **Financial institutions.** The fourth and last aspect of the financial system that must be included in any over-all view is a description of the institutions or organizations that hold, create, and exchange financial instruments. An important part of government financial policy consists in the regulation, the creation, or even the destruction of financial organizations. The willingness to hold financial instruments, and therefore their prices, and the willingness and ability to create or destroy financial instruments, depend to a very large extent on the nature of the organizations in the society, for most financial instruments are held, exchanged, and created by organizations, not by individuals. Table 4 lists the major types of financial organizations in the United States, and in most developed countries, together with a note on their characteristic balance-sheet structure and activities.

Objectives of financial policy. This rather long introduction, sketchy as it is, has been necessary to delineate the *field* of financial policy. We must now turn to the problem of the *objectives* of financial policy. What is a "good" financial system, and how do we tell it from a bad one? Once we move beyond certain rather obvious and elementary criteria in regard to the prevention of deliberate swindling and misinformation and the ensuring of uniformity and quality in various moneys and financial instruments, the appropriate criteria are by no means easy to formulate. Indeed, criteria for financial policy can be developed only in the light of over-all standards of performance for the economic system as a whole, and in the light of a clear understanding of the function that the financial system performs within the larger framework. Let us examine briefly,

TABLE 4

Institution	Principal Assets	Principal Liabilities	Financial Activities
Federal government	No balance sheet: assets consist mainly of taxable capacity of nation. Some real capital.	The national debt (government securities)—mostly bonds.	Creates and destroys government securities; may issue money.
State and local governments	Same as for federal government.	State and local government securities (mostly bonds).	Issue and repay bonds.
Government corporations (*e.g.*, T.V.A.)	Mostly real capital.	Securities (those in private hands, mostly bonds).	May issue bonds.
Private "operating" corporations	Mostly real capital; some bonds and bank deposits. Some consumer credit. Some accounts receivable.	Stocks and bonds. Some accounts payable.	Issue stocks and bonds. Some buying and selling other stocks and bonds.
Holding companies and investment trusts	Stocks and bonds of operating corporations.	Their own stocks.	Issue stock; buy and sell and hold other stocks and bonds.
Insurance companies	Bonds and bank deposits.	Unexpired policies.	Issue policies. Buy and sell securities, mostly to hold for income.
Savings banks; mortgage and loan companies	Mortgages and bonds. Some commercial bank deposits.	Savings deposits.	Sell savings deposits; buy mortgages and bonds.
Pension funds	Stocks and bonds.	Pension claims.	Hold stocks and bonds. Create and extinguish pension claims.
Specialized banks (*e.g.*, land banks, farm credit banks), co-op banks	Mortgages, bonds, promissory notes.	Equities, bonds.	Hold and issue specialized assets.
Commercial banks	Bank loans. Government securities. Central bank deposits and notes.	Bank deposits. Central bank loans.	Maintain checking system. Create deposits. Buy promissory notes and bills and some bonds.
Federal Reserve Banks	Gold certificates. Government bonds. Acceptances. Rediscounted bills.	Central bank deposits.	Purchase and sell government securities. Lend to commercial banks. Rediscount.

therefore, possible contributions—or impediments—offered by the financial system to the achievement of our four goals of economic policy—progress, stability, justice, and freedom.

Contributions of the financial system to economic progress. The great contribution of the financial system to progress is, first, that it facilitates exchange and therefore specialization, and second, that it permits the separation of ownership of property from its control, and so enables those who are skilled at administering property to administer more than they personally own. Without financial instruments of some sort any complicated system of exchange is impossible. Various media of exchange (such as cattle and metals) develop at a very early stage in civilization, and the use of a widely acceptable medium of exchange is a necessary condition of any society above the level of the most primitive tribe. Bills of exchange, bank deposits, paper money, checking accounts, and clearing arrangements are all part of a long process of development by which multilateral exchange has been facilitated. We might even look forward to a future state in which physical money virtually disappears and all transactions are cleared in a universal clearing system—all money being reduced to money of account. Indeed, internally we are not very far from that state now. The one remaining obstacle is the system of national money units, foreign exchanges, and the lack of free convertibility of different currencies one into another at stable and uniform rates of exchange.

Difficulties of assessment. It is hard to assess the contributions of specific financial organizations and institutions to the rate of economic progress. In the nineteenth century most economists and men of affairs would have defended the Gold Standard (and the consequent stability of foreign exchange rates and free convertibility of the various national moneys into one another at these fixed rates) as the most important generator of world economic development. Today we are not so sure. Especially in a world of wide gaps between the rich and the poor nations, and in a world that has been subject to shattering international fluctuations and disruptions, the appeal of national economic insulation is strong. Some unfortunate experiences of nations dependent on one-crop economies or extractive industries lend support to those who advocate "balanced growth" on the national level. Nevertheless, these "neo-mercantilists" may easily overlook the very great gains of international specialization, and the gains of integration into a large economic system. The rapid growth of the United States, for instance, owes much more to its own great size and large internal market than to its isolation from the rest of the world.

The sources of economic growth, however, are so complex, and so interwoven with all the elements of a culture and with the "spirit" of a society, that it is very hard to attribute effects to specific institutions. One hesitates to affirm even whether from the point of view of rapid growth a controlled, central banking system is preferable to an undisciplined "free banking" system, or whether a highly planned economy is preferable to a more *laissez-faire* system, or whether a "passive," conservative banking system is preferable to an "active," entrepreneurially minded banking system. Sometimes the function of the financial system and institutions is simply to provide a *setting* or framework for the activities of the developers and the entrepreneurs; sometimes its function is actively to propagate change and development within a system that lacks such movements.

The destructiveness of deflation. One conclusion we may venture: that deflation is an important handicap to short-run economic development, and that long-continued inflation may be a handicap to long-run development. This relates economic progress to the second of our great objectives—stability. Deflation is destructive because it destroys profits and hence destroys the incentive for investment. It is also likely to lead to unemployment, surplus stocks, and weak markets. An important question to ask of a financial system, therefore, is whether it contains within itself safeguards against deflation. On this count a simple Gold Standard is clearly inadequate. Even though, as we have seen, there is a certain tendency for deflation to correct itself under such a system by making gold production profitable, this process is much too slow and uncertain. There is, as we have also seen, a danger of inherent instability in a completely unregulated financial system, because of the speculative nature of the willingness to hold various kinds of assets. A general belief that prices of nonmoney assets are going to fall will lead to a general desire to diminish asset holdings and increase money holdings. In the absence of any agency that can bring about rapid changes in the relative quantities of assets and money, this fall in the willingness to hold assets can lead only to a general decline in their prices, which in turn may lead to still less willingness to hold assets, and so a deflation justifies itself and gathers momentum as it proceeds. Because of the interrelatedness of asset values through the system of balance sheets, if this process goes far enough it will collapse into a "panic" in which there is a desperate scramble for liquid assets, and in which everyone is trying to sell securities and nobody wants to buy them.

The central bank as a stabilizer. The basic instability of financial markets is one factor that has led to the establishment of central banks. In the nineteenth century the Bank of England developed the habit of being a "lender of last resort"—an agency entrusted with the preventing of the worst manifestations of financial panic by being able to create liquid assets in indefinite quantity on stringent terms. By 1913 with the founding of the Federal Reserve System in the United States the functions of the Central Bank were conceived more broadly as not merely the prevention of crises and panics, but the smoothing of the fluctuations that culminate in these crises and panics. This leads to the concept of the Central Bank as a continuously operative control, operating to restrict or to expand the private creation of financial instruments according as the system seems to be expanding or contracting beyond some rather ill-defined limits of tolerance.

Instruments of central bank policy—(1) bank rate, (2) legal reserve ratios. There are four major instruments of such central bank control. Two of these—the "bank rate" (or the rediscount rate) and the legal reserve ratio—operate directly on the commercial banks (called "member banks"). Under the Federal

Reserve System, for instance, commercial banks (if they are members of the Federal Reserve System) can obtain reserves by borrowing from a Federal Reserve Bank, for member bank reserves consist of their deposits at the Federal Reserve Banks. The Federal Reserve Banks can discourage such borrowing by raising the interest rate that member banks have to pay, so making it more profitable for them to replenish their reserves by restricting their own lending to their customers rather than by borrowing from the central bank. The Federal Reserve also has limited powers of changing the legal reserve ratio of the member banks—*i.e.*, the legal minimum ratio of their loans to deposits. By the raising of this legal minimum, banks may be forced to restrict their lending in order to increase their reserve ratio. Insofar as the "expansiveness" of a bank's policy depends on the volume of its "excess reserves" (*i.e.*, the excess of its actual reserves above the legal minimum requirement for its volume of deposits) raising the legal minimum destroys excess reserves, and so discourages expansion of loans and deposits. Lowering the legal minimum creates excess reserves and so encourages expansion. This device is in practice rarely used, and the rediscount rate likewise has declined in importance as a direct instrument of control, though it has importance as a symbol: a rise in the rate is regarded as a storm warning!

(3) **Open market policy.** The other two major instruments of central bank control are "open market policy" and a heterogeneous group of regulations loosely termed "direct control." Open market policy involves the purchase or sale of securities (usually government bonds) by the central bank on the open market. The importance of this activity lies in the fact that when a central bank buys securities it pays for them with its own deposits (known as "federal funds"), which increases the total volume of these deposits. These deposits may originally come into the possession of nonbanking firms (*e.g.*, dealers in government securities) but most of them will end up in the possession of member banks, where they become reserves. When the central bank buys securities, therefore, it almost automatically increases the reserves of member banks and so gives them

a greater potential for expanding their own loans and deposits. Similarly, when a central bank sells securities it diminishes the reserves of member banks and so diminishes their loan and deposit potential.

(4) **Direct controls.** Direct controls are regulations that prohibit or limit certain types of lending and borrowing. Thus there may be restrictions on borrowing for special purposes, such as for house purchase or for consumer durables. These direct controls are apt to be regarded as emergency measures rather than as a part of permanent, long-run policy; nevertheless, they may be increasing in importance. There is also a class of direct controls that set up certain legal limits on the composition of balance sheets. The legal reserve ratio itself is an example. The "margin requirements" for borrowing to purchase stocks is another; this limits the amount that an individual can borrow to buy stock to a certain proportion of his equity. This type of control would seem capable of considerable expansion if circumstances arose to require more direct control of nonbanking institutions by the financial authorities. Certain legal limitations might be imposed, for instance, on the relative proportions of different kinds of assets in corporation balance sheets.

Conflict between central bank and treasury. A problem that almost inevitably arises in a developed financial system is the conflict of roles between the central bank and the government treasury. The relation between these two agencies is bound to be intimate, and presumably their ultimate objectives are much the same. Nevertheless, because of the somewhat different areas within which they operate, and the divergences of their more immediate objectives, conflicts sometimes arise. The over-all operations of government, especially where, as in all modern societies, government arrogates to itself a substantial part of the total economic activity, inevitably produce substantial effects on the financial system. By its cash surplus or deficit, government changes the total volume of liquid assets in private hands. By its debt-management policy government changes the total volume of various forms of government securities in private hands. Thus the raw material of an important segment of the financial system originates in government and is in part controlled by it. Consequently the policies of a central bank may be reinforced or may be contradicted by what is happening in government. A central bank will be helpless to control inflation if government is running heavy cash deficits, and it will be helpless in the face of severe depression unless there is a vigorously expansionist policy in the treasury.

The "government bond standard." An interesting example of the conflict of "immediate objectives" is that between the desire of the treasury to keep interest rates low and maintain the price of government securities and the desire of the central bank to control inflation through open market policy. This conflict has been much in evidence in the United States in the years during and since the second World War. Up to 1951 the "treasury" position dominated, and the Federal Reserve System found itself operating almost on a "government bond standard"—that is, it stood ready to buy (and perhaps to sell) government securities at a fixed price. This meant, of course, that the price in the market could not vary appreciably from the price at which the Federal Reserve Banks were buying. This, however, meant fixing the interest rate on an important financial instrument, which had a tendency to bring the prices of all other financial instruments into a fairly stable relationship with the interest on government securities. If, for instance, the prices of other securities were low enough so that the rate of interest on them was "too high" in relation to the fixed rate on government bonds, people would sell government bonds in order to buy the better-yielding securities, and this would raise the price of these other securities, and lower interest rates yielded by them. As long as the central bank stands ready to buy government bonds in unlimited quantities at a fixed price, therefore, rates of interest can hardly be raised.

—conflicts with inflation control. This means, however, that the ability of the central bank to control inflationary movements in the private economy is practically nil. It has to stand as an unstanchable fountain of funds—and what is worse, of funds that serve as member-bank reserves and so permit themselves to be multiplied several times. It is powerless to raise interest rates or to cut down bank reserves by the sale of securities, as long as it dares not permit a fall in the price of these securities. It is clear that the cost of an active "monetary policy" by the central bank is a certain instability in the price of government securities. This in a sense is the significance of the so-called "accord" between the Treasury and the Federal Reserve System in 1951, which gave the Federal Reserve greater freedom to use open market policy in the interest of controlling inflation.

Monetary and fiscal policy as alternatives. From the point of view of the control of instability, fiscal and monetary policy are to some extent alternatives. If inflation threatens, for instance, we can deal with this *either* by raising tax rates and increasing the cash surplus of government, *or* by raising interest rates and reducing bank reserves. We may, of course, have some combination of the two policies. From the point of view of over-all control of immediate movements in prices or outputs, it may not matter much which we use. From other points of view, however, there are important differences.

Thus, if inflation is fought by increased taxes, this operates mainly by reducing consumption. If it is fought by restricting credit, this operates mainly by reducing investment. If it is fought by "government economy" and restricting government expenditure, this operates mainly by reducing government absorption. Insofar as inflation is a symptom that the economy is trying to "absorb"—in household and government purchases or through additions to capital (investment)—more than it can produce, a reduction in any of these three items will reduce the inflationary pressure, and simply from the point of view of stability there is not much to choose between the three methods. In regard to other objectives of economic policy, however, there are important differences. Thus the avenue of fiscal policy is likely to lead to reduced consumption and increased investment in time of inflationary pressure; this is more favorable to the goal of economic progress than the alternative financial policy of restricting investment through credit restriction. In times of deflation and depression, on the other hand, financial policy aimed at increasing investment, insofar as it can be successful, is more favorable to economic progress than fiscal policy aimed at increasing consumption. The situation here is complicated by the phenomenon of "induced investment," for an increase in consumption owing, say, to lower taxes and budget deficits, may also produce an increase in investment.

Our logic inclines us therefore to a certain prejudice, from the point of view of economic progress, in favor of a combination of fiscal and financial policy in depression, with emphasis on fiscal rather than financial policy in inflation. This conclusion runs somewhat counter to current trends, and we must be careful, of course, not to suppose that anything that favors higher rates of investment is always desirable. Nevertheless, unless increased investment is clearly shown not to be desirable, there remains a certain prejudice in its favor.

Effect of monetary policy on distribution. Further complications arise when we look at the problem from the point of view of economic justice, for here also the effects of the different policies may well be different. In a period of inflation, for instance, a policy of credit restriction and high interest rates inevitably shifts distribution towards the receivers of interest. In the period 1946 to 1956, the proportion of national income going to net interest rose from 1.7 to 3.5 per cent. There is something to be said for a prejudice against such a movement. Interest is the price (and not really a very high price) that we pay for the function of the financial system. These functions are complex, but important, and if they are not performed somehow in a society, trouble ensues. There is, for instance, the important function of enabling active and productive individuals to control more resources than they own. Important as these functions are, however, there is no point in paying any more for them than we have to. It is quite possible that interest might fall to a point where the functioning of the financial system was threatened—something like this happens in long but unforeseen inflations, as in Brazil and France, where the real rate of interest in terms of purchasing power has been sharply negative. Nobody knows, unfortunately, where this minimum point is. If the system seems to be functioning reasonably well, with 2 or 3 per cent of national income going to interest, there seems to be no point in raising this proportion. These considerations, therefore, would again give us something of a prejudice towards the control of inflation by fiscal rather than financial policy. Here again the situation might be quite different in a period of deflation and depression, when financial policy requires a sharp lowering of interest rates.

Who gets interest? We do not know enough about the impact of these various policies on the inequality of income to make good judgments on this score. We cannot be sure, for instance, that a rise in interest rates will make income more unequal, though we have a suspicion that this is so. Insofar as a rise in interest rates results in lower bank charges, in higher income for foundations and charitable institutions, or in higher interest on small savings, the effects might be actually more favorable to the poor, or at least to the middle income groups, than to the rich. There is some suspicion also that credit restrictions fall more severely on small business and on people who are in a somewhat disadvantaged position than on large corporations and on the rich. This, however, is no more than a surmise.

Freedom and finance. Turning now to the more ambiguous, but still important objective of economic freedom, we find again that financial institutions and policies are not neutral, but that the ever-present dilemma of reconciling individual freedom with social control presents itself, not so much in the form of fiscal versus financial policy (which seems to be neutral on this issue) but in terms of the forms of organization of financial institutions. In the United States, for instance, branch banking has been discouraged by state laws, mainly out of fear of the potential power of large, nationwide branch banking systems. In Britain and Canada, on the other hand, there have been no such discouragements and in both countries there are a few large banks with branches throughout the nation, as over against the several thousand small local banks of the United States. Both systems seem to rub along fairly well; the United

States has had in the past a worse record of bank failures, but on the other hand the local banks have been more active in promoting and encouraging local enterprise, and it may well be that the greater dynamism of the American economy may be in part a result of the high degree of local autonomy in the banking system. In this case greater "freedom" (dispersal of power) may have been somewhat favorable to economic progress.

The democratization of credit. A very interesting development in financial policy has been the gradual extension of credit facilities to larger (and poorer) groups in the population, largely under the stimulus of government-sponsored institutions. This movement has important implications for the wider involvement of the mass of the people in the processes of capitalist society—what might be called the "deproletarianization of the masses." A hundred years ago it would not have been unfair to say that access to credit on reasonable terms was a mark of privilege. Sometimes, of course, the poor had credit thrust upon them—as in the iniquitous truck system of wage payment, or in the sharecropper system, where the worker became bound to a single creditor. This is still true in many parts of the world, where the peasant is chronically in debt to a single landlord or moneylender. This situation is deplorable from almost every standpoint; it prevents economic progress, and it is repugnant to our ideas of elementary justice and freedom. Once a society has embarked upon a course of rapid economic growth, however, it seems gradually to be able to lift this burden of "debt-slavery," partly because the growth of income itself beyond the bare subsistence level permits increasing numbers of the poor to save, and partly because of a great proliferation of financial organizations and institutions directed towards extending "creditworthiness" further and further down the economic strata of society. Some of these "democratic" credit institutions are private; the rise of consumer credit, household finance, automobile finance, and mortgage finance until they have become available to a very large proportion of the population is a quiet, almost unperceived movement which is gradually working a remarkable revolution, at least in most Western countries, through the break-up of old monopolies of credit and the opening up to increasing numbers of people of the facilities of a reasonably competitive credit market. Government institutions, or governmentally sponsored institutions, have also played an important part in this movement, especially in agriculture and in housing. Land Banks, Intermediate Credit Banks, the Home Owners Loan Corporation, the Farm Security Administration, and now the Farm and Home Administration are all essentially devices for the democratization of credit, and on the whole they have been very successful. Even the older institutions, however, have played an important part in this movement. Commercial banks, for instance, have been constantly broadening the field of their lending operations. Government has made some contribution here through such institutions as the Federal Deposit Insurance Corporation, which, in the 'thirties at any rate, played an important role in restoring public confidence in the commercial banking system.

The instability of democratized credit. The democratization of credit has its dangers, of course. It may lead to careless credit expansion with subsequent collapse when the uncollectable nature of many of the loans becomes apparent. There may be a certain conflict here between the objectives of progress, justice, and freedom, which are clearly furthered by this movement, and the objective of stability, which may not be. I doubt, however, whether this is a serious objection. There is a certain cost of "democratic credit" in the form of bad debts—these are a not inconsiderable item in the national accounts, having a magnitude of about a billion dollars a year, or about 1/400 of the Gross National Product. This cost is fairly well routinized, however, and can be regarded as a rather sloppy form of income redistribution towards the possibly somewhat less deserving poor. The instability of credit is a problem no matter whether the credit base is broad or narrow; there is not much reason to suppose that a mere broadening of the base makes this problem much more difficult to solve.

Problems may arise, however, as household rather than business debt becomes a larger and larger proportion of the total volume of credit. Households do not respond in the same way as businesses; they are almost certainly less responsive to small interest changes, and more responsive to salesmanship. The control of household credit therefore may require a different set of instruments from those that have proved successful in the case of businesses. There may be a case here for more selective and direct controls than seem appropriate in the business area. The size of the down payment is a particularly important quantity in determining the growth of household credit, and it might be possible to use legal regulation of this fairly simple and observable quantity as the fulcrum from which the general rate of expansion of household credit may be regulated. The main difficulty here is the absence of any satisfactory, simple criterion for determining the "ideal" rate of expansion. It is clear that there must be some rates of expansion of household credit that cannot be maintained, and that must be followed by a contraction, or at least a marked slowdown in expansion. Such a contraction or even slowdown would have sharp deflationary effects which might be hard to offset. At present, however, there seem to be no clear standards, either in theory or in practice, by which the growth of household credit might be regulated.

10

Income maintenance policy

The young, the old, the sick, the crazy
Even the shiftless and the lazy,
Eat at the common human table
Spread by the Active and the Able.
The problem is, to organize
This monumental enterprise
So that—to see that all are boarded—
Both Need and Virtue get rewarded.

The responsibility for income maintenance. All modern states find themselves accepting increased responsibility for the protection of their people from personal economic breakdown. The acceptance of this responsibility leads to the development of a series of somewhat related, and often rather elaborate programs, all of which may be lumped together under the head of "income maintenance." All modern states accept the principle that there is some minimum level of real income below which its individuals or households cannot be allowed to fall. This led, at quite an early date, to the development of "poor laws" or public assistance programs. These provide a certain "floor" of subsistence which is in a sense a "right" of every individual.

In the development of this "right," however, a strong feeling arose that it was somehow shameful to have to exercise it, and those who found it necessary to accept public assistance fell under the stigma of "pauperism." Consequently we now find above the floor of public assistance a complicated set of social security programs—unemployment insurance, old age and survivors' insurance, disability insurance, medical insurance, workman's compensation, widows' and orphans' pensions, aid to dependent children, family allowances, and so on. These programs have grown up in rather piecemeal fashion, partly under the influence of social philosophers like Sidney and Beatrice Webb and Sir William Beveridge in England and John R. Commons in the United States, partly under the influence of social workers, administrators, and civil servants. One suspects that the motivation has come from above rather than below: this was clearly the case in Bismarck's Germany, which pioneered in this field, and where the motivation was nationalistic and antisocialist. In no country does there seem to have been strong pressure from the electorate for the specific plans that were put into operation. Political pressure and dissatisfaction of course there was, but it took the form of broad movements rather than specific pressures—the social democratic movement in Germany, the socialist movement in England, the various radical movements in the United States—and perhaps it is not unfair to interpret the social security program that developed as an essentially "conservative" program to forestall pressures for something more radical. From this point of view the programs have been highly successful; they have contributed a great deal towards "deproletarianization"—the integration of the mass of the people into the general economic fabric—and have greatly increased the degree of general acceptance of the existing institutions. If we no longer live in a revolutionary era, social security must be given a good deal of the credit (or blame, if one is concerned about the soporific effects of security).

Two problems—poverty and redistribution. If now we try to look at the problem in a broad setting it becomes apparent that there are really two rather different problems that these income maintenance programs set out to solve. One is the problem of *poverty* as such—how to prevent any individual or group in a society from falling below some level of economic welfare that is regarded as the acceptable minimum. The other is the problem of "support" or redistribution, not from the rich to the poor, but from the earners (producers) to the non-earners (nonproducers). These problems are not unrelated. The more productive the society, for instance, the easier it becomes to solve both problems. Nevertheless, they are not the same problem, and institutions directed towards solving one will not necessarily solve the other.

Redistribution in the tribe and family. We will consider the problem of support first, as this is the main concern of social security programs. Any society, no matter how primitive, must solve this problem in some way, and it is perhaps the necessity for solving it, at least in the case of mothers and young children, that forces men into societies, and all animals into some device for protecting and raising the young. Among all living creatures there must be a period of growth—in the egg, the womb, the nest, or the family, when the young consume more than they are themselves capable of producing, and their excess consumption must be provided for out of the excess production of the adult members of the group. Among the simpler forms this excess consumption is often provided at or before birth—this is the egg-yolk, the host insect, the wasp larder. In birds and mammals, however, there is almost universally a period when the young are fed and protected by the mature. In human societies this problem is extended to the support of the sick and the old. The sense of solidarity of the group—the sense also, perhaps, of the active producers that the time might come when they themselves would no longer be able to produce—has led to an almost universal institution of group support.

The earliest, and still an important channel for this kind of redistribution is the family itself. Where the family is an extended kinship group comprising tens or perhaps hundreds of persons, or where the tribe takes on many of the social characteristics of the extended family even beyond the boundaries of kinship, this problem is taken care of by the communal organization of such groups. The producers—the food-getters, the clothing-makers, the house-builders—produce for the whole tribe. An individual is not thought of as a unit, rather the whole group is thought of as a single organism, and the problem is taken care of in an "organic" way. Just as in the body the stomach shares with the rest of the system the food that it digests, so in the family or tribe all production is brought into a common pool from which all share.

The "sharing group" as social insurance. Even in quite complex civilizations this problem of sharing the product of the producer with the nonproductive has been left to the family. If the family or the "sharing group" is large enough the group in itself provides a kind of "social insurance"—the sick, the aged, the widows and orphans are taken care of in the larger group. It is when the "sharing group" becomes too small to ensure that there will always be enough producers in it to support the unproductive that devices for "social insurance"—which really involve an extension of the "sharing group" to the whole society—become necessary. When the "sharing group" is small there is always a danger that sheer accident will bring the proportion of earners to non-earners to a level at which the group cannot function properly. Thus, if the sharing group is limited to the "conjugal family"—man, wife, and their children—there is a possibility that the death or incapacity of the principal earner (usually in this case the man) will bring the group below the poverty line. In some cases this problem can be handled by an enlargement of the sharing group beyond the confines of the family, but still short of the society as a whole. Thus many religious groups have "taken care of their own"—

the Mormons are a conspicuous example in American society. The theory of the English Poor Law, which still carries over to a considerable extent in public assistance programs, is that the local community is the sharing group, and the support of the poor must therefore come out of local taxes.

Social security as an extension and formalization of "sharing." Social security therefore represents the coming together of two movements in dealing with the redistribution problem. It represents in the first place an *extension* of the sharing group from the kinship or local or religious community to the national state. Then, mainly because of the size and complexity of the operations involved, it also represents a *formalization* of the sharing arrangements.

In the small group, and especially in the family, the sharing arrangements are informal. No contracts are involved, no precise statement of rights and duties. When needs arise they are taken care of because of certain tacit agreements and understandings—the earning members voluntarily share their earnings with the aged, the children, and the incapacitated. The larger the sharing group the more difficult it is to maintain these informal arrangements, which depend essentially on face-to-face contacts and intimate knowledge of the persons involved. Hence we get an inevitable movement from informal to contractual arrangements, in which the rights and duties are clearly specified and limited, in which the individual pays and receives amounts that are clearly defined by law or by contract.

Private insurance as a contractual sharing group. The formalization of the sharing arrangement permits the growth of *private* insurance, and one of the important problems in this field is the delimitation of the areas in which private and social insurance are most appropriate. Private insurance represents the development of a *contractual* sharing group. The policyholders of an insurance company are in no sense a community—they do not know each other and may never meet each other. Nevertheless, they do form in a sense a sharing group—the premiums constitute payments into a common pool by the "earners," and the benefits represent payments out to "dependents."

If the group is large enough, the premium payments (together perhaps with a certain accumulated reserve) can always take care of current benefits paid. Thus fire insurance is a device for formalizing the contribution of the people whose houses do not burn down to the relief of the people whose houses burn; life insurance is a device for enabling those who survive in a given year to contribute to the estates of those who die, and so on. The insurance company can thus be thought of as a kind of middleman, organizing an exchange by which everybody gives up something (the premium) in return for a right to receive benefits out of these premiums if the event against which he is insured, whether fire, sickness, accident, liability, or death, occurs during the period of the contract.

Social security as a contractualization of "informal" insurance. The contribution of private insurance to the "sharing problem" is an important and a growing one, and must not be neglected in any appraisal of policy. Nevertheless, it is generally felt that the problem is larger than can be dealt with by purely voluntary private insurance, and that therefore private insurance needs to be supplemented, and perhaps in some cases replaced, by a system of compulsory social insurance. The main argument for this proposition is that society has a noncontractual obligation anyway to provide support for those who by reason of accident, illness, youth, or age are nonproductive, and that if it is made a contractual arrangement this contributes to the dignity and self-respect of those who receive the support, and also prevents anyone from evading his obligation to contribute to this support.

Insurance *vs.* support. There are really two principles involved here. The first is the principle of compulsory *versus* voluntary insurance. Here it is assumed that the insurance programs, though compulsory, are actuarially sound—that is, that everybody pays approximately the present value of the chance of his receiving benefits, so that in the mass premiums and benefits (neglecting costs of operation of the program) are equal. The second is the principle of *general support,* by which members of the society receive a contractual right to certain benefits not by reason of the contributions they have paid but by reason of the acceptance by society at large of the obligation to make provision for their "need." In practice almost all social-insurance schemes combine both principles in some degree.

The compulsory insurance principle. The compulsory insurance principle assumes that each individual, or more accurately each primary "sharing group" (*e.g.*, family) in the society can, over its whole lifetime, earn enough to cover its support in both earning and non-earning periods, and for both earning and non-earning members. If everyone in such a situation were rationally motivated, private insurance could take care of the whole problem; everyone would be aware of the evils that might beset him, and would insure against them. It is argued, however, that many people are not so motivated, and that hardly anyone is completely motivated by these rational considerations, and that therefore under a purely voluntary system some will insure and some will not. This means, however, that those who do not insure will have to be supported anyway—perhaps at lower levels and in humiliating and respect-destroying ways—when they are in the nonproductive phase of life, but that they will escape the burden of paying premiums when they are in the productive phase. In fairness to those who insure voluntarily, and in order to maintain the self-respect of those who would not otherwise insure, insurance should be compulsory.

Private *vs.* public insurance. We may accept the principle of compulsory insurance and still leave open the question whether the insurance should be carried out by a state monopoly, by private companies, or by some combination of the two. In practice a great variety of methods are used. In the United States, for instance, Old Age and Survivors' Insurance is carried out by a nationwide government monopoly. Unemployment insurance is carried out by *state* government monopolies. In Workman's Compensation, however, a great variety of plans exist. The insurance is made compulsory (usually on the employer) by state law. Some states, however, rely entirely on private insurance companies, insisting merely that the employer insure, but leaving him free to choose his insurer. Some states have state monopoly insurance organizations with which they compel employers to insure. Some have a mixture of the two systems, and run a state insurance office in competition with private insurance companies, leaving the employer free to choose among them.

The question as to how compulsory insurance should be carried out is quite distinct from the question whether insurance should be compulsory. The case for or against a government monopoly of insurance rests partly on questions of general preference for public as against private enterprise—questions which we shall discuss in the following chapter. It also rests on a certain matter of fact—whether or not there are important economies of scale in the insurance business. If there are these economies—that is, if the cost of administering the insurance declines with every increase in the amount of insurance written—then a state monopoly will almost inevitably be cheaper than a number of competing private companies. If, on the other hand, costs begin to rise beyond a scale of operations that still permits a number of companies to occupy the field, the case for a state monopoly is much weaker. We may venture a hypothesis that where the operations of insurance are fairly routine, the case for state or national monopoly is stronger than where the operations involve great difficulties of *definition* of rights. Thus in Old Age and Survivors' insurance it is usually a fairly routine matter to determine who should get how much in benefits: in the vast majority of cases the fact of death or of age is easily established by a doctor's certificate or a birth record. Here, therefore, we should expect few obstacles to large scale, and the case for a national monopoly is strong. At the other extreme, Workman's Compensation or Disability Insurance involves many difficulties of definition and great opportunity for legal wrangling; it is often very unclear just who is entitled to what. In this case, therefore, the argument in favor of private companies is stronger, though not necessarily conclusive.

The inadequacy of insurance and the need for support. In practice, the principle of compulsory insurance never turns out to be adequate to meet the problem of dependency-redistribution, and always has to be supplemented by some general support. The reason is clear: compulsory insurance can only solve the problem of dependency if everybody belongs to a family or similar sharing group in which over the whole life of the group income is sufficient to take care of dependency needs. Many people do not belong to such groups; moreover, it cannot always be assumed that people who are in this category are in some sense "at fault" or undeserving. There is, of course, some tendency for those in need of general support to belong to "problem cultures" within the society which inhabit depressed areas in both city and country. The problem of general support, however, is by no means confined to the problem cultures, and in the absence of general support many people sink down into the problem cultures who would otherwise not be in them. Thus a family in, say, the lower middle brackets may receive blows of fortune—a chronically sick or incapable child, a serious illness or death of the father, hopeless dependency of aged parents—which in the absence of general support will tend to sink the family below the level of living at which it can "get along" and push it towards criminality or other forms of disorganization. The family income, however, over its whole life, might be quite insufficient to enable it to insure against these calamities at actuarially sound rates. It is considerations such as these that have induced most modern governments to include large elements of general support in their social security programs. Or at least, these considerations which can be used to justify such general support.

Special problems of OASI. We may now turn to some special problems relating to particular income maintenance programs. Probably the most far-reaching of these programs, and certainly the one that involves the greatest sums of money, is the Old Age and Survivors' Insurance, often abbreviated to OASI. Several problems of interest arise here. There is first the problem of how—and from whom—the contributions should be assessed and levied, assuming—as seems to be universally accepted—that the scheme should be contributory. Somewhat related is the question of the amounts and conditions of benefits. Then there is an instructive controversy regarding the necessity—or lack of necessity—for accumulating a reserve fund. Finally, we may raise some questions regarding the over-all impact of such a program on the economy, especially from the point of view of our four standard objectives—progress, stability, freedom, and justice.

The incidence of social security contributions. It is the common practice in many social insurance programs to collect contributions both from workers and from employers, and in some programs (for example, in Great Britain) from the general funds of the government. No matter what the formula for collection, however, the contributions are virtually indistinguishable from taxes and should be considered as part of the tax system. The problem of incidence—that is, "who really pays" the taxes—is a difficult one, perhaps the most difficult problem in the whole of economics, and we cannot go into it deeply here. We must distinguish between the "impact effect," which is what happens when the taxes are newly imposed, and the long-run effects after all the various adjustments that people can make have been made. The situation is complicated because the *total* effect on the economy of such a program depends on the size and distribution of the benefits as well as of the contributions. There is certainly no expectation that the ultimate effects will correspond to the apparent or legal basis of the payments.

Thus, suppose that the contribution is paid half by the worker and half by the employer. When the tax is first imposed, the impact effect may fall about half on the worker and half on the employer—the worker finds his take-home pay is immediately reduced by the amount of *his* contribution, the employer finds his costs immediately raised by the amount of *his* contribution. If, however, there is a general inflationary trend in the economy, the employer will not find it hard to raise the prices of his product, especially as all his competitors likewise find themselves in the same position of having to pay the tax, so that the employer's tax may be shifted to the purchasers of his product —who may, of course, be workers in other industries. Similarly, the workers may press for increased pay to offset the tax, which may in turn be passed on. It is almost impossible to say where this comes out in the end. One thing, however, we can be fairly sure of: it will not make much difference to the final result as far as the distribution of income is concerned whether the tax is levied wholly on the employer, wholly on the worker, or is divided between them.

Psychological effects of various modes of payment. The psychological effects of the method of assessing contributions, however, may be important, even if the economic effects are seldom what they seem. Where the worker has a contribution assessed as a deduction from his nominal wage he seems to feel more deeply associated with the program—the money that has been collected is "his." The rights to benefit seem to be "earned" in a way that is not perceived when the contributions come out of the general amorphous tax collections. For this reason alone it is probably worth while to continue the "fiction" of contributions from workers, in spite of the doubt about the ultimate incidence of these contributions and the greater simplicity of a program of finance out of general taxes. There is a perceptible difference, for instance, between the attitude of workers towards Old Age and Survivors' insurance (to which they make a formal contribution) and their attitude towards Workman's Compensation, where the premiums are paid wholly by the employer.

Reserve funds in private pension plans. The question of a reserve fund for an OASI program has been a matter of great controversy, with many facets. The concept of a reserve fund arises from the analogy with private insurance and pension funds. If a private pension fund is to be actuarially sound it should at all times have a net worth at least equal to the present value of the future benefits to which the existing contributors are entitled. It is possible, of course, to run pension funds—and some labor unions have actually tried this—on a purely current basis, collecting each year from the contributors an amount sufficient to pay the benefits. The difficulty with such a scheme is that if it ever ceases operation a grave injustice has been done to those who have been paying contributions through the years and who will now be deprived of benefits. In order to avoid this possibility, it is considered wise for a private pension plan to accumulate reserves in its early years when collections are high and benefit payments low, so that in later years even if the plan ceases current operation those who have built up an equity in the fund by contributing will be able to receive at least the present value, at compound interest, of their contributions.

The "fiction" of a social security reserve fund. The arguments that are so cogent in the case of the private pension fund are much less applicable, however, when we look at the economics of a compulsory security program covering the mass of the population. Here, presumably, the continuance of the plan into the indefinite future, short of the kind of collapse of society that would also make any reserve fund worthless, is almost to be taken for granted. Furthermore, when we look at society as a whole, it is clear that the old, the sick, and the indigent are in fact supported out of the current production of the working population. The bread that the old eat was baked yesterday, from wheat sown last year, it was not "saved up" from what they abstained from consuming a generation ago when they were young, active, and thrifty!

An even more weighty argument against a reserve fund is that even if one is set up on a national scale it must take the form either of government securities or of private securities. If it takes the form of government securities it becomes, in effect, a device for paying off the national debt. Government securities are, in effect, repurchased by another agency of government (the social security fund); government pays itself interest out of one pocket into another, and the whole procedure takes on a curious air of unreality. If the plan were to cease operation, while maintaining the rights of existing participants in the equity they had accumulated through their years of contributions, the benefits paid to these residual beneficiaries would still have to be financed largely out of current taxes or by the sale of government securities to the public (that is, by increasing the national debt). Though there may be some case, therefore, for paying off the national debt out of the excess contributions of a social security fund, the purchase of government securities by such a fund would seem to be a purely paper operation, in no way analogous to the funds of private pension plans. If the fund tried to build up a portfolio of private securities the very size of the operations of such a national fund would play havoc with the securities markets, would force up the price of private securities to inappropriate levels; and again, any attempt to liquidate such a fund would cause a collapse in the price of private securities and therefore in the value of the fund itself.

Psychological value of a social security fund. The main justification for a social security fund, held in the form of government securities (which seems to be the only practicable plan), is again largely psychological. It gives the contributors, especially those (the great majority) who are not sophisticated in ways of economic reasoning, a sense of security, of having something "there" which represents an equity they have built up out of their contributions. It may be doubted, however, whether the psychological value of a fund approaches, say, the psychological value of a "worker's contribution." In fact, fund or no fund, there is very little sense among the contributors to social security funds of building up an "equity," simply because the accounting is not done in this way. Only that very small minority of contributors who request it receive any statement of their present accumulations from the Social Security Board. In fact, such a statement would be almost meaningless, because of the increasing shift from the pure saving or insurance principle to the "general support" principle mentioned above. Under the present plan, the present value of the future rights to benefits are much greater, for young people and for people who have not been working long, than the accumulated value of their contributions. This came about largely out of a desire on the part of Congress to avoid a long period of a generation or more when most current contributors would not be provided with even the very modest level of benefits that the plan contemplated. In a sense, therefore, we have moved to what is almost a currently financed plan, although the form of the accumulating fund remains. In strict logic it would seem sensible to advocate a frank recognition of this fact and the abandonment of any attempt to build up a reserve fund. Strict logic, however, seldom governs political affairs, and at least in the present condition of mild inflation there is a lot to be said for building up a social security reserve—not for its intended purpose, of course, but as a measure against inflation. It seems to be one of the ironies of economic policy that frequently a device that is quite useless for its avowed purpose turns out to be very useful for some purpose that was never in the minds of its inventors.

Evaluation of OASI. Let us now take a look at OASI from the point of view of the major policy objectives. On the score of economic progress we find ourselves adrift on a large sea of ignorance. It has been argued that social security will destroy incentives to progress, and that by making people "security minded" it will produce a stagnant, timid generation, unwilling to take risks for improvement, content to jog along in a comfortable rut with a little pension at the end of it, and the end of it all will be that we will all be engulfed by the rentier mentality. On the other hand, it can be argued that by putting a floor, as it were, under failure, we induce people to take more risks and to be more enterprising, knowing that society at least provides them a cushion if their risks turn out to be bad. There is very little evidence for either of these views, though I confess I incline to the second. In the absence of further information the best guess would seem to be that as far as the motivational aspects of economic progress are concerned, social security makes little difference. A case for building up a social security reserve can be made on the grounds that it will help capital formation by enabling us to maintain a higher rate of investment without inflation. This argument, however, really carries us over into the second objective—economic stability.

Has social security made for *instability* of the economy? It is in connection with the impact of social security on the stability of the economy that the most interesting questions arise. There is little doubt, for instance, that the depression of 1937-38 in the United States was set off largely by the introduction of the social security plan. In the first few years of operation the plan involved much larger collections than benefits. It amounted, therefore, to a substantial increase in tax collections and in the cash surplus of government. Indeed, social security collections actually moved the government from a cash deficit in 1936 to a substantial cash surplus in 1937. At a time when there were still over ten million unemployed this was sheer fiscal foolishness, and we thoroughly deserved the depression of 1937. On the other hand, during the inflationary war and postwar years social security acted as a somewhat deflationary force—again through its excess of collections over benefit payments—and so was all to the good. Unfortunately the liberalization of social security has come along again in a somewhat inflationary period, and makes control of the inflation all the harder. Looking over the years, therefore, one can argue that the contribution of social security to the stability of the economy has been somewhat negative. This is particularly true of OASI; it is not true of unemployment insurance, as we shall see.

Justice and freedom furthered by social security. In regard to the third and fourth objectives—justice and freedom—there can be little doubt that social security scores high. Indeed, the quest for social security has on the whole been motivated by a search for justice—by the feeling that without some plan of social security society is desperately unjust to great numbers of those who have served it well, but who by reason of age, infirmity, illness, or accident are no longer in a position to earn income, and who have not been able to provide for these contingencies by their own efforts. Social security is a symbol of the acknowledgement of the responsibility of each for all, the "brotherhood of man." It is, of course, a formalization and bureaucratization of brotherhood; it lacks the deep human relationships that are found in the small group and that are so necessary to the full and rich life. It does not solve the problems of loneliness, of unwantedness, and the consequent disintegration of character that comes over people in old age or in chronic disability, especially when they do not have the affection and support of a small group.

Some have worried about whether social security might not undermine the small sharing group, especially the family, by taking the burden of support of the aged from those most immediately involved in giving psychological support—the children. There is much to be said, however, on the other side. The necessity for economic support, especially where this involves "doubling up," with grandparents, for instance, living in the same household as grandchildren, often creates tensions that undermine the psychological support and have seriously disruptive effects on the family unity. The "freedom" that social security gives to the aged and the dependent, small as it is, should help rather than hinder the development of that psychological support without which economic support is little more than the perpetuation of misery.

The problem of coverage. The main problems of "justice" in social security are, first, in regard to the coverage of the plan, and second, in regard to the *level* of benefits (and indirectly, of contributions). No existing social security plan covers the whole population. The usual history of such plans is that they start with the industrial working population; here the collection of contributions is fairly easy to organize by way of payroll deductions—the employer in effect can be made to administer many of the more routine details of the plan. Once a plan is in operation, however, the demands of simple justice press for its extension—to the self-employed, to professional groups, to agricultural workers, and so on. The ideal is clearly that the plan should cover the whole population, and though no plan so far has quite achieved this objective, we have been moving fairly rapidly towards it.

The problem of adequacy. The problem of what is an "adequate" level of benefits is more difficult. The answer inevitably depends not on what would be desirable if there were no economic problem—that is, no scarcity of resources—but on what society feels it can "afford," and this depends on a very complex set of factors—its actual income, the strength of the sense of obligation towards the dependent, and the strength of the claims of alternative uses of resources, for progress or for national ambitions. The higher the level at which the dependents are supported, the less resources are left for other uses. It is clearly conceivable that a society might support its dependent population at such a high level that its ability to invest, or its incentives to productivity, or its military potential, might be seriously impaired. It is highly doubtful whether any modern society is even within sight of such a situation; however, it must be carried in mind as an upper limit.

Even in rich societies like that of the United States the problem of the size of dependent population grows constantly in importance because of the very success of modern medicine in keeping people alive. The proportion of old people, for instance, continuously grows and will grow much more if present trends continue. It is probable that the proportion of people incapacitated by sickness will likewise grow—people who in former times would have died at an early age now are enabled to live on in sickness without quite being restored to health. We thus have the paradoxical result that the more and better medical care we have, the more sickness there is. Unfortunately, the incapacitating diseases of middle and later life seem to be most resistant to modern medicine and seem to be most encouraged by modern habits of living. In previous times only the tough and disease-resistant lived on into middle life, and only the very tough into old age. We have now largely conquered the diseases that used to carry people off in youth and early adulthood, with the result that degenerative and incapacitating disease is likely to become an increasingly serious social problem.

Inflation and "adequacy." There is no golden formula for quick and simple decisions on what constitutes an adequate level of benefits. If the level of benefits in a social security program is so low that a substantial proportion of the people whom it is supposed to protect fall in fact into poverty, or disorganization, or pauperization, obviously something is wrong, and levels should be raised. If, on the other hand, a society shows a chronic tendency to inflation, this is a symptom that it is trying to "live beyond its means" and to devote to *all* the competing uses—support of dependents, wages, investment, profits, and national government—more than it is capable of producing. One of the principal effects of inflation is the erosion of the real income provided for the dependent population, whether this be social security benefits, private pensions, or income from bonds and private savings. In a sense, therefore, we might say that inflation is a symptom that society is spending too much on *something*, and is a tacit undertaking to cut down on the most "expendable" use of resources, which turns out to be the support of dependents. Inflation is a refined method of taking bread out of the mouths of the aged, the infirm, the widows and the orphans, and feeding it to soldiers, to productive laborers, or to profit-makers. After every rise in the cost of living, of course, there is strong pressure to increase the money benefits (and less enthusiastically, the contributions) of the social security plan. If this pressure is successful, and if the other commitments of the society are not reduced, the problem of "overcommitment" is still unsolved and inflation will continue; the system is fundamentally unstable, and will remain so until a more honest and conscious decision in regard to what the society can afford is made.

"Private" social security by collective bargaining. One final phenomenon should be noted before we leave the subject of provision for old age and disability. There is an increasing tendency in American society for labor unions to press for, and to obtain, pension plans and health and disability insurance in their union contracts. This movement arises partly out of a widespread feeling that the government social security plans provide an inadequate level of benefits and need to be supplemented by private plans, and also because of a feeling that wage increases in the form of these "fringe benefits" are easier both to get and to give than straight wage increases. The growth of these private pension plans has been spectacular, and their impact on the economy is substantial. The movement for a "guaranteed annual wage" likewise can be interpreted as motivated in part by a sense of the inadequacy of unemployment insurance benefits.

Dangers of private plans. There are real dangers in this movement for private pensions, especially from the point of view of the worker who apparently benefits. Insofar as the plan is confined to a particular employer, the worker loses his rights under the plan when he changes his employer. This means that he is financially tied to his present employment and that his freedom of action in the labor market is very severely curtailed. This may lead eventually to a weakening of the bargaining position of the union, especially if the industry is declining relative to the rest of the economy. It is possible, of course, to guard against this feature of the plans—generally speaking, the more firms and industries are involved in the plan, the less objection there is to it on the score of the above considerations. It is also possible, of course, to provide for withdrawal from the plan by giving the worker the right to his accumulated equity at any time, after perhaps a reasonable minimum period, when he withdraws from the employment that entitles him to participate. It would not be necessary to have the withdrawal take the form of a cash payment, but rather the form of a pension right equivalent to the amount withdrawn. There are also strong possibilities of misuse of union pension funds, and there have been some unfortunate cases.

There is much to be said, therefore, for taking these funds out of the control of the union (or the company) officials and setting them up as an independent agency. There is much need for legislation on this matter. The problem of the impact of these large pension funds on the financial markets, and the implication for financial policy, is also extremely interesting, and has not received adequate study. Insofar as saving becomes increasingly institutionalized either through private pension plans or through life insurance, the "institutional investor"—the pension-plan administrator or the life insurance company—plays an increasingly important role in financial markets. His standards and patterns of behavior are different from those of the private investor, and he may not respond to the more traditional methods of monetary and financial policy.

The "special" insurances—unemployment, disability, etc. We must now go on to take a look at some of the special problems involved in other forms of social insurance. Unemployment insurance, health and disability insurance, and Workman's Compensation differ from Old Age and Survivors' mainly in the fact that the events that call for benefits are much less universal. Everyone can look forward to getting old, if he does not die first. Not everyone necessarily becomes unemployed for long periods, or becomes disabled, or has an accident. Most of the special problems of these other forms of social security arise out of the lack of universality of the contingencies against which they insure.

Experience rating: the "social cost" argument. This lack of universality leads to a demand, for instance, for *experience rating*. By this is meant the attempt to proportion the contribution at least roughly to the risks involved by basing it on the past experience of the contributor. Any attempt to apply the "pure insurance" rather than the "general support" principle will lead to some kind of experience rating. The economic case for this is strongest when the insurance covers different "social costs" in different industries. Thus, suppose one industry is much more liable to industrial accidents of a disabling nature than another. It is argued that the dangerous occupations should pay the full social costs of the dangers involved; otherwise these occupations are in effect being subsidized by society at large, and they will attract more resources than is socially desirable. Thus a dangerous industry should bear the costs of supporting and rehabilitating those whom it disables, and the dependents of those it kills—otherwise the price of its product will be too low, and people will be too much encouraged to buy it.

Suppose, to take an extreme example, that we have two industries, *D* (for dangerous) and *S* (for safe), and that their products compete for the same use (for example, lumber or brick in the building of houses). If *D* is not charged with its "human cost" the price of *D*'s product may be lower than *S*'s product, and *D* will tend to expand at the expense of *S*. This low price of *D*'s product, however, is a fraud: it hides a subsidy that society is paying in the form of general support of the disabled and the dependents that the industry creates relative to *S*. Industry *D*, therefore, should certainly be taxed to the point where the price of its product is sufficient to cover the full social cost, and people will not be deceived by its apparent cheapness. One way to do this is force industry *D*, based on its previous accident and disability experience, to pay a much higher premium or contribution in any plan for disability insurance or Workman's Compensation.

The self-improvement argument. Another argument for experience rating is that it encourages firms and industries that have a "poor" rating to improve themselves, because improvement in their record will lead to a lowering of their contributions or premiums. If these "social costs" are taken care of by general support and do not fall on the firm, there is no incentive for the firm to reduce them. If, however, the firm has to pay for the human losses and dependencies that result from its operations, it will gain by investment in reducing them. In the case of Workman's Compensation there is evidence that experience rating, as reflected in differential insurance premiums, has motivated a good deal of investment in safety.

The case is much less clear in regard to unemployment insurance. There is not the same close connection between the experience of a firm in regard to fluctuations in its labor force and its policies that there is between its safety record and its policies —that is to say, fluctuations in employment may not lie within the power of the individual firm to correct. There may be an exception to this in the case of seasonal fluctuations. It is argued, for instance, that just as a firm with a high accident rate incurs a social cost that should appear in its books, so a firm with highly seasonal employment incurs a social cost, because the workers must be supported by society when they become unemployed, and it is only fair that the firm or industry that causes the unemployment should bear the cost. Unfortunately the matter is not so simple; part of the seasonality of employment is compensated for by higher wages, and part may be offset by counterseasonality in other occupations. Thus professors were once supposed to earn enough in nine months' teaching to enable them to devote themselves to self-improvement during the summer; building-trades and construction workers are compensated in some degree for the seasonality and irregularity of their occupation by a higher hourly wage; men who work in lumbering in the winter often work on farms in the summer, and so on. The problem of measuring the "true" contribution of a single firm or even an industry to the social cost of unemployment is therefore very difficult, and almost any administratively practicable plan for experience rating in this area is likely to run into as many inequities as it proposes to rectify.

Unemployment insurance as a stabilizer. The problem of unemployment insurance is further complicated by the fact that up to the present, at least, general depressions have been a much more important source of unemployment than the seasonal or even long-run vicissitudes of particular industries. Insofar, therefore, as serious depressions are a result of a failure of economic policy, what we are really insuring against in unemployment insurance is incompetence or ignorance in government. This is a contingency for which it is hard to develop empirical probabilities! Consequently, it is almost impossible to say whether any unemployment insurance plan is actuarially sound. A serious depression will bankrupt any plan; long-continued prosperity leads to absurd accumulation of reserves. However, unemployment insurance has the great virtue of being "regulative" of fluctuations, or "anticyclical." When output turns down and unemployment rises, the unemployment insurance fund automatically begins to show a deficit, as contributions decline and benefits rise. The unemployment insurance fund, therefore, operates to pump money into the economy and to maintain incomes when deflation is threatening. Similarly in periods of full employment the fund runs a persistent surplus, which operates as an anti-inflationary force. Unemployment insurance is a "built-in stabilizer" for the economy. It should be observed that once any social security plan is in steady operation, in which contributions depend on income, it acts as a built-in stabilizer in a milder degree, because a decline in income automatically leads to a decline in contributions without necessarily any decline in benefit payments. Thus, even though as we noted earlier Old Age and Survivors' Insurance has actually been an antistabilizer in the period of setting up, once this is in steady operation it, too, will act in some degree as a stabilizer.

Health and disability insurance. Perhaps the thorniest problems in the social insurance field revolve around health and disability insurance. Great Britain has an elaborate scheme of health insurance which virtually ensures the population a minimum standard of free medical care purely on a basis of self-perceived need. The United States has not yet seen fit to enact such a program, in spite of several attempts to do so, largely because of the very vociferous opposition of the American Medical Association. The problem of administering a nationwide plan of health insurance is much more difficult in a large, heterogeneous country like the United States than in a small, homogeneous country like Great Britain. Nevertheless, it cannot be claimed that the existing system of medical economics is satisfactory. It is a curious mixture of extremely socialized medicine under the Veterans Administration, and extremely private medicine for much of the rest of the population, with an important and increasing in-between sector of what might be called "privately socialized medicine"—labor union health plans, Blue Cross hospitalization and White Cross surgical insurance, private health and disability insurance, Workman's Compensation, various state disability and rehabilitation schemes, cooperative clinics, and so on.

It can be argued that for the mass of the population the problem of medical economics is being worked out privately and locally, without the need for national intervention. One cannot feel wholly satisfied with this argument, however. There is always the minority of the population who cannot, or do not, take care of their medical needs through private action. The British scheme when it first went into operation after the war revealed a hitherto unsuspected backlog of medical, dental, and optical needs which had not been met under the previous system; there is little doubt that any society would find the same, and that the investment in taking care of these needs would almost certainly pay off in terms of human happiness and productivity. Even for the mass of the population whose needs are at least partially met by private methods there remains one quite unsatisfied need—the need for what is called "major medical" insurance. Most people in the United States, it is argued, can take care of casual or minor medical needs; a major medical bill, however, of several thousand dollars is a catastrophe almost worse than the disease, and the medical profession itself is faced with the charge of preserving people only to pauperize them.

The problem of poverty: the "poverty-culture." At the beginning of the chapter I distinguished between the redistribution-dependency problem on the one hand and the more fundamental problem of poverty on the other. Up to this point most of the discussion has related to the first problem, because most of the policy has been in this direction. We have conceived the problem on the whole as one of protecting the individual from inability to share in the blessings of an essentially productive and rich society. When we look at the world as a whole, however, and even when we look more closely at certain subcultures within the rich societies, we see that the problem of poverty is not merely one of accident, or old age, or some temporary condition of the individual. There are what might be called "poverty-cultures"—whole nations, or groups within a nation, where the *average* level of income is inadequate to maintain a "decent" life even on very minimal standards. As a world problem poverty is not so much the result of exploitation, or of a failure of generosity towards the dependent and the temporarily unproductive; it is the result of the existence of whole cultures where per-capita output is inadequate to sustain a decent minimum standard. Even within American society the poverty of the southern tenant farmer, of the northern slum, of the "hillbilly," is a problem of self-perpetuating subcultures, secreting poverty as bees secrete honey, rather than the kind of problem that is dealt with by social insurance.

The stability of poverty-cultures. The forces that create, perpetuate, or improve these poverty cultures are complex in the extreme, and we cannot hope to deal with them here. Indeed, to a very large extent we do not know what these forces are:

we can only surmise that they extend deep into the religion and the family life of the culture as well as into its economic institutions, and that a full account of these forces cannot be given by economics alone. Where these cultures are stable—and many of them are deplorably stable—it often seems to take a considerable force from outside to stir them out of their miserable equilibrium into a process of steady improvement. This force may be a missionary bringing a new religion, a trader bringing new opportunities for exchange, a national government bringing schools, roads, teachers, doctors. Occasionally, of course, a prophet or innovator arises from inside a culture—as Mohammed arose, for instance, within the stagnant culture of the Arab tribes and set off a revolutionary process of change that carried the Arabs to world dominance in the space of a century.

We understand all too little of these forces. The persistence of poverty and disorganization, not only in the poor nations but also in the depressed and substandard cultures even within rich societies, is proof of our ignorance. Crime, poverty, and social disorganization persist in spite of—or perhaps even because of—the elaborate apparatus we have set up to deal with it. One has an uneasy feeling that the whole system of courts, police, and prisons, social work agencies and charities, detention homes, poor relief, and so on actually helps to perpetuate the condition that it is intended to cure. Yet in our present state of knowledge it is hard to propose any substitutes, or even any very radical reforms of the existing system. One can only hope that if the problem is perceived as a whole, one day we will be able to deal with it as a whole.

11

Commercial policy and international economics

Economists have long portrayed
The excellent effects of Trade,
And frown upon the wayward nation
That seeks to live in isolation,
And though their arguments declare
That Trade should not be free as Air,
Yet broad considerations lead 'em
To have a prejudice for Freedom.

"Foreign" and "international" economic policy. Many of the most difficult and pressing problems a government has to face arise out of the circumstance that the government is not universal—that is, it is not a world government. Its sovereignty extends only to a limited area of the earth's surface and to a portion of the human race. It is surrounded by other nations of varying degrees of hostility or friendliness. Consequently, it usually feels obliged to make provisions for national defense and for the maintenance or expansion of its economic and military power. It also must face that fact that its economy is not a closed, self-contained system, but that it is intimately bound with the economies of other nations through imports and exports of commodities, people, money, and securities. The effects of its economic acts therefore will "leak out" to other countries, and the effects of economic policies and movements in the rest of the world will "leak in."

Under these circumstances almost all national governments indulge in measures for "economic defense." These generally involve attempts to create a certain degree of isolation from the rest of the world through deliberate restrictions of immigration, trade, foreign exchange, or investment. It is these attempts at economic defense against unwanted impacts from the rest of the world that constitute what might be called "foreign" economic policy—that is, unilateral policy on the part of one nation directed towards regulating its economic relations with foreigners. Because the "system" of foreign economic policies tends frequently towards mutual impoverishment on the "beggar my neighbor" principle, there has been an increasing demand for *international* economic policy which would coordinate foreign economic policies for the mutual benefit of all nations. This demand finds expression in the creation of international economic institutions such as the International Monetary Fund, the World Bank for Reconstruction and Development, and the Economic and Social Council of the United Nations.

Immigration policy. Foreign economic policies on the part of a single nation revolve around the four major items of input and output of the national economy—people, goods (including services), money, and securities. The input or output of people is controlled by immigration policy. The problem here has both a quantitative and a qualitative aspect. Quantitatively, we might divide countries into those that are below their optimum population and those that are above. Those that are below will certainly wish to encourage immigration, and those above may be expected to encourage emigration. If the world were culturally and economically homogeneous we might suppose that people would move from the overpopulated to the underpopulated countries, thereby raising per-capita incomes in all countries, and the interest of each would be the interest of all. Unfortunately, such an idyllic harmony is a highly special case. It may be, for instance, that all countries are beyond their optimum population, but some more than others. In this case if migration is unrestricted people will move from the *relatively* overpopulated countries to the *relatively* underpopulated ones, but this movement, while it raises the per-capita incomes of the first, may reduce the per-capita incomes of the second, if these are now beyond their optimum populations. In this case national interest may demand immigration restrictions on the part of the receiving countries in order to maintain their differential advantage in income. The less populated countries may thereby preserve incomes above the world average by keeping people out, even though this lessens human welfare as a whole. Here a conflict between the national and the world interest arises.

Emigration cannot solve the Malthusian problem. The above model is essentially static; when we take dynamic considerations into view the problem becomes much more complicated. Thus a country that is in a Malthusian equilibrium, where only the low level of living keeps the population from expanding, may be quite unable to solve its population problem by emigration. Every adult who emigrates releases foodstuffs and other necessities that will permit one or even more extra children to survive—hence emigration may even increase the growth of population, and the country becomes a perpetual source of emigrants. The emigration merely spreads the poverty that the unlimited reproduction has produced to other parts of the world, and does nothing to relieve the problem of overpopulation at home. Even on the criteria of world interest, therefore, there is something to be said for restricting migration from countries of genuine Malthusian pressure and for protecting countries that maintain reasonable population control from floods of immigrants. The problem is further complicated by the dynamics of the short run. Paradoxically, it may be easier to maintain full employment with a large than with a small volume of immigration. A large volume of immigrants creates demand for new investment. On the other hand, a large volume of immigrants of working age creates a distortion in the age distribution which may have an unfavorable effect on consumption—the immigrants may be "high savers." The over-all effects are thus very complicated, though it should not be too difficult to offset any unfavorable effects by fiscal or monetary policy.

Qualitative aspects of immigration. The qualitative aspects of immigration are very difficult to reduce to simple terms, and carry us beyond the usual boundaries of economics. Nations have varying degrees of desire for cultural or racial homogeneity, and this may affect their immigration policies. The occupational and social status of immigrants is also frequently a matter of concern; those immigrants whose special skills are in short supply are naturally welcomed more enthusiastically than those whose services are a drug on the market. Sometimes the need for special occupational groups overcomes any prejudice that might exist in favor of cultural homogeneity, and immigration of people of different culture or color from the predominant group is encouraged, or even forced—the African slave trade is an unsavory example of such "forced" migration; the immigration of indentured Indian laborers into South Africa is another. At other times the desire for cultural homogeneity or racial purity is so strong that groups are excluded who would be a valuable asset to the economy—the immigration policy of the United States since 1924 seems to be a case in point.

The protectionist controversy. Regulations affecting the import or export of commodities are even more common than those that affect the migration of people. A long dispute has been going on both inside economics and between economists and the "men of affairs" ever since the eighteenth century on the question of "free trade" versus "protection." The economists, on the whole, have been free traders; businessmen and politicians have just as consistently been protectionist. The literature is enormous, and the arguments are frequently subtle. The outlines of the controversy, however, are simple.

The case for free trade—that is, for a minimum of governmental interference with imports or exports—is by and large the case for specialization. The tariff—that is, a tax levied on imports—is equivalent to an increase in the cost of transport of the taxed commodity at the national boundary where the tax is imposed. Bastiat, a famous (and rather dogmatic) French free trader called tariffs "negative railroads"—a railroad being a device to diminish the cost of transport between two places, and a tariff being a device to increase it! The analogy is not quite fair, as a railroad presumably decreases the cost of transport in both directions between two places, whereas a tariff only increases it in one. Still, the general effect of a system of tariffs is to increase the economic distance of nations one from another. This inevitably diminishes the degree of local specialization, as we can see very readily if we imagine the process carried to the extreme where the distance becomes infinite and the nations are completely cut off from economic intercourse. In that case each nation would have to produce everything that it needed at home, and would not be able to benefit from resources outside its boundaries.

The case for free trade. The advantages of trade and specialization are twofold. In the first place, it enables the special resources of each to be used for the mutual benefit of all—the fruits of the tropics turn up on breakfast tables all over the world, and the products of local mines similarly enjoy a wide distribution. In the second place, it permits the concentration of production of particular commodities in particular areas, such as automobiles in Detroit, and so enables us to enjoy the economies of large scale, where these exist. The case for free trade, then, rests on the simple principle that it is foolish to produce at home directly things that can be obtained more cheaply (that is, with a smaller expenditure of real resources) by specialization and exchange. That is, if we can get commodity *A* cheaper by making *B* and exchanging it for *A* with someone else, it is foolish to cut ourselves off from these benefits by insisting on making *A* directly at home. It should be noted that this is not an argument for reciprocal free trade, but for unilateral free trade: no matter what tariffs are imposed by other countries, on the above argument it would still pay any one country to adopt free trade, because no matter what the system of exchange opportunities may be, *any* restriction of these opportunities makes *everybody* worse off in the long run—including the nation imposing the restrictions.

Arguments against free trade. This argument, of course, is much too strong, and various modifications—some very elaborate and sophisticated—have been accepted by economists. Most of these come down to showing that there are disadvantages as well as advantages of specialization, and that free trade may lead to too much specialization. Even Adam Smith, who is usually thought of as the great advocate of free trade, recognized many exceptions. His famous statement that "defense is more important than opulence" indicates that specialization, while it increases the wealth, may diminish the power of a nation, by placing it in too great a degree of economic dependence on others. Adam Smith was also worried about the effects of too-great specialization on the character of a people—he preferred the virile and adaptable character of the relatively unspecialized farmer to the narrow and cramped personality of the specialized machine operator.

When dynamic considerations are taken into account, the case for pure free trade becomes still weaker. There is, for instance, the "infant industry" argument. This argues that certain industries that could not survive in a particular locality (for instance, an underdeveloped country) without some protection or subsidy might be able to grow to the point where they no longer needed protection, as their costs would fall with increasing scale and cumulating experience. There is the even more important "external economies" argument, which says that certain industries, which again might not be able to survive without some form of support, yield benefits to the rest of the economy that are not reflected in the price of their products, and hence should be supported for the sake of these unpriced benefits. This is closely linked with the "balanced growth" argument, that a national economy that becomes too highly specialized does not grow as fast as one that is less specialized and contains a number of mutually complementary components. An argument of a somewhat different nature is the argument from uncertainty—that specialization exposes the specializer to the uncertainties involved in dependence on others, and especially in the possibilities of serious loss owing to "sudden changes in the channels of trade." The question as to how far one wants to be safely poor rather than insecurely rich is, of course, a difficult one.

The concept of "desirable distortions": subsidies *vs.* tariffs. Most of the objections to freedom of trade involve what might be called "desirable distortions" of the economy away from that distribution of resources among industries and occupations that might be expected under free trade. The mere demonstration that some distortions might be desirable, however, is not in itself an argument for trade restrictions, for there might be other, and more satisfactory ways of bringing about the same distortions. Thus, a direct subsidy to an industry which it is desired to preserve—either for defense, or for its possible nonfinancial contributions to the society, or for its importance in economic growth—might be preferable to a tariff. Here, however, we get into very difficult welfare considerations involving the political process. Trade restrictions once established are hard to change, but subsidies have to be appropriated yearly. This fact cuts both ways; regulations, like tariffs, can more easily become obsolete than subsidies, and many quite unnecessary trade restrictions survive simply because of inertia. Subsidies, on the other hand, because of the usual necessity for annual renewal, involve a great deal of energy in lobbying and political activity which might better be spent in technical improvement. Also the history of the agricultural subsidies indicates that when there is a powerful pressure group behind a subsidy this also is extremely difficult to get rid of.

Political reasons for protection: concentrated gain *versus* diffuse loss. The reasons why on the whole protection is popular whereas free trade is not lie in the nature of the political system rather than in any strictly economic arguments. Indeed, the arguments that might be used by an economist to justify protection on the ground of the general interest are much too subtle, and too little capable of factual and political content to have much influence on the decisions of governments. The success of protection therefore does not rest on these subtle arguments, but on a very simple principle of politics—that concentrated and present benefits and losses have much more political influence than diffuse and remote ones. The benefits of trade restriction are concentrated and present; they are confined to a small and frequently a well organized group. The losses are broadly diffused over the whole society in the form of higher prices of the protected articles, and do not hit anyone severely. The gains moreover are in the near future; the losses may be spread over a long time to come. Thus if there are no restrictions on entry into a protected industry, it cannot indefinitely preserve the superior incomes and profits that the imposition of protection gives it, for these superior incomes will attract resources into it until rewards are once more reduced to normal. This time, however, may be a long way off, and in the interim the protected occupation enjoys real gains. The political influence of these concentrated gains, simply because of their visibility, more than outweighs the influence of the losses, even though these may substantially exceed the gains *in the aggregate,* because the diffuseness of the losses renders them politically invisible and therefore impotent. The diffuseness of the losses, however, does not mean that they are unreal: when everyone tries this game of getting concentrated gains at the cost of diffuse losses, eventually everybody loses. As a child I had a fantasy in which I imagined that everybody in the country gave me a penny; nobody would be any the worse off, for who would miss a penny, whereas I would be a millionaire! Clearly this is a principle that cannot be applied universally, and yet it is a principle according to which many political decisions are made. This, indeed, is precisely the principle of log rolling, whereby congressmen trade support with each other for their own pet projects for raiding the public purse.

Tariffs *vs.* quotas. Within the general category of trade restrictions there are several varieties from which to choose, so that even if it has been decided as a matter of policy that trade restriction is desirable, the mode of restriction still remains in question. The principal methods of restriction are the tariff and the quota.

The tariff has the great advantage of simplicity and relative freedom from administrative entanglements—though even here the definition of a commodity, in order to determine which tariff scale it falls under, is often an arbitrary matter involving much red tape and even litigation. The tariff also has a certain advantage, provided that it is not prohibitive, in that it brings in revenue to the government. If the supply of the imported commodity is inelastic, the real incidence of the tariff may fall mostly on the foreign suppliers; from the national point of view this is presumably very desirable!

The quota, on the other hand, has the disadvantage of all quotas—that it can only be administered by allotting previous importers' licenses to import restricted amounts, and these amounts generally are determined with reference to some past experience—for instance, imports for some previous year or group of years. A quota system always tends to "freeze" an existing structure, and to create property rights that are based merely on the accident of having been in the field at the appropriate time. Moreover, if the demand for the imported goods is inelastic, and the imported goods are differentiated in the minds of the buyers from the home-produced article, producers of the imported goods will be able to get a monopoly price, and this monopoly is quite unshakeable as long as the quota system is in effect, for no "outsiders" can get a quota! The effect of the quota in this case is simply to organize the exploitation of the home consumer by the foreign producer—surely a very odd result of a presumably nationalistic policy!

Negotiable quotas. Some of the worst effects of quotas can be mitigated if they are negotiable—that is, if these rights or licenses according to which the quota is allocated can be freely bought or sold. In that case there is some possibility for newcomers to break into the select circle of licensees by buying a quota from a previous owner. This still further accentuates the stupidity of the system in regard to distribution, however, as the result is simply to give existing importers a free gift of a "turnstile"—a license to exploit, a valuable piece of property the value of which is the capitalized monopoly gain. Only the original holders of quotas then get any good out of them; newcomers are forced to pay any monopoly gains to the original holders, in the price of the quota, and presumably therefore do not make monopoly gains themselves, though of course they may reap the gains (or losses) of uncertainty.

The foreign exchanges. The problem of trade restrictions is closely related to the regulation of the financial flows into and out of a country, which may be flows either of money of various kinds, of securities, or of financial instruments. When exports are sold abroad they are in the first instance converted into holdings of foreign currencies. Similarly, when imports are sold at home they are converted first into holdings by foreigners of the domestic currency. In the foreign exchange market these various currencies are exchanged one against the other; thus people who have pounds and want dollars exchange their pounds for dollars with people who have dollars and want pounds. The sale of securities abroad likewise results in the previous owners of the securities coming into the possession of foreign currencies. These various claims are "cleared" in the complex apparatus of the financial and money markets of the world. The "foreign exchange rate" is the price of one currency in terms of another; it follows the general principle of price determination in a competitive market, in that there will tend to be some system of foreign exchange rates at which, on balance, people are content to hold the amounts that are present "in the market."

It is not always easy to define the limits of the market, especially when they are speculative opportunities—holdings of funds that might be in the market at one time might not be at another. If, however, any currency becomes "scarce" in the market—that is, if it becomes hard to find sellers of it to accommodate those who wish to buy it—its price like any other in such circumstances will tend to rise; at higher prices buyers are discouraged and more sellers come into the market until the buyers can be satisfied. Conversely, if any currency becomes "plentiful" its price relative to others will tend to fall until holders can be found for it.

Stability in exchange rates. The maintenance of stability in foreign exchange rates has been a concern of economic policy-makers for many generations. The principal argument for stable exchange rates is that fluctuating rates introduce an element of uncertainty into international transactions so great as to be a serious handicap to international trade, and still more to international investment. The trader has to consider not only the risks of fluctuating prices in one currency, but of fluctuating exchange rates when he wants to "bring his money home." The investor has to consider not only the general risks attendant on investment but the additional risks that exchange rates may have moved against him by the time he wishes to repatriate his capital. When exchange rates are stable and the various currencies are freely interchangeable there is, in effect, a common international monetary standard. If pounds and dollars can be exchanged freely one for another at all times at a rate of $2.80 to one pound, then one pound is virtually equivalent to $2.80, and it matters little to a person operating in international markets whether he holds pounds or dollars. If, however, exchange rates can fluctuate freely, the markets become subject to speculative fluctuations that may be quite unrelated to the underlying conditions of international trade. Up to a point, for instance, a rising price for one currency would create speculative demand for it which would push the price up still further.

Methods of stabilizing exchange rates. There are many ways of ensuring a reasonable stability in foreign exchange rates. A bilateral gold standard will ensure stable exchange rates between two countries within the limits of the gold points. This is a rather indirect mechanism, however, and direct "pegging" of the exchanges is just as effective, if not more so. By this we mean a standing offer—say by the central bank—to buy or sell foreign exchange at a fixed price in terms of the national currency. As long as this offer is maintained the exchange rate in the market cannot differ from the official rate by more than a very small amount, for if it rises above the official level buyers will prefer to buy from the exchange authority rather than in the market, and sellers in the market will be forced to reduce the price for lack of buyers. Similarly if the rate in the market falls below the official rate, sellers will sell to the exchange authority rather than in the market, and buyers will have to bid up the price for lack of sellers. Under these circumstances if there is a scarcity of the foreign currency this does not cause a rise in its price, but rather a drain of the reserve of this currency held by the exchange authority. Similarly an abundance of the foreign currency does not cause a fall in its price, but rather will be drained off the market into the holdings of the exchange authority.

The ability of the exchange authority to maintain the official price depends, of course, on its ability to maintain holdings of the foreign currency; there is not usually much difficulty about maintaining holdings of the domestic currency. If there is a prolonged drain on the foreign currency holdings the authorities may defend these in various ways. Interest rates on short-term loans may be raised, which may have the effect of attracting foreign currencies through the sale of short-term securities to foreigners. The currency may be *devalued*—that is to say, the officially maintained price of foreign currencies may be raised (or what is the same thing, the price of the domestic currency lowered). Or various restrictions in the free exchange of currencies may be imposed.

Restrictions on exchange of currencies. Currency restrictions have become extremely popular in recent years, and seem to be an almost permanent part of the economic landscape, although they are generally conceived as a "crisis policy" in war and postwar years. The simplest form of such restriction is the prohibition of transactions in currencies at other than official prices, and the rationing of foreign exchange by the official agencies. This is known as "exchange control." It almost inevitably results in the development of extensive black markets. It is difficult to detect illegal exchanges of an item as portable as money, and the abstract nature of money seems to inhibit the development of a widespread conscience in the matter of illegal exchange transactions. A more elaborate device is the development of multiple exchange rates for different purposes. In Hitler's Germany, for instance, there were at times up to forty different exchange rates for different people and purposes. This is an attempt to exploit the monopoly position of the exchange authority through price discrimination, or "charging what the traffic will bear." Where the demand for the currency (whether foreign or domestic) is inelastic, a high price can be charged for it, and where, for another purpose, the demand is elastic, only a low price can be charged. This game can only be played, of course, if the markets can be kept separate—otherwise the people who buy in the low-price market will be able to resell to the victims of the high-price market, and so undermine the high-price market altogether.

Difficulties of exchange control. One difficulty with exchange control is that it seems inevitably to lead to unjust discrimination and to bribery and corruption of the authorities who have the power to grant permits to exchange. Like the quota system which it resembles it is apt to freeze existing situations and to give quite undeserved windfall gains to the people who happen to be "in on the ground floor." Exchange control is also a powerful agency of internal taxation and redistribution of income. If the price of the domestic currency in terms of foreign currencies is held down by the exchange authorities, this means that the exporting industries get less income, in terms of the domestic currency, than they otherwise would. Thus, suppose a bag of coffee is sold by a Brazilian exporter for $50. If the exchange rate is held down to, say, 20 cruzeiros to the dollar, he gets only 1,000 cruzeiros for the bag: if the "equilibrium" or free market rate would have been 30 cruzeiros to the dollar he would have got 1,500 cruzeiros for the bag. As people do not generally understand the mysteries of exchange control it is rather easy to swindle them in this way without their knowledge, and hence without their disapproval.

The sale of exchange permits. As the official exchange rate gets closer to the equilibrium rate, exchange control can be "liberalized" by increasing the rations of foreign exchange, by liberating certain types of transactions, and so on. One ingenious method of maintaining an apparatus of exchange control while at the same time ameliorating many of its major defects is to regularize—and exploit—the black market itself by creating a market in exchange permits. Thus in Brazil exchange permits are auctioned, and go to the highest bidder. This in effect restores a free market in foreign exchange, plus a tax (the price of the exchange permit) which is greater, the greater the divergence between the official and the "free" price of the currency. This eliminates the "quota" feature of exchange control, which gives rise to so many objectionable consequences, and it permits the state to absorb much of what otherwise would be windfall gains.

International flows of capital. The problem of the regulation and encouragement of the international flow of capital covers the fourth of the broad types of input and output of national economies. There is an intimate relation between the flow of commodities and the corresponding movement of securities or indebtedness. Whenever a good is exported a short-term security is created in the form of an account receivable in the foreign currency. Similarly, when a good is imported, an account payable is created. For any nation therefore the excess of exports over imports (services included) creates directly an increase in its total claims on foreigners—*i.e.*, an export of capital. Similarly, the import of capital signifies an excess of imports of goods and service over exports.

The problem now, however, is that of the *form* of these claims. People are rarely content to hold accounts receivable for very long! The foreign exchange market is a device for clearing the accounts receivable from abroad against accounts payable to foreigners. Some of the claims, however, may be transferred into more formal obligations—loans or bonds—in which case they acquire a semipermanent status and are removed from the clearing operation of the foreign exchange market. Thus, suppose the United States lends Brazil 100 million dollars. This will enable the Brazilians to import 100 million dollars worth more than they export (neglecting now effects on the rest of the world, and supposing that Brazil and the United States are the only two countries), and they will still be able to maintain the same exchange rate. If Brazil tried to import more than it exported *without* the loan this would result in the first instance in an excess of accounts payable to the United States, which would soon bring the excess of imports to a stop, either through a drain of Brazil's holdings of United States dollars or through a rise in the cruzeiro price of dollars. The flows of securities across international boundaries are therefore of great importance in determining the flows of real capital in the form of excesses of exports over imports or of imports over exports. These considerations are summed up in the balance-of-payments identity, which states that the payments into a nation from the sale of exports, securities, or gold abroad must equal the payments out from the purchase of imports, securities, or gold from abroad.

The balance-of-payments problem. If now the balance of payments is an identity, why is it so often conceived as a *problem?* A great deal of discussion of this problem followed the second World War, especially in regard to what was known as the "dollar shortage." Europe and other war-devastated areas had great need for imports, especially from America, but had very little to export in return. What they needed clearly was an import of capital, especially from the United States. This was difficult—indeed, apparently impossible—to accomplish by the sale of securities to Americans; hence the "dollar shortage." This was solved for a period at any rate by the Marshall Plan, representing a substantial gift of capital to Europe by the United States—

a remarkable expression of human, or at least of Atlantic, solidarity.

The foreign investment problem. The problem of the organization of the export of capital to underdeveloped areas remains one of the major problems of the world economy, even though the problem of the recovery of the war-devastated areas no longer looms so large. In the nineteenth century the "advanced" countries of Western Europe made a substantial contribution to the development of certain parts of the rest of the world through the export of capital—this was an important, though not perhaps the dominant, factor in the development of North America, Argentina, and Australia and similar areas of European settlement. The European influence was much less successful in promoting development in the tropics and in the more strictly colonial countries, where the plantation economies remained alien enclaves in the culture and did not feed back into the surrounding territory. Nevertheless, the over-all record of the nineteenth century system was a good one; the twentieth century has not done nearly as well as an international economy.

The great problem here is to assess the conditions under which private investment can succeed in creating an adequate flow of capital from the rich to the poor areas, and the conditions under which it cannot be expected to succeed in this task and must be supplemented by governmentally organized investment. The question is a controversial one. It seems clear, however, that the political instability of the twentieth century has created an environment where private foreign investment in sufficient volume has not been forthcoming, and where there is a strong case for supplementary activity on the part of government. However, even within nations that have wide differences of economic development in different areas the problem of organizing flows of capital from the developed to the less developed areas has proved extremely difficult. Within the United States, for instance, the flow of capital from the developed North to the less developed South has been slow, and while the Federal Government has assisted the process to some extent (for example, through the Tennessee Valley Authority), the political resistances to such policies are very strong. There is even less reason to be optimistic, therefore, about substantial intergovernmental assistance, except in emergency situations, in view of the very limited sense of world solidarity that prevails today.

International Economic Organizations. Nevertheless, there are some international economic organizations that have had a moderate success.

The International Monetary Fund is primarily conceived as an agency for minimizing fluctuations in exchange rates, mainly through granting credit to countries that find themselves in temporary shortages of foreign funds or their equivalents. It has not been successful in achieving full convertibility of the major currencies (notably the British pound, which is still subject to fairly stringent exchange controls), but it has unquestionably been useful in minor crises.

The International Bank for Reconstruction and Development is mainly an agency for granting small to medium-sized loans for public works and developmental "overhead" to the less-developed countries, and for mobilizing the resources of the world capital markets to be channelled in this direction by selling its own securities on world financial markets. It has therefore something of the aspect of an international investment trust: investors who might hesitate to lend money for development in a single country because of the special risks involved might be more willing to lend for a world program in many countries.

These two organizations were products of the wave of enthusiasm for international organization during and just after the second World War. The atmosphere is now less favorable, and proposals for the setting up of "Sunfed" (Special United Nations Fund for Economic Development) to supplement the work of existing agencies has not up to the time of writing (1957) shown much prospect of success. The "Point Four" program of the United States is a small but generally useful effort on the part of a single nation to assist the development of others.

The technical assistance program of the United Nations is likewise a small step in the direction of human solidarity. We seem to be moving into an age, however, when generous impulses and large ideas are at a discount, and it is hard to visualize any concerted effort on the scale that seems to be demanded by the need.

The coordination of internal and external policies. Perhaps the most basic problem in international economic policy is that of the coordination of internal national policies with foreign policies. No matter how well conceived a foreign economic policy, it can be wrecked if the internal policies are not consistent with it. A good example of this is the impossibility of maintaining a stable system of exchange rates if different countries are having unequal rates of internal inflation or deflation. Suppose, for instance, that a single country is having a noticeable inflation at a time when the rest of the world is maintaining stable prices. The inflating country will be increasing its money supply, either by cash deficits of government or through expansion of private bank debt, and its currency therefore will become plentiful. Some of this superfluity of currency can hardly help finding its way into the possession of people and institutions that operate in the foreign exchange market. If the market is free, the price of other currencies will rise as the owners of the plentiful currency bid for the relatively scarcer foreign currencies: which is to say that the price of the home currencies will fall. If there is a gold standard, or if the exchange rates are pegged, or if there is exchange control, the reserves of foreign currencies will decline, and will go on declining as the inflation proceeds until there is danger of their being exhausted.

We may put the same series of events in a more conventional way by saying that the inflation encourages imports and discourages exports, and so leads to a drain of the foreign currency or gold stock to pay for the excess of imports. The upshot is that if the inflation continues, all foreign exchange holdings will be drained away, and long before that happens measures will have to be taken to protect these holdings. Either the currency must be devalued to correspond roughly to its new internal value, or exchange control will have to be tightened, with the inevitable development of black markets, individual inequities, and the discrimination against the export industries.

Real *vs.* monetary adjustments. It is clear that there is some validity in the notion of an equilibrium set of exchange rates under given conditions of internal incomes, money stocks, and international capital movements. It is this which makes the ideal of stable exchange rates a reasonable one, provided there is an adequate degree of internal stability in the nations concerned. We may observe that most nations have achieved this ideal internally—New York dollars, for instance, are now always exchanged for Chicago or San Francisco dollars at par, though this was not always the case prior to the establishment of the Federal Reserve System. This stability in internal exchange rates for balances in different localities produces little sense of strain, and little sense of a "balance of payments problem." Kansas, of course, may have a "New York dollar shortage" if there is a failure in the wheat harvest or a sharp fall in the price of wheat. This dollar shortage, however, is met by short-term loans and by restricting consumption in Kansas as incomes fall off. Suppose now, however, that the State of Kansas had enough sovereignty to create its own money, and to try to compensate for the decline in Kansas incomes by increasing the number of Kansas Dollars. In the face of the real adjustments it is clear that the Kansas Dollar would have to go to a discount. There is no way by merely internal monetary management that a region or a nation can avoid the loss in real incomes that comes from a decline in the quantity or in the value of its exportable products. Under these circumstances, however, the decline in the aggregate income would not immediately be reflected in personal incomes, and there might not be the decline in personal consumption that would follow from a direct fall in personal incomes. That is to say, a nation may for a while insulate its people from the worsening of their real terms of trade or real income derived from trade. What this means is that for a while individual consumption can stay up because the "collective" foreign reserves are declining. This cannot go on for ever, however, and is likely to result in a "crisis" when reserves decline below some point that is perceived as dangerous. The "cushion" is then drawn sharply away from under consumption, and drastic reorganizations of consumption, taxation, and so on may follow.

The conflict between exchange stability and full employment policy. The problem is somewhat reversed when we consider depression and unemployment. Here the problem is not so much how to prevent an internal instability from upsetting the external stability, but rather how to prevent an external stability from *creating* an internal instability. This problem is not wholly absent even in the case of inflation—an American inflation, for instance, by building up the dollar reserves of other countries, may set off inflations abroad, if these increased dollar holdings are interpreted as a signal to expand credit. Many of these relationships, however, are like a chain, which pulls very effectively and directly but which develops a lot of slack when it is pushed. The accumulation of reserves does not produce a "crisis" in the way that a depletion does—we can sit back and admire our coffers filling, but we are constrained to rapid action when our coffers are emptying!

The problem of the conflict between internal and external stability presented itself in the 'thirties, therefore, mainly in the form of how to protect various national economies against deflation and depression originating in the United States. The United States enjoys such a large proportion of world production and trade, that even quite small downward movements of income in the United States may produce disastrous results in smaller countries: "When America sneezes the rest of the world gets pneumonia." Confidence in this proposition was shaken somewhat by the experience of the small depressions of 1948 and especially 1953, when if anything the rest of the world helped America recover from a slight economic cold in the head. However, the experience of the 'thirties certainly indicated that a major depression in the United States could propagate itself through the whole capitalist world in a very short time. The machinery of transmission here is partly psychological—a collapse of stock prices in New York, for instance, may produce pessimistic feelings in London—and is partly mediated through changes in the flows of goods and securities. Thus, if there is a depression in the United States the rest of the world will find it more difficult to sell both securities and commodities in the United States; this will cause a drain of dollar (or gold) reserves in the rest of the world, and if the main object of policy is to preserve stability in foreign exchange rates, this will force countries in the rest of the world to take internal deflationary measures, which may lower incomes and create unemployment.

The "neomercantilist" revolution. The experience of the 'thirties—and the interpretation of that experience by economists, and especially by J. M. Keynes—led to something of a revolution in the principles of foreign economic policy, especially in Europe. Whereas in the nineteenth century the maintenance of the Gold Standard and of stability in foreign exchange rates was the principal ideal objective of foreign economic policy, in the 1930's this ideal was gradually replaced by the objective of insulating domestic economies from deflationary disturbances originating abroad—especially, of course, originating in the United States. A whole battery of policies that would have been regarded as morally reprehensible in the nineteenth century now became respectable. Devaluation of currencies became fashionable. The case for restrictions on imports took on a new respectability, for the imposition of such restrictions, whether by tariff or quota, would have an inflationary effect within the country imposing them, by checking the loss of foreign funds and gold. The old mercantilist concern for the balance of payments and for encouraging an excess of exports over imports in order to bring money into the country, which Adam Smith had derided almost into oblivion, was revived, and an export surplus hailed, from a strictly national point of view, as the export of unemployment. From the point of view of employment theory an export surplus is as good as internal investment—the first gets rid of accumulations of goods, the second accepts them; both have multiplier effects on income.

Neomercantilism and the international economy. It was recognized, of course, that this "neomercantilism" could be, and indeed was, disastrous from the point of view of the international economic order, however much it might give temporary benefits to national economies. If everybody tries to solve his unemployment problem by "exporting" it, everybody gets more of it: it is as if everybody tried to solve his sewage disposal problem by spreading his own wastes on the neighbor's lot. Fortunately in the case of unemployment there are much better alternative solutions in the form of internal fiscal and monetary policies, as we have seen in Chapters 8 and 9. These solutions may not, especially in the case of a severe depression originating in a major country, be compatible with absolute stability in foreign exchange rates. There is no reason, however, why they should involve trade restrictions: a country can take full advantage of the opportunities of foreign trade, and can accept all the imports it can pay for, without getting itself into an internal deflation, provided that it offsets the increased imports with policies designed to increase aggregate consumption or investment.

The three international systems—(1) mutual aggression. There seem to be three main systems of international relations, or indeed of the relations of any set of interacting, distinct, and more or less independent organizations. The first, and worst system is that in which each organization tries to solve its own problems at the expense of others. This is the sewage-on-the-neighbor's-lot system; this is neomercantilism: this is the system of national security through national armaments, which increases the security of one nation only at the cost of creating insecurity for another. These systems tend to be unstable, though they are not necessarily so; when they are unstable they lead to arms races, "trade restriction races," and an increase in general nastiness apparently without limit short of the breakdown of the system. Under special circumstances there may be equilibria in these systems, as shown by Lewis

Richardson [1]—this is the "balance of power"—which might better be renamed a balance of nastiness. The balance of power, however, is treacherous and unstable, and the circumstances that give rise to it are usually transient.

(2) **The self-sufficient system.** The second system is that in which each organization tries to solve its own problems at home without creating problems for its neighbors. This is the septic-tank system, where each organization disposes of its wastes at home. In economic policy this corresponds to the system of internal defenses against unemployment and inflation, for instance, which do not involve the export of trouble. In national security this corresponds to systems that are strictly "defensive" in the sense that they merely lessen the neighbor's ability to damage you without increasing your ability to damage the neighbor. These systems are clearly preferable to the first, but they are not always possible. The septic tank may not work, the internal stability measures may not be adequate, the means of aggression may be superior to the means of defense. Under these circumstances if we are to avoid falling back into the first system we must move to the third.

(3) **The superior-organization system.** The third system is the system of superior organization, or coordination of the component organizations. This is the city sewer system. In economic policy it corresponds to the development of world economic organizations with some degree of authority over national policies, at least at the point of vetoing unacceptable solutions (sewage on the neighbor's lot). In national defense this means security through national disarmament and world government.

These systems of superior organization are not costless. Sewer systems mean increased taxes. International authorities mean a certain surrender of national independence of action, whether in the economic or in the political sphere. The choice between systems of the second and of the third kind depends on their relative costs and workabilities; if anarchy will work, by all

[1] Lewis V. Richardson, "Generalized Foreign Policies," *British Journal of Psychology,* June, 1939.

means let us have it. If it will not work, then let us be willing to pay the price of as much government as is necessary to prevent falling back into the unworkable anarchy of the first system.

Difficulty of evaluating foreign economic policy. Foreign and international economic policy is peculiarly difficult to assess, even with the aid of our fourfold set of objectives. Part of the difficulty arises because of the question on whose behalf we are making the assessment. A policy that might be "good" from the point of view of the welfare or interest of a particular nation might be "bad" from the point of view of the world as a whole. It is unrealistic to be either a pure nationalist or a pure world citizen in our evaluation of policies at this stage of the world's history. The pure nationalist criterion, according to which any policy is good if it serves the interest of the nation that makes it, no matter what the repercussions on others, is incompatible with the growing sentiment of human solidarity which is a perceptible phenomenon of our day, and without which such institutions as the United Nations, or such national policies as the Marshall Plan or the Point Four program, would be quite incomprehensible. On the other hand, we still do not have an effective world government, and national policymakers are responsible *to* their national constituency in a way in which they are not responsible to the great constituency of the human race. Consequently, they can hardly be blamed if national considerations weigh heavily with them, and if a national gain seems more important to them than an equivalent foreign loss. Somewhere between irresponsible nationalism and utopian world responsibility the national policymaker has to pick an uneasy way, and it would be surprising if we could come up with neat answers to all his dilemmas.

Evaluating protectionism: (1) the economic-progress objective. Nevertheless, it is still worth while to examine very briefly the possible contributions of our four basic objectives to the evaluation of foreign and international economic policies. Let us consider first the general free-trade and protection continuum. The cause-and-effect relationships here are not easy to disentangle. We cannot say unequivocally, for instance, that free trade always leads to a higher rate of progress, or that protection leads to stagnation, for some of the arguments for protection are based on the possibility of distorting the national economy in directions that will encourage more rapid rates of development. Nevertheless, the political forces making for protection are so clearly of the beggar-my-neighbor system that the economist may allow himself the feeling that a general prejudice in favor of free trade is likely to move policy in the right direction. When one contemplates the frequent technical stagnation of protected industries one is all the more inclined to advocate the bracing effects of foreign competition as a spur to domestic economic development. A classic example is the technical vigor of unprotected British, Dutch, and Danish agriculture by contrast with the backwardness of the protected agriculture of France and Spain. It is clear that we have here a delicate problem of "how much." The case for some protection for the early stages of growth cannot be ruled out; on the other hand, the political forces always seem to be on the side of having too much rather than too little.

(2) **The stability objective.** From the point of view of stability we have already noticed that there is some case for insulating a domestic economy from world fluctuations by means of suitable trade restrictions. Here again, however, it is easy to get into a beggar-my-neighbor system, and trade restrictions may not be the best way of ensuring domestic full employment. There is a question of the politics of stabilization here, too—whether it is not easier to set up effective stabilizers for small than for large systems. There is some evidence that medium-sized countries, like Sweden and Canada, do a somewhat better job of economic stabilization than large countries like the United States or—in a very different way—Russia. There may be diseconomies of scale in economic policy. If there are, there is a case for trying to stabilize semi-isolated economic areas rather than trying to do the job for the world as a whole. There is a possible case here for a degree of economic isolationism,

just as there is a case for a degree of cultural isolationism. The case, however, is based on impressions rather than on exact knowledge.

(3) **The justice and freedom objectives.** From the point of view of justice and freedom, trade restrictions are hard to justify, though here again we cannot rule out possible exceptions. Restrictions of any kind result in redistributions of income and assets—to the detriment of some groups and the advantage of others. From a pure nationalist viewpoint, of course, a detriment to foreigners and an advantage to nationals would presumably be regarded as an act of justice, though it is hard to maintain this view in all its purity! Even from a nationalist viewpoint, however, it is virtually impossible to devise restrictive policies that do not injure some domestic groups, and here the principle of diffuse injury previously noted would give us a strong prejudice against the likelihood of "just" redistributions through trade restriction. There is, furthermore, in general not the slightest reason to suppose that trade restrictions lead to more equal incomes—indeed, because of the concentration of gain and the diffuseness of loss there is a certain reason to suppose that restrictions will generally redistribute income towards the rich and away from the poor. From the point of view of freedom all restriction in itself constitutes a limitation of freedom, and the burden of proof is on those who argue that other freedoms are extended because of the limitations on freedom to trade.

The evaluation of other restrictions. The assessment of other forms of restriction—for instance, on the migration of people, or on the flows of money and securities—follows much the same lines. The restriction of migration is perhaps the most difficult to assess. Here again the political forces that give rise to such restrictions are likely to be of a narrow and selfish kind. Nevertheless, as we have seen, there is a case for such restrictions even from the point of view of the world interest. Indeed, the freedom to migrate and the freedom to propagate are related freedoms, and for both of these it can be argued that the unrestricted exercise of these freedoms may lead to the enslavement of future generations by poverty. Just how these freedoms can be limited in the mass without causing intolerable interference with individual rights is, however, a problem which we have not yet solved.

12

Government and business enterprise

Business is a useful beast,
We should not hate it in the least;
Its profits should not be sequestered,
And yet it should be mildly pestered.
To pester, rather than to bust,
Should be the aim of Anti-Trust,
For business best can serve the nation
When pushed by gentle irritation.

In the next three chapters we shall take up various aspects of government policy in regard to what are thought to be the three main economic interest groups of modern society—business, agriculture, and labor. The interests of these groups of course overlap, and they by no means exhaust the economic groups of a society.

Nevertheless, they represent three convenient divisions of policy, and in the United States government at least they are represented by three departments—Commerce, Agriculture, and Labor.

Government policy towards business has two rather different aspects. There is, first, the problem of the regulation of business by government—that is, the setting up of a legal and administrative framework to limit what are regarded as undesirable activities or forms of business enterprise. Then there is the problem of government enterprise itself—how far should government "go into business," and what rules of conduct should it adopt if it does? This question merges into the more general question of socialism or private enterprise as a method of organizing economic life.

Government regulation of business. Government regulation of business focuses around three main problems. There is, first, the problem of the control of monopoly and monopoly practices; this resolves itself into the more general problem of placing social limitations on the power of businesses. Secondly, there is a rather vague, but nevertheless important, problem which might be called the "unfair practices" problem. This, of course, is related to the monopoly problem, but it is by no means the same thing, and certain apparent (or perhaps real) contradictions in policy towards business may be explained by the tension between these two problems, for frequently some policy that may be directed towards solving one may actually create difficulties for the other. Thus there has been a constant tension in American policy, for instance, between the notion of "getting rid of monopoly" and the notion of "making monopolies well behaved." Then, in the third place, there is a group of related problems about the form and structure of business enterprise—the corporate *versus* the unincorporated form, the stock corporation *versus* the cooperative, and so on. In this category might also be placed the controversy regarding the *size* of the business enterprise—whether we want a large number of small enterprises or a small number of large ones.

These three problem areas are, of course, closely related. The conditions that lead to the growth of large firms are also likely to lead to monopoly, unfair practices may also lead to monopoly, and so on. Nevertheless the problems are fairly distinct. Thus we may dislike (or like) large-scale enterprise simply for its largeness, quite apart from whether it leads to monopoly. The apparent confusion that lies over the legal history of the regulation of business, especially in the United States, may be attributed in part to the confusion of these three problems, as well as to the constant necessity to interpret an eighteenth century constitution to meet the needs of an increasingly complex society.

Sources of antimonopoly feeling. The ideological roots of antimonopoly feeling undoubtedly lie mainly in Adam Smith's doctrine of the "hidden hand" and the protection that competition provides against unjust concentrations of economic power. One can trace some roots back much further, however, in the Anglo-Saxon tradition, to the animus of the common law against "conspiracy"—the feeling that a group of conniving men are much more danger to society than a single rascal operating in isolation—and to the mediaeval restrictions on "forestalling," "regrating," and "engrossing," which are activities of a quasi-monopolistic nature in the grain trade, which in turn go back to the mediaeval concept of the "just price" and the feeling that it was peculiarly sinful to make personal gains out of the exploitation of a temporary scarcity. The antimonopoly feeling also contains a large element of "Jeffersonian" democracy—the preference for a society of widely distributed property and many small property-holders rather than one in which property is concentrated in few hands and most of the people are proletarianized.

The dilemma of monopoly and economies of scale. The great dilemma of monopoly policy arises out of the principle of increasing returns to scale. If over a substantial range of size of the single enterprise the principle holds that "the bigger the cheaper," this may come into sharp conflict with the principle of "the bigger the nastier" or "the bigger the more dangerous." We see this dilemma cropping up in many different fields: we shall see in the next chapter, for instance, how it crops up in the problem of land reform, and what difficulties develop when large estates are broken up into small farms. This dilemma also plagues anti-trust legislation, and the judicial interpretation of this legislation, the course of which may be compared not unfairly with the weavings of a drunkard. A further dilemma is that the attempt to solve the monopoly problem by breaking up large enterprises into a number of competing smaller enterprises is likely to result not in "perfect" but in highly imperfect competition, or in oligopoly. This condition as we have seen is unstable, and is likely to lead to "wasteful" competition in the form of price or advertising wars, unless this is again checked by formal or informal monopolistic arrangements.

Monopoly in deflation and in inflation. A further complication of the monopoly problem is that there is a striking (but often unobserved) difference between the role played by monopoly in periods of deflation and depression on the one hand and in periods of inflation and boom on the other. The main distinction between monopolistic and competitive markets from the point of view of dynamics is that monopoly prices tend to be much more stable through time than competitive prices. There are good reasons for this. In a competitive market, such as we have had in times past for most agricultural commodities, the principal holders of the stocks of the commodity have no direct control over output. Consequently, if a deflationary situation arises, let us say, either because of a fall in national income or because of unusually large crops, the only possible recourse of holders of the commodity who find themselves with unsaleable stocks is to lower the price in order to try to unload them. Similarly, in an inflationary situation there is nothing to prevent buyers from bidding up the price, and these movements take place very rapidly. In monopolistic markets, on the other hand, either the price-setters have a great deal of control over the volume of output, or prices are determined by a bargaining process (as in collective bargaining for wages) which is time-consuming and likely to operate only with substantial lags. Price policy is conceived as a rather long-run affair, and prices are changed only when considerable pressure for change has accumulated. Hence a deflationary situation is likely to be met by cutbacks in output and employment, by short-time working hours, or by accumulations of inventory, rather than by price changes, until of course the inappropriateness of the existing price structure becomes so glaring that fairly large changes have to be made. Similarly, in inflation, output is increased along with sales, often well beyond what would be thought of as "capacity" in quieter times, overtime is used, inventories are depleted, and so on, before the accumulating pressures force an increase in prices.

Evils of monopoly greatest in deflation. It is little wonder, then, that interest in the monopoly problem is likely to be greater in times of deflation than in times of inflation. In deflation monopoly is an obvious monster; it holds up prices that should fall, it clearly exploits the public, it creates unemployment, and it seems to occupy a peculiar position of power in society. In inflation, on the other hand, monopoly seems relatively benign; if anything it operates, if only by the sheer inertia of its pricing processes, to "hold the line" against inflation. In consequence it loses income relative to the more flexible competitive sectors of the economy, and it seems no longer to be a great exploitative power. It is not surprising, therefore, that many of the major pieces of antimonopoly legislation have come out of periods of depression. It is not only that monopoly makes a fine scapegoat but that the problem manifests itself more acutely in such periods.

The Sherman Act. Thus the Sherman Act of 1890 was in part a product of the economic discontent arising out of the great depression and deflation of the 1870's and 1880's. This period also saw the beginnings of what I have elsewhere called the "Organizational Revolution" [1]—the rise in the scale of organizations of many kinds and in many different fields as a result mainly of certain improvements in the skills and techniques of organization. This movement manifested itself in business in

[1] K. E. Boulding, *The Organizational Revolution* (New York: Harper & Brothers, 1953).

the rise of large corporations and also in the rise of "trusts"—the financial union of previously separated concerns through the device of forming a trust fund to hold stock of the previously independent companies. The "trusts" formed a convenient target for the reformers, and the Sherman Act is usually referred to as the "Anti-Trust" Act. It prohibits "every combination in the form of trust or otherwise, or conspiracy, in restraint of trade or commerce. . . ." Thus it harks back to the old common law doctrine of conspiracy in restraint of trade. It also goes a step beyond the notion of combination or conspiracy, however, and prohibits "attempts to monopolize" whether conducted by a single person or a group. This section of the Act seems to look to some "act" of monopolizing, or perhaps to a motive of trying to monopolize, rather than to a combination or conspiracy as such.

The Act is a superb example of the difficulty of reducing subtle economic concepts to terms that are definable in law. It has given rise to an enormous volume of litigation and judicial interpretation—perhaps more than any other Act of Congress, and the vagueness of the wording and the extreme difficulty of defining exactly what the Act prohibits has permitted a great latitude in judicial interpretation. The indeterminacies of the Constitution have added to the vagueness of the Act itself, and the shift in the judicial interpretation of the Constitution, particularly in regard to what constitutes "commerce" and in regard to the jurisdiction of the federal as over against the state governments, has also permitted great changes in the interpretation of the Act. It is hard to trace a clear direction in the shifting currents of judicial interpretation, but on the whole the direction has been towards stricter interpretations of the Act. One of the early decisions (later reversed), for instance, ruled that manufacturing combinations were not "commerce" and so were exempt! [2] The famous "rule of reason" of 1911 established the principle that "mere" bigness was not a crime, but that some kind of "monopolizing" activity had to be proved.[3] The

[2] *United States v. E. C. Knight Co.*, U.S. 1 (1895).
[3] *Standard Oil Co. of New Jersey v. United States*, 221 U.S. 1 (1911).

interpretation of the Act thus tended away from the "conspiracy" or "combination" doctrine towards the prohibition of certain specific *practices* which were regarded as evidences of monopolistic intent. One might almost say that the interpretation led in the direction of preventing firms from *acting* like monopolies rather than prohibiting them from "being" monopolies.

The Clayton Act. The Clayton Act and the Federal Trade Commission Act, both of 1914, represent a further legislative move in the direction in which the interpretation of the courts had been moving. These acts were not depression-spawned legislation, for the preceding years had been prosperous. Rather they came out of certain dissatisfactions with the administration of the Sherman Act, especially on the part of labor unions, whose legal position had been made somewhat more dubious by the codification of the conspiracy doctrine in the Sherman Act. The Clayton Act therefore attempted (as it turned out, not too successfully) to exempt labor unions from the antimonopoly elements of the law. It also strengthened and codified the penalties against many "monopoly practices," such as price discrimination, and "tying clauses" (by which a manufacturer, for instance, *rents* equipment to its users with the proviso that certain other products also have to be purchased). The Clayton Act in turn proved to be ineffective in some respects, and the next wave of depression-induced antimonopoly legislation produced the Robinson-Patman amendment of 1936, which strengthened, and made surprisingly effective, the prohibition against discriminatory pricing not based on "cost differences." This amendment is sometimes known as the "anti-chain store act," as it was particularly inspired by opposition to certain practices of chain stores.

The Federal Trade Commission Act. The Federal Trade Commission Act carries still further the legislation against certain business practices falling roughly under the head of "unfair competition," and hence is directed not so much against monopoly as such as against the "unfair practices" aspects of business life. These unfair practices center around various forms of misrepresentation or false claims—especially in advertising or labelling—and around various malpractices involving corruption or coercion or "bad faith." Experience with the operations under this Act, as with the Clayton Act, led to further legislation (the Wheeler-Lea Act of 1938) to strengthen the position of the Federal Trade Commission and plug various loopholes.

Effects of antimonopoly legislation. Perhaps the most significant aspect of this legislation is not so much the specific prohibitions it spells out, as the setting up of specialized enforcement agencies to police them. The Sherman and Clayton Acts are policed by the anti-trust division of the Department of Justice, and the Federal Trade Commission Act by the Federal Trade Commission. This means that businesses operate continuously under a watchful pair of eyes whose business it is to ferret out misbehavior. The enforcement may not always be particularly vigorous—it seems to have alternated from little more than a holding operation under some administrations to very vigorous and not always well directed activity under others. The over-all effect, however, has been to create a climate of operations of business in the United States that is very different from that in European countries which have not had such legislation or even an antimonopoly ideology. Things that European businessmen do (or do not do) almost as a matter of course in the way of agreements, cartels, and general gentlemanliness are not part of the American pattern in anything like the same degree. Indeed, the contrast between the American and the European scene in this regard is very striking, and unquestionably has something to do with the faster rate of economic development in the United States. In Europe restraints on competition, cartels (which are organizations for the joint sale of the product of otherwise independent producers), and monopolistic restraints of all kinds have even been extolled as creators of "order" in the anarchy of the market, or even as models of community spirit! Only very recently has concern about these restrictions developed: Britain, e.g., adopted an antimonopoly law in 1948.

Public utilities as "natural" monopolies. It has long been recognized that certain types of monopolies were "natural," in the sense that economies of large scale operated so strongly and over such a wide range of outputs that there was no point in having more than a single supplier. The classic examples are the industries known as public utilities: railroads, gas and electric light and power companies, oil pipe lines, street car or other public transportation systems, and now the coming atomic power industries. The concept of a public utility has its roots in the common law concept of an industry "affected with the public interest." The general course of legal development has been to broaden the concept of a public utility into almost anything the public, as expressed through the legislatures, want to regulate. As in these cases the automatic regulation of economic power that is provided by competition is absent, a political check on possible abuses is provided by setting up a regulatory commission, of a quasi-judicial character, to set prices and rates and to regulate the nature and conditions of the services of commodities provided. Sometimes this is done at the local level, as when a municipality grants a franchise to a public transportation system and retains certain rights of regulation. Most states have public service commissions, with varying degrees of effectiveness. The Federal Government has set up a number of such regulatory bodies, the granddaddy of them all being the Interstate Commerce Commission (1887), which regulates railroads and certain other carriers. The names of the Federal Power Commission (1920), and Federal Communications Commission (1934), the Civil Aeronautics Board (1938), and the Federal Maritime Board (1950) are self-explanatory. The work of the various boards and commissions extends far beyond the setting of rates or prices; the Civil Aeronautics Board, for instance, has power to regulate the routes of commercial air lines and the conditions of flight. There is even an international regulatory agency in the field of air transportation, the International Civil Aviation Organization.

The principles of regulation. It is one thing to set up a regulatory commission, and it is another thing to develop principles by which it should operate. This subject has aroused a voluminous controversy, both at the technical level among economists and at the practical level among lawyers and men of affairs. The practical discussion has been dominated by the concept of "fairness" to the investor. Under theoretically perfect competition the operation of the market itself would tend to bring that amount of capital into each occupation that would make the rate of return (modified by various nonmonetary advantages) equal in all occupations. If regulation, then, is to stimulate competition, it is argued that the investor should be allowed a rate of return at least equal to what he could have obtained in some other occupation, and that if regulation is so severe as to cut the rate of return below what is regarded as a "fair" level, this will be in effect a theft of the investor's property.

The difficulty here is twofold. There is first the problem of defining what is a "fair" rate of return in an uncertain world. Obviously, investors in unregulated industries are not guaranteed any "fair" rate of return without regard to what happens to demand or technology. Similarly, we cannot undertake to guarantee, let us say, the investors in a street car system 6 per cent in perpetuity, merely because it happens to be a regulated industry, if street cars become obsolete owing to the rise of the automobile. Indeed, the whole problem of regulation has taken on a curious change of emphasis insofar as many of the regulated industries have in fact suffered from "competition" of alternative commodities to such an extent that the problem of regulation has shifted from that of protecting the public against rapacious monopoly to the problem of protecting the industry from the impact of technological obsolescence. In a society as dynamic as ours there is no telling what substitutes may not be found even for the services of the best-established utilities. Individual household solar power units, for instance, *might* make all our massive electric utility companies obsolete, and some new channel of communication might even undermine the giant network of American Tel. and Tel.!

In an industry that is facing the competition of technological substitutes, moreover, the demand for its product is likely to become more elastic, and there may be *no* price or rate at which a "fair" rate of return can be earned. The railroad passenger service may well be a case in point; any attempt to recoup losses by raising the price of passenger transportation will simply drive still more passengers to the busses, roads, and airways and result in still further losses. Generally speaking, quite insufficient attention has been given to these elasticity problems—though it is true that in the 1930's the Interstate Commerce Commission actually raised the revenues of the railroads by forcing them to charge lower passenger fares!

The valuation problem. Even if a "fair" rate of return has been decided upon, and we think we know how to get it, a controversy arises on the question of the *valuation* on which the rate is based. Thus, suppose that by charging a certain price for its product or service a public utility can earn $1,000,000 per annum. If the property of the company is valued at $20,000,000 this is a return of 5 per cent per annum, which may be regarded a "fair" rate (6 per cent seems to have been the most popular number historically). If, however, the property were valued at only $10,000,000, the rate of return would be a rather excessive 10 per cent, while if the property were valued at $40,000,000 the rate of return would be a meager 2½ per cent. It is clear that utilities are interested in having their property valued highly for purposes of a regulatory rate base, for the higher the value the larger the income a "fair" rate of return implies. For purposes of local taxation, of course, they would like to have a *low* value of their property, which places them occasionally in a curiously schizophrenic dilemma!

Original *vs.* reproduction cost. The instability of the general price level has led to a long and still unresolved controversy about "original" *versus* "reproduction" cost as a basis for a fair rate of return. In a period of inflation the original cost of installations, having been made at an earlier date when dollars would buy more, is likely to be less than the reproduction cost—that is, what it would cost to reproduce the installation at the present moment. There is force, then, to the argument of the utilities that the original cost grossly underestimates the present value of their plant, and therefore would yield them, at the "fair rate," an income quite insufficient to maintain the plant at the present price level and also pay out "fair" dividends. In a period of deflation, of course, reproduction cost will tend to be less than the original cost incurred in an earlier period of higher prices, and the utilities lose their enthusiasm for reproduction costs as a valuation principle. The legal situation has been splendidly vague, as it probably should be in the face of an essentially bargaining type of situation where the actual rates always have to be reached by compromise among the conflicting views.

The marginal-cost controversy. While the legal fraternity has been debating "fairness" to the investor, the academic fraternity of the economists has been engaged in a long, and also rather inconclusive, debate about the fundamental principles of regulated prices, known as the "marginal-cost controversy." The general principle of legal regulation has been, on the whole, that prices should be set at some "average cost," where the cost includes a fair return. This whole principle has been challenged by a substantial group of economists, beginning with Hotelling,[4] who have argued that the socially best price is that which covers the *marginal* cost—that is, the addition to total cost that results from the last unit produced. It is hard to explain the reasons for this without getting involved in technicalities. The basic idea is that if some commodities are priced above the marginal cost of the product, additional production of the commodity would be worth more, as measured by the price, than the value of resources transferred into this use, as measured by the marginal cost. Hence wherever price is above marginal cost production should be expanded until the price falls to the marginal cost, or marginal cost rises to the price. If, however, average cost falls with increasing output—that is, is smaller at larger outputs—marginal cost will be below the average cost.[5] A price

[4] Hotelling propounded the principle in its modern form, but the core of the argument goes back to Marshall's proposal to subsidize industries of increasing return and tax industries of decreasing return.

[5] Suppose at an output of 100 units average cost is $10 per unit; total cost is $1,000. Then at an output of 101 units average cost is $9.95; total cost is $1,004.95. The marginal cost—*i.e.*, the addition to total cost that results from going from 100 to 101 units—is $4.95. The mathematical reader can easily prove that this is a general proposition.

that is set to cover average cost then will be too high from the point of maximum social benefit, because it will exclude customers who could only afford to purchase the commodity or service at some lower price that would still cover marginal cost. Thus, suppose an electric light company priced its power at 3 cents per kilowatt hour and at this price just made a "fair" rate of return. It might still be possible to supply electricity at a marginal cost, say, of 2 cents per KWH, and if the pricing policy cut out customers who would be willing to purchase further increments of power at a lower price, this seems like a clear social loss.

The "fair return" conflicts with the "marginal cost" standard. A difficulty arises, however. If a flat price is charged that just covers marginal cost, the price will be below average cost, which means that the company will not be making a "fair return." There is conflict here, therefore, between the "fair return" standard and the "marginal cost" standard. There are two principal ways out of this dilemma: one is to subsidize the public utility out of general tax funds (provided that additions to taxes do not distort the allocation of resources too severely) and the other is to permit discriminatory pricing—that is, charging different prices to different types of customer or for different amounts to the same customer. Thus, suppose the electric power company of our previous illustration were to charge 5 cents per KWH for certain classes of customers or for, say, the first 200 kilowatts per month, and then 2 cents for all subsequent amounts used; it might then be able to raise an average return of 3 cents per KWH, which would yield a fair return, and still charge a marginal price equal to the marginal cost. This practice is widespread in the power and light field.

Price discrimination: in freight rates. The problem of policy towards price discrimination is a very difficult one, and is found in a great many fields. It is worth examining it a little more closely. We find it, for instance, in railroad freight rates, where the principle of "charging what the traffic will bear" has a long history. What this means in practice is that those commodities of high value and small bulk, for which the cost of transport is a small proportion of their final price, are charged high freight rates, whereas those commodities that are bulky and of low value per unit weight or volume, such as wheat, coal, gravel, and so on, where the cost of transport is a high proportion of their final price, enjoy low freight rates because without these low rates they would not move at all, or would move in much diminished volume.

The principle employed here has been well worked out in the theory of monopoly.[6] The general idea is that more revenue can be obtained from a given volume of sales when high prices are charged in those markets in which the demand is inelastic—that is, in which a high price has only a small effect on restricting sales—and relatively low prices are charged in those markets where demand is elastic—that is, where a high price would have a severely restricting effect on sales. This principle can only be employed, of course, where the markets in which different prices are charged are separated—that is, where there is no or little possibility of resale by those who enjoy low-priced markets.

The "basing point" system. Another aspect of the general problem of price discrimination of a rather different kind is what is known as the "basing point system." This is the system whereby producers of a commodity enter into an agreement—which may be either explicit or tacit—to charge a price at any point equal to the "mill price" at some basing point (hence the name of the system) plus the cost of transport from that basing point, no matter from what source the commodity comes. The classic example of this system was "Pittsburgh Plus" in the steel industry, where the price of steel everywhere was equal to its price at Pittsburgh, plus the cost of transportation from Pittsburgh, even though the steel might be produced and delivered in Chicago. By comparison with a system of charging costs of transport from the point of actual origin of the steel, this amounted to discrimination against customers who were remote from Pittsburgh in favor of those who were close. In some in-

[6] See K. E. Boulding, *Economic Analysis,* 3rd ed. (New York: Harper & Brothers, 1955), pp. 608-615.

dustries such as cement there have been several basing points, since cement, being bulkier and of low value density, does not travel as far as steel. Nevertheless, any basing-point system implies geographical discrimination of some kind. It was probably not the discriminatory aspects of the basing-point system that led to its adoption, though it may well have been that the demand for steel was more elastic in the older industrial areas closer to Pittsburgh than in the newer and more distant areas where capital needs were more urgent. The main motive seems to have been a desire to escape from the instability of oligopoly into a form of price leadership. It is noteworthy, for instance, that those industries where this system has been common have been characterized by few firms selling a rather standardized commodity. This is a situation where price wars are possible, especially in periods of deflation, which may be ruinous to all concerned. A convention whereby one firm becomes the price leader and the others follow is a simple way out of this dilemma. Such a convention, however, runs afoul of the "conspiracy" notion of the anti-trust laws, and the discriminatory aspects of the system run afoul of the "unfair practices" notion. Consequently the system in a naked form has been abandoned as a result of an unfavorable Supreme Court decision in 1948.[7] It has been revived in somewhat more disguised form, however, in the shape of the adjustment of mill prices for distant sales.

Government operation of business. Government policy towards business extends far beyond its mere regulation and the provision of a legal framework, towards the *conduct* of business operations by government or by some form of governmental agency. The problem of the extent to which political agencies are suited to the conduct of business is perhaps the great controversy of our age. At one extreme, of course, is the communist position, which holds in effect that *all* business should be operated by political organizations and that "private" business should be abolished except perhaps for very insignificant and marginal cases. At the other extreme is the "anarchist" position

[7] *Federal Trade Commission v. Cement Institute,* 333 U.S. 683 (1948).

which holds in effect that *no* functions should be performed by governmental agencies. Somewhere between these extremes various parts of the world find uneasy positions of equilibrium, varying from the totalitarian communist regimes—in which a very large part of economic activity is in the hands of organizations actively responsible to the hierarchy of the state rather than to private owners—down to what are thought of as "capitalistic" countries like the United States, where at least the major part of economic activity is in the hands of private organizations. Even in the capitalist countries today it is usual to find at least a quarter of the Gross National Product accounted for by government activity, though the larger part of this in turn is accounted for by the somewhat "uneconomic" activity of national defense.

The "politicizing" of business. The "politicizing" (this seems to me a more accurate word than "socialization") of economic activity takes place at all levels of government. There are, for instance, municipal enterprises of many kinds—electricity, gas, public transportation systems. There are specially created political authorities at the local level—port authorities, river authorities, turnpike authorities. There are state universities, state hospitals. Then there are large national enterprises such as the Post Office, or in some countries the nationalized railroads or mines. Finally there are the communist countries where the state is itself a gigantic firm or holding company covering almost the whole economy, of which the separate industries and enterprises are merely branches.

Political *vs.* market environments. If we are to be able to evaluate intelligently the degree to which business should be politicized, we must first be clear as to the essential differences between economic organizations that operate in a political environment and those which operate in a "market" environment. The most essential difference is the source of the revenue of the organization—roughly, the source of its money receipts. A "market" organization (that is, a business in the usual sense of the word) receives its revenue almost wholly from the sale of its product to customers—usually, though not necessarily, to many different customers; if it sells to only one customer it approaches the "political" type of organization. A politicized enterprise, such as a government department, an armed force, a municipal school system, and so on, derives its revenue mainly not from the direct sale of its product, but from a "budget grant" by some higher authority, which in turn usually obtains revenue from taxation, or from some kind of ability to commandeer the incomes of individuals. There are, of course, government enterprises, such as the Post Office, that derive a large part of their revenue from the sale of goods and services to customers. There are other quasi-governmental enterprises, such as the Tennessee Valley Authority, that derive capital from the government but virtually all revenue from the sale of goods and services.

Five types of enterprise. We may therefore distinguish two degrees of politicizing, or independence from the market, and therefore four types of enterprise. The *capitalist enterprise* depends on the market both for its capital and for its revenue. The *government enterprise* depends on the market for its revenue, but on government for its capital. The *government department* depends on government authority both for its revenue and for its capital. The fourth class seems to be practically an empty one: it is conceivable, however, that we might have organizations that would be financed by private capital but that would find their whole revenue coming from government. Certain firms that specialize in armaments might almost be placed in this category. On the analogy of the above nomenclature we might call these *capitalist departments!* Yet a third dichotomy might be added, for in all the above we have supposed that the enterprise relies on the market for its factors of production other than capital: it hires labor and land, and buys raw material and equipment. There are enterprises such as conscript armies, however, which rely on coercion to supply their labor force, and occasionally (under stress) on requisitioning (which is the military term for the conscription of property) to supply other needs. These might be called "conscript departments."

The budget as an instrument of organization. A good deal of internal organization and control is common to all four, or even five types of organization. All organizations beyond a certain size must be broken down into departments, and must develop a hierarchy of "line" authority and responsibility. The primary internal economic control is the "budget"—a fairly detailed plan of expenditure for a period ahead—usually a year, though it may be longer for more grandiose plans and shorter for departmental details. Budgets are characteristic of *all* organizations—whether capitalist or governmental—beyond the simplest and most informal level. They are prepared by a process originating in the various departments and subdepartments, one of the principal responsibilities of a departmental chief being the preparation of a tentative budget which goes up the hierarchy and the fulfilment of a final budget which comes down. As budgets go up the hierarchy they are simplified and condensed, and a final budget is approved at the top of the hierarchy, usually in terms of over-all sums allocated to different sections of the organization. The administration of the budget involves the carrying out of the over-all plan by the various departments, subject to increasing interpretation in detail as it goes down the hierarchy. This process may, of course, be a fairly continuous one—there is no law that it must happen only once a year, though in government enterprises and departments the annual budget acquires the character of an intense seasonal ritual.

The budget process as a source of diseconomies of scale. One may venture on a proposition that the larger an organization the less "rational" is the budget process likely to be, simply because more levels of authority have to be interposed, and the people who make the final decisions know less and less about the ultimate consequences of their acts. Consequently the apportionment of the total resources (that is, total expenditure) among the various departments and divisions depends more on the abilities and skills of the department and divisional chiefs than on any objective rational principle. An aggressive and ambitious department head will get a larger slice of the budget than a cautious and perhaps even more conscientious one. Budgets get padded, ambitious department heads get more skilled in justifying a large budget than in turning out a product. The greatest danger that besets any large organization is that the only product of a department that the higher members of the hierarchy ever see is *reports,* and on the whole it pays better to devote energy to producing "information" in the proper channels than it does to producing "product." This is not to say, of course, that other channels of information do not exist; indeed, there must be sources of information to the higher echelons of the hierarchy other than the reports of the lower members if an organization is not to collapse into a mass of falsehood and illusion. A department that does not produce "the goods" or that has an inflated budget, or that is corrupt, eventually, no doubt, gets found out through the long and diffuse processes of feedback from the societal environment of the organization (its customers, its workers and their families) and its watchdogs (policemen, anti-trust officials, and so on). Nevertheless, these processes are painfully slow, and especially if the organization has control of the coercive power in the society may be positively glacial in their operation. It sometimes takes the death of the scandalous to expose the scandal!

The market environment as a source of rapid "feedbacks." From the point of view of internal organization there is no particular reason why any large organization, whether capitalist or governmental, should escape these difficulties; the problem of imperfect internal feedbacks and distorted information systems is common to them all. Nevertheless, when an organization derives its revenues from a market—that is, from the sale of its product to many customers—there is a directness and rapidity of feedback here that is not usually present in the cases of "departments" who derive their revenues from some superior organization. This is because revenues derived from the market can *only* be obtained by, in some sense, "delivering the goods" —that is, by producing something for which people are willing to part with their money.

It may be, of course, that the public can be deceived, by fraudulent advertising or by flashy design, and can thereby be persuaded to buy something that it later regrets having bought. It is difficult, however, to build up a continuing business on such a basis, and with some exceptions the market is an environment in which "delivering the goods" and being serviceable "pays off" in the long run, or even in the medium run. Only the fly-by-night operator can hope to make money by pure deception. A possible qualification of this optimism lies in the lack of expertness of the household purchaser, which renders him (or her) more open to deception or even to manipulation of preferences than would be the case with a small number of expert customers. Even in this connection, however, organizations like Consumers Union exist to give expert advice to the inexpert buyer, and if a fool and his money are soon, and unwisely, parted, perhaps it is not wholly inappropriate to have a few penalties for foolishness.

Feedbacks to budgets are slow and indirect. The government department gets its revenue not by directly pleasing the people to whom it renders service, but by pleasing its superiors in the organization. It is true, of course, that strong dissatisfaction with the services rendered by the department will eventually percolate, by way of the political processes of lobbying and electioneering, to the department superiors and so down to the department. These processes, however, are indirect and circuitous. Once a department has been established it is remarkably difficult to get rid of it, even after its usefulness has passed. One of the fundamental theorems in the theory of the budget is that it is easier to take a new item into a budget than to get it taken out, and easier to accept an increase than to enforce a decrease. Unless severely checked by the absence of revenue, therefore, budgets have a chronic tendency to expand. This may not raise a serious problem in periods when there is a strong case for the expansion of budget-directed activities; it makes contraction, however, very difficult.

The market as a coordinator of small-scale enterprises. The great case for the market as a mode of economic organization is that it permits the coordination of relatively small-scale organizations, and hence enables us to enjoy the economies of specialization without involving us in the diseconomies of scale. This is a crucial point in the evaluation of "capitalism" *versus* "socialism"—that is, of more market-oriented systems *versus* more politically integrated and planned systems. The difficulties and diseconomies of a budget-controlled system increase—probably more than proportionally—once we pass a certain size of organization, simply because of the increasing difficulty of establishing an adequate information and communications system. We see these difficulties in their extreme form in the communist state, which ideally and to a considerable extent in practice is a "one-firm society." If we imagine General Motors, for instance, expanding until it covered the whole of the American economy, we would have a situation, at least from the point of view of organizational structure, very similar to that which prevails in the Soviet Union. Indeed, I have sometimes twitted my friends in General Motors by pointing out that they run a "communist" state about the size of Jugoslavia, as measured by national income! Up to a point, of course, there are economies in size, especially in concentrated lines of production. One can hardly doubt, however, that a firm the size of General Motors that produced a complete cross-section of the products of the American economy would not exhibit the economies of scale that are present in the relatively homogeneous operations of that corporation!

Diseconomies of scale under communism. The "plan" in a communist society is nothing more than a rather elaborate budget, and the system of economic organization is essentially that of budget control—that is, the performance of any department, whether this be a small shop in a plant or a great All-Union Trust, is measured by its conformity with the plan—that is, with its budget. The budget under the five year plans is of course more elaborate than the budgets of capitalist governments (though probably not any more elaborate than the budgets and plans of large capitalist enterprises). It includes not only a financial budget but a materials budget, a labor budget, and so on. The principle of allocation among the parts of the organization by a process of budget bargaining, however, holds as much in the communist case as it does for capitalist budgets. It is hardly surprising, therefore, that communist societies are insensitive to consumer needs, and that they tend to run into bureaucratic inefficiency, the production of reports rather than of goods, and a constant tendency to cover up the mistakes of authority by the use of coercive and police-state methods.

The cooperative society. We should not leave even this very sketchy survey of business organization without noticing an important mutant from the capitalist form—the cooperative society. The problem of what government policies should be adopted towards this form is still a current issue in American politics, and has been with us for several decades. The cooperative enterprise is distinguished from the capital-stock enterprise mainly by the different location of the ultimate bearers of responsibility and risk and the recipients of residual "profit." In the capital-stock enterprise the *stockholder* bears the ultimate responsibility for the success or failure of the enterprise, and is the recipient of residual profits (or the payer of residual losses) after all contractual obligations have been met. In the cooperative society the *member-customers* have the ultimate responsibility and receive the residual profits. In both cases residual losses may be (and usually are) limited by the device of limited liability, and continuity is ensured by incorporation, so that the mere corporate form of organization in itself does not serve to distinguish them. In the stock enterprises, however, the profits are distributed among the stockholders in proportion to the amount of stock held—that is, in proportion to their degree of participation as *capitalists.* In the cooperative society the profits (or, as cooperators prefer to call them, "savings") are distributed among the members in proportion to their degree of participation as *customers,* not in proportion to the amount of stock held. Cooperative societies are financed almost exclusively by fixed-interest "shares" which have more the character of "bonds" than of "stock," and by the accumulation of undistributed profits.

Workers' cooperatives. There are roughly three types of cooperative enterprises. In the producers' or workers' cooperative the workers themselves put up or borrow the capital, and distribute the earnings in proportion to the amount of work done —that is, in proportion to the degree of participation as workers. This form has had little success in the capitalist world, in spite of many experiments with it. It exists under Soviet communism in the form of the "artel," or artizans' cooperative. The main difficulty seems to be that the specialization between employer and employed is highly effective from the point of view of efficiency of internal organization. Workers' cooperatives, therefore, have not generally been able to provide their members with as good a standard of life as they could get in more conventional employment, and hence have tended either to disintegrate or to become more conventional enterprises.

Marketing cooperatives. The second form is the marketing cooperative. This has enjoyed a substantial success in agriculture, where it has permitted farmers to integrate their enterprises forward into the marketing and processing fields in a way that no farmer by himself would find possible. Here a group of sellers combine for the joint sale or processing of their product—for instance, a group of milk producers may join together to establish a cooperative creamery. The earnings of the cooperative are then divided among the members in proportion to the sales made to it, or through it.

Consumers' cooperatives. The third form is the consumers' cooperative, in which the members are householders who take responsibility for organizing a retail outlet or store. The profits of the store are then divided among the members in proportion to *purchases*. The consumers' cooperative has been very successful in many European countries, but has only enjoyed a very qualified and local success in the United States. The main reason seems to be the more rigid class structure in Europe which led to the underutilization of managerial talent in the working class. The cooperatives were able to exploit this talent, and so use the abilities of many able people who could not rise to managerial positions outside the cooperative movement because of their class origins. In the United States the relative fluidity of classes has made it necessary for the cooperatives to compete on relatively equal terms with the chain stores and "capitalist" enterprises for good management. As there seem to be no very large efficiencies in the actual form of organization this has made it hard for consumers' cooperatives to compete with their very efficient rivals.

Cooperatives as educational institutions. The case both for and against the cooperatives rests largely on the fact that they demand a greater degree of *participation* in the enterprise on the part of those people who constitute its "environment," whether as workers, sellers, or buyers. It can be argued that this greater participation is socially desirable, in that it avoids the extreme impersonality that characterizes the relationship of a stock enterprise to the people it hires or serves. Greater participation produces greater understanding, and it can certainly be claimed that experience with cooperatives gives the ordinary person a much better understanding of the problems of business than any amount of formal instruction. Thus the cooperative can be defended as an educational institution, producing desirable changes in knowledge and character as well as performing a more strictly economic function in providing goods and services. This alone might be sufficient to justify a small amount of discrimination by government in its favor. In the United States cooperatives enjoy certain tax advantages (not of very great magnitude) and agricultural cooperatives especially enjoy certain legal privileges such as exemption from the anti-trust acts.

Economic progress under various institutions. When we come to try to evaluate government policy towards enterprise and business organization we find ourselves faced with a great diversity of views and experiences, ranging all the way from extreme laissez-faire to totalitarian communism. One difficulty seems to be that many of the objectives of economic life can be served almost equally well by a wide range of different types of organization. One is sometimes almost tempted to think that the key to the success of an economic system lies not in its particular forms of organization as in the "spirit" of the culture in which these organizations are embedded. We cannot so easily separate the "spirit" and the "forms," however, for they act and react one on another in a most complex way in the interminable conversations of history.

Thus, take first the objective of economic progress. We find rapid rates of economic progress in the most diverse societies —in the democratic capitalism of the United States, in the feudal capitalism of Japan, and in the totalitarian communism of Russia or China. Each society seems beset by its own special set of Furies: capitalism by depression, communism by purges and famines. Each of these three types of society at its most successful, however, seems to reach about the same rate of economic growth.

Initiative *vs.* imitative progress. We may argue, however, that the *initiation* of technological change requires a uniquely free and optimistic society and could not be expected under a universally planned communism. That is to say, the economic growth under communism may be largely a matter of *imitation* of techniques worked out in freer societies—a "catching-up" process in which the diseconomies of scale are not so apparent and in which a high concentration of economic power in the hands of the state (or the Party) may actually assist the processes of technological and cultural change. Against this argument it is maintained that change can be institutionalized, as for instance, in the resources that are devoted to research both in larger corporations and in communist states. Some of this may be admitted; nevertheless, unless there is freedom somewhere in the society for the "maverick"—and unless there is opportunity for "playfulness" in ideas and in innovations—change will proceed along fairly well established lines, and we will not get truly revolutionary innovations in *method*—like, for instance, the method of science itself. We will certainly expect du Pont to give us Better Living through Chemistry; we would be somewhat surprised if it gave us Better Living through Sociology, and even in chemistry some of the far-reaching innovations like antibiotics have not been developed in the great laboratories either of corporations or of governments, but in the minds of unusually creative individuals often working in relative isolation.

Economic stability under various institutions. Looking now at the problem of stability, one again has the feeling that many different forms of enterprise and organizational structure are compatible with either stable or unstable societies. Communism has not proved itself any more stable than capitalism; indeed, the absence of self-correcting mechanisms is even more striking under totalitarian regimes, where the mistake of the dictator may involve the death of millions before they are corrected. Thus in Russia the period of "war communism" (1917-21) and the first period of collectivization (1928-32) led to disastrous famines and economic collapse and had to be followed by easier and less extreme policies. Within the framework of capitalism neither monopolistic nor competitive markets are capable in themselves of ensuring stability. Competitive markets are subject to wide cyclical swings of a speculative nature. Monopoly *prices* are more stable than competitive prices, but for this very reason monopoly *outputs* (which are what matter most) are less stable than competitive outputs. It is monopoly, under capitalism, that turns deflation into depression by maintaining prices in the face of falling incomes. There is no substitute for monetary and fiscal policy in this area; neither cartels, nor cooperatives, nor anti-trust actions, nor any other scheme of business organization can in itself do much to ensure the stability of the whole economy.

Economic justice and business institutions. Differing ideas of what constitutes economic justice are the main source of the wide divergence of judgment on forms of business organization. There is widespread hostility to private business *as such,* even in capitalist countries, where the governments tend to regard themselves as defenders of the public against business rather than as defenders of business against the public. Thus even in the United States the prevailing tone of government policy towards business might be described as one of mild hostility, as reflected for instance in the anti-trust laws, the corporation tax, the regulation of public utilities, railroads, insurance companies, and banks.

This is not to deny, of course, the power of the business lobby in Congress, as represented, for instance, by the United States Chamber of Commerce or the National Association of Manufacturers. On the whole, however, this lobby has been fighting a rearguard action; frequently the measures that it opposes eventually become law, and the measures that it supports have rough going in the legislatures. It is not particularly helpful in reelection for a Congressman to get too much of a reputation as a partisan of business, especially of big business, though there seems to be a certain amount of political kudos in the support of *small* business!

We appear curiously two-sided in our attitude towards business as an institution, especially towards big business: we admire it, we admire the "businesslike virtues," and yet we distrust it. The reasons for this lie deep in our culture and education. We are taught to admire "service," and to regard "public service" as a peculiarly praiseworthy activity. Our attitude towards government is still tinged with some of the "divinity" that "doth hedge a king." In their extreme form these attitudes lead to a naive socialist faith—what is "private" is bad, what is "public" is good, income from work is "good," income from property is "bad." Unfortunately the moral order is more complex than this, and as one contemplates the heroics and the villainies of governments and the vulgarities and much milder villainies of business, one gets an increasing affection for workhorses like Standard Oil and General Motors, and a slight nausea in the contemplation of "people's governments." Even from the point of view of equality in distribution it is very hard to demonstrate any clear relationship between forms of organization and the distribution of income. Monopoly may make incomes more equal if the monopolist is poor! Certainly communism is no guarantee of equality of income, and in concentration of economic power it exceeds the wildest dreams of the Rockefellers and Insulls!

Economic freedom and business organization. On the score of freedom certainly both monopoly and communism are to be indicted; if to be free is to have many masters, there is nothing like a good competitive market for providing it! One doubts whether any system of political checks and balances can ensure personal freedom in the way that is provided by an active labor market, where the individual can go where he wants, and always be reasonably sure of finding a job. If states had to compete for citizens in the way that firms have to compete for their labor force they might be much better behaved! On the other hand the freedom to be poor is very poor freedom, and the communist argument that freedom must be sacrificed to high rates of economic growth in order that men may be freed from their prison cells of poverty is not to be taken lightly. It can only be answered by showing that economic freedom is not incompatible with economic growth—which means, perhaps, that the freedom of the backward-looking and content-with-things-as-they-are part of the population may have to be limited in favor of increased freedom for the innovator and the daring young man. This is a part of the subject where there are no easy answers.

13 Agricultural policy

The Farmer is obsessed with Price:
So Parity's his pet device;
But now, alas, we find in Parity
The nation's most expensive charity.
Those generous contributions which
Should help the Poor, support the Rich,
Because, when Prices we uphold,
We pay the more, the more is sold.

Agriculture as a declining occupation. The agricultural sector of every economy has always presented special problems and has usually enjoyed special treatment in government policies. The peculiar position of agriculture arises partly because of social and political structures. The rural vote, for instance, is almost invariably overweighted in legislatures based on local representation, and farmers—in the past fifty years at least—have become well organized and active politically.

There are also, however, fundamental economic reasons for the special position of agriculture as a "chronically depressed" occupation. Paradoxically enough, the economic difficulties of agriculture arise in large part out of its technological successes. Most agricultural products have a low income-elasticity; that is to say, a rise in household income leads to a less-than-proportionate rise in their consumption. The proportion of income spent on food, for instance, falls almost continually with increase in income. This means that as techniques in agriculture improve, and a society gets richer in consequence, the *proportion* of its resources devoted to agriculture continuously falls. In a society in which the food producer is able to produce barely enough for his own family it is clear that close to 100 per cent of the society will be in food production, and there will be no manufactures, and no cities. If the food producer can feed himself and one other family then only 50 per cent of the people have to be in food production, as they can produce enough for the whole population; this releases 50 per cent for producing other things, and permits the development of cities and civilization. In the United States today we can produce all the food we need with about 15 per cent of the population: this means that we can spare 85 per cent to produce automobiles, cities, atom bombs, and the other luxuries and conveniences of life. The real income of a society, therefore, depends to a very large extent on the productivity of agriculture—no matter how productive the techniques in industry, if the society cannot spare people from food production it will not be able to have a very large industrial output.

The income disadvantage of agriculture. However, the very rise in agricultural productivity that is the foundation for the wealth and power of a society creates *relative* difficulties for agriculture. This is because, as we have seen, in a progressive society the *proportion* of resources devoted to agriculture continually declines. In the United States, for instance, this proportion has fallen from something like 90 per cent in the eighteenth century, to 50 per cent by about 1870, to the 15 per cent of today, and undoubtedly will fall further. In another few decades we may find ourselves able to produce all the food we need with only 5 per cent of the population. The only way to achieve a relative decline of any occupation, however, is to squeeze people out of it—that is, to make it somewhat less attractive than the relatively expanding occupations. We shall not be surprised, therefore, to find that agricultural incomes (per capita) have been persistently below urban incomes for similar qualities of work. In the United States, for instance, according to the calculations of the Department of Agriculture, the per-capita income of persons on farms from all sources has rarely exceeded *half* the per-capita income of persons not on farms, and in depression has fallen to *one third*. These figures must be interpreted carefully, as we shall see, but they indicate at least a perceptible income disadvantage for agriculture.

The need for movement of people out of agriculture. The income disadvantage of agriculture is a result of the inadequate rate of migration out of agriculture. The amount of economic pressure (as measured by the income differential) that is necessary to get people out of agriculture depends on the ease or difficulty of getting them out! A very slight pressure will squeeze a thin and mobile liquid out of a tube, whereas it takes heavy pressure to squeeze out a heavy grease or paste. The mechanics of the discrimination against agriculture is very simple. A technical improvement increases agricultural output; the price elasticity for agricultural products is low, hence quite a small excess of production causes a sharp fall in the price, and therefore in agricultural incomes. If this results in a rapid shift of resources out of agriculture, agricultural output diminishes, industrial output grows, and very soon agricultural prices and incomes rise again. If, however, it is difficult for resources to move out of agriculture the excess of agricultural product persists, and agricultural incomes remain low for a long time. The faster the rate of technological improvement the greater must be the relative movement out of agriculture to maintain agricultural incomes at par with industrial incomes. An additional source of low incomes in agriculture is the almost universal phenomenon of a higher birth rate (and natural rate of population growth) in agriculture than in industry. Even if the relative proportions of the people in agriculture and industry were unchanged, then, there would have to be a migration from agriculture to industry—the surplus production of people in the country replenishing the deficit in the towns. This would again necessitate a real income differential between agriculture and industry, for if there were not such a differential the additional agricultural people would not migrate to industry, the agricultural population would increase relative to the industrial population, and this would soon cause an excess of agricultural production and a fall in agricultural prices, resulting in lower incomes for the farm families.

The parity concept. American agricultural policy for the past generation has been dominated by the concept of "parity." This concept originated in the Bureau of Agricultural Economics of the Department of Agriculture and is an interesting example of how a statistical concept can become a powerful symbol, capable of organizing large political movements around it. The Bureau had prepared an index of prices received by farmers and another index of prices paid by farmers, and someone had the bright idea of dividing the first by the second: so the parity index was born. The base years of the original index comprised the period 1909-14, for which years, therefore, the index stands at 100. When the index of prices received by farmers ("farm prices") is relatively higher than the index of prices paid, the parity index is above 100; when farm prices are relatively lower than prices paid the parity index is below 100. Thus in the depression years 1930-34 the prices-received index was 90, the prices-paid index was 135, and the parity index was therefore $\frac{90}{135} \times 100$, or 67. In the war years 1945-49 the prices-received index was 250, the prices-paid index was 230, and the parity index was therefore $\frac{250}{230} \times 100$, or 109.

The parity index as a measure of agriculture's terms of trade. In order to understand why the parity index is low in depression and high in prosperity we must see it as a measure of the *terms of trade* of agriculture. The "terms of trade" is an expression used in the study of international trade to mean the ratio of a country's physical volume of imports to its physical volume of exports; it is the amount of imports it can get per unit of exports. The higher this ratio the more "favorable" the terms of trade—the more the country gets for a unit of what it gives in exchange. Now let us think of agriculture as one "country" and industry as another, and consider the trade between them. Agriculture "exports" agricultural products to industry and "imports" industrial products from industry. Let P_r be the price index of its "exports" (this is the same as "prices received by farmers") and Q_e be the quantity—*i.e.*, the volume of produce sold off farm. Then gross farm *income* is P_rQ_e. Similarly, let P_p be the price index of farm "imports" of industrial goods and services, and Q_i their quantity. Then P_pQ_i is equal to farm expenditures for goods purchased from industry. If now farm income and expenditures are equal, which will at least be approximately true, we have

$$P_rQ_e = P_pQ_i, \text{ or}$$

$$\frac{P_r}{P_p} = \frac{Q_i}{Q_e}.$$

That is, the parity index is equal to the index of the terms of trade of agriculture. The equality is not quite exact, but is exact enough for the present argument.

Why do the terms of trade of agriculture deteriorate in depression? The question therefore as to why the parity index falls in depression is practically the same question as to why do the terms of trade of agriculture worsen in depression? The answer to this question can be found in the different behavior of industrial and agricultural *outputs* in depression. Agricultural markets are usually highly competitive, and agricultural output is produced by large numbers of independently acting producers. When money incomes decline, or markets weaken, the effect is felt immediately in a fall in prices, not in a fall in output. Indeed, in a severe depression agricultural output may even increase, in spite of the low incomes, partly because farmers work harder trying to maintain their incomes when prices fall, and partly because people with rural connections often drift back to the farm when unemployment rises in the towns. In industry, on the other hand, markets are more highly organized and monopolistic; the reaction of industry to weak markets is to cut back output and lay off men rather than to reduce prices. In a depression, therefore, agricultural output stays up, and industrial output declines.

The *trade* between agriculture and industry, however, consists of the exchange of the excess of farm production over farm consumption of farm products, for the excess of industrial production over the nonfarm consumption of industrial products. In depression, farm production and consumption of farm products do not change much: the farmer has just about as much to sell as before—which is just as well for the urban population, who at least by and large eat about as well in a depression as in prosperity! Industrial production is down, however, and the consumption of industrial products by nonfarm people does not fall proportionately: hence industry has less to offer the farmer in depression than in periods of full employment. That is, farm exports to industry stay up, but what industry has available for the farmer to import declines. Thus the farmer gets less for what he gives up than before—the terms of trade turn against him. If the farmer cannot buy much in depression it is because the stuff that he otherwise would have bought is simply not being produced, and the resources that might have produced it are standing idle.

Why farmers are "price conscious." It is not surprising, in view of the obvious and intimate connection between farm prices and farm incomes, that the farmer is "price conscious" and that agricultural policy tends to be "price centered." A depression hits the industrial worker in the form of unemployment, rather than in the form of low wages. Indeed, the real wages of the employed frequently rise during a depression.

The industrial worker, therefore, as we shall see in the next chapter, is "job-conscious." A depression hits the farmer, however, not in the form of unemployment (there is never any lack of things to do on the farm) but in the form of low prices for his product, and therefore a low return on his labor and capital. The farmer therefore tends to see his problem in terms of low prices, and the appeal of the parity concept—which seemed to put this ancient grumble into focus and give it a kind of "scientific" standing—is not hard to understand.

Deficiencies of price-centered policy. Nevertheless the parity concept is extremely unsatisfactory as a goal of agricultural policy, however valuable it may have been—and still is—as a political symbol. There are two fundamental arguments against a price-centered agricultural policy. The first is that it is an extremely ineffective means of tackling the problem of *poverty* in agriculture. The second is that the administrative measures that have been taken to try to raise agricultural prices are wasteful and self-defeating, and frequently aggravate the problem instead of alleviating it.

The problem of agricultural poverty not solved by price policy. The problem of poverty in agriculture, even in a rich country like the United States, is a real one. There are between a million and two million farmers out of the approximately six million farmers of the United States who might be classified as "poor." These are concentrated heavily in the south, especially in the Appalachians and in the Mississippi valley. When we look at the world as a whole, of course, there are hundreds of millions of farmers, especially in Asia and Africa, who live at a level of poverty so deep that the Kentucky mountaineer or the Mississippi sharecropper live in luxury by comparison. Nevertheless, the million or so "poor farmers" of the United States live far below the standards of their urban compeers, or of their more fortunate farm brethren, and so present what looks like a problem of economic injustice.

Raising agricultural prices, however, does very little to help the poor farmers, because the main reason why they are poor is that they have very little to sell, and they have little to sell because they produce very little. Also, the poorer the farmer, the smaller the proportion of his produce he sells off the farm and the more he consumes at home, and farm prices are significant only for the portion that he sells. In the extreme case of a completely self-subsistent homestead which sells nothing off the farm the level of income is completely unaffected by prices, for nothing multiplied by anything is still nothing! So a policy of raising farm prices through some artificial means—that is, by some kind of a subsidy from the rest of society—helps the rich farmer much more than it helps the poor farmer. Agricultural policy is sold to the nonfarm population (which after all is now in a large majority) by appealing to its sense of charity; the argument goes that the poor should be helped, farmers are poor, and therefore farmers should be helped. The fallacy of the argument is that only *some* farmers are poor and some even are quite rich, and that a policy designed to help farmers, especially by raising prices, helps the rich farmer more than the poor one. Agricultural policy has been described as a "charity racket,"[1] in which about a tenth of the "take" goes to the poor farmer on whose behalf the policy is ostensibly supported, and about nine tenths goes to the promoters—the wealthy and middle class farmers who constitute the backbone of the agricultural organizations and pressure groups.

Techniques of price policy: the nonrecourse loan. The second argument against price-centered policy is that many of the methods employed to raise prices result in severe social wastes. These methods all involve devices either for restricting the quantity of the commodity sold through ordinary domestic markets, or for increasing the demand in these markets. The simplest device for restricting the quantity entering the market is government purchase and storage. We have seen earlier that a government can fix a market price for any storable commodity by the simple device of offering to buy and sell the commodity in unlimited quantities at the desired price. We have seen how this operates to fix the price of gold under a gold standard; the

[1] I am indebted to Dr. A. G. Hart for this brilliant analogy.

same principle can also be applied to farm commodities, such as wheat or corn. The device used to carry out this price support is known as the "nonrecourse loan." A farmer can borrow from the government, using say his stock of corn as security, an amount equal to the amount of corn so pledged multiplied by the "support price" of corn. Thus if he has 1,000 bushels of corn and the support price is $1.50 per bushel, he can borrow $1,500. If the market price of corn rises above $1.50, he can sell the corn and repay the loan, and have something left over (not counting interest). If the market price is below $1.50, however, at the time he decided to pay back the loan, he gives title to his corn to the government and does not have to repay the loan in cash. Thus the farmer is sure of getting $1.50 a bushel for his corn no matter what the market price when it is sold, for if the market price falls below $1.50 he can in effect sell the corn to the government at that price. This means, however, that the market price cannot fall much below the support price, or the quantity coming to market will fall off sharply as farmers turn in their corn to the government.

Agricultural surpluses related to high support prices. There is, under any given set of circumstances, some average level of the support price at which stocks in the hands of government will neither rise nor fall in the long run; this is what is known as the "normal price." If, however, the support price is above the normal price for any considerable period a gap will develop between production and consumption. Production will be encouraged and consumption discouraged by the high price, and stocks will accumulate in the hands of the government. This is the phenomenon of "agricultural surpluses." It is clear that the government cannot go on piling up stocks of these commodities for ever; hence, though price supports can keep prices above the normal level for a while, they will inevitably lead to a breakdown of the system through the accumulation of stocks.

Solutions to the surplus problem: (1) destruction, (2) dumping abroad. Four possible solutions present themselves for the problem of surpluses—assuming, that is, that we still wish to maintain the price above normal. The simplest solution is just to destroy them. This, indeed, is precisely what Brazil has done at times with coffee, preferring to dump it into the Atlantic in order to keep up the price rather than trying to dispose of it in any other way. This solution, however, is perhaps too barefacedly simple, and it arouses resistance; there seems to be something peculiarly wicked about destroying food in a hungry world. The second solution is to dump it on foreign markets, and so feed it to foreigners rather than to fish. This is the principle of a "two-price system" which still has its advocates, and has even been tried to a limited extent in the case of cotton. This was the principle of the McNary-Haugen bills which represented the best Congressional thinking on this subject of the 1920's, but were vetoed by the even better Presidential thinking of President Coolidge. A two-price system (that is, selling cheap abroad and dear at home) is an example of price discrimination such as we have already noticed in the case of railroad rates. It can only work if the exports of the country are a fairly small proportion of the world market; otherwise the world market will not be able to absorb the increased exports without a substantial fall in the world price, which will cause all manner of international difficulties.

(3) **Dumping at home.** The third solution is that of expanding domestic consumption, again usually through a two-price or multiple-price system, such as the food-stamp plan, whereby families on relief or assistance can get surplus foods at low prices, or the school lunch program under which school children are provided with a free or a below-cost lunch heavily spiked with surplus foods. This is certainly the least objectionable of all methods of disposal of an agricultural surplus; however, it is limited in scope, as it can succeed only if there are highly elastic domestic markets that are untapped at the support prices. The scheme then involves maintaining the support price by tapping these low-price markets without giving up the high prices in the markets that can afford to pay them.

(4) **Production and marketing controls.** The fourth solution is control of production or of farm marketings. Production control has on the whole been rather unsuccessful—unsuccessful,

that is, from the point of view of controlling production! It is usually based on a system of acreage quotas: each farmer is allowed to plant only a given percentage of his acreage under the crop in some base period. Inducements to participate are generally in the form of denial of price-support privileges to nonparticipants. The failure of these schemes arises mainly because they invariably stimulate a rise in the yield per acre, as farmers tend to put as much, if not more, labor and fertilizer into the restricted number of acres. If the land has been farmed too extensively before, this may even *increase* the total production, as the rise in yields per acre more than compensates for the diminished acreage! There is some evidence that this actually happened in the case of cotton in the 1930's.

The restriction of marketing by means of marketing quotas is more apt to be successful, as a device for maintaining the price, than attempts at restriction of production. Marketing quotas (which again have to be based on the amount the farmer sold in some base period) are not too difficult to administer and very effectively restrict the amount that comes to market. Marketing quotas are also usually more effective in restricting production than are attempts to restrict production directly, for there is not much point in growing what cannot be sold through the regular channels.

The very success of the marketing quota, however, is a strong argument against it from the broader point of view. Restrictionist policies may be tolerated as long as they are inefficient; they soon become objectionable once they start to work. The great objection to the marketing quota is that any gains to the producer soon become capitalized, as we have seen, in the value of his quota, if that is salable, or in the value of his land if the quota is based on land ownership or use. The best example of the marketing quota in American agricultural policy is probably that of tobacco. The result of the scheme has been to increase enormously the value of the land that enjoys a quota, so that anyone now wishing to enter the tobacco-growing industry must in effect pay a large tax to someone who was fortunate enough to be in it at the time the quota scheme went into operation. It is difficult to justify such an artificial creation of "property."

Income-payment proposals: the Brannan Plan. The difficulties of price-centered policy have led to proposals to substitute "income payments" for price supports. This was the central idea of the "Brannan Plan," proposed by the then Secretary of Agriculture Brannan in 1949, but never adopted by Congress. The proposal is that instead of supporting prices by purchasing the commodities, the government should allow prices to fall to the level at which all the output is disposed of in the usual channels, and then make up the difference between the market price and the "support price" by a direct cash payment to the farmer. Thus, suppose that the "support price" for wheat were $2.00 per bushel, and that the market price were $1.50. Then for every bushel of wheat the farmer sold he would get $1.50 from the buyer and $0.50 from the government.

Price supports distort relative outputs— The principal arguments in favor of this proposal are, first, that it would automatically avoid the problem of agricultural surpluses, and would permit the disposal of products through usual commercial channels, and second, that it would avoid those distortions in the structure of *relative* outputs that are an inevitable consequence of purchase programs. The second point needs further explanation. In the first place, price-support programs based on purchase and storage must inevitably concentrate on easily storable commodities that do not depreciate much in storage and are not expensive to store. This means in practice the major "grain" crops—wheat, corn, and so on—plus cotton, plus a few minor crops like peanuts and flaxseed. The program has been extended to refrigerated products like butter and cheese, but this is difficult, and spoilage and cost of storage present grave problems. This means, however, that the perishable commodities—fresh vegetables, milk, meat—do not receive support, and the *relative* price structure of agricultural products gets distorted in favor of the storable crops. Consequently the relative *output* structure likewise gets distorted—too much of the storable crops being produced and not enough of the perishable ones. This is doubly unfortunate, because it is precisely the perishable crops that are most in need of expansion from the point of view of a nutritionally balanced diet. In effect we are subsidizing corn pone by a tax on milk and fresh vegetables; folly can hardly go further.

—even within the supported commodities. Furthermore, not only is there a distortion as between storable and nonstorable commodities, but even within the group of supported commodities the relative prices tend to be frozen at the base-date structure, if the support prices are based on a parity ratio for *each commodity*. Thus, suppose the "parity price" for wheat was $2 per bushel. This would be calculated by taking the average price of wheat in the base period (say, 1909-1914) and multiplying it by the ratio of the present index of prices paid by farmers to the same index in the base period. If the price of wheat in the base period was $1, and if the index of prices paid by farmers was 200 now and 100 in the base period, the parity price would be $\$1 \times \frac{200}{100}$. That is, the parity price for any particular commodity is the price that gives a unit of *that commodity* the same purchasing power it had in the base period. There is no reason to suppose, however, that there is anything sacred about the purchasing power of a commodity in the base period! Indeed, as time goes on, some commodities get relatively cheaper to produce, some get relatively dearer, because of the unequal incidence of technical change and factor scarcities. If the relative prices of the base period are maintained, those commodities that have been favored most by cost reductions will be priced too high, and those that have not will be priced too low. Thus, suppose that the average cost of production of wheat in the time since the base period had fallen by half, while that of the other commodities had not. It would be absurd to maintain the same purchasing power for a bushel of wheat that it had in the base period, for this would give the wheat producers unreasonably high incomes.

The income-payments plan reveals the basic incongruity of agricultural support. Both these arguments for an income-payments plan are sound in themselves; it would avoid surpluses, and it *could* avoid relative price distortions within agriculture, though it would have to be framed very carefully in order to do this. Nevertheless, the very elimination of the more obvious defects of agricultural support reveals all the more clearly the fundamental incongruities that are involved in supporting "agriculture" as such. An income-payments plan based on support prices reveals almost blatantly the principle of to him that hath shall be given; it will be the rich farmer who sells a lot who will get the biggest check from the government, and the poor farmer, who is poor because he sells so little, will get a very small check, if any. There is some possibility of making the payments discriminate against the large farmer, either by setting an upper limit as in the original Brannan Plan, or by a sliding scale. Proposals of this kind, however, make the plan unacceptable to those farmers who are politically the most influential, and in any case cannot do more than modify the inequity.

Cumulative instability of income payments. Furthermore, an income-payments plan based on support prices that are on the whole above "normal" is just as likely to run into cumulative difficulties as a purchase and storage plan. As we saw, a purchase and storage plan is likely to run into ever-increasing surpluses if the support prices are above normal. An income-payments plan would not run into this difficulty, as excess production would result in a fall in market prices to the point where it would be disposed of through normal channels. If, however, the support prices are above normal, an income-payments plan will run into ever-increasing *payments*. The high support will encourage production, and will discourage the migration from agriculture to industry, which we saw was a necessity in a technically progressive society. The more production, the lower will be the market prices necessary to dispose of it, and the higher will be the income payments. We might even find ourselves in a few years having to give away all our agricultural produce for nothing in order to dispose of the ever-mounting production, meanwhile paying the whole of farmers' income out of the public treasury! Long before this absurd position, of course, there would be a public outcry against so outrageous a use of public funds, and the scheme would break down through the unwillingness of Congress to appropriate enough money. Another difficulty of the scheme is that because of the relatively inelastic demand for most agricultural commodities a small excess of output may produce a very large fall in market price, and consequently very large income payments. The income payments therefore would fluctuate wildly from year to year—a phenomenon which would also be regarded coldly by the legislators called upon to appropriate the money.

Flexible price supports. One modification of the price-support principle, in either its purchase-storage form or the income-payments form, that would go partway to eliminate the objection that it leads to cumulative disequilibrium, is the "flexible" or "sliding scale" price-support proposal. This was embodied in the Agriculture Act of 1948, but has never been put into application. The principle here is that the level of price support should fall according to some formula related to the "normal supply," so that the larger the excess production above some defined normal level, the lower the level of price support. This reintroduces the principle of a downward sloping demand curve for these products, and relieves the government of the obligation of purchasing—or of subsidizing—indefinite amounts at a fixed support price. Such a system would eventually find an equilibrium where the support price was about equal to the normal price.

Forward prices. The question might be raised: why bother to support the price if it is not supported above normal! There is, however, a strong case for what are called "forward prices"—that is, a government guarantee in *advance* of a minimum price for a crop or a product, made sufficiently far in advance of the harvest so that the farmer can make his decisions as to how much to produce in the light of these forward price "floors." Flexible forward prices, adjusted period by period in response to surpluses or shortages, would eliminate that degree of uncertainty in the farm enterprise that arises from purely speculative fluctuations in price. Uncertainty is a real social cost of these operations, and if some unnecessary price uncertainty can be removed, without destroying the essential function of price as an adjuster of supply to demand, this lowers the real cost of the commodities concerned and it should be possible to obtain them at a lower price. The system now moves sedately towards equilibrium by periodic adjustments of the forward price, rather than through the cat-on-hot-bricks oscillations of the speculative market. The difficulty, however, with reasonable systems is that they are seldom popular, and the political fate of the sliding scale indicates that it is probably not part of a stable political system.

Support of education and research. Price supports are not, of course, the whole of agricultural policy, and we should at least mention some other aspects. The support that government has given to education and research is probably the part of agricultural policy that has paid off best from the point of view of society as a whole, even though as we have seen it may not help the *relative* position of agriculture. An important part of the almost constant improvement in agricultural productivity that we have enjoyed in the past hundred years is a result of the Morrill Act of 1862 which set up the Land Grant Colleges, out of which grew the agricultural experiment stations. These institutions, together with the county agent system which they fostered, must be given a great deal of credit for what amounts to a technological revolution—a revolution, moreover, on which the *industrial* power of the United States is largely based, for it is the labor power released from agriculture that mans the industrial occupations.

Land problems: owner-occupancy *vs.* tenancy. Agriculture is peculiar in that it uses much more land than any other sector of the economy, and some special problems arise from this. Should we, for instance, aim at owner-occupancy as an ideal—that is, aim at a situation where the average farmer owns his own land? The ideal picture of the independent proprietor, secure on his acres, as the economic base of a healthy democracy, as over against the economy of large estates and insecure tenants, has been an important image, especially in American political life. Owner-occupancy, however, is unstable, simply because there is nothing in the processes of inheritance that ensures that the people who own land are going to be those best able to farm it. Even if we started off with a system of pure owner-occupancy (which was the object of the homesteading system by which the states west of the Alleghenies were settled), it would not last: farms would come into the possession of maiden aunts and city cousins as the original proprietors died off and property got reshuffled in the long slow process of inheritance. Soon we would find that only a proportion of the equity in farms and farm land was owned by people who actually wanted to operate the farms.

There are two solutions to this problem. One is the development of credit, or what is the same thing, debt—that is, financial institutions and instruments that permit the farm operator to "own" a farm without having much equity in it. The lender or the mortgage holder now "owns" most of the value of the farm, but has little or no part in operating it. The other solution is tenancy in one form or another—that is an arrangement whereby the owner of the land "hires" it to the farmer for some consideration. There are several kinds of tenancy, depending on the type of "consideration." In sharecropping (called "metayage" in Europe) the tenant delivers to the landlord a proportion of the crop, or of the proceeds from the crop. In cash tenancy the tenant pays the landlord a money payment fixed by the contract. There are many intermediate forms.

Effects of inflation and deflation on farm mortgages. Given the institutions of property and the freedom to dispose of property by wills, it is impossible to achieve "pure" owner-occupancy (that is, where the operator of the farm owns the whole equity in it) beyond a certain rather small percentage. The choice is between tenancy and "mortgaged ownership," and government policy can, especially over the long pull, favor one or the other substantially. Thus in Denmark mortgaged ownership is predominant, in England tenancy, as a result of decades or even centuries of fairly deliberate policy.

Mortgaged ownership has the great advantage of security in possession for the operator, barring failure to pay on the mortgage contract and subsequent foreclosure. The danger of mortgaged ownership is that it is peculiarly vulnerable to deflation. In the United States, for instance, many farmers lost their mortgaged farms in the great depressions of the 1870's and the 1930's. The reason is clear. Suppose a farmer buys a farm for, say $50,000, pays $10,000 in cash and takes out a mortgage for $40,000, with annual payments for interest and amortization of, say $4,000. If the gross income of the farm is $12,000 the mortgage payments are no great hardship. Now suppose, however, that the price level halves. The annual income is now only $6,000, and the value of the farm, is now, say, only $25,000. The farmer's own equity is completely wiped out, and the mortgage payments have become an almost intolerable burden. Foreclosure and loss of the farm are all too likely. The converse of this gloomy picture is, of course, that in a period of inflation farmers rapidly reduce their burden of debt, and those who were fortunate enough to buy their farms at the beginning of the inflation are apt to find themselves in full possession by the end. Those who buy at the beginning of a deflation, however, are almost doomed to failure. Many of the difficulties of agriculture have arisen out of a certain inclination of farmers to get into debt at the wrong time—for instance, in 1919, or even worse in 1929.

The evaluation of tenancy. Tenancy has a bad name in the United States, largely because of the disastrous effect of the sharecropping system in the South, which at its worst has bred poverty and soil erosion, and even at its best is the economic foundation of a social system that is not compatible with the spirit of an independent citizenry and a democratic society. Tenancy, however, should not be condemned outright. It has been fairly successful in England, and given laws that provide reasonable security of tenure and compensation for improvements, there is no reason why tenancy should not represent a reasonable division of labor between landowner and operator. There are studies showing that a young farmer with limited capital does a little better when he rents a farm and puts his capital into equipment than when he tries to buy a farm and so perhaps has to skimp on equipment.

Agricultural credit policy. Government policy in this field involves setting up the legal framework of tenancy and mortgage contracts. It also may involve creating specialized institutions for agricultural credit. Two kinds of institutions of this kind have been sponsored by the United States government: Federal Land Banks and Intermediate Credit Banks.

Intermediate credit is needed for the finance of long processes of production, such as the raising of cattle or the maturing of wines and cheeses. The establishment of government-sponsored institutions reflects a dissatisfaction with private institutions in the field. The dissatisfaction may not be wholly unjustified, as private credit institutions are mostly of urban origin and their directors and managers tend to be city folk who may not be adequately sensitive to rural needs. The government credit institutions, however, have also been very conservative, especially in this long inflation, and their contribution can hardly be regarded as outstanding.

Probably the most interesting experiment in government credit, used as a positive tool for human and social reconstruction, was the Farm Security Administration (1937-1946) and its successor the Farm Home Administration. Here credit to low-income farmers was used combined with a program of advice and counsel as a lever to raise levels of living. The possibilities of combining credit management with social work in this way are still far from exploited, either in rural or even in urban communities. Debt can be a powerful breeder of respectability if the conditions are right.

"Family farm" policy. A problem of the structure of agriculture that has received much attention is the maintenance of the "family farm." The contrast is drawn between the independent farmer, operating his enterprise mainly with the help of his family or at most with a hired man, and the large "factory in the fields" employing many day laborers or migrants. In Europe the same contrast is drawn between the independent peasant and the great landed estate; in Asia between the small native proprietor and the plantation.

The virtues of the family farm depend largely on its size and efficiency. There is an enormous contrast between the "family farm" of 300 acres in Iowa, operated by a single man with the aid of tens of thousands of dollars worth of machinery, and the peasant holding of an acre or two of rice in China operated entirely by hand. We may run into a real dilemma here of efficiency *versus* desirability of the social structure. Thus "land reform" that involves a mere break-up of great estates into peasant farms that are too small for efficient agriculture may be a disaster for the society, for it diminishes the food supply and sets back the rate of economic development. We see in the United States, however, especially in the Middle West, that large-scale, highly capitalized, efficient agriculture is not inconsistent with family-sized enterprises. Except in one or two fields like truck farming and range livestock there do not seem to be any startling economies of scale in American agriculture, and the family farm, though it is itself getting larger both in area and in the amount of capital required, is at least holding its own against the so-called "large" farm.

The key to the persistence of the family farm is the difficulty of routinizing the operations of agriculture, especially in livestock enterprises. Livestock seem to require a certain amount of loving care, and almost have to be part of the family to thrive! We must not, however, make a fetish of the family farm. It should not be impossible to solve some of the social problems that go along with large-scale enterprise without giving up the benefits in terms of efficiency, and concentration on the family farm as an ideal in itself may lead to too little imaginative thinking about more satisfactory conditions of wage labor.

The migrant labor problem. Migrant labor presents a human problem of unusual difficulty. Migrants tend to lack "roots" and community. They tend to be rejected by the communities through which they pass, and their conditions of work and life are often poor. On the other hand, we must beware of attempts to solve this problem by simple exclusion—a solution made easier by the circumstance that many migrant laborers are aliens, either from Mexico or the Caribbean. The migrants *may* be better off than if they had stayed at home, and the fact that they make us uncomfortable by the visibility of their poverty is no good reason for confining them to the greater, but less visible poverty of their home countries.

Soil conservation. Another important aspect of agricultural policy is soil conservation. This issue was dramatized by the great droughts and dust storms of the mid-1930's, when samples of Kansas and Nebraska started to show up quite literally on the steps of Congress. It is hard to appraise the many conflicting viewpoints on this issue.

On the one hand there are the extreme "viewers with alarm" who feel that man is rapidly making the planet uninhabitable; ecologists and naturalists have a certain tendency in this direction, for it is undoubtedly true that man always upsets the existing balance of nature. At the other extreme are the optimists who can see no limits to man's ingenuity or his ability to solve problems as they arise. The economic issue is fortunately simpler than this grand philosophical controversy. Soil conservation practices are those that increase the value of the land more, or decrease it less, than alternative "nonconserving" practices. Thus contour ploughing and terracing are more conserving than straight up-and-down ploughing, soybeans are a more conserving crop than corn, and so on.

There are then two problems. First, is there anything in the culture or in the institutions of rural life that prevents the farmer from following conserving practices which are to his *own* advantage? This is the problem of ignorance on the one hand, and short-term unprotected tenancy on the other. It is also a problem of the "time-horizon" of the farmer; will he take quick returns on crops that ruin the land, or is he out to maximize his advantage over a long period? This is the sort of problem that is tackled by education and propaganda, and perhaps also by tenant-right laws which give the tenant property in his improvements.

Then there is a second problem: do the interests of society

require a greater degree of conservation than is in the interests of the individual farmer? Society generally has a longer time-perspective than the individual. It may be of advantage to society, therefore, to push the individual, by a judicious system of subsidies and encouragements, towards a more conservationist set of practices than he would follow if simply left to his own interest. What might be called the "ethic" of conservation is of importance here. A good deal of soil conservation ideology is devoted to building up an ethic of "stewardship" for the land and its resources, so that people will individually willingly forego some present advantage for the benefit of the continuity of the society.

The level of conservation. An important consideration in conservation policy is the *level* at which it pays to conserve. Conservation practices exhibit diminishing returns like almost everything else. It would certainly not pay us, for instance, to try to conserve virgin soils or virgin forest at their pristine level of fertility. There is a case here for "soil-mining" down to a more easily maintainable level. The problem of conservation is made more difficult, in general, because of uncertainty about the technological future. This is particularly clear in the case of exhaustible resources; should we freeze on top of our coal mines for fear of using them up, or should we spend these resources without inhibition in the hope of finding continual new sources and substitutes? In a sense we can regard the present era of high civilization based on the exploitation of fossil fuels and concentrated minerals as an experiment in the transformation of natural capital into knowledge. We do not at present have the knowledge to establish a permanent high-level civilization free from dependence on exhaustible resources. There are indications, however, that such knowledge is not impossible to obtain, and the long-run future of man depends on his ability to use this happy inheritance of fuel and minerals which he is now running through rather rapidly, in order to acquire the knowledge that can put his civilization on a firmer long-run foundation. Invention, born of necessity, provides new sources of fuel to augment or conserve dwindling supplies.

The confusion of conservation and income payments. To return to more mundane matters: conservation policy in the United States has been confused somewhat because conservation has been used as an excuse to make what are essentially income payments to farmers. Thus, when the original Agricultural Adjustment Act of 1933 was declared unconstitutional, the Soil Conservation and Domestic Allotment Act of 1936 was passed as a substitute, largely to get around the unconstitutionality of the processing tax by which payments under the 1933 act were financed. As a result of this history there are two agencies in the field of soil conservation—the Production and Marketing Administration, which administers the Agricultural Conservation Program, which is a centralized, Federal program, and the Soil Conservation Service (set up also in 1936) which encourages the formation of local soil conservation districts under state law. As a result of this duplication of authority the whole picture is somewhat confused, and the farmer sometimes finds himself getting different sets of advice from the two agencies! The Soil Conservation Service has done excellent work in creating an "ethic" of conservation, and has been inspired by almost a religious zeal. The activities of the ACP are more open to question, as the mixture of income payments with conservation leads to a good deal of waste.

Agricultural marketing problems. There are many other aspects of agricultural policy which we must pass over lightly in this brief survey. There is, for instance, the whole problem of agricultural marketing. Some people have seen the difficulties of agriculture as caused by the high costs of processing and marketing, and have sought means for reducing this, for instance by the establishment of agricultural marketing cooperatives. There is this much truth in the above position, that the difficulties of farmers in depression may be aggravated by the relative "stickiness" of marketing costs in a deflation, so that a fall in retail prices of farm produce is reflected in a greater proportionate fall in farm prices. There is not much evidence, however, to show that the marketing and processing of farm products are either less efficient, or more profitable, than the general run of occupations—indeed, both processing and retailing have at least kept pace with the general technological improvement in the United States, and perhaps even have improved faster than the average. One cannot feel certain that there is any serious problem here, especially in an age of supermarkets and packing plants, and whatever problems there are are certainly not responsible for the farmers' difficulties.

The contributions of agricultural policy: (1) to economic progress. We now come to evaluation. From the point of view of economic progress there is much to be said for a rather special emphasis on agriculture, if only because it is the sale of food from agriculture that feeds the rest of the population. In underdeveloped areas there is the additional consideration that at an early stage of development agriculture is by far the most important single occupation. There has been much misunderstanding of this point. Economic development has been thought of too much in terms of industrialization, and it has not been realized that industrialization can only be based on an increase in the food sales from agriculture. The success of economic development in Japan may be largely due to the emphasis placed on agricultural as well as industrial development in that country, and failure in other parts of the world may be due to an overemphasis on industry and a neglect of agriculture. In poor countries with primitive agricultural techniques often relatively simple improvements in agricultural methods will lead to enormous returns to the society; long-handled hoes and improved plows may be much more important at this stage than tractors!

United States policy scores well on this account. The support given to agricultural research and education, and especially the splendid device of the County Agent have paid off magnificently as far as the general progress of the society is concerned. The homesteading principle as a means of settling the frontier, and the general absence of restrictive feudal land laws also must get some credit for the progress of the American economy. There is a very real magic in fee simple, and the energy and productivity of small-capitalist agriculture is a marked contrast to the inertia of collectivized agriculture. Agriculture seems to be the one place where individualistic institutions, especially when placed in a setting of wise collective action and an ethic of community responsibility, are more conducive to rapid development than collective farms. The one exception that might be made to this principle is the Kibbutzim or cooperative farms of Israel. Here, however, a very unusual social situation prevails, and there are signs already that as the enthusiasm of the first generation recedes into the past the Kibbutzim will run into increasing difficulties.

(2) to economic stabilization. Insofar as agricultural policy supports the incomes of farmers in times of depression, it makes some contribution to economic stabilization. It usually makes no contribution whatever to the problems of inflation, and indeed rather tends to aggravate them. It is one of the least savory features in the farm group as a political force that it not only makes money out of war and war inflation but that it actively resists any attempt to diminish its carrion profits. It can be argued with much force that if a *general* stabilization policy can be developed there is little need for general income or price-support policies for agriculture, and, indeed, very little justification for them. Although it is no doubt a good thing for the government to give out money, and even perhaps to increase its holdings of commodities during a period of deflation or threatened deflation, there seems to be no reason why farmers should be singled out for these benefits exclusively. Indeed, insofar as a deflationary situation may be caused by a disproportion in the amount of resources devoted to storable goods as against services, leading to the piling up of unwanted stocks of these goods, a policy of support prices for agricultural storables, or even of supporting agricultural income, may actually prevent or at least delay the kind of adjustments in relative outputs that are necessary.

Thus we have seen that in a progressive society the proportion of resources devoted to agriculture must decline. If the decline is not fast enough not only will agricultural incomes be low relative to the rest of society, but there may be a chronic tendency for the accumulation of stocks of agricultural storables which may set off a general deflation and depression. There is something in the claim that great depressions start in agriculture, at least to the extent that an excess of resources in the basic storable crops creates a constant threat of deflation and consequent depression. The remedy is not, however, to subsidize farmers—and especially wheat and corn storable-crop farmers—to stay where they are, but to subsidize them to get out! Price and income supports have precisely the effect of preventing the desirable output adjustments, both within agriculture towards the perishables, and from agriculture into industry and the service trades. Consequently, while these devices may have a palliative effect, they do nothing to correct the underlying disequilibria, but rather make the necessary adjustments all the more difficult.

(3) **to economic justice.** From the point of view of economic justice it is still more difficult to justify a price-support policy. As we have seen, price supports always give more aid to the rich than to the poor. There is a very real problem of poverty in agriculture, even in the United States. It can be solved, however, only by measures that attack poverty as such, not measures that protect agriculture. We cannot do justice to a commodity, nor to an industry; only to people. At no point perhaps has the substitution of a commodity- and price-centered policy for what should be a people-centered policy led to more confusion than in agriculture.

(4) **to economic freedom.** From the point of view of economic freedom, also, the score on price supports is a low one. If they are effective in raising farm incomes they almost invariably lead to various restrictions on the freedom of the farmer to produce what he likes and to sell what he likes, insofar as price supports lead to production or marketing controls. These might be stomached in the interest of a larger freedom; the "larger freedom" in this case, however, is largely a freedom to exploit the public and gain monopoly rents. The problem of maintaining small but efficient farm units and of avoiding the spread of large estates and plantations is a real one in some

parts of the world, and is not unrelated to the general problem of economic freedom. Fortunately this does not seem to be a pressing problem in the United States except for one or two limited areas.

Towards a better agricultural policy. The somewhat negative tone of this chapter may prompt the reader to ask what would be the elements of a *good* agricultural policy! The question is easier to ask than to answer, and any answer must be tentative. Nevertheless, one might venture on the outlines of a policy that would not violate the canons of good policy quite as flagrantly as current policies do. It should include the following main headings: (1) The maintenance of high levels of employment and the prevention of deflation. This would deal with at least three-quarters of the legitimate sources of agricultural discontent. (2) A program of "development credit" for poor farmers to consolidate farms and get them established on a better capital basis. (3) A program to assist migration from agriculture, which again might be somewhat concentrated at the level of the poor farmer. (4) A program to mitigate purely speculative fluctuations in prices by a system of forward pricing, the forward price being on a sliding scale so that the appearance of surpluses automatically lowered the forward price.

14

Labor policy

Labor is a thing of price,
Yet it is not wise or nice
To buy it merely by the hour
As if it were a sack of flour,
And so Collective Bargaining
Becomes the well-accepted thing,
And though economists may grumble,
Pure Competition takes a tumble.

The "labor group" in society. In the history of the past hundred years or so the rise of "labor" as a group in society and the rise of the "labor movement" as the self-conscious expression of this group are striking phenomena. By "labor" we mean the group in society whose income depends mainly on wages—that is, on the sale of labor to an employer—and which does not regard itself as part of "management." We thus see the rise of the labor group as another example of specialization. In a society of independent craftsmen and artisans or small farmers the laborer is his own employer, and the labor and management functions are united in a single person. In a business society these functions become separated. In the extreme case the worker performs no management functions and accepts no responsibility for the enterprise; he sells his labor to it just as a man might sell raw materials.

The industrial relationship. Over a large field of economic activity this division of labor between employers and employed has clearly paid off in terms of productivity and economic development, if only because it seems to be the easiest way of organizing large-scale enterprises with a high degree of specialization of operations. It has, however, created social and emotional problems which do not come to the surface in a less specialized society, and which have provided a great deal of the "steam" behind the rise of the labor movement. This is because of the nature of the "industrial relationship"—that is, the "job"—which relates the employer to the employee.

A job is in part an exchange relationship like any other. The employee gives up something (his time and energy) in return for something else (the wage and other perquisites). The employer gives up the wage in return for the work, or rather for the *product* of the work. So far labor is a commodity, and its wage is a price like any other. The circumstances that surround this exchange, however, are different from those that surround the exchange, say, of wheat for money. In the first place, the transaction looks different from the point of view of each party. The employer views the transaction as essentially an exchange of money for the real assets that are the product of the work. Thus at the end of a week's employment the employer has less money but more cloth or yarn or whatever it is the worker has made. The worker, on the other hand, gets not only money but a "job" with all that this implies in terms of status, conditions of work, associates, and so on, and he gives up the alternative uses of his time. He who sells labor sells life, and sells the right to organize at least part of his life. For the eight hours a day that he works the worker is at the disposal of the employer. What he sells therefore is eight hours of "freedom." What he gets is "status" as well as wages.

Labor as something "more than a commodity." This means that labor is much more than a commodity, although it is *also* a commodity, and that the industrial relationship involves personal and social problems which are not usually found in simple exchange. It is a more complex relationship than that involved in the casual purchase of a shirt; it is a less complex relationship than that involved in the family. The problem of achieving the right degree of complexity in the relationship, and proper institutions for governing it, is the heart of the labor problem. The "pure market" solution in which labor is treated purely as a commodity is unacceptable because it neglects the complexities of the relationship, the need of the worker for status and security in a job, and the need of the employer for adequate channels of communication with his staff. The "familistic" solution is not acceptable either because it overlooks an essential looseness and abstractness in the relationship which is not present in the family. The "right to quit" is a very important right which is impaired by the familistic solution. A firm is *not* a "big happy family," and the employer who thinks it is deludes himself.

The Boss should neither be a brute,
Nor yet a father-substitute.

Motivation for joining unions: (1) better economic conditions. The rise of the labor movement and of labor unions is in part a response to the personal needs generated by the growth of the labor group and the industrial relationship, and in part a result of the general improvement in the skills of organization which I have called the Organizational Revolution. There seem to be three main motivations that lead workers to join and support unions. The first is the very simple economic motivation—the belief that by joining a union the worker can get better wages, shorter hours, easier conditions of work and so on. This appeal has been of great importance in the ideology of the labor movement. The delightful blues song "Talking Union" puts the appeal succinctly:

> Now, if you want higher wages let me tell you what to do
> You've got to talk to the workers in the shop with you,
> You got to build you a union, got to make it strong,
> But if you all stick together boys, it won't be long—
> You get shorter hours—better working conditions—
> Vacations with pay—take your kids to the seashore—
> It ain't quite this simple, so I better explain
> Just why you got to ride on the union train,
> 'Cause if you wait for the boss to raise your pay
> We'll all be a-waitin' till judgement day.[1]

The workers' economic gains from unionization are limited, except where the union has monopoly power. There are enough cases where unionization—or even the threat of it—has resulted in wage increases to make this ideology plausible. The cold fact is, however, that there is little evidence to support the view that the labor movement as a whole has been able to shift the distributional shares appreciably in favor of labor. Here we run into the brute fact that wages are part of the price system, and real wages especially are determined by a vast array of decisions all through society in the ramified processes of general equilibrium, of which collective bargaining and union-determined wages are only a very small part. The great movements of inflation and deflation are much more important in determining distribution than the rise of collective bargaining. Thus in the period from 1933 to 1943, when membership in labor unions rose from under four to over fifteen million and a large proportion of American industry was brought under collective bargaining contracts, the proportion of national income going to labor declined steeply from 74 per cent to about 64 per cent! The situations where unionization is most likely to result in real wage increases for the unionized—not merely money wage increases which are soon lost in higher prices—are in those cases where a small craft can exercise a degree of monopoly power, especially in local situations, by controlling

[1] Folkways Album, "Talking Union and Other Union Songs." FA5285 (85/1).

entry into the occupation through licensing, high entrance fees, or a closed shop. The success of the American Federation of Labor in the 1880's, by contrast with the failure of the Knights of Labor a decade earlier, is not unrelated to its concentration on small economic gains in craft unions rather than on grandiose schemes for organizing everybody.

Motivations for unionization: (2) security in the job. The second great motivation to support unions comes from the need for security in the job. Workers are "job-conscious" in the way that farmers are "price-conscious." This is partly a result of experience with depressions. As we have seen, a depression is reflected in agriculture by a fall in prices, and in industry by a fall in output and employment. Unemployment is the nightmare of the worker; it deprives him not only of income, but of a place in society. It makes him feel unwanted, and it has a corroding effect on his self-respect. Without organization, however, the worker feels defenseless against the unrestricted right of the employer to hire and fire. Consequently, unions have placed a good deal of emphasis on devices for securing continuity of employment and for protecting their members' jobs in periods of declining employment. The seniority device is the one most frequently employed, whereby the employer who must diminish his labor force is obliged to lay off or to dismiss first those who have been with the firm the shortest time. This has the effect that the burden of unemployment is likely to fall mainly on the young or on the footloose, and there is perhaps a certain rough justice in this which appeals even to those who suffer from it.

Motivations for unionization: (3) the need for status. The third main motivation to join unions is the need for "status" in society, or the fear of inferiority in personal relationship. This need is not unrelated to the need for job security, as especially in Western society a person's status is determined to a very large extent by the kind of job that he holds. When we ask of a man "what *is* he" we often expect the answer "a janitor" or "a professor" or "an executive," and our rating of his importance depends largely on our rating of the importance of the job. The status problem is also related to unemployment. In periods of full employment when there is an active labor market, and a man who does not like one job can easily get another, the sense of "inferiority" of the worker as over against the employer is lessened. On the other hand, in periods of unemployment the loss of a job is a very serious matter, and workers feel the superior power position of the employer acutely. In these periods the problem of "industrial democracy"—the development of orderly and acceptable procedures for hiring, firing, industrial discipline, and for resolving the human problems of employer-employee relations—becomes acute. It is worth noting that unionism is not merely a protest against the "bad" employer. It may also be a revolt against the paternalism of the "good" employer, when this is felt as oppressively powerful or as interfering with the dignity and independence of the worker.

There is an interesting analogy here between the labor movement and the feminist movement. Just as the movement for woman's rights represented a demand for equality of status with men, while preserving differences in function, so the labor movement represents a demand for equality of status in the industrial relationship with the employer, again without denying the difference in function. The difference in function (that is, the specialization between employers and employed) has such obvious advantages that revolutionary unionism, for instance of the Industrial Workers of the World in the period from 1907 to 1919 (which denied the validity of this difference in function and tried to abolish the "wage system"), never came to anything. "Business Unionism" on the other hand, which accepted the basic division of function between employers and employed, but sought to improve the status of the employed within this system, has been a success.

The trend of labor history to the Wagner Act. The history of the labor movement, and of labor law and administration in the United States, follow much the same pattern. Before about 1880 labor organization is sporadic, and the law is hostile. From the 1880's to 1933 there is a slow, rather uneven growth in the number of workers organized, mostly into craft unions. With some ups and downs the attitude of the courts and of the legislatures becomes more friendly during this period; the first World War, for instance, brings the first legislation that is distinctly friendly to unions. Unlike the situation in England and some European countries the labor movement did not try to form a political party, though largely because of its ethnic and urban composition it worked more with the Democrats than the Republicans. Under the leadership of Samuel Gompers the American Federation of Labor remained uncommitted to party, and even rather unpolitical in outlook, following the policy of trying to "reward its friends and defeat its enemies" in Congress of whatever party.

The Great Depression of the 1930's produced a marked shift of public opinion in favor of labor organization, reflecting perhaps dissatisfaction with a business system which had been impotent in the face of so great an economic disaster. The result was a number of laws designed to make the organization of labor unions easier. Thus the Norris-LaGuardia Act of 1932 restrained the use of the injunction in labor disputes, thus denying to employers a powerful legal weapon against the unions. It also outlawed the "yellow-dog contract" by which employers sought to make their employees promise not to join unions. The great "charter" of the labor movement was the Wagner Act of 1935. This declared the encouragement of labor unions and collective bargaining to be part of public policy. It defined many "unfair labor practices" on the part of employers. It set up machinery for elections whereby the employees of a particular plant or firm could vote on whether they wished to be represented by a union, and if so, which union. Most important of all, perhaps, it set up an agency, the National Labor Relations Board, to administer the Act in a quasi-judicial manner, and especially to hear complaints from unions in regard to noncompliance on the part of employers.

Effects of the Wagner Act. The Wagner Act was deliberately weighted in favor of the unions, the theory being that this was necessary to counterbalance the existing economic power of the employers. Thus while employers were prevented from doing a long list of things that might discourage their employees from joining, or from voting for a union, and were also restrained from setting up "company unions" under their domination, there were no similar restraints placed on unions. The Wagner Act unquestionably assisted substantially in the great drive for organization which carried the labor movement from four to fifteen million members in a little over ten years. However it also changed, in a subtle but important way, the character of union drives and even of union leadership. The kind of qualities that carried a union to success before the 1930's—a curious combination of militancy and willingness to compromise—were not necessarily the qualities that made for success in the new environment. Under the Wagner Act a softer, more legalistic approach often paid better than the strongarm methods of the early period. This is not to deny that there was "industrial warfare" in the 'thirties. The great mass-production industries, for instance, were not organized without bitter strikes. Nevertheless, one detects a change in atmosphere; this is the era of the labor lawyer rather than of the militant leader.

Industrial *vs.* craft unionism. An important feature of this period was the rise of industrial unionism. There are roughly two ways of classifying workers for the purpose of organization. Craft unionism seeks to organize all members of a craft, such as carpenters or plumbers, into a single union, no matter by whom they are employed. Industrial unionism seeks to organize all employees of a given industry, such as steel or automobiles, into a single union no matter what their craft. It is clear that these two principles may conflict, and the struggle between them did in fact produce a split in the labor movement in 1935 with the formation of the Congress of Industrial Organizations, or C.I.O., dedicated to organizing the unorganized workers into industrial unions rather than trying to parcel them out among the crafts. The sheer logic of the situation forced the A.F. of L. also to set up industrial unions, for especially in the newer industries the old craft lines became less and less meaningful. With the death of some of the leaders associated most personally with the split, a reunion became possible, and the two federations united into the A.F.L.-C.I.O. in 1955. The Wagner Act probably favored the industrial form of organization more than the craft form, as it was easier to hold a single election in a plant for an industrial union which would include everybody rather than to try to hold many little elections among many employers to organize the crafts.

The rise of industrial unionism is to be welcomed as lessening the danger of labor monopolies. It is the small craft, the wage bill of which constitutes only a small part of the total value of the product, that offers the best opportunity for monopoly, for here the demand for the craft's particular form of labor may be quite inelastic, and wage gains can be made without much reduction in employment. A large industrial union, on the other hand, faces a fairly elastic demand for its labor, and cannot raise wages much above what the free labor market would give.

The Taft-Hartley period. With the continued prosperity of the 'forties and 'fifties the memory of the dark days of the 'thirties receded, and it is not surprising that the tide of public opinion turned somewhat away from favoring labor organization. Relative to the great expansion of the period 1933-43, the years from the mid-'forties on have seen a relative stagnation of the labor movement quantitatively, with a rather slow increase over-all and an actual decline in some sectors. There has also been an appreciable decline in the friendliness of the law and of government agencies towards labor unions. The Taft-Hartley Act of 1947, though it did not repeal the fundamental intention or machinery of the Wagner Act, nevertheless modified it in the direction of making things a little harder for unions. It added to the list of unfair labor practices on the part of employers a similar list on the part of unions, and it made it somewhat harder for unions to bring cases before the National Labor Relations Board. The Taft-Hartley Act has probably not had much effect on existing and well established unions: it has made it harder, however, to extend organization to the unorganized industries and areas, especially in the South, where the hostility to unions that once characterized the whole country still in many places persists, and where the race issue divides the labor group and is a great handicap to effective organization. The National Labor Relations Board itself has also changed from the almost aggressively pro-union organization of the 'thirties to a relatively ineffective agency. In the state legislatures there has been a drive for what are called "right-to-work" laws, the main object of which is to outlaw the union-shop clause in union contracts, under which all the employees of an employer have to become members of the union. In 1957 a wave of scandals concerning misuse of funds by high union officials further hardened public opinion against unions.

The significance of collective bargaining. Some special problems connected with the labor movement deserve brief attention. First, we should note the significance of collective bargaining and the union contract itself, as the key instrument of organized labor. In an unorganized labor market each individual makes his own contract with the employer; this is "individual bargaining." There may not, of course, even be any "bargaining" in the usual sense of the term, any more than there is in a retail store. The employer offers jobs on certain terms on a take-it-or-leave-it basis, just as a store offers goods at a price that the consumer may either take or leave. It may well be that one of the most significant things about collective bargaining is not that it is collective but that it is bargaining. The rise of organized labor has led to a great increase in palaver, in negotiation, in economic gamesmanship. In an unorganized labor market, as in agriculture, a labor shortage results in a rapid upward drift in the wage through the quiet processes by which farmers in desperate need of help bid away workers from each other—individual employers going to individual workers and saying "come and work for me and I'll pay you $5 a week more than you are getting now." Similarly, a labor surplus results in a rapid decline in wages. In an organized labor market, on the other hand, wages are set by a process of bargaining which may be long, public, noisy, and dramatic. The process results (if it does not break down) in a contract, which not only sets forth a schedule of wages, fringe benefits, and conditions of work, but usually sets up an elaborate system of industrial jurisprudence embodied in "grievance procedure." Once made, the contract is not easily altered; it runs for a year, or in some cases like the General Motors contract for as long as five years.

Collective bargaining contracts as a "dam" against inflation or deflation. We can see that the organization of the labor market by collective bargaining has a great impact on the course of inflation or deflation. Collective bargaining acts like a set of dams. It dampens the movement of wages in both inflation and deflation. In inflation it operates to prevent wages rising as fast as they otherwise would have done, simply because of the difficulty involved in reopening contracts; in fact, the contracts become obsolete as soon as they are signed. In deflation it operates even more strongly the other way. There are very strong emotional resistances to lowering wages by collective bargaining. John L. Lewis of the United Mine Workers, for instance, established his reputation and almost wrecked his union in the 1920's by his famous slogan of "no backward step." In deflation, therefore, when there is a fall in aggregate incomes and in money demand, organized labor maintains its hourly wage but suffers severely from unemployment.

Does labor organization lead to an inflationary bias? A very important question, which does not admit of a definite answer at present, is whether the organization of the labor market introduces a tendency for long-run inflation into the economy. No matter whether the labor market is organized or competitive, industrial relations are apt to run more smoothly in periods of inflation than in periods of deflation. The reason is that in an inflation there are continual increases in money wages, even though prices may rise still faster so that there is no increase—or even a decrease—in real wages. What happens to prices, however, is not perceived as something that is the "fault" of the employer. A rise in prices is an act of God and a rise in wages is an act of the employer, or a "gain" by the union. A fall in wages similarly creates ill will for the employer and is perceived as a "loss" by the union, even though prices may be falling proportionately. The organization of the labor market probably accentuates this phenomenon. If the union is to hold the allegiance of its members it continually needs to register "gains" of some kind, even though these gains may be illusory. In a period of inflation this is relatively easy; every time the contract is renegotiated the union can point with pride to the increases it has "won," and its members are less conscious of the erosion of these gains through price increases. In a period of deflation, on the other hand, industrial strife becomes acute, for every money-wage reduction looks like a defeat, even though in fact real wages may be increasing.

Organized markets make deflation difficult. This is not to say that unions should necessarily be blamed for inflation. It is true that there may be "wage-induced inflation" if industrial peace is bought at the cost of wage increases, which are followed by price increases and monetary expansion to finance the higher level of wages, prices, and incomes. There is some evidence that this has happened in Britain over the past decade; there is much less evidence for it in the United States. On the whole, however, wage pressures are only one out of many forces that make for inflation, and historically, unbalanced budgets due to wars and to an excess of investment plans over savings potential are much more important.

It must also be pointed out that many other sectors of the society get along better during inflation—the pressure of farmers for inflation, for instance, is probably as effective, if not more effective, than that of the labor groups. What the organization of markets in general, and of labor in particular, implies is that *deflation* becomes almost impossibly destructive. If we can never have a deflation, however, this means that we can never *correct* an inflation, so that if long-run inflation is to be prevented, short-run inflation must also be prevented. We may be faced with the choice of either learning to live with long-run inflation (not an impossible solution, though a tricky one) or of learning to be much stiffer in controlling short-run inflations.

Union security: union shop and checkoff. Another problem of great importance to the labor movement is known as "union security." This is the attempt to write into the contract with the employer conditions that tie the "job" in with union membership. In the "closed shop" (now outlawed by the Taft-Hartley Act) the employer was allowed to hire only workers who were already members of the union. In the "union shop" the employer may hire anyone, but anyone hired must become a member of the union within a certain period. During the second World War a compromise known as "maintenance of membership" became popular, which stipulated that any employee who was a member of the union at the time of the signing of the contract must remain a member of the union for the duration of the contract. The "checkoff" by which the employer deducts union dues from the paycheck and hands them over to the union is also a device for union security.

The evaluation of union security provisions. The union security problem presents real dilemmas. The case for measures of this kind is first that it eliminates "free loading"—that is, the acceptance of the benefits of unionization without the acceptance of the responsibilities. The "good union man" who pays his dues and takes his responsibilities not unnaturally feels aggrieved when his fellow workers accept the gains but refuse to pull their weight. There is also a case for union security from the point of view of the employer—that it relieves the union of the necessity for militancy, and leaves the way open for peaceful and constructive industrial relations. Indeed, a case can be made that union security provisions actually weaken the union in the long run. A union which does not have to "fight" to keep its members, and which grows fat on the checkoff, is also apt to grow lazy. There is an analogy here with the established church —when one contrasts, for instance, the established and state-subsidized—and lackadaisical—Lutheran churches of Scandinavia with the vigorous "free" Lutheran churches of the United States, one can see the dangers of too-great security for an organization. In view of this consideration it may be rather short-sighted of many employers to press for "right to work" laws which would outlaw the more effective forms of union security, and it may even be short-sighted of labor to take too much advantage of these provisions. There also is a real problem here of individual rights in a collective organization. There are some individuals, for instance, who are conscientiously opposed to joining unions for religious or other reasons; the better unions respect these scruples, but not all do.

Internal democracy within unions. This raises the larger problem of internal democracy within unions, and the rights of individual members in relation to possibly corrupt or ineffective or dictatorial leadership. Unions range over the whole spectrum of forms of political organization. At one end we have the active two-party parliamentary democracy of the typographers, and at the other end there are corrupt dictatorships and oligarchies. The greater the power of unions, the more important becomes this problem, and the more justification there is for some kind of governmental "policing" of union organizations, though it is very hard to draw the line here between legitimate protection of the rights of members and of the public on the one hand, and the destruction of the independence of unions and making them subservient to the state on the other. The problem has been accentuated in recent years by the great growth of union-sponsored pension plans, which accumulate large sums and which may offer temptations to both union officials and to employers if the administration of these funds is not carefully safeguarded.

The jurisdictional dispute. Another problem of the labor movement is that of the jurisdictional dispute. There are some two hundred independent unions, most of them loosely federated into the A.F.L.-C.I.O. The "domain" of each union is a certain set of jobs, defined either by craft or by industry, or perhaps simply by who gets there first! Inevitably there are disputed areas—that is, jobs whose occupants are claimed by more than one union. We might compare a union to a nation, impinging on other nations at rather ill-defined boundaries. These boundaries, moreover, are continually shifting with changing technology—the earthquakes and floods of social and technological change are continually changing the very landmarks and are constantly eliminating "natural" boundaries between different kinds of jobs. Each union comes to think of certain jobs as its "right," and challenges to these rights by another union are strongly resisted. The machinists and the carpenters, for instance, have been fighting for decades over certain kinds of mill work; the brewers and the teamsters have had a similar long drawn out battle. The employer and the consuming public who are caught in these inter-union fights are like the innocent civilians in a battle area, and it is little wonder that this kind of dispute creates ill-will for unions.

The federations (the A.F.L. and the C.I.O., and now the combined organization) operate as a kind of United Nations for the settlement of these disputes. It is a common disease of federations, however, that they find it easier to mete out justice to their smaller members than to their larger, and the federations have not been very effective in solving the disputes among the larger unions. On the whole the industrial unions have had a better record in this regard than the craft unions—perhaps because the industrial unions were expanding into a larger unorganized field, and hence could afford to be generous with each other, or perhaps because technological change does not erase boundaries between industries quite as rapidly as it does between crafts.

Industrial warfare. The jurisdictional dispute is a special case of the larger problem of industrial disputes in general, or of what might be called "industrial warfare." This is frequently perceived as a great problem, and in some places and at some times it is. To quote another labor song:

> They say in Harlan County
> There are no neutrals there
> You'll either be a union man
> Or a thug for J. H. Blair.[2]

The conditions that lead to industrial warfare at one time and place, and to industrial peace at other times and places, are at least as complex as those that lead to international war and peace. It is important to realize that *conflict* does not necessarily lead to *warfare*. There is in any social situation an elaborate set of habits and institutions designed to prevent conflict from erupting into warfare. Warfare only results when the con-

[2] Folkways Album FA5285 (85/1).

flict is too great for the restraining forces, and there is a "break" in the social fabric. The break does not depend merely on the intensity of the conflict, but on the relation between the intensity of the conflict and the strength of the restraints. Strong conflict does not lead to a break if there are strong restraints; weak conflicts may lead to a break if the restraints are weak.

Conflicts of interest in the industrial relationship are not great. There are, of course, real conflicts of interest between workers and employers and between different groups of workers. Industrial warfare, however, is to be interpreted not so much in terms of the intensity of these conflicts as in terms of the varying strength of the restraints. The real conflicts of interest in industrial relations are not very great. There is an important community of interest in the *fact* of the industrial relationship—workers and employers need each other, and their relationship is mostly a symbiotic one. There may be some conflict about the *terms* of the relationship. Within limits, workers want a higher wage and employers a lower. The limits, however, are important, and may be quite narrow. The worker does not want a wage so high that it would drive his employer out of business and deprive him of a job; the employer does not want a wage so low that it would deprive him of the power of attracting labor. Under conditions of theoretically perfect competition these two limits approach each other, and the range of conflict shrinks towards zero. If there is some wage below which the employer will get no labor, and above which the workers will have no jobs, clearly there can be no conflict about the wage—that is, the range of conflict has shrunk to nothing. In practice, of course, we never find so "perfect" a situation and there is always some range of possible conflict. The more one studies industrial relations, however, the more one feels that industrial warfare is "about" very little in substantive terms—a few cents one way or the other, some minor losses or gains in managerial prerogative or union power. They may lead, however, to intense warfare.

The intensity of warfare may have little to do with the realities of the conflict, if the social structure is too weak to prevent "breaks." The break comes when the parties to the conflict lose the sense of community which binds them together, and begin to visualize each other as "enemies." Here destructive dynamic processes may be set up, analogous to arms races, in which hostility on one side creates more hostility on the other side, which creates further hostility on the first side, and so on until the situation explodes in warfare—that is, in organized attempts on the part of each side to damage the other.

The principal expression of warfare in industrial conflict is the strike or the lock-out—the first, a concerted refusal to work on the part of the employees; the second, a concerted refusal to employ on the part of the employer or employers. There are, however, other expressions—the "slow-down" and sabotage on the part of the worker, the "stool-pigeon" (informer) on the part of the employer, and overt violence—the "goon squad" may be employed by both sides.

The significance of strikes. Because the strike is a colorful and visible phenomenon, it is easy to exaggerate its importance in the general picture. In the United States, for instance, the year of highest man-days lost by strikes since records began in 1927 was 1946, with 116 million man-days lost. Even this impressive total, however, represents only 1.43 per cent of total working time, and in more than half the years the loss due to strikes was less than 0.25 per cent, or 1/400 of total working time. Losses due to unemployment, to sickness, and even perhaps to fishing fever greatly exceed the over-all losses due to strikes. The losses due to the more subtle forms of industrial warfare, especially in unorganized industries—to slowdowns, to "soldiering," to bad human relations—probably are very much greater than losses due to strikes, though naturally no estimates of these hidden losses are available.

Although it is true, therefore, that the rise of labor unions may mean a greater direct loss by strikes, the very fact that the conflict becomes overt rather than hidden may diminish rather than increase its total impact. One important result of unionization is to bring out into the open conflicts and practices which previously were hidden. This is true even of restrictive practices; there is a famous study[3] showing that virtually all the restrictive practices that show up under unions exist, in a more clandestine and informal way, among unorganized workers. In this respect unionization has some analogies with psychoanalysis, in that it dredges up into public view things that previously were in the social unconscious. This may look bad in the short run, but it offers hope of more creative and intelligent long-run solutions of these problems than would be possible if they were to remain covered up.

Typical sequenccs in the industrial relationship. We may perhaps distinguish four periods in an "ideal type" of the industrial relationship. The first is the unorganized period, when industrial warfare is hidden, when discontents may be building up, but when the employer is able to suppress most of the overt expression. This is the period of "monarchy," of the undisputed sovereignty of the boss, checked only by the activity of the labor market.

The second is the period of union-formation, when the accumulated discontents rise to the surface and the workers organize —sometimes spontaneously, but more often under the leadership of professional outside organizers. This is the period of "revolution": it is characterized by much overt industrial warfare, by strikes, often by violence, by injunctions, by legal maneuvering on both sides. It culminates in recognition of the union as a bargaining agent and in the beginnings of collective bargaining. Since the Wagner Act, of course, the law has encouraged this development, and has assisted it materially.

The third period might be called the period of "cold war"; the two sides continue their hostility in spite of recognition; there are still strikes or threatened strikes to mark the end of every contract; there may be a lot of "unofficial" strikes, or officially unofficial stoppages which are winked at by the union. The employer is still not reconciled to the permanence of the union; the union still does not feel secure in its position.

Then, as the parties get used to each other, the cold war

[3] Stanley B. Mathewson, *Restriction of Output among Unorganized Workers.* New York, Viking Press, 1941.

sometimes passes over into a fourth stage of "industrial peace" in which there is genuine cooperation among the parties, in which strikes become practically nonexistent, in which the employer accepts the union as a permanent feature of the landscape, in which the union feels secure, and in which, we hope, morale and productivity are high.

Contributions of unions to industrial peace. I do not mean to imply that this is a necessary or universal pattern, though it is not an uncommon one. It may be possible, for instance, to pass over into a genuine condition of industrial peace without unions and without the second and third stages. This requires, however, a very unusual degree of ability on the part of management. Perhaps the main reason why the union seems to be necessary in so many cases to the establishment of industrial peace (as opposed to the mere industrial quiet of the first stage) is that the nature of the industrial relationship itself renders communication between the parties difficult. Intimate communications flow only between equals: only formal communications pass between unequals. Both management and the workers therefore frequently have quite distorted images of each other. The union here acts as a telephone; the union leader has both an ear and a mouthpiece in both camps. This is a peculiarly difficult role to play, and indeed sometimes leads to his undoing; too much industrial peace may lead to the union leader's "growing away" from his members as he comes to have more and more the management point of view, until discontent grows to the point where there is a new revolution and he is displaced by someone more aggressive and closer to the workers.

Conciliation, mediation, and arbitration. A great many different proposals have been made and experiments tried to develop a legal and administrative framework that shall minimize the cost to society of industrial warfare. Most modern governments have set up machinery for conciliation and mediation, by which skilled "outside" mediators are able to go into a dispute situation and try to bring the parties to voluntary agreement. The function of the mediator is to soothe tempers, to convey information, and to see that possible areas of agreement are known by both parties.

Where mediation fails, recourse is sometimes made to arbitration. In voluntary arbitration there must be an agreement to arbitrate—that is, to accept the decision of a third party, the arbitrator. Some countries, notably Australia and New Zealand, have experimented with compulsory arbitration; this involves making the strike illegal. American opinion on the whole is unfavorable to compulsory arbitration, as involving too great a degree of state interference in what are regarded to some extent as "private" disputes. There is a real value in the right to strike, and the social value of the strike is not entirely negative.

A special problem arises in the case of "essential" industries where work stoppages may endanger the health or safety of the public. There is a tendency to develop special institutions for these industries, such as the special boards for the arbitration of disputes on the railroads. There is a strong tradition in the United States against strikes by government employees, who are expected to express their grievances by lobbying in Congress. So strong is this tradition that one solution to the "essential industries" problem seems to be to have them taken over, at least temporarily, by the government, as President Truman did with steel. This can hardly be regarded as a permanent or satisfactory solution.

Government regulation of the labor bargain. To conclude this sketch of the problems of labor policy we should outline the area of what might be called direct government regulation of the wage bargain. This would include such matters as minimum wage and hours legislation, legislation affecting discrimination in employment, child labor laws, laws regulating migrant labor, and so on, and would include at the extreme direct government control of wages. These are regulations that limit the *nature* of the bargain that may be struck, whether by collective or by individual bargaining in the industrial relationship, mainly by direct prohibition of certain types of labor contracts.

Minimum wage and hours laws. Minimum wage and hours laws have been a prominent part of labor legislation, first in Europe and then in the United States since the Fair Labor Standards Act of 1938. Minimum hours legislation has a particularly long history, going back to the first British Factory Acts. The arguments in favor of this type of interference with the freedom of contract are related to those used for the protection of infant industries; it is argued, with much force, that if complete freedom of contract is allowed in the labor market certain low-level equilibria will be established which need to be "jolted." Once people are jolted out of these positions by the legal prohibitions they soon find superior situations which they would never otherwise have reached. Thus in the early days of the Industrial Revolution the sheer weight of custom, carried over from agriculture, imposed a twelve-hour day on the factories. Reduction of this by law proved beneficial not only to the workers' health, but to productivity; the worker often produced more in nine or ten hours than in twelve. Obviously there are limits to this process, but there is a strong case on health grounds alone for an eight-hour day.

The case for the minimum wage is, oddly enough, that it will create unemployment and so force adjustments and improvements that otherwise might not have taken place. Thus the modest minimum wage of 40 cents per hour of the 1938 law is credited with having destroyed the peanut-shelling industry, in which peanuts were shelled by hand and productivity was so low that the industry could afford to pay barely 25 cents an hour. This was followed, however, by improvements in the industry and the development of peanut-shelling machines, which raised productivity to the point where the industry could now afford to pay the minimum wage. Another justification of minimum wage laws is that they bring to light "hole and corner" exploitation where workers are exploited through ignorance of other opportunities. One difficulty of minimum wage laws is that they tend to lag behind inflation and so become obsolete.

Child labor laws. Child labor laws, it is argued, are necessary in order to prevent the exploitation of the ignorance of children or the selfishness of parents, especially insofar as the education of children may be hampered by starting work at too early an age. Education is still, in the mass, one of the best investments even for the individual, and greatly increases his chance of higher incomes later in life; it is probably an even better investment for society at large. Children, and even their parents, are not good judges of the value of education above the more immediate income from work; hence there is a case for interference with freedom of contract in this case also, for the betterment of all concerned.

Antidiscrimination laws. A similar case can be made for the regulation of the labor of certain disadvantaged groups in the society, such as migrants, racial minorities, and so on. Laws against discrimination in employment again jolt us out of a lower-level equilibrium and force us to seek more satisfactory solutions. Discrimination in employment, especially against negroes and against women, is a serious source of loss in the United States, simply in terms of the wastage of human resources. Fair Employment Practices Acts, which seek to prohibit such discrimination, have much to recommend them (provided that the social climate is such that they can be effective) both from the point of view of elementary justice and from the point of view of economic progress. There is a very interesting problem here of the degree to which legislation and administrative machinery can improve social customs and habits that are deleterious to the broader interests of the people. It is reasonable to suppose that there is an optimum degree of pressure from the law on custom, and that up to a certain point legal measures, by the slow, steady pressure they exercise, are effective in changing customs. Beyond a certain point, however, the divergence between law and custom becomes too great, and the law actually intensifies adherence to the custom that the law is supposed to change. Prohibition seems to have been a case in point, where the legal prohibition of alcoholic beverages actually seems to have reinforced the custom of drinking them. Just where the point of optimum legal pressure lies in any one case is very difficult to determine.

The evaluation of labor policy. The field of labor policy is so large and complex that it is impossible to evaluate it as a whole in the light of our analytical scheme. The best we can do is to point out some questions that must be raised in any such evaluation, many of which in the present state of knowledge do not admit of definite answers. Policies in the field fall under two principal headings: first, policy in regard to the encouragement or discouragement of particular forms of organization—unions, employers' associations, and so on; and second, policy in regard to the regulation and limits of the industrial relationship itself—for instance, should union security clauses be outlawed, should there be minimum labor standards, and so on.

(1) **Effects on economic progress.** In regard to economic progress, the influence of unions is somewhat doubtful. Unions rarely initiate technical improvement—this is not their function—though there are unions, like the Amalgamated Clothing Workers, that have cooperated actively with employers in the introduction of more productive methods. Sometimes unions have opposed technical change; sometimes they have sought to control it and to protect their members from its impact. There is an interesting question as to whether the *indirect* effect of unionization has not been to stimulate labor—saving improvements by making labor scarce, or more difficult to handle, or even by making wages less flexible. Employers, like everyone else, tend to follow lines of least resistance; in an unorganized labor market the employer's easiest way out of a difficult situation may be to cut wages. In an organized labor market this solution is in part barred to him, and his attention is forced towards cost-saving and labor-saving devices. This may create temporary unemployment, but it is more beneficial to labor in the long run than wage-cutting.

Essentially the same case can be made out for minimum wages and labor standards. A classic example of the evils of unorganized labor markets was the miserable fate of the hand-loom weavers in the early nineteenth century, who maintained their employment in the face of machine-loom competition only by a process of continual wage reduction almost to the point of starvation. If their market had been organized and their wages had stayed up they would have suffered widespread and permanent unemployment, but this would have forced them out into other occupations and solved the problem of adjustment more rapidly than the long drawn out agony of wage reductions. On the other side of the argument there are many cases—for instance, in the building trades—where the impact of unionization has been to slow down or even to reverse the movement of technical improvement, and if unions are too secure, too powerful, and too security-minded they may act as a serious brake on economic progress. The problem of discrimination in law between the constructive and the destructive attributes of unionization in this regard is a very difficult one, and we cannot claim to have solved it successfully.

(2) **Effects on economic stability.** In regard to economic stabilization, it seems pretty clear that unionization intensifies the evils of deflation, in the sense that with organized labor markets a deflation will be taken out in unemployment rather than in a simple lowering of the price-wage level. If deflation were unavoidable this would be a very black mark against labor organization. However, deflation is not unavoidable, and the existence of organized markets in general simply means that even greater efforts must be made to avoid it. Furthermore, deflation would be fairly destructive to the economy even in the absence of organized markets because of its shifting of distribution away from profits towards rentier incomes, so that deflation should be avoided in any case. The fact that something makes an avoidable disease worse if it is not avoided is no argument against it. In short-run inflation, organization of labor markets may even be favorable to slower price and wage increases than organized markets.

A real question arises, however, whether the organization of the market does not introduce a long-run tendency towards inflation, partly because of the "ratchet effect"—if we cannot have a deflation we can never correct any inflationary excess—and partly because of the lubricating effect of inflation on industrial relations. Then the question resolves itself into two further ones: first, how hard do we have to work to prevent long-run inflation; and second, if we can't prevent it, how can we learn to live with it? One may hazard a guess that in a given situation there is some degree of strength and militancy of the labor movement above which inflation cannot be prevented, below which it can. This critical value itself may not be stable, and it must not be thought that the labor movement is the only, or even the principal source of inflation. Britain seems to be clearly above this critical point, the United States somewhere close to it.

Organized labor and "built-in" stabilizers. The political influence of organized labor in the development of "built-in" stabilizers—notably the progressive income tax and the unemployment insurance system—should not be overlooked, though it is difficult to assess. The development of supplementary unemployment benefits (which is the reality behind the so-called "guaranteed annual wage") also has an effect in the stabilizing of consumer purchases. Its over-all effect is harder to assess, for as the payments come from private firms rather than from government, they may create a shift in liquid assets *away* from firms at the very moment when liquidity is needed by them to reorganize production or to make new investments. This might cause a decline in investment which would in part offset the maintenance of consumption, so that the over-all effect of private unemployment benefits on the stability of income might be less favorable than that of government benefits.

Should there be a "wage policy"? The question whether there should be a "wage policy" is difficult. During wars most countries have a rather active wage policy; in the United States, for instance, an elaborate machinery was set up in the War Labor Board for the processing of labor disputes and the discouragement of too rapid wage increases. In peacetime "wage policy" falls into discard, as involving too great a degree of government interference with what is regarded as an essentially private and domestic matter. Like price control, wage policy is wrecked on the rocks of particularity—the job of translating a general policy into hundreds of thousands of individual wage contracts is too great to be done without administrative wastes and serious impairments of individual freedoms, which only seem justifiable in times of crisis. As an instrument of stabilization, wage policy is clumsy and inept compared with the swift and general adjustments that can be made in taxes, and one may conclude that on the whole it is an unsuitable instrument except when the more delicate devices fail.

(3) **Effects on justice and freedom.** On the even more difficult problems of justice and freedom there is again some uncertainty about the contribution of labor organization. The labor movement has derived much of its support, both by those inside it and those outside it, from a belief that it is an agent to correct certain injustices both in regard to the distribution of income as between the labor group and the rest of society, and in regard to the personal dominance of the employer in the industrial relationship. The effect of labor organization on the distribution of income is much in dispute. The view that wages would fall to subsistence levels were it not for labor unions is somewhat mythological, and the impact of the organization of the labor market on the over-all distribution of income has certainly been exaggerated. The forces that determine the distributional shares are many and complex; the great movements of inflation and deflation certainly have a much more immediate impact than does collective bargaining. There is a ticklish question as to the extent to which the gains of organized labor are made at the expense of the unorganized, or at the expense of pensioners and small rentiers, rather than at the expense of the employers. In certain cases the gains of labor organization may simply be a division of the spoils of monopoly with the employers. Certainly one cannot say for certain that collective bargaining leads to a more equal or to a less equal distribution of income.

Contributions of the labor movement to the integration of society. On the matter of the industrial relationship itself the picture is clearer. The great accomplishment of the labor movement is that it has given the worker *status* and has helped to integrate the labor group into the community at large. In this respect the labor movement is a profoundly conservative force in capitalism, deeply committed to the perpetuation of the system especially when the main expression of its activity is collective bargaining, union contracts, and the administration of a system of industrial jurisprudence. In the "deproletarianization of the proletariat" which has taken place in the United States and some other Western countries the labor movement has had a critical role to play. In this there has been a real gain of both justice and freedom. Like all gains, it has come with certain costs. The worker sometimes finds that he has exchanged the tyranny of the employer for the tyranny of the union boss. The problem of internal democracy within unions remains acute in many cases. Once these problems are recognized, however, they should not be destitute of solution.

Perhaps the greatest problem the labor movement faces today is the loss of a certain air of idealism which sustained it in its more militant and formative period. In the growth of any new type of organization there comes a critical period when it passes from being a "movement" into being a "sect"; this involves painful readjustment of its images of its functions and its future. The labor movement in the United States may well be going through this period now. The very mobility of American society, however, puts an additional strain in this adjustment. All "underdog" movements tend to suffer an erosion of leadership and potential leadership into the "upper dog" groups. The greater the mobility of the society, the greater this erosion tends to be. This may be the most difficult single problem the labor movement will face in the decades ahead.

The present state of industrial relations. One cannot help feeling a certain sense of satisfaction in contemplating the industrial-relations scene in the United States. There is a great contrast between the bitter industrial warfare of fifty years ago and the relatively constructive industrial relations of today. Some of this comes out of the social sciences—the growth of industrial relations as an academic and as a "clinical" discipline has been a remarkable feature of the past twenty or thirty years. Some of it comes from the good fortune of statesmanlike leadership on both sides of the industrial relationship. Some of it also comes from what has been on the whole a wise legislative and administrative policy. We must beware, however, of thinking that the millennium is here; new difficulties may well lie ahead. Nevertheless, when in a difficult situation, and especially when our ignorance of so many important questions in this field is so great, we feel we have not done too badly, gentle congratulations seem to be in order.

15 The economics of war and peace

War produces an immense
Increase in Government Expense.
This in turn brings Debt, Inflation,
Price Control, and Allocation.
Even after Victory Day
There's the Devil yet to pay.
What we sow we often reap,
So war is seldom very cheap.

Why war dominates the modern economy. The institution that dominates the economic life of the twentieth century is war. By far the largest movements of the world economy were due to the two world wars, and even the smaller wars had a noticeable effect. We have already taken note of the principal reason for the increasing proportion of national product that is devoted to war and war preparations. It is that in an unstable arms-race situation there is a constant tendency for the absolute amount of resources devoted to armaments to increase, and in an all-out war the amount devoted to war tends to rise towards the whole economic surplus of the country and even beyond this limit. Even as late as the eighteenth century this economic surplus was relatively small, as witness the passage from Adam Smith in an earlier chapter. Hence only a small proportion of the resources of a nation could be devoted to war; it took most of the resources just to keep the society fed, clothed, and supplied with bare necessities. In the developed nations of the twentieth century, on the other hand, the society can be kept going with half or less of its total resources, and half or more can be spared, if necessary, for making war. This is why war seems to be such a far-reaching phenomenon and why society seems to be dominated by it, even though the general culture is not particularly favorable to it, and by contrast with many previous epochs war is looked upon with feelings akin to horror, and threatens to destroy not only civilization but life itself.

War as an "industry": three aspects—(1) military strategy. The economics of war are simply the economics of the growth of one "industry"—the armed forces—at the expense of others. It is peculiar because of the magnitude of the transfers involved, which make it difficult or impossible to rely wholly on the market mechanism. It is peculiar also because virtually the only customer of the war industry is the national government, so that its product is not sold to households through the usual channels of the market, but to a single buyer which derives its revenue from taxation, borrowing, or the creation of money.

There are, then, three main economic aspects of war. The first is what might be called the "planned economy" of the armed forces themselves—the business of moving the instruments of destruction to the place, and at the time, and in the form where they will have the greatest impact on the opponent. This is the more purely military phase of the operation, and is beyond the scope of this book, though it involves many problems that are essentially economic in nature, such as the distribution of forces among various types and in various places, the organization and logistics of keeping forces in the field, and so on.

(2) **Economic warfare.** The second economic aspect of war is "economic warfare"—that is, measures designed to hamper the opponent in marshalling his resources for war, for instance through trade or other economic relations with neutrals, or even with private citizens of the belligerents. In modern war it is hard to draw the line where economic warfare ends and military operations begin. Thus air forces are rather specialized in the killing and wounding of women, children, and civilians, and in the destruction of homes, cities, works of art, and so on. This is economic warfare, designed to diminish the economic surplus of the opponent by forcing him to spend a larger proportion of resources for the sheer maintenance of the population. Submarine warfare likewise has come to be concerned with the sinking of merchant ships bringing food and supplies to civilian populations as well as with attacks on the opponent's armed forces. This also is economic warfare. Indeed, in modern war the distinction between the civilian and the military population has become completely blurred, and with it the distinction between economic and military operations.

Economic warfare in "cold war." In the "cold war" which seems to have become a permanent feature of our landscape overt military measures are avoided, and so of course economic and psychological warfare become more important. In this case economic warfare takes the form of building up friends and tearing down enemies. One of the difficulties with this process is that one is never quite sure of one's friends, or even of one's enemies: the international scene is a shifting kaleidoscope, and nations that are bosom friends today may be bitter enemies tomorrow, and vice versa. Consequently we may find ourselves building up some nation as a friend, only to find our own resources turned against us later when it ungratefully becomes an enemy. The polarization of the moment always seems more permanent than it turns out to be. This makes the strategy of economic warfare in a cold war peculiarly difficult. If one could simply assume that the existing coalitions would be stable, the rational thing to do would presumably be to encourage trade within the allied group, remove barriers to imports and exports, and let each partner specialize in what he does best. Unfortunately the world is not so simple, and each partner must carry at the back of his mind the possibility of doublecrossing and being doublecrossed.

Example: the materials policy of the United States. An example of the above dilemma is the materials policy of the United States. No nation, not even the United States, is self-sufficient, and there are strategic materials which every nation must import or export. The United States, for instance, must import virtually all its chromium, nickel, tin, and natural rubber. A self-sufficient defense policy leads to the maxim of exporting as little and importing as much of these materials as can conveniently be managed, and especially to the building up of stockpiles of scarce materials. The attempt on the part of the United States to follow a fairly self-sufficient materials policy prior to and just after the outbreak of the Korean war in 1950 led to serious difficulties with her allies, and to a spectacular rise in the price of many of these commodities. This led to the formation of an International Materials Conference in 1951, to organize the allocation of these scarce materials among the allied nations, through the formation of Commodity Committees. All these were dissolved by 1953, when conditions were less stringent. The problem is complicated by the pressure of domestic producers in the United States, especially of lead and zinc, for stockpiling to keep up the price of their commodities without much regard to actual defense needs; the principle of price supports and surpluses is not confined to agriculture!

(3) **The domestic economy in war.** It is the third economic aspect of war—its impact on the internal economy of a nation—with which the economist is most at home. Here we do not face the difficult and unpredictable problems of military and political strategy, where even the theory of games throws only a fitful light on the overwhelming uncertainties of the situation. In domestic policy the "game" is with a reasonably compliant

and predictable partner—the home population—rather than against an unpredictable outside opponent. Hence the principles of policy are more like those to which the economist is accustomed.

The breakdown of the price system: conscription. The problem here is how to achieve a large and rapid redistribution of economic activity away from the industries producing for domestic consumption and investment and into the war industry —meaning by this both the armed forces proper and all those industries and occupations that produce things to sell to the armed forces. Some of this shift can be made fairly easily—a clothing manufacturer, for instance, can shift fairly easily from making civilian clothing to making uniforms for the army, and food producers do not have to shift their occupations at all, for roughly the same kinds of food will feed soldiers as will feed men in corresponding civilian occupations. In these cases the market mechanism suffices; the government simply buys the things it needs by bidding them away from civilian purchasers. The structure of demand is altered by the entry of government into the market, and perhaps also by the exit of private purchasers as taxes are increased and private disposable income declines. The new structure of output then simply follows the change in the over-all structure of demand.

Some shifts, however, are difficult; the supply into the war industry is inelastic. Where this is the case the price system inevitably begins to break down and increasingly the government comes to rely on its powers of direct regulation and coercion in order to achieve the desired transfer of resources. The first example of this breakdown of the price system is usually the conscription of men for the armed forces. Under a system of voluntary enlistment the armed forces must attract men in much the same way that an industrial employer attracts them, by bidding them away from other occupations. In time of war the armed forces have an appeal to patriotism (and less overtly, to sadism) which an industrial employer does not have, and so for small forces may find a highly elastic supply of manpower. In order to build up large forces, however, the unpatriotic, the unsoldierly, and even the plain shirkers have to be attracted to the armed forces, and to continue to rely on the market for these large numbers would require either impossibly high pay or impossibly successful propaganda. The community therefore accepts conscription as a substitute for the market, and so relieves its young men of the intolerable burden of deciding for themselves where their duty lies.

Why war raises employment—It is not generally feasible to conscript other resources in the way that young men can be conscripted, partly because of their complexity and the sheer administrative problem that would be involved, and partly because it is easier to conscript the young and propertyless than it is to dragoon the old and propertied. War therefore involves the government in large purchases from private suppliers. If these are of moderate dimensions it may be possible to pay for these increased government purchases by increased taxation. As we have seen, however (p. 196), even if the cash budget remains balanced, so that there is no increase of money in the hands of the public, an increase in government purchases is likely to be inflationary in its effect, and will increase the national money income. If the increase in government purchases—whether for war or merely for rearmament, or, for that matter, even for welfare—comes when there is less than full employment, the rise in money income will be reflected in a rise in real output, and an absorption of the unemployed, rather than in a rise of prices.

—and causes inflation. At some point, however, as employment and output rise, limitations of capacity begin to be approached in one commodity after another, and prices begin to rise. If a war starts from a condition of high employment, as did the Korean War of 1950, a price inflation is likely to start immediately, not only because it is most unlikely that taxes will be raised sufficiently to offset the inflationary effect of the increase in government expenditure, but also because people expect inflation during a war and this causes a rise in the velocity of circulation of money. If the increase in government expenditure is *not* to be inflationary the increase in tax collections must exceed the increase in expenditure, so that the reduced volume of civilian goods now available to the public meets a correspondingly reduced disposable income. Financial virtue as extreme as this is too much to expect of any country in time of war. Nor is this merely a matter of virtue; most tax systems are only tolerable as long as the amount of tax collected is a fairly small percentage of income. An effort to increase tax collections accentuates the inevitable strains and injustices within even the best of tax systems. There are, therefore, administrative and political limits to the proportion of income that can safely be collected in taxes; these limits seem to be below the proportion of real output that can be devoted to war. So inflation seems to be an absolutely necessary concomitant to any major war. It can be regarded as a form of taxation—as we have seen, inflation redistributes income and wealth away from the people with fixed money incomes, and as these are likely to be the less productive members of society, in a major war inflation may be the method of real taxation—that is, of reducing real incomes and consumption—that has the least adverse effect on productive effort and output.

Price control. Inflation is never left to itself, however. It is invariably associated with some form of price control, rationing, and allocation. Historically this has frequently been the result of economic ignorance on the part of governments; they look at the symptoms (rising prices) rather than the cause (inadequate taxes) and first attempt to treat the symptoms by imposing a set of maximum legal prices. This soon leads to trouble, however. Either the maximum prices become ineffective through the development of black markets and widespread evasion of the law, or else if the coercive instruments—or the habits of obedience—are strong enough to enforce the legal maxima, the regulated commodities begin to disappear from the market. When part of a price system is controlled and the prices of some commodities held down below "normal," prices in the uncontrolled part will rise still further, and it will become much more profitable to produce the uncontrolled than the controlled commodities.

Price control, therefore, especially when it extends over only part of the price system, inevitably leads to controls over consumption and production. Consumption controls are attempted through *rationing*—that is, through the allocation of maximum amounts that may be purchased by each individual. Rationing may also be done for raw materials and producers' goods; in this case it is called *allocation*. Production controls are more difficult; it is easier to stop people doing something that they would otherwise have done than it is to make them do something that they would otherwise not have done. Something can be done, however, with manpower, especially by making it difficult for people to leave jobs in what are regarded as essential occupations. Most democratic states have hesitated to conscript all their manpower even in major war, though governments frequently have been granted extensive powers in this direction.

Rationing. Rationing of consumer goods presents some interesting problems, some of which have been discussed earlier in the book. The simplest way to ration is to calculate the total amount of the commodity that is expected to be available and then divide this by the total population, so obtaining a figure for per-capita available supply, and then give every person a ration card entitling him (or her) to buy just this amount in the given time. This initial simplicity is soon destroyed, however, by the difference in tastes and *needs* of the people. It is absurd, for instance, to give a small child the same food ration as a man doing heavy work. Consequently there soon develops a complex system of special rations for special classes. No matter how complex the system, it can never take care of all difference in individual needs, even for calories, so that it is a fundamental principle of rationing that some major source of calories (*e.g.*, bread or potatoes) must be left unrationed, and its price controlled if need be by subsidies.

Points rationing. A very ingenious invention of the second World War was "points rationing." This is in effect a supplementary price system, applied to the more complex commodities such as canned foods and clothing. Instead of allocating specific quantities of each commodity to each person, the individual is given a certain number of "points," and each commodity is given a "point price"—*i.e.*, a number of points that must be given up in order to purchase it. The individual is then free to allocate his quota of points as he wishes among the various commodities. If any commodity tends to disappear from the market this can be remedied by raising its point price, thus discouraging its purchase; if a commodity becomes too plentiful in the market its point price can be lowered, thus encouraging purchases.

The great advantage of this system is that it allows a certain amount of consumer choice, so that commodities tend to go to the people who want them most. Thus suppose a commodity, say canned salmon, becomes unusually scarce. Under simple rationing the allocation to each person is diminished. This may cause no hardship at all to people who are allergic to salmon, and great hardship to people who are very fond of it. Under points rationing the point price is raised; the people who do not care for salmon then refrain from buying it altogether, and those who are very fond of it, and who are willing to sacrifice other things to get it, will be able to purchase the whole supply. Thus goods tend to go to those who have the greatest demand for them.

Allocation of materials. The allocation of scarce materials among producers has to follow rather different principles. Here equal distribution makes no sense at all, as needs are so varied. What is developed therefore is a system of priorities, with those industries that are deemed most essential to the war effort at the top of the list and the quota allotted by a central board in accordance with its scale of priority. This in effect substitutes the administrative process for the market process; the firm that finds itself short of some essential raw material now no longer has the option of bidding it away from others by offering a higher price, but must convince the official hierarchy of the essentiality of its claim. The system is subject to the besetting sin of all administrative systems—that skill in the persuasion of administrators may not correspond to the actual needs of the society. Consequently nonessential but persuasive users may get more than their share, and the essential but tongue-tied get less. There is much to be said for combining an allocation system with a peripheral "grey market" which is either legalized or winked at, where the exceptional and difficult cases can be served through the market mechanism, even at very high prices. This is equivalent to the "one unrationed foodstuff" in the theory of food rationing.

Defects of price control. Price control suffers from another defect of any administrative system—that it can only be established by "freezing" a price structure which existed at a certain date, and that the administrative adjustments never catch up with the constant shifts in economic conditions and cost structures which make the old structure of relative prices obsolete. When price control is imposed it is usually in the form of a "roll-back"—some date in the recent past is selected, and the maximum legal price of each commodity is fixed by its price on the base date. Any such list of prices, however, will show anomalies—some commodities, for instance, may have been in unusually short supply on the base date, and their maximum price therefore will be "too high," whereas other commodities may have been in temporary glut, and their maximum prices will therefore be "too low." These anomalies will increase rapidly as time goes on, especially in an economy that is thoroughly disturbed by a major war, where all the old landmarks are shaken and where rapid shifts in relative price structures may therefore be expected.

The problem is complicated by the necessity for establishing not merely a legal structure of maximum prices for a long list of commodities, but also a *geographical* structure of prices for these commodities at a long list of key places. There is a "normal" geographical structure of prices determined largely by costs of transport and the direction of commodity flows; thus in a smoothly operating competitive market we would expect the difference in price between two places to be roughly equal to the cost of transport between them—the higher price being at the place towards which the commodity flows. If now under price control the geographical structure of maximum prices no longer comes to correspond with the costs of transport, we may find goods piling up in one place and not moving to another.

It is reported that at one brief period during the second World War the structure of meat prices was such that it did not pay anybody to ship meat east of Cincinnati! It is true, of course, that the legal price structure is not rigid, and that there is always an elaborate machinery for making adjustments. By comparison with the swift adjustments of the market, however, any administrative machinery is clumsy and slow. Consequently the legal maximum prices become less and less realistic as time goes on, and price control rarely survives more than a few years. Curiously enough, it is most likely to be abandoned precisely at the moment when some control is needed—in the period of delayed inflation which almost always follows a major war.

Wage control. The control of wages and of industrial disputes presents problems related to, but perhaps even more difficult than those of price control. Shortages in the labor market are an inevitable result of the diversion of large amounts of manpower to the war effort. If these shortages are allowed to exercise their full impact on money wages, the rise in wages will soon undermine any attempt at "holding the line" on prices. On the other hand, a failure to hold the line on prices results in strong pressures for wage increases. Price and wage control must therefore go hand in hand. Wage control, however, creates difficult political and psychological problems of consent, especially as most democratic states eschew the direct conscription of labor. It becomes difficult therefore either to use wages as a means of shifting workers into occupations of high priority, or to employ direct compulsion. An indirect compulsion hangs over the labor force in the shape of the draft—this indeed may be one of the important functions of conscription in time of war. Wage control, however, remains a ticklish matter, and the control of work stoppages even more so; much here depends on the degree to which the labor unions feel identified with the aims of the war effort. One may venture on the hypothesis that wage control can only be successful in a war with wide popular support.

Control of the cost-of-living index. A curious by-product of wage control is the control not of the cost of living, but of the cost-of-living index. One of the principles that commands wide acceptance among unions, employers, and wage boards is that a wage increase may be "justified" by appeal to a rise in the cost-of-living index. If the cost-of-living index is an accurate measure of the price level of the goods that workers buy, this principle would mean that inflation could not result in a reduction of real wages. In a major war a reduction in the real consumption of the working class may be essential, simply because so much is being absorbed by the war effort that the goods of worker consumption cannot be produced for lack of resources. We cannot consume what is not there to be consumed. When this happens a reduction in real worker consumption is inevitable. In part this may be done by taxation, in part by savings drives, but in part it may have to be done by denying wage increases equal to the actual rise in the cost of living. This may sometimes be done by subsidizing articles that figure prominantly in the cost-of-living index, so that this index underestimates the true rise in the cost of living. Wage increases based on increases in the cost-of-living index then still permit some reduction in real wages.

War finance: taxation. The control of civilian consumption is one of the basic problems of war finance. In part this is done by increased taxation. One of the major economic accomplishments of the second World War was the development of "pay as you go" or current income taxes. This removed a serious defect from the income tax system—that previously the taxes paid in one year were based on the income of the previous year. In an inflation this meant that income tax payments were based on the smaller incomes of the previous year, and hence it was difficult to get an adequate yield. With the coming of current income taxation this difficulty has been removed, and the income tax has become a very sensitive and easily adjustable method of controlling disposable income, and therefore of controlling consumption.

Borrowing from households and businesses. There are limits, however, to tax yields, as we have seen, and in a major war there must be extensive recourse to government borrowing. The effects of this differ greatly, depending on whether the borrowing is from households, from producing firms, or from banks. Borrowing from households—that is, the sale of government securities to households—tends to reduce household consumption, though not necessarily by as much as the amount borrowed, for households tend to regard government securities as liquid assets and hence treat them as substitutes for money. The sale of government securities to households, therefore, is usually offset in part by a decline in the willingness of households to hold cash. If the sale of government securities means simply a replacement of cash holdings by government bond holdings, the effect on consumption may be negligible, and the anti-inflationary effect correspondingly small. This, however, is an unlikely and extreme case.

The sale of government securities to businesses and corporations likewise may have some effect on reducing their expenditures, and hence in diminishing the inflationary pressures.

Borrowing from banks. The sale of government securities to banks does nothing to reduce inflationary pressure, and may actually increase it. The banks pay for the securities by the creation of new deposits, which government then pays out to its suppliers and its labor force. In the first instance, therefore, if government borrows from the banks and then spends the borrowed money, the total of bank deposits in the hands of the public is increased by roughly the amount of securities sold. The process is thus roughly equivalent to the printing of government paper money. The inflationary effect may actually be even greater, because banks regard government securities as liquid assets, and hence may lend more freely to business and diminish their excess reserves; this will increase the total of bank deposits even beyond the amount of government borrowings.

There is a real dilemma of policy here. The transfer of resources from peaceful to military uses requires a good deal of new investment, some of which is appropriately financed by bank loans. A general expansion of bank loans facilitates the transfer of resources into the war effort. If, therefore, the government follows too restrictive a banking policy—for instance, raising reserve requirements as the bank's holdings of government securities rise—the transfer of resources may be delayed. If, on the other hand, its policy is not restrictive, the operations of the banking system intensify the inflation. The more money can be raised by taxes, of course, the less serious this dilemma becomes, and ideally a system of high taxes and liberal bank loans would seem to be in order.

The economist's view of war finance. Nothing illustrates the difference between the "sophisticated" and the "unsophisticated" attitude towards economics better than attitudes on war finance and war borrowings. The economist looks at the problem in terms of the transfer of real resources: "finance" is merely the intermediary machinery for accomplishing these real transfers. The money raised in taxes and in bond drives does not "buy" the armaments; its sole economic purpose is to prevent inflation, or to allow only that degree of inflation which is necessary to the smooth operation of the real transfers. Even if no money were to be raised in taxes and bond drives the government could still "buy" its military supplies either by printing money or selling bonds to the banks. In this case, however, there would be a rapid inflation of prices, which might damage the economy. The unsophisticated attitude by contrast sees the government as dependent on bond sales and taxes to buy the armaments it needs, as if there were a large shop full of arms and government had to come to it with money derived from the people.

Restriction of consumption through shortages. A restriction of private consumption also takes place during a war because of the very development of shortages. Certain commodities such as consumer durables tend to disappear from the market, mainly because they are produced by the industries that are most easily turned over to war production. Consequently, households find that there are gaps in their pattern of expenditures simply from the lack of things to buy. Then, because of a certain stability in conventional patterns of expenditure, they do not immediately divert the money to other uses, but increase their money balances, relative to their income. This is the phenomenon known as a fall in the velocity of circulation of money, and though it is quite irrational in times of inflation or expected inflation when stocks of money are declining in value, the persistence of old habits outweighs more economic considerations in the minds of householders and the phenomenon is frequently observed. This is usually followed by a rise in velocity once the war is over and the restriction of consumption is no longer either patriotic nor fashionable. Then people spend their money stock freely, with the result that there is a sharp rise in prices and money incomes. Thus there were sharp inflations in 1919 after the first World War and in 1945-47 after the second.

The national debt. A major war inevitably results in a sharp increase in the national debt, and certain problems arise as to its management. Here again we may notice a marked contrast between the unsophisticated and the sophisticated view on the subject. The economist views the national debt as a fairly minor problem. It consists of a volume of government securities which are useful in the financial system in that they provide a convenient form of assets not quite, but almost, as liquid as money. If there is a demand for these assets, as there is, there seems to be no reason why government should not provide them, and if the national debt were to be entirely paid off a quite inconvenient gap would appear in the structure of financial instruments.

It is true that interest on the national debt may be something of a burden, in that it represents a form of redistribution of income which may not be altogether in accord with general redistribution policies. If, for instance, the national debt were mostly held by the rich, and taxes were paid by the poor, the redistributive effects would be adverse. As it is, however, the debt is widely distributed, and especially insofar as it is held by banks interest on the debt amounts to a government subsidy to the banking system, a subsidy much of which is passed on to depositors. On the whole, then, it may be said that interest on the debt is not a serious burden; that it consists for the most part of our paying taxes out of one pocket and interest into another pocket. This might not be true if the debt were held by foreigners; then the interest would be a real national burden, in the sense that it would be represented by an excess of exports over imports. However, only a very small proportion of the United States debt is so held.

The economics of postwar reconstruction. The economic problems of a postwar reconstruction period are in some ways rather similar, though in a reverse direction, to those of mobilization for war. There is again a problem in real terms of transferring a large volume of resources—this time from warlike to peaceful uses. The armed force must be demobilized, large numbers of its personnel returned to civilian employments, and the industries that have been producing the means of death and destruction must now turn to production of the means of life and enjoyment. Here again the economic problems may be divided into two categories. First there are the military and political problems—such matters, for instance, as the military government of a defeated nation, reparations, and the economic terms of the peace settlement. Secondly there are the problems concerned with domestic policy—demobilization, the control of postwar inflations or depressions, and so on. Domestic postwar policy soon merges into the general economic problem of a peacetime economy.

The economy at the end of a war. The transition from war to peace differs from the transition from peace to war, however, by reason of the different initial position. At the outbreak of a war a nation is likely to be in a condition very different from its condition at the war's close. At the outbreak of a major war, especially if there has been a long period of peace, nations are usually well supplied with material resources. At the conclusion of a major war these resources are likely to be very much depleted. The experience of the United States here is not typical. The United States emerged from both world wars with an industrial plant at least as good as when she went in, if not better, and with agricultural productivity unimpaired or even improved; her cities were undamaged, and her losses of men relatively slight. The only serious deficiencies were in consumer capital—automobiles, household equipment, and houses—and even here the stock was so large that the deficiency did not much impair the productivity of the household. In Europe, on the other hand, and in the other theaters of war, devastation was widespread, cities were destroyed, transportation was disrupted, there had been great losses in men, huge displacements of population, and the whole fabric of economic life was strained to the point of collapse.

The real cost of war: the city-country exchange. The real cost of war is greater than the obvious destruction and loss of life; it consists in those things of peacetime use that were *not* produced by the resources devoted to war. Thus war has a double cost; there is the destruction itself, and on top of this there is the unseen cost of the destruction—the unborn children, the unmade investments, the unmaintained equipment and land. In a major war these unseen costs may be greater than the visible destruction. This is particularly true if the war has strained the economy of a nation by using more than its economic surplus, so that it has been financed in a real sense by disinvestment. Paradoxically enough, if a nation is too successful in mobilizing its resources for war it may find itself not only defeated, but utterly prostrate in defeat.

Russia in the first World War was a good example. The strong centralized government of the Czar mobilized such a large proportion of Russian manpower and Russian industry for war that the whole system collapsed, largely because of a breakdown in exchange between agriculture and the rest of the economy. The extreme mobilization of industry meant that the rest of the economy had nothing to exchange with the agriculturalist for food except rapidly depreciating money! Consequently, farmers held on to their food and the whole system collapsed into revolution. Even in Germany something of the same phenomenon appeared; the starvation that followed the first World War was not so much a result of the absence of food as a result of a breakdown of trade; the cities again had nothing to give the farmers, so the farmers ate their own food plentifully and the cities starved.

Reconstruction as capital accumulation. The problem of postwar reconstruction then is essentially a problem of investment—that is, of capital accumulation—in both human and material resources. This is in part a quantitative problem, in part structural. The quantitative problem is that of how to get the widest possible excess of production plus imports over consumption plus exports; production and imports represent additions to the total stock of real capital, consumption and exports represent subtractions from it. If real capital is to grow as fast as possible, then, the problem is to increase production and imports, and to diminish consumption and exports, with the exception of that consumption and those exports that lead to still greater production and imports. To put the matter in another way, we need to get an excess of production over consumption and of imports over exports. For a thoroughly devastated and disorganized country, however, this may be very difficult. Production is very low; it is hard even physically to push consumption below it, and there are additional psychological difficulties in that after the strains of the war people are in a mood to relax and try to enjoy themselves rather than to continue to work, scrimp, and sacrifice. If imports are to exceed exports there must be either an ability to sell securities in other countries—an unlikely possibility if the nation is defeated and disorganized—or there must be subsidies and gifts from other countries.

Postwar hyperinflations. It is not surprising that under these circumstances defeated and disorganized countries have lapsed into hyperinflation; this happened in Russia and Germany after the first World War, and in Hungary and China after the second. The tax system tends to be disorganized along with the rest of the economy, and government expenditures for reconstruction will be large. Consequently there will be large budget deficits, which can be met only by printing money or by borrowing from the banks and thus creating bank deposits. At first the inflation may have some effect in restricting consumption, as the real incomes of pensioners and bondholders shrink. It will also, in its early stages, assist the recovery of production, through shifting incomes towards profit-makers and making it easy to finance investment. Wages may or may not lag behind the rise in prices; if they lag there will be some restriction of consumption by the working class; if this does not go far enough to impair their productivity it assists the reconstruction process. At some point, however, inflation passes over into hyperinflation; all confidence in the stability of prices is lost, and there is a rapid rise in the velocity of circulation towards the physical limit imposed by the fact that it takes a little time to run from the pay window to the store! In severe hyperinflations prices double every week or less, and the price level rises to billions of times its former level. The faster prices rise, of course, the less tax collections can keep up with the mounting value of government expenditure, and the increasing deficits add fuel to the inflation.

Currency reform. Hyperinflation, or even threatened hyperinflation, can be stopped only by a "currency reform." This consists usually of issuing a new kind of money, often in a different denomination, and destroying the old kind by refusing to accept it in payment of obligations to government and denying it the right of legal tender. To be successful the new money should be substantially less in quantity than the old, so that the operation really amounts to a large once-for-all tax on the whole population. If this is large enough it may restore the functioning of the tax system, and so destroy the government deficits that are the continuing source of the inflation. The German currency reform of June 1948 was a spectacular success from this point of view, and led to a rapid and remarkable recovery of production and trade.

Recovery through an import surplus: relief. Capital accumulation in postwar reconstruction—and, indeed, at any other time—can be materially assisted if a country can import more than it exports. Insofar as the problem of recovery is treated as a world problem this means organizing an export surplus from the rich and undevastated countries to appear as an import surplus in the poor and devastated countries. In the first stages of reconstruction this shows up as relief. After both world wars extensive international relief organizations, both governmental and private, were set up, financed mainly by contributions from the richer countries. Even in the organization of relief the needs of reconstruction should not be overlooked, and may indeed be complementary with the objectives of relief. Thus, supplying fertilizer to farmers in a devastated area may not only contribute towards the food supplies of the next and subsequent years, but may increase the food sold off the farms and so contribute to the feeding of the cities, where the most serious problems are likely to lie.

Reconstruction: the first World War. Once the more immediate needs are met the interest shifts towards problems of long-run reconstruction. After the first World War the reconstruction of Germany was assisted mainly by private loans from the United States. This turned out to be an unstable and unsatisfactory solution. France and England had borrowed extensively in the United States during and just after the war, and were burdened with these obligations. They tried to recoup by imposing reparation payments on Germany, which Germany proved quite incapable of paying out of her disorganized economy. A temporary solution was found in the years 1924-30, after the German mark was stabilized. The United States made private loans to Germany, Germany paid reparations to France and England, and France and England paid installments on their war debt to the United States. Thus in effect the United States was paying herself back her war debts. This happy arrangement broke down during the great depression, when American loans to Germany dried up, Germany defaulted her reparation payments, and Britain and France defaulted on the payments of their war debts.

Reconstruction: the second World War. The lessons of the first World War were not lost. After the second World War the United States expressed its sense of world solidarity through the Marshall Plan, as embodied in the Foreign Assistance Act of 1948, and in subsequent acts and appropriations, in making gifts rather than loans. The total of these gifts from 1945 to 1956 amounted to over $38 billion. Tragically, what was originally an expression of human solidarity became transformed, by way of reaction to Russian intransigence and hostility, into an instrument of cold war. One may hope, however, that happier world situations in the future may lead to a recovery of the larger aims. At this point the problem of reconstruction after war merges into the broader problem of world economic development. The essential economic problem, indeed, is the same—that of starting up a process of capital growth from low levels—though the sociological and psychological conditions are very different. Reconstruction after a war is helped by the memory of the "old days"; the essential skills of the people remain, and if the culture has not been too much shaken by the war experiences the material embodiment of the culture can swiftly be reconstructed, and in surprisingly few years the physical scars of war are healed. It is easier, however, to rebuild than to build; if the culture does not contain an image of a better state than the present, or even if it only contains an unclear image, there will be no sustained drive for improvement.

The foreign exchanges in a postwar reconstruction. The problem of exchange stability and exchange control takes on peculiar importance in periods of postwar reconstruction. When a country has an internal inflation its foreign exchange rates reflect the inflation in some degree; the value of the national monetary unit falls in terms of more stable foreign currencies as well as in terms of domestic goods. If exchange control prevents the exchange rate from falling far enough, there will be "shortages" of foreign exchange—that is, people who wish to purchase foreign currencies with the domestic currency will not be able to find sellers. In the case of the German hyperinflation of 1923 the operations of speculators outside Germany actually subsidized the German economy to some extent. After the mark had fallen a fair way many speculators bought marks to hold them for a rise; actually the mark became almost completely worthless, so that these speculators lost their whole investment. What the speculators lost, however, the Germans gained, as the foreign currencies which they bought with the half-depreciated marks in fact turned out to be a virtually "free gift"—a very unofficial and unintended Marshall Plan by the speculators!

A devaluation—as when the official dollar price of the pound sterling, for instance, was lowered from $4.04 to $2.80 in 1949—may assist the international economic position of the devaluing country, at least temporarily, especially if the devaluing country has had an internal inflation relative to the rest of the world. Devaluation only helps, however, if the demand for a country's exports is elastic. Devaluation amounts to a general price reduction of a country's exports in terms of foreign currencies. Thus before the devaluation of 1949 an item costing £1 in England would sell for $4.04 in the United States (neglecting costs of transport); after the devaluation it would sell for $2.80. If this results in a large increase in exports from England, the ability of England to import essential foodstuffs and capital equipment will also be increased. If the demand for exports is inelastic, however, devaluation may make a negative contribution to a country's recovery.

Structural reconstruction. There is an apparent paradox here. We have stressed the importance of an excess of imports if a war-weakened country is to recover quickly. In countries like England and Germany, however, which rely heavily on exports to purchase essential foodstuffs and raw materials, great stress is laid on increasing exports and on developing the export industries. The paradox is explicable in part by the consideration that the growth of an economy is not merely a quantitative matter—the mere piling up of random commodities—but is a structural problem. That is to say, investment is not the accumulation of commodities in general, but a pattern of specific accumulations of particular goods—agricultural implements, human skills, steel mills, special machinery, transportation systems, retail outlets, civic and national services, and so on. An economy grows as a body grows, not as a sandpile grows. It may be worth while, therefore, to export unessentials in order that essentials (such as food and raw materials) may be imported, even if this means that fewer imports in general can be made.

The economics of disarmament. In 1957, when this is being written, we seem to be a long way from a settled and peaceful world. The burden of armaments is great even for the United States, where national-security expenditures account for about 10 per cent of the Gross National Product. It is an even worse burden in poorer countries, and is an almost intolerable burden for countries like India which need to devote as much of their resources as possible to economic development. Nevertheless, there is some hope even in the very terror which now threatens the world. Not even the largest nations can now be defended against the annihilation of their cities, and it seems clear that the only road left to real national security is through universal policed disarmament and at least enough world government to do the policing. Whether this goal can be achieved in view of the enormous obstacles of mistrust, hostile ideologies, and national pride that block the way is not a question within the scope of this work.

Nevertheless, it is within the purview of a work on economic policy to ask what would be the effects of disarmament on the economy, and especially on the American economy. The question is all the more important because there is a widespread belief—which is not confined to communist circles—that the American economy depends on a high level of armaments expenditure for its continued prosperity, and that universal disarmament down to the level of internal police (which is the only kind of disarmament that makes sense in terms of security) would create a major depression in the United States. This belief is an important weapon of communist propaganda; it is a commonly held view even within the United States, and is a real obstacle to popular support for disarmament proposals.

Why disarmament *need* not lead to depression. There are really two problems here. One is that of preventing general depression. The other is that of the local shifts and structural changes in the economy that disarmament would involve.

The first problem does not present serious difficulties to the economist, though it often seems like a very difficult problem to the non-economist. To take round figures, suppose that a

$400 billion Gross National Product (GNP) is regarded as "full employment," and that $40 billion of this is absorbed by national security. If this $40 billion is reduced to zero, substitutes for it must be found if the value of the GNP is not to fall. Suppose now that tax collections are reduced by $40 billion. This will expand household purchases, as it expands disposable income even out of the same GNP, but not, probably, to the full extent of $40 billion. Suppose the expansion in household purchases is only $30 billion: there would then be a fall in GNP, with a resulting fall in income, with a further fall in household purchases, and we might end up with a GNP of only $380 billion. If the poor outlook caused a decline in investment this would further lower GNP, incomes, and household purchases, and we might find ourselves in a moderate to severe depression, especially if counteracting monetary and fiscal measures were not taken.

The problem, however, is simply to find some set of increases in the other components of the GNP that add up to $40 billion. We might, for instance, reduce taxes by more than the reduction in government expenditure and so run a budget deficit. This would increase household purchases, as it would increase disposable income. Then we might expand government expenditures for nonmilitary objectives—better schools, roads, parks, research, public works. We might also expand foreign loans or grants for economic development. Or we might even encourage an increase in private investment. If the sum of these increases —say 33 more for household purchases, 5 more for nonmilitary government expenditures, 2 more for world development grants —add up to 40 (all these in billions), the GNP will remain at $400 billion, and there will be no general depression.

The particular combination of increases we set out to achieve will depend, of course, on the other objectives of policy. If the country were badly in need of roads and schools, and if we decided on a grand program of world development, we might divide it, say, 25 to household consumption (which would probably mean a smaller tax reduction), 8 to nonmilitary government expenditures, and 7 to world development. All that is necessary to maintain the GNP, however, is that the sum of the various increases in the components should equal the decrease in arms expenditure.

Structural problems in disarmament. Structural changes present important problems for certain localities, especially those dependent on the aircraft industry. This is probably the only major industry that is dependent for a large proportion of its sale on armaments. The technical changes in armaments themselves might, of course, make this obsolete, but at present disarmament would create serious problems for those communities heavily dependent on aircraft—especially where there are few alternative sources of employment. The flexibility of the American economy, however, is remarkable, as the transition after the second World War showed. In a single year expenditure on national security fell from 38 per cent of the GNP in 1945 (it was 44 per cent at the peak in 1944) to 10 per cent in 1946, with only a small decline in the GNP itself and no large-scale unemployment. An economy that can take a turnover of this magnitude in its stride should not be fazed by a reduction from 10 per cent to zero—provided that it is not allowed to fall into general depression. The transition needs much more thought and planning than it is getting—or than it will get if it ever looks imminent—but we may safely conclude that it could be accomplished without serious disturbance.

16

The world perspective: communism and development

The Russians might not have a Cycle,
If governed by the Archangel Michael,
But they had cycles deep and mean
When ruled by Stalin and Lenin.

When Noble Words like "Just" and "Free"
Mean different things to you and me,
There is enough potential trouble
To level all the world to rubble.

Poor countries are inclined to dicker
With those who'll make them richer quicker:
This gives the conflict added zest
Between the Russians and the West.
And they might well be Doubting Thomases
Who trust in other people's promises,
When all development must roll
On Thought, Work, Thrift, and Self-Control.

Up to this point our attention has been focused mainly on the economic policies of the United States or of similar, highly developed, democratic countries. When we look at economic policy in a world perspective, however, it is clear that the developed, democratic world covers only part, and not a very large part, of the human population. At a generous estimate not more than 350-400 million people live in developed, democratic societies. About 250 million live in the semideveloped, communist societies of Russia and her satellites. About 600 million live in the undeveloped, communist society of China. And about 1,200 million live in the undeveloped, noncommunist rest of the world, under a great variety of governmental forms ranging from the advanced democratic system of India to fascist and military dictatorships and colonial subjugation.

It is impossible in a few pages to give more than the briefest outline of the problems of policy in a communist state. Nevertheless, the challenge of communism in the world perspective is so important that we would do less than justice to the world situation if we neglected it entirely. The difference between communism and democratic capitalism runs deeper than a mere disagreement over means. There are deep disagreements about the *objectives* of economic policy. In some form or other we might say that the four objectives we have identified—progress, stability, justice, and freedom—are important for both systems. The interpretation each gives to these objectives, however, is very different.

There is least disagreement, perhaps, about the first: economic progress is an ideal of both systems. But even here there are subtle differences of interpretation. Because of their materialist ideology communists have a tendency to neglect services, and especially household and personal services, in their concept of the economic product. Consequently their ideal—and their policies—are more heavily weighted on the side of increasing the production of material goods rather than of "utilities." This bias is also likely to be reflected in the weight given to the development of heavy industries in communist planning. In their educational system this bias is reflected in the emphasis placed on science and engineering, to the detriment of the social sciences and the humanities. Even within the technical fields the scientist who promises quick material results, like Lysenko, is likely to have an advantage over the more "pure" and conscientious worker in basic research.

The differences between Russia and the West, and especially between Russia and America, on this score can, of course, be exaggerated. Communists have "parks of culture and rest," and lay great stress on literacy and education; our own society is not wholly innocent of the charge of materialism! We have our Lysenkos in the laboratories of our corporations, and Russia at present shows some encouraging signs of greater liberty. The difference in the ideological bases of the two societies may be much greater than the differences in their practice. Nevertheless, the ideological difference exists, and operates in either case to produce a certain bias.

Communists are not generally aware of the problem of stability in their own system, being under the illusion that this is merely a problem of capitalism! It is true that the business cycle as it exists under capitalism cannot manifest itself in the same form is a centrally planned economy. Nevertheless, the history of the Soviet economy exhibits a cycle even more devastating than that of capitalism, and (perhaps only by a coincidence) with much the same timing.

The period of "war communism" (1917-21) ended in a famine and a shocking economic collapse in 1921. This was not merely due to war and civil war, but was due in large part to the severe application of communist principles, and the disorganization of economic life that resulted from the divorcement of "payoffs" from "production." Lenin had the genius to recognize the source of the debacle, and in 1921 introduced the New Economic Policy, with a limited return to private trading and private ownership. Under this there was a substantial recovery up to 1928. Then policy took a sharp turn towards strict communism again in the first five-year plan and the collectivization of agriculture. The forced collectivization of agriculture involved the "liquidation" (that is, murder or exile) of millions of

Russia's best farmers, the "kulaks," the herding of peasants into large collective farms, and the loss of more than half the country's livestock. This culminated in another famine in 1932 in which millions died. Again, after Stalin's famous "drunk with success" speech there was a relaxation. Peasants were allowed to have tiny plots of their own; collectives were allowed some security of the collective property and consequently their members could enjoy at least some of the fruits of increased productivity. In industry likewise managers were given more incentives, and plants might enjoy some of the fruits of increased efficiency. Under this regime there was again a substantial recovery, though agriculture continues to be a very weak spot in the whole Soviet system, and is an ultimate limiting factor on Soviet economic growth.

It may of course be mere coincidence that the troughs of the Soviet cycle—1921 and 1932—and even the peak of 1928—correspond so exactly with the troughs of the American business cycle. There is certainly no direct connection between the two cycles, as there is, for instance, between American and European cycles. The Soviet economy is heavily insulated from the rest of the world, and is highly self-sufficient; fluctuations in Soviet trade are not closely related to the general cycles in other parts of the world. The critical question, however, is whether cycles of this political nature are an essential part of the Soviet system as at present constituted, that is, whether there is a real "cybernetic" problem in Soviet policy.

The cycle can be interpreted as a result of a conflict between ideology and reality. The communist ideology in a pure and rigid form is a very imperfect picture of the world of real human relationships. Consequently when this ideology is applied in a pure form it is bound to result in some degree of breakdown or failure.

The "cycle," then, in communism takes the following form. Communists are impelled by their ideology to policies which, if applied rigidly, will divorce all marginal reward from marginal productive effort, and so will lead to some sort of failure or breakdown. It takes a while, however, for this information to penetrate to the policymakers, especially as in a totalitarian regime these are likely to be surrounded by "yes-men" and so are cut off from reality. The dictator controls the sources of his information so that in order to retain their jobs (or even their heads) the information-providers *must* delude the dictator with "favorable" information even when the truth is unfavorable, and when the information-providers know this.[1] Eventually, however, the situation grows so desperate—as it did in Russia in 1921 and again in 1932—that the communist policymaker can no longer be insulated from the realities of the world around him, and he is forced to compromise his ideology in the interests of economic recovery. This compromise rankles; so that after recovery has proceeded for a while, ideology reasserts itself over reality, a new experiment in rigid communism begins, and the cycle starts all over again.

If, of course, the communist policymakers are wise enough, and realistic enough, and informed enough, to sense immediately when their policies are too rigid and are creating economic breakdown, the cycle might be eliminated. The very centralization of decision-making, however, which is an inevitable concomitant of a centrally planned economy, makes it hard to set up the political checks and balances that would correct the tendency towards cycles. In such a system there is a tendency for the ruthless and the uncompromising to rise to the top, and the very Stalin-like qualities that enable them to rise are precisely the qualities that produce the political cycle. There is some evidence that the present rulers of Russia are aware of this problem, and that the reorganization after the death of

[1] For a superb illustration of this principle, see the following passage from Khrushchev's secret report to the Twentieth Congress: "All those who interested themselves even a little in the national situation saw the difficult situation in agriculture, but Stalin never even noted it. Did we tell Stalin about this? Yes, we told him, but he did not support us. Why? Because Stalin never travelled anywhere. He knew the country and agriculture only from films. And these films had dressed up and beautified the existing situation in agriculture. Many films so pictured *Kolkhoz* life that the tables were bending from the weight of turkeys and geese. Evidently, Stalin thought that it was actually so." Quoted by Robert C. Tucker in "The Psychology of Soviet Foreign Policy," *Problems of Communism* (U.S.I.A.), Vol. IV, No. 3, May-June 1957, p. 6; reprinted by permission of the Rand Corporation.

Stalin represents some effort to deal with it. In a centrally planned economy, however, it is very difficult to set up any institutions that are independent of the centralized state. Where there are no private employers and no private property, everybody is ultimately dependent for his livelihood and even his life on the favor of the central concentration of power. Any system of checks and balances therefore is likely to prove weak.

The greatest divergence in economic objectives between communist and noncommunist systems lies in the interpretations given to economic justice and freedom. Economic justice as communists understand it involves the elimination of all income derived from the private ownership of the means of production. This is a basic value system of the communists; it not only governs much of their policy but also colors their view of the realities of human relations and historical development. In socialist thought, and especially in Marx, this view of economic justice is derived from a certain aspect of the Labor Theory of Value. This is the view that the total product of economic life is derived from acts of labor, either present labor or past labor embodied in physical capital. If, then, labor *made* everything, labor ought to *get* everything. Under capitalism, however, the product is divided between labor income and nonlabor income, the latter going to the owners of property, simply in their capacity as owners. The argument is then that the owners didn't make it, so why should they get it! This is the theory of "surplus value," affirming that nonlabor income, which is the excess or surplus of the total value of the product over the real wage bill, or what goes to labor, is a result of the exploitation of the working class by the owners of the means of production, and is therefore an unjust and illegitimate form of income. The remedy is the "expropriation of the expropriators"—the seizure of the means of production by the state in the name of the dictatorship of the proletariat, and the subsequent elimination of the owning class either by liquidation or by their absorption into the labor force.

This concept of justice colors the whole view of reality of the communist. Thus he sees history as a great cyclical process of class warfare, in which the lower classes are continually rising to dominance and overthrowing the upper classes. This process mysteriously enough comes to an end when the last class—the proletariat—comes to dominance, and in a sense history then ceases and mankind enters an earthly paradise—or perhaps Nirvana! This is the "dialectical" view of the historical process. In a broad form there is some truth in it; the communist, however, narrows it into a dialectical materialism, which is the view that history is governed essentially by the dynamics of material technology, and that all other aspects—ideas, religions, politics, and so on—are merely cars attached to the great engine of technical change.

This view is closely related to the essential materialism of the Labor Theory of Value, which discounts the human and intellectual aspects of the economic process and sees it just as a mechanical transformation of acts of labor into products. It leads to a drastic oversimplification of the complexities of social life. The true dynamics of history is a process of enormous complexity, in which technical systems, ideological systems, latent and manifest dynamic movements, act and interact in a bewildering network of intricate cause and effect. It is just as true—and as false—to say that everything depends on the dynamic of material productive processes as it is to say that everything depends on ideas, or on religion, or on climate, or on heredity. Each of these interacting systems has a certain dynamic of its own, but they all also contribute one to another. Yet it is the very oversimplification of the Marxist system that has given it its appeal to many minds who seek a short cut through the bewildering complexity of the real world.

The Soviet Union has been successful in virtually eliminating income derived from ownership of the means of production—at the cost, of course, of transferring this ownership to the state. This does not mean that it has eliminated inequality. Indeed, the degree of inequality of income is very substantial, and there are marked signs of the development of a new ruling class in the professional and managerial groups. The degree of inequality of power is much greater than in a capitalist society, where private property and constitutional rights act as checks on the power of the state. The elimination of income from "surplus value," therefore, does not mean the elimination of privilege, or of exploitation. Indeed, the Soviet Union has probably exploited its farmers and workers more ruthlessly than any capitalist country, in the sense that a large proportion of the product of the society has been channeled into the single control of the state, and farmers and workers have received only a fraction of what they have produced.

The problem here is a clear case of the difficulty we have discussed in Chapter 6—that of confusing means with ends. Private property is a means, and neither its abolition nor its unrestricted right should be an end in itself. The system, and its alternatives, should be judged by their fruits and their costs, not by any absolute principle of rightness or wrongness. Private property is no more "wrong" than any tool or implement is wrong, unless it is devised exclusively for wrong ends. We do not denounce hammers as such because they may occasionally have been used as instruments of murder. Insofar as the cost of abolishing private property is the centralizing of all economic power in the hands of the state, and insofar as this almost inevitably leads to totalitarianism and a grievous loss of liberty and basic human rights, it is reasonable to adjudge the cost too high, and to look for systems that permit, at the same time that they may restrain, the rights of private property and private enterprise.

There seems to be little doubt that in many fields the denial of rights to private property and private enterprise has been extremely costly to the Soviet Union. Especially is this true in agriculture. The collective farm has certain technical advantages over the very small-scale peasant agriculture that preceded it, especially in grain or cotton growing, where the consolidation of small and scattered holdings into large fields makes it possible to use mechanized methods of farming. It has very few technical advantages in livestock production or in garden crops. Had it not been, indeed, for the relaxation of communist principle which permitted the peasants to have a little garden and a cow or a pig or two on the side, with the right to dispose of their own produce personally in the city markets, the Russian food situation would have been desperate indeed.

Furthermore the technical advantages, where they exist, have often been dissipated by the sociological disadvantages. It takes an unusual degree of idealism for a large body of people, not related by ties of kinship or by a common religious faith, to work together in a common enterprise when the rewards of work are pooled and where good work receives no special reward. In some cases this can happen, and it has happened. There are some kolkhozes (collective farms) that have a high morale and where there is great pride in the accomplishment of the collective as such. These, however, seem to be rare. In agriculture there is a very real magic of property; there is nothing like allowing the individual to receive the product of his individual labor if we want to produce the goods. Soviet agriculture, therefore, compares very unfavorably with the agriculture, say, of the American Middle West, where family farms are large enough to take full advantage of the economies of mechanization and where there seems to be a reasonable proportion between private and public institutions.

Another field where the prejudice against private enterprise is very costly to the Russians is in the distributive trades. Nowhere does the prejudice against "profit" manifest itself in such absurdity as here. If a grower takes his produce to the town market himself and sells it, this apparently is at least winked at as not involving *serious* "exploitation"! If a merchant were to save the grower the trouble of carrying his produce to town, and were to buy it on the farm, and sell it in the town, this would be capitalist exploitation—one of the worst crimes in the Soviet code! The state monopolies of distribution are evidently inefficient in the extreme, as we might expect in an industry that involves widely scattered operations and an immense dispersal of decision-making. It apparently pays a grower of oranges in Georgia to fly to Moscow with four crates of oranges and sell them on the open market—this more than pays for his trip! The whole system gives one the impression of fantastic waste, and the increase in the over-all product that the introduction of a few capitalist middlemen would create might be many times their profits. This fact illustrates the fallacy of the theory of surplus value admirably; if the introduction of some private capitalists into the system would increase the total product by more than the capitalists' profits, there is clearly no exploitation: everybody is better off than before, except those people whose narrowness of vision cannot bear to witness any "private" success.

In regard to economic freedom the communist record is poor. Under the Stalin regime, at any rate, there was a good deal of forced labor of political prisoners. This aspect of the regime seems to have been considerably moderated since the death of Stalin, though naturally it is not easy to get the facts. The abolition of almost the whole area of private enterprise is a serious limitation on the freedom of those who might have abilities in this direction. The forcing of peasants into collective farms was one of the greatest violations of human freedom of the twentieth century. It is true that there seems to be a reasonable amount of freedom to change jobs, which is an important check on the power of the managerial group.

In spite of certain limitations on political freedom in the United States and various degrees of oppressiveness among the allied and colonial powers, the term "free world" is not wholly inappropriate, at least by comparison with the communist bloc. There is a peculiar atmosphere of spiritual oppression about the communist world which stems mainly perhaps from the deadly lack of humor to which the communist seems to be condemned. It is the oppressiveness of Byzantium without even the grace of religion.

The problem of China deserves special mention. The success of the communists in China was undoubtedly more a result of the total failure of the previous regime than it was of any special virtue of communism in the Chinese situation. China has been a country in turmoil for the past hundred years, suffering the breakdown of an old, beautiful, but prescientific civilization under the impact of the modern world. She has been bullied by the European powers and half-conquered by Japan, and has been rent with internal warfare for decades. The Revolution of 1911 which deposed the Manchu emperors and set up a republic should have set off an era of economic development as, for instance, the Meiji restoration of 1868 did in Japan. Between civil wars, the Japanese invasions, incompetence and nepotism in government, and an apparent incompatibility between the "imported" institutions of capitalism and the matrix of Chinese customs, morals, and family-centered culture, the regime of Chiang Kai Shek lost the confidence of the people and was driven out of the mainland by a communist regime under Mao Tse Tung. This regime seems to be firmly established. It has at least brought internal peace, has controlled inflation, has restored internal communications, and has begun the development of heavy industry. All this, however, has been bought at a heavy price in the destruction of an ancient culture and the spiritual oppressiveness of a grimly puritanical and totalitarian regime. There has been a heavy price, too, in loss of life—though probably no heavier than in previous revolutions and civil wars.

The critical question for China is whether the Chinese communists will be any more successful in solving the problem of agriculture than the Russians. China cannot industrialize successfully unless she can obtain a surplus of food from agriculture. Under previous techniques this surplus was very small: the Chinese land had been divided and subdivided till in many areas the average size of the farm was less than two acres! With these meager resources in both land and equipment the Chinese peasant could barely raise enough for himself and his family, and it took something like 90 per cent of the Chinese to raise enough food for the population. If economic development is to be successful in China there must be a large migration out of agriculture, and the reorganized farms must be able to produce more food than before. The present regime seems to believe that collectivization is the way to achieve this end. The experience of Russia is not encouraging. Whether the Chinese experience will be any better remains to be seen.

We now turn to the problem of the noncommunist, but poor, countries which include about half the world's population. There is great variation here in the nature of the problem and in the resources that are available to meet it, so that we cannot apply any single rule to cover all these countries. Nevertheless, some broad generalizations apply. We can say, for instance, with a good deal of confidence, that the greatest source of world poverty is subsistence agriculture, especially under conditions of uncontrolled population pressure. By subsistence agriculture we mean a condition in which the cultivator is able to produce barely enough food for himself and his family. Where this condition obtains, the society must inevitably have a large proportion of its population—perhaps 90 per cent—engaged in scratching the bare means of subsistence from the soil, and these cultivators will have little or no surplus with which to support industrial occupations and purchase industrial products.

The forces that produce subsistence agriculture are many—ignorance, superstition, traditional modes of life, the lack of energy that follows on malnutrition and disease. There is one pattern of culture, however, that seems to produce subsistence poverty with sickening regularity. This is the type of culture—of which there are innumerable variations in detail—where the essential patterns of the culture are transmitted only through the family or the small kinship or tribal group, where there are no—or too few—schools to break the continuity of family tradition, where there are no checks on the growth of population except rising mortality from starvation and disease, and where the land is subdivided among the children on the death of the owner or the operator. There may be various land ownership or tenure patterns within this general framework: the land may be owned by the cultivator, or may be nominally held in common by a kinship or tribal or village community, or may even be owned by an absentee landlord. The dynamic of poverty, however, is the dynamic of land-splitting, under whatever institution of ownership and tenure. Where adequate size and shape of the farm is not protected by law or custom, there is an inevitable tendency for farms to be split up, and even for fields to be split up. There are places even in Europe where a peasant will cultivate perhaps forty tiny patches of land scattered throughout the village landscape. This problem of "fragmentation" or "parcellement," as the French call it, is common to many parts of the world, and exists wherever there are heavy populations and old cultures, whether in Europe, in Asia, or in the Andes.

Areas of subsistence agriculture are inevitably weak in a political and military sense, as they cannot possibly support large armed forces, nor the industry that is necessary to supply modern means of coercion. They tend to fall prey therefore to colonialism in one form or another, either through outright conquest by a developed power or through more subtle forms of domination which permit a nominal independence within the limits of "good behavior."

There are a great many grades and varieties of colonialism. There is a frankly exploitative type, which is much less common than it used to be, but which has by no means disappeared, in which the colonies are regarded as simple appendages of the imperial power; the imperial power tries to get as much out of the colony and put as little into it as possible. These countries are usually not interested in economic development, especially in their colonies. Development for them simply spells trouble—rising discontent, nationalism in the colonies, and eventual loss of colonial possessions. They may very well be right in this diagnosis; the only stable colonialism may well be a very low-level system in which there are no surpluses to tempt aggressors or potential revolutionaries, and the level of energy of the colonial populations is too low to permit them the luxury of thoughts of independence. There is some truth in the proposition that it is precisely those countries that try to develop their colonies that are most likely to lose them!

On the other hand, the low-level stability is bought at a very high price. In spite of the exploitative philosophy the imperial power actually gets very little out of the colonies, simply because they produce so little surplus above subsistence. Moreover the colonies may actually be a drain on the imperial power, because they necessitate keeping up a much larger armed force than the mere defense of the mother country would require. They may also drain off capital and human resources from the mother country which could actually be more advantageously employed at home. When one compares the economic status, for instance, of the various European countries as measured, say, by their per-capita income, the returns of colonialism seem very doubtful and meager. Those countries that have not had colonies, or have had only very small-scale colonial enterprises, like Sweden, Norway, Denmark, Germany, and Switzerland, compare very favorably in per-capita incomes with countries that have maintained large colonial empires like Holland, Belgium, France, Portugal, and Great Britain.

The economic equivalent of political colonialism is the plantation economy. This is common in many countries that are politically independent, like the republics of Central America. We can extend the concept beyond agriculture to the extractive enterprises—the oil wells of Venezuela and Arabia, the mining industries of Bolivia and Central Africa, the nitrate industry of Chile, and so on. The typical pattern of these areas is the large enterprise, operated by a foreign company located in some richer country, built by foreign capital, managed on the whole by foreign personnel at the top, with native labor and some native management, producing mainly a raw material for export. This merges into what might be called the "indigenous" plantation pattern, where the owners of the plantation (or extractive enterprise) are nationals of the country where the enterprise is located, but where the enterprise still produces mainly for export, and where there is still a sharp social and economic differentiation between the owning and managing class and the laboring class.

The social balance sheet of the plantation system is mixed; there are real assets, and yet heavy liabilities. There is a sense in which the plantation is a spearhead of civilization. We may not, of course, think much of civilization! However, it is easy to romanticize the idyllic beauties of primitive cultures, and though there is always some loss when a weaker culture is exposed to a stronger, there seems to be a certain irreversibility about these processes of development which we may regret but which we must accept. There is, of course, a great deal of difference in plantation systems. At one extreme we have plantations worked by slaves, which are purely exploitative, and which are doomed to ultimate failure simply through their corrupting effects on both owner and slave, and through their incompatibility with the rising conscience of mankind. At the other extreme we have "model" plantations where much consideration is given to the health and comfort of the workers, and where the standards are unquestionably much higher, in a material sense, than the standards of the surrounding culture. Even the most model plantation, however, is subject to the criticism that it is essentially an enclave, and that it does little to raise the standards or to integrate the culture of the region as a whole.

Even where the plantation is not exploitative, therefore, in the sense that it does not leave the people of the region any worse off than they would be without it, or with some alternative mode of economic organization, it still is likely to be "disintegrative," in the sense that it remains an "alien" body, sustained essentially by activity and by a culture that originates outside the region where it is located. It does not, therefore, produce a locally self-sustaining culture, unless the region can pass over into a somewhat higher stage of economic organization in which the local culture can produce the managerial and organizational ability to sustain the more advanced methods of production.

The very class differentiation which the plantation economy involves, however, militates against an integrated development of the culture of the region, unless special measures are taken to overcome it. The plantation worker lacks the incentive and the independence of the small proprietor. Because he does not have to exercise initiative in his daily task, the capacity for initiative deteriorates. This is a consequence of the division of labor which, as we have already noticed, had worried even Adam Smith! But we must beware of sweeping social judgments. As we have seen, peasant proprietorship under many conditions—perhaps under most conditions—is an appalling producer of poverty and misery, and it is certainly not beyond the wit of man to devise techniques of management in large organizations that do not have the deleterious effects on character that a purely authoritarian or exploitative regime seems to produce.

There is no doubt that the age of colonialism is passing. The American Revolution and the separation of the South American countries from Spain and Portugal showed that colonial domination could not be maintained over semideveloped societies, as these countries were at the time of their revolutions. The extensive liquidation of colonialism in Asia as a result of the second World War is a further step in this process, and we see the same process now extending to Africa. All this is in ultimate accord with the ideal of a democratic and free world society. Domination turns out to be almost as bad for the dominant as for the dominated, and we see from innumerable examples in history that societies based on the domination of one class, color, race, or culture by another are essentially unstable. Domination corrupts the dominant and frequently purifies the dominated! Once man has experienced the possibility, therefore, of a truly free society that is not based on domination and the coercion of one group by another, he cannot be satisfied to be either dominating or dominated.

Nevertheless, the passing of political colonialism before the world is economically integrated presents some very grave problems. The advantage of political colonialism was that it relieved the colony of the costs of independence—which can be sometimes very high. Thus colonies did not have to maintain the apparatus of the sovereign state, especially in the shape of armed forces, and were often able to devote most of their budgets to public works and education. The present situation in the Indian subcontinent is a sad illustration of the costs of independence. The two countries into which it has been divided, India and Pakistan, feel obliged to spend a large proportion of their meager national resources for defense against each other

—resources which are desperately needed for economic development.

A further advantage of political colonialism was that private investors in the imperial country were usually willing to invest in the colonies for fairly moderate rates of return, because of the close political and social connections between the colony and the mother country, and because of the lessened degree of risk which this connection implied. The greater uncertainty that independence implies is paid for by the limitation of foreign investment only to those enterprises that yield very high rates of return. American investors, for instance, who might be willing to invest, say, in Texas, for a return of 6 per cent, may require a prospect of 30 per cent before they will invest in Venezuela, and may require 75 per cent before they will invest in Indonesia! The prospect of political instability and possible expropriation of foreign properties in these independent countries is great enough so that foreign investors are prudent in restricting their investments to those that earn very high rates of return, to compensate for the risk. This is a case, however, where private prudence may be public imprudence; the restriction of investments to those that offer a very high rate of return means that the amount of foreign investment is very small, which means in turn that the development of these countries is too slow to give them much confidence in Western methods; and this, of course, makes the possibility of revolution greater. A belief in the political instability of these countries may therefore to some extent be self-justifying.

It must not be thought, however, that foreign investment is the only, or even the most important key to economic development, though it can certainly be a help. Foreign investment without some kind of internal reorganization may be of very little help, and even without foreign investment internal reorganization of these countries might be able to set them on the road of economic growth. A major example of economic development accomplished almost entirely by internal reorganization is Japan. As we have observed earlier, the economic development of Japan after 1868 was accomplished by diverting an existing economic surplus derived from agriculture, which previously had supported the "unproductive labor" of servants and courtiers, into supporting "productive laborers"—workers who built factories, railroads, machines, and so on. Foreign investment played a very small part in this development, though in the early stages it contributed a little. Foreign "information" played an important part; the Japanese imported European technicians in considerable numbers to train their own people, and also sent their students abroad to learn what techniques the West had to offer. Japan also had the great advantage of being an island, accessible to ocean navigation and world trade; she was therefore able to take advantage of specialized production for a world market.

The internal reorganization of overpopulated, subsistence-agriculture countries like India and China presents problems of mountainous difficulty. It is not difficult to visualize the end product of an economic reorganization that would give these countries at least a "Low European" standard of life. This would involve—to use India as an example—getting some 200 million people off the land, and reorganizing the tiny farms into larger holdings. Then some—say 50 million—of the 200 million removed from agriculture could produce machines and implements with which the 100 million or so left on the land would be able to produce more food, in toto, than the 300 million or more who are now cultivating it. This would leave 150 million people who might produce additional conveniences and small luxuries—better houses, schools, water systems, bicycles, and so on. This is a very modest model; it might almost be called the "decent poverty" model. It is, however, a situation so much better than the mass of indecent poverty that now prevails that it is worth setting up as a not impossible aspiration.

The difficulties in the way of achieving even this modest goal are very severe. The sheer social and human upheaval involved in displacing 200 million people from agriculture is not pleasant to contemplate. There is a special difficulty here in that when people leave the villages there is a tendency for those who are left to increase their meager food consumption, so that there is little or no additional food to go from the villages to the towns. As long as the villager remains in the village the sense of communal and family responsibility insures that the available food supplies are shared with him; once he leaves the village he no longer is the direct responsibility of the community, and especially if he is not engaged in producing things that can be exchanged with the village for food, there is no reason to suppose that his leaving the village will much augment the food supply to the towns.

For this, and other reasons connected with the nature of Indian culture, the Government of India has launched an experiment in village development the results of which may affect the future of Asia for many generations to come. The theory is an essentially sound one: that economic development in a country like India must begin at the village level, because in Indian society the village, rather than the individual or the conjugal family, is the "organic" unit of social behavior. Development must begin within this unit, and in an integrated pattern, with public health, agricultural improvement, better roads, schools, wells, and sanitary arrangements, and improved local cottage industries, all moving forward together as a single front. Thus instead of thinking of uprooting 200 million people from their ancestral village homes and transplanting them in great—and inevitably ugly and congested—industrial cities, we think of taking a village of a few hundred people and shifting people out of agriculture within the village, or at least into neighboring communities and small towns, so that the people released by the reorganization of agriculture can still form part of the village community.

The obstacles even to this degree of reorganization are great. There are the encumbrances of ancient tradition—caste, sacred cows and monkeys, the whole fatalistic, "Oriental" attitude towards life and change in which man is seen as merely adjusting to nature rather than as mastering it. There is the ever-present problem of population increase, as we noted in Chapter 2, constantly threatening to eat up in the avalanche of new mouths the gains of improved techniques. The Indians seem to be well aware of this problem. It is one thing to be aware of it, however, and another thing to be able to do much about it! Nevertheless, in spite of the obstacles, one feels a surge of hope in India, that perhaps a way can be found for economic development that will not follow strictly the pattern of the West, but will move more within the framework of an ancient, more organic way of life.

One of the trickiest questions of a more purely economic nature in the development of the poor countries is that of land reform and land tenure. The plantation system, as we have seen, seems to go so far and no further; it runs up against a dead end in its inability to be more than an enclave of advanced techniques in a non-integrated society. "Domestic" plantations run into the same difficulty—the "latifundia" of ancient Rome, the great estates of East Europe, Hungary, Britain, South America, and so on. By creating a class society, with a small, propertied upper class of owners and managers and a large, generally rather poor, lower class of landless laborers, these systems spell their own eventual doom—there is at least this much truth in Marxism! On the other hand a "land reform" that merely involves splitting up the great estates into small, poor farms may do more harm than good, and may condemn a country to the miserable state of subsistence agriculture. The American solution by means of the *large,* highly capitalized family farm certainly seems to be much superior to either the inefficient, small-scale peasant agriculture or the not much better compulsory collectivization of Russia and China. Nevertheless, the American solution comes out of American culture and history, and it cannot simply be transplanted to other cultures and other histories. Here is a case where we may still be looking for new social forms and social inventions, and where new imaginative solutions are still to come.

In thinking about economic development we must not assume that the problem is merely one of the spread of the *existing* best techniques to those areas that do not practice them. In the first place, many of the particular techniques of the rich countries are not applicable to the peculiar physical or psychological conditions of poor countries. An amusing, though also rather tragic illustration of this point is the story of the American agricultural expert in Jordan, who persuaded the cultivators of some dry and stony fields to clear out the big stones so that more modern implements could be used—to find that crops could only be grown on these fields because the stones condensed the morning dew and mist and so gave the soil a little moisture just sufficient to raise the meager crop! Techniques that seem primitive often are the result of many centuries of adaptation to peculiar and difficult physical environments, and should not be hastily dismissed.

Then we must remember that the world is still in the middle of this amazing era of rapid technical and scientific discovery, and that new techniques are on the horizon which may revolutionize economic life and which may even be of particular application to poor countries. The development of atomic power promises to overcome some of the difficulties of countries that are deficient in other power sources, though one can easily be too optimistic about this in view of the fact that only rich countries at present can afford the high technology required to develop atomic power. Certain developments which may be just round the corner—food and fuel from algae, by use of solar energy; birth control by simple pills; new methods for detecting and treating the sources of violence—may lead to a technology in the underdeveloped countries that will be quite different from what we now have in the West.

In the face of the present world situation, then, it is extraordinarily difficult to prescribe economic policy for the underdeveloped countries, especially at the level of social institutions and legal frameworks. It can be argued with much cogency that in a society where private enterprise is not enterprising, much more in the way of government enterprise is necessary for economic development, and that at least in the early stages policy has to be much more "socialist" than would be appropriate in a country like the United States where there is a long tradition of development by private institutions. On the other hand, what does one do when the government itself is not enterprising! Or, if government is *too* enterprising, how do we ever raise up a generation of energetic and enterprising private entrepreneurs? When the meager economic surplus of a poor country is absorbed by the foolish extravagance of a Maharajah or an Arab Sheik, one can see point in the Marxist claim that the expropriators must be expropriated and the economic surplus devoted to the general use—especially to investment for economic development. On the other hand, it is impossible not to see in the ruthlessness and sheer human inefficiency of brontosaurian communism an almost Shakespearian tragedy of corruption—in this case the corruption of a not ignoble ideal by its inadequate social and ethical theory.

When one looks at the sheer geography of poverty—its extreme concentration in the tropics—one is tempted to acquiesce in the climatic determinism of Ellsworth Huntington or Markham,[2] which sees civilization as simply a by-product of human energy, and human energy as a simple function of the climate. To parody Pope—

> For forms of government let fools contest,
> Wherever climate's bad enough, is best!

If this is true, then the only effective source of economic development will be the air conditioner—the space heater has already pushed civilization about as far as it can go towards the poles, and the air conditioner must now complete the job towards the equator, to keep mankind at his most energetic 70° Fahrenheit! Like all other simple explanations, however, this too must be treated with the utmost reserve. Civilization is the result of information rather than of energy, and information is an enormously complex structure, not to be equated with any simple variable. Genetic, cultural, and institutional factors all play large roles in the over-all human complex. Nevertheless, the climate theories have this importance—that they do direct our attention to man himself as the source of all his creations, his institutions and his cultures, his wealth and his poverty.

[2] Ellsworth Huntington, *Civilization and Climate,* 3d ed. (New Haven: Yale Univ. Press, 1948); S. F. Markham, *Climate and the Energy of Nations* (Toronto: Oxford Univ. Press, 1947).

17

To Utopia – and beyond

We travel—faster than it seems—
Towards the substance of our dreams.
A world is almost at our door
Devoid of poverty and war.
But won't Utopia be dull?
Won't human nature soon annul
The tenuous gains of Social Science?
To that dim thought I shout defiance,
For at the end of every rope
There lies a little loop of hope.

The reader who penetrates this far will, it is hoped, have the impression that there is at least enough substance to the general principles of economic policy to write a book about it. Even though there are many questions which remain unanswered, and even though all conclusions must be qualified with *ifs* and *buts,* the book will have failed if the reader has not by this time received an impression of a substantial body of useful knowledge.

The growth of "science" of economic policy. A surprising amount of this knowledge is the product of the past thirty years; by far the greater part of it, at least in explicit form, is the product of the past two hundred years. This is not to say, of course, that those who directed the destinies of ancient or even of medieval nations were totally ignorant of economics, even if their knowledge may have been more implicit than explicit. Nevertheless, in the ancient and medieval world, success in government was more an accident of the wisdom of the governor rather than the product of a well-established and explicit body of knowledge. Government, in other words, was a craft rather than a science.

The skills of the craft *versus* the skills of science. The distinction is an important one. The skills of a craft are personal and implicit; they are passed on by apprenticeship, by the face to face transmission of a culture from the old to the young. Because of this they are unstable; the transmission may fail, especially where the skills are secret and scarce. The skills of a science, by contrast, are impersonal and explicit. They are passed on by teaching and reading; they are embodied in books and are widely accessible. Because of this these skills cumulate in a way quite impossible for the skills of a craft. The world of science literally operates as a superorganism, accumulating knowledge—and actually applying it—far beyond the powers of any one man to know or to apply. A single craftsman can make an exquisite violin, or a Damascene sword, or a Greek vase. It took an army of specialists to split the atom, not one of whom possessed all the knowledge necessary.

Is government becoming a science? The rise of the social sciences raises the question of whether government is not now in process of passing from a craft to a science. If this is so it represents one of the most important revolutions in the history of man, and the implications of such a change are far-reaching almost beyond present imaginings. There is still room, of course, for the sceptic. The social sciences present unusual, and perhaps insurmountable difficulties. The fact that man is himself part of the system he studies creates "noise" which may make it impossible to detect the subtler harmonies of man's nature and interactions. Man as a system, and still more therefore society as a system, is almost inconceivably complex; the crude machines of science, even the most elaborate guided missiles and electronic calculators are systems of a low order of complexity compared with the "fearfully and wonderfully made" machinery of the human organism. We are a long way from really explicit knowledge of man, although from our inside track we have a good deal of implicit knowledge of ourselves, as expressed in the humane crafts of literature, art, music, and even history. In spite of councils of economic advisors and institutes of social relations, then, government—whether of the state, of a business, or even of the personal life—will remain largely a craft for many generations to come, and hopes of reducing it to a science are premature, and perhaps even illusory.

Signs of progress: the economics of the two world wars. Yet when the sceptic has said his say and received his due, "the world still moves." Explicit knowledge about society and social processes does accumulate. As we look back on history we see mistakes which could have been avoided had those in power possessed some of the explicit knowledge which is now available to us. We get a sense of movement even as we contrast the economic history of the first and second World Wars, and the subsequent periods of reconstruction. The second World War, though much larger than the first, created less economic disturbance, and the reconstruction after it was smoother and faster. This is particularly evident in Germany. After a defeat in 1919 Germany staggered through a hyperinflation in 1923, a very delayed recovery up to 1929, and then a disastrous depression—even deeper than the general world depression—which played a great part in producing the pathological growth of National Socialism. After a much greater defeat in 1945 and almost complete internal collapse, the loss of almost half her territory, and the influx of millions of refugees, West Germany has made a recovery which now puts her in a position superior to that of her victorious neighbors. England, in spite of an intrinsically unfavorable world position, has avoided the mistakes of the 1920's and maintained full employment in the years following 1945—at some cost in terms of inflation and restrictions, it is true, but still the contrast with the 1920's is striking. One gets an even stronger impression of progress in economic thought when one compares the reports of the economic conferences which followed the first World War with those which followed the second; there is a curious air of emptiness about the first, of failure to understand the essential nature of problems which were pretty clear by 1945.

What is our Utopia? We must not be too self-congratulatory, of course. The great problem of world economic development still remains unsolved. International trade and (even more so) international investment are hampered by restrictions and uncertainties. And of course the great unresolved dilemma of the split world hangs over our heads and threatens us with total destruction. It is not that we have arrived. But to say this is not to deny movement, and while there is movement there is hope. We shall now examine the nature of this hope.

Suppose, for instance, that even such knowledge as we now have were applied on a world wide scale; what kind of a world would we have? What, in other words, is our Utopia? The word *Utopia* is not free of unfavorable connotations. It has an overtone of unreality, of speculative dreaming, out of touch with the hard realities of the world. Yet utopias are of enormous importance in directing the energies of men. If we move anywhere, it is because the reality we perceive does not conform to our ideal. The nature of the ideal more than anything else determines our direction of movement. It is our image of the future which draws us on into the future,[1] or even which repels us in other directions. Thus the utopias of the socialists have had a great effect on the history of the last century or so: the

[1] For this simple yet profound idea I am indebted to Dr. Fred Polak, whose great work, *De Toekomst is verleden tijd* documents in great detail the importance of the prevailing image of the future as the main driving force in cultural change and historical development.

"anti-utopias" represented by Aldous Huxley's *Brave New World* and George Orwell's *1984* have had an equally profound effect in checking the movement towards socialism.

It is by no means idle, therefore, to dream of the ideal, especially when there seem to be roads going towards the ideal, for it is these roads that we shall try to take.

The abolition of poverty. The first dream is that of a world in which poverty shall be no more; in which nobody shall go hungry, or lack adequate shelter and clothing, or be deprived of those things which are necessary for the development of the personality, for sheer lack of means. This is one of the great objectives of economic progress, and without economic progress this objective cannot be reached. The constant search for better ways of doing things, and the constant willingness to try new ways in the hope that they will prove better than the old, is the only road to economic power. Economic power in itself, however, will not automatically lead to the abolition of poverty. The fruits of progress, as manifested in the economic surplus, can be diverted to the purposes of a small group—to the extravagance of a court of the magnificence of a church, to the luxury of the rich, even to the pomp of death. If the fruits of progress are to be widely distributed there must be an active concern for economic justice, embodied in institutions which prevent the undue concentration of economic power. Here the economic problem and the political one go hand in hand; unless the political institutions of society grant power to the masses, there is no guarantee that economic power will be used to abolish poverty.

Obstacles to progress: (1) *War:* For the first time in history, with the possible exception of a few isolated and highly favored communities, the abolition of poverty seems to be a practicable ideal, and a world seems possible in which even the poorest will have enough to eat, a roof over his head, and the minimum means for health and decency. There is, however, a long road to tread before this happy condition is reached. Today perhaps a quarter of the world's population lives in societies where the abolition of poverty is feasible and within sight of being accomplished. But the other three quarters live in societies where the great majority of people are ill fed, ill clothed, ill housed, and tens—perhaps hundreds—of millions are constantly on the edge of starvation. The great human enterprise will be to raise the productivity of these societies to the point where they too can abolish poverty. Even under the most favorable circumstances this will be a long and difficult task. There are, moreover, great obstacles in the way, the greatest of which are war and procreation. Even in this period of relative peace, war and the threat of war tie up in armaments resources desperately needed for investment in economic development. Indeed, if we could devote to economic development half the resources which are now devoted to instruments of destruction, the problem of poverty might be solved in fifty years. What is worse, the more resources are devoted to armaments, the greater the threat of war. As we all become less secure the probability of a catastrophe of cosmic proportions becomes ever larger. The solution of this problem is beyond the scope of this book, and possibly beyond the present intellectual and emotional capacities of mankind. Unless it is solved soon, however, man may be written off as what has been called an unsuccessful experiment in curiosity.

(2) *Population:* Even if we succeed in solving the problem of war, the problem of population remains with us. The fruits of economic progress can be wasted in two ways—in extravagant uses of the economic surplus in war and luxury, or in disappearance of the economic surplus through unrestrained growth of population. If a permanent high-level society is to be achieved it must have either a stable population or a growth of population that does not outpace the growth of output. It is one of the ironies of our age that many of the modern techniques which are most easily introduced into the poor areas are those which reduce the death rate, especially the infant death rate, without affecting the birth rate. A few relatively simple and cheap public health measures, especially in tropical areas, can bring about spectacular declines in the death rate; this has happened in Ceylon, in Formosa, and in many parts

of the world; as a result a population explosion is in progress which threatens catastrophic famines in another generation or two. The history of Ireland may be repeated in many parts of the world. Nor is this a phenomenon which affects only the poor countries. In the United States and in Europe a new population explosion is also under way, produced in this case not so much by a fall in the death rate as by a change in attitudes towards the family and the consequent rise in the birth rate. If this continues it will raise serious problems of overpopulation even for the United States in a period, say, of a hundred years.

The difficulty here is that no developed society has produced any control mechanism for population to substitute for the crude control of food shortages in poor societies; if people in the United States, for instance, suddenly decide to have families of four and five children instead of two or three, there is no machinery to counteract this decision short of economic pressures which might not manifest themselves for decades. Furthermore, any such controls would be repugnant to the spirit of free and progressive societies. The only two "natural" population controls are food shortages and "place" shortages. If a population is pressing on the means of subsistence a rise in birth rate simply results in fewer children surviving to maturity. Similarly, if the society has a set of well defined "places," so that anyone who fails to find a place does not survive, excess children are killed and the society simply fills each place as death renders it vacant. Both these solutions are unacceptable to high-level societies. Just how to reconcile population controls with high ethical standards and a high degree of personal freedom remains an unsolved problem.

(3) *Exhaustion of natural resources:* The third great obstacle in the way of the establishment of a permanent high-level society is the possible exhaustion of natural resources. Present high-level societies are based on techniques which involve the using up of "geological capital," especially fossil fuels and mineral deposits. The exhaustion of many of these resources is not indefinitely remote, and especially if the rest of the world

begins to catch up to American standards of consumption, the exhaustion of conventional fuels and of most important mineral deposits may be a matter at most of a few hundred years—a brief span even in the perspective of human history. Permanent high-level society therefore must rest on somewhat different techniques from those we have at present. The power outlook actually is fairly bright, with the development of atomic energy and the probability of great technical advances in the use of direct solar energy. The problem of mineral deposits may be more difficult; the result of most economic activity is to diffuse the useful elements present in nature in concentrated form; this process of increasing economic entropy cannot go on forever. With sufficient energy and appropriate techniques, however, the reversal of this process of diffusion is possible, and processes such as the fixation of nitrogen from the air and the extraction of magnesium from the sea are anti-diffusionist even now, and perhaps foreshadow an age which will be independent of natural concentrations. The technical prospect therefore seems to encourage at least a moderate optimism, provided that the sources of human ingenuity and inventiveness do not dry up.

Utopian institutions *versus* ideal functions. The goals and the general conditions of our Utopia—the permanent high-level society—are fairly clear; the particular institutions are much less so. This is unavoidable, and for a very fundamental reason. The utopias of man's imagination, from Sir Thomas More on, are all static societies, repeating themselves in a stationary state of endless and unchanging perfection. This perhaps is what not only gives them an air of unreality, but makes them slightly repulsive. I have never read of any Utopia, imaginary or attempted, in which I have had any longing to live. The Utopia of economic policy, however, is dynamic; it encourages economic progress and individual freedom, and it moves forward into an ever uncertain future. It is neither a self-contained spinning ball of the stationary state nor a train on the track of a planned future; it is a mighty vessel provided with a rudder, radar, and a compass to keep it from going on to the rocks, but free to roam the great seas of the future wherever the fancy of its crew may lead. Thus, we do not emerge with a clear picture of the future institutions of the society, but with the notion of a set of *functions* which must be performed, but which might be carried out by a wide range of different institutions. There is the function of *government*—the great art of steermanship, whereby the cumulative processes that lead to disaster are avoided by countervailing action. There is the function of *enterprise*, whereby new combinations of resources are tried out and new techniques of doing things are developed. There are the functions of *justice*, whereby discontents are brought to the surface and expressed in ways that lead to creative resolutions of conflict. There are the functions of *integration* which must underlie the institutions of justice—the processes in society which bind people one to another, which create a community of loyalties and concern, so that the good of all becomes the quest of each. The particular institutions which embody these functions are likely to vary from time to time; unless they are embodied in some institutions, however, the society will not survive.

Can Utopia produce Utopian characters? Behind all the dreams of Utopia are the aspirations of man himself. Insofar as all man's institutions are reflections of his inner life—his ideas and knowledge and values—one of the critical questions for human betterment is the extent to which "human nature" itself has within it the seeds of destruction of the best institutions which man can construct. There is a complex process of action and reaction at work here; man's institutions are created by him, and yet he is created by his institutions. The problem of how the institutions of society determine the character of its members through the experiences which they channel, especially in childhood, and how in turn the character of a society's individuals molds its institutions is the whole problem of social dynamics. It is a problem however which admits of no simple solution. We know something, for instance, of the effects of various types of childhood experience on adult character, but the processes by which character is built up are complex and we cannot pretend to more than a most superficial understanding. If we put the question in a bald form: "What government policies would promote the development of fine, generous, well rounded, sensitive, responsible persons?" the complexity of the problem and the extent of our ignorance becomes immediately apparent. Without further insights into the formation of character and personality economic policy may be self-defeating: increased riches may lead to degeneration of character (it frequently has); increased security may lead to sloth and boredom; increased freedom may lead to licentiousness and irresponsibility; and the most excellent institutions may in time be perverted because they do not produce the types of personality which enable them to survive. There is a modicum of truth in the Marxist contention that institutions determine character, but the narrowing of this general principle to the proposition that private property is the source of all vice and that man's nature will flower to perfection under the institutions of socialism is naive in the extreme!

The need for ethical theory. It is clear, therefore, that economics is not enough; we must have an ethic, or at least an ethical theory. Simply at the level of social science we must know more about how the ideals and value systems of individuals are formed, for it is these ideals—whether conscious or unconscious—which largely determine individual behavior in particular situations. If a society produces by its operations ideals and value systems which are incompatible with its institutions, then it cannot survive. From a more fundamental and philosophical point of view we cannot avoid raising the question of the *validity* and objectivity of ideals and value systems. The social scientist perhaps can avoid this issue, treating values simply as part of the social landscape to be investigated—social species to be classified, described, and pursued to their origins and their consequences. If we rest here, however, we face the possible nightmare of the manipulative society, in which ideals can be manufactured at will by a sufficiently knowledgeable, unscrupulous, and powerful elite. It is this fear of the manipulative society which lies behind many of the "anti-utopias" of today—the fear that knowledge leads to damnation-through-manipulation, not to the extension and purification of essential human freedom. The deep pessimism of existentialism likewise reflects a loss of faith in the objectivity of values, in the "essences" of truth and goodness. This existentialist despair, however, is self-justifying; it produces a negative image of the future, resignation to evil, and a loss of faith in human betterment; while it is in many ways noble, it is destructive of hope, because it is destitute of faith, and eventually destroys charity.

It is clearly beyond the scope of this volume to solve the great problem of the objectivity of values—a problem which has baffled philosophers and theologians from the beginnings of speculative thought, and in which there are still no solutions which command immediate and universal acceptance. Nevertheless, a brief glance at what might be called descriptive ethics—ethics treated at the level of social science—will at least throw light on some of the problems which must be faced, and on some of the deeper issues which confuse and frustrate man in his search for betterment.

Value systems as simple orderings. The economist starts with the value concept as a *simple ordering*. We have some kind of "field" which sets out various *possible* situations, or elements—A, B, C, etc. If, then, these possible situations can be arranged on a line, with "better" ones at the top and "worse" ones at the bottom, we have a simple value ordering. Such an ordering involves two concepts: the concept of "nextness" and the concept of the "superior direction." The first is satisfied if we can simply arrange the elements in order, say from left to right, without any implication that "leftness" is superior to "rightness." For the second to be satisfied one direction must represent "improvement" and the other "worsening." That is to say, we look over a field of possible situations and arrange them in a "class list" with a "top" and a "bottom." Any situation which is nearer the top than another one is "better" than it. This is what we mean by a "value system" in its simplest form.

Numbers as a value system. One of the simplest systems which has this property is a set of numbers, for any set of arbitrary numbers can be arranged in an unequivocal order of "nextness," and if we adopt a convention such that, for instance, big numbers are "better" than small, the ordering also has *value direction.* Thus take any arbitrary group of numbers, say 8, 3, 25, 2.8, π, $\sqrt{2}$. These can be arranged in a simple order, ranging from the smallest to the largest: $\sqrt{2}$, 2.8, 3, π, 8, 25, and if we adopt as a convention, the bigger the better (the smaller the better will do just as well, as for instance in golf scores!) we can tell immediately which of two figures is "better." This property of sets of numbers is the main reason why quantification is a great help in the making of value judgments, and why, for instance, we find it helpful to reduce complex situations to numerical indices such as "incomes," "price levels," "marks," and so on. The concept of a value system, however, is much more general than that of a set of numbers, and many situations are submitted to value orderings which cannot be matched with a set of numbers. Sets of numbers also have properties which value systems do not have. Thus, in the example given above the interval between 8 and 25 is greater than the interval between 2.8 and 3; given a set of numbers we can arrange the intervals between them in a value ordering, and the intervals between the intervals, and so on. A simply ordered value system does not have this property. Thus, if value systems are expressed by sets of numbers we stand in some danger of reading into the value system properties which belong to the set of numbers but not to the value system which it matches. For example, the difference between an income of $50,000 and an income of $51,000 is not the same as the difference between incomes of $5000 and $6000, though numerically the intervals are identical.

The ethical problem arises out of the conflict of value systems. As long as a value system is thought of as describing the private preferences of an individual, the problem of ethics does not arise. Tastes are tastes, and nothing more can be said about them. Some economists have taken the position that individual preferences must simply be taken as the data of economics, and can neither be judged nor compared. This position is an abdication from ethics, though at a certain level of abstraction it makes sense; it is a useful exercise, at least, to see how far we can get in social theory without ethics. In matters of social policy, however, we cannot get very far without ethics—that is, without considering the interrelations, conflicts, and hierarchies of value systems.

The hierarchy of value systems. Even a single individual does not usually have only one value ordering. He may say, for instance, "A is better than B for me, but B is better than A for my family, or for the nation, or for the world at large." An individual thus may have a number of value systems, each corresponding to a certain level of responsibility or interest—the person, the family, the town, the firm, the nation, the world. Then the question arises as to the value ordering of the value systems themselves. This may not be a simple ordering: under some circumstances he may value his personal value ordering more than his social value ordering; that is, he says, "A is better than B for me, and B is better than A for society, but in this case I prefer what is better for me to what is better for society." Under other circumstances the social value ordering may dominate; the individual sacrifices his personal interest for the sake of the interest of the larger group. Some of the tension between "ethics" conceived as a set of obligations and the hard realities of personal interest arise perhaps from the complexity and overlappings in these ratings of value *systems*. In what might be called "preaching" ethics—the sort of thing which is inculcated by sermon and precept—there is a common assumption that there is a simple ordering of value systems—that the "higher" value systems are those which involve the greatest degree of responsibility; thus, the family interest should predominate over the individual, the nation over the family, and though many are not prepared to go the next step it would seem logical to make the world interest predominate over the national interest. The ethical problem is therefore posed in terms of an obligation to serve the larger interest which conflicts with the "sinful" desire to act according to the smaller interest. There is a great deal of truth in this picture; nevertheless, it is perhaps oversimplified. There are certain situations when the dominance of the smaller interest might be defended—the great artist, perhaps, who sacrifices his family and friends to his personal artistic development, and some would no doubt add the patriot who in certain circumstances puts his nation above the world.

What determines the dominant value system? The extent to which the larger interest will dominate the smaller in the behavior of an individual depends on the degree to which he *identifies* himself with the larger interest. This raises the whole difficult problem of the sources of identification and integration in society—a problem which is very far from solved and to which we can give no more than passing mention. What is it, for instance, that makes one person generous and selfless and another mean and selfish? Ordinary theories of conditioning, or even the game-theory view that behavior moves towards the highest "payoffs" (a reincarnation of the old economic doctrine of the maximization of utility) are quite inadequate here because the question is not what are the payoffs but in what currency should they be paid! What is it that makes one man accept the currency of personal power and pleasure, while another accepts the currency of the general good? This is a question to which at the present time there seems to be no good answers.

The contribution of role theory. The role theory of the social psychologists offers a clue to this problem, though it does not have enough content to yield a satisfactory solution. According to this view people do what is expected of them; a man has an image of the role which he is supposed to play in society and adjusts his value system to fit this role. Thus, a quite ordinary and selfish person who becomes President of the United States will find himself acting in a large and responsible manner, simply because the requirements of the role impose themselves on him. There is, of course, always some interaction between the person and the role, and the role itself may be changed in some degree by the nature of the person occupying it. Nevertheless, society and social organizations are structures of roles rather than of persons, and if we want to build good characters we must create the roles which call forth the desired personal qualities. In this view, then, the organizational structure of society plays a large part in creating characters appropriate to it. The view must not be pressed too far, for it would almost deny the possibility of human freedom; there must be a place for the innovator and the nonconformist who is a creator of new roles and who is not simply shaped by the slot in which society has placed him. Nevertheless, there is enough truth in it to make the search for proper organizational structures an important one. It is no use preaching responsibility if the role structure creates irresponsibility; it is the life situation which is always the most effective preacher.

Responsibility *for* and *to* others: tyranny, paternalism, democracy. As an illustration of the above principle consider the difficulties which arise when people are responsible *for* persons without having responsibility *to* them. Wherever the actions of a decision-maker affects the lives and fortunes of others he is, in a sense, responsible *for* them. When those who are affected by the actions of a decision-maker have some control over these actions, can express their approval or disapproval to him, and can if necessary remove him from his position, then the decision-maker is responsible *to* those who have this ultimate power over him. We may distinguish three cases. The first is tyranny, in which the decision-maker is neither responsible *to* those who are affected by his decisions, nor does he accept responsibility *for* them, but makes his decisions without regard to their welfare. The second is paternalism, in which the decision-maker is not responsible *to* those who are affected by him, but nevertheless accepts responsibility *for* their welfare, in the sense that he makes his decisions *on behalf* of those who are affected. The weakness of paternalism is that the judgments of the decision-maker regarding what he thinks is the welfare of those whom he affects may not correspond to the judgments of those who are affected. The third condition is democracy, in which the decision-maker is responsible both *for* and *to* those affected by his decision. In this case he must act not only according to his private notions of what constitutes the welfare of others, but at least in some degree according to notions of the affected persons themselves—that is, if he wishes to remain in the role. It might be of course that a man who did not feel responsible for those whom he affects might act in such a way that those to whom he was responsible still were willing to keep him in the role. Nevertheless, institutions which make people responsible *to* those whom they affect are likely to set up role expectations in which responsibility *for* is encouraged.

The "institutions" and the "habit" of responsibility. It seems to be impossible, however, to organize society so that everyone is responsible *to* the people who are affected by his actions. The actions even of ordinary men may have repercussions far beyond their immediate circle. The actions of chiefs of state, of heads of corporations, of union leaders, and so on may affect the lives of millions of people far beyond the circle of their particular organizations. This terrible absence of institutions of responsibility is seen most clearly in international relations, where the whim of a minor potentate may plunge the whole world into war, and where national governments are constantly making decisions which affect profoundly the lives of millions who are "foreigners" and to whom, therefore, these governments are not responsible. On a smaller scale one sees the same principle operating in economic organizations, where, for instance, a decision reached by a great corporation or by an important union may affect the lives of millions of people who have no say in the matter at all, and who are not even remotely connected with the organizations to which these decision-makers are responsible. Some of the burden for responsible decision-making therefore must rest on the general "habit of responsibility" and the over-all sense of community. The stronger this sense of community becomes—the more, that is to say, people take account of influences beyond their immediate power complex in making their decisions—the less likely we are to run into the arbitrary and tyrannical exercise of power and the easier it becomes to set up institutions of responsibility. It is by a combination of good will and good institutions that society moves forward; neither alone is sufficient. In our Utopia, then, the institutions of responsibility are sufficiently broad to enable the sense of community and the institutions of integration to perform the residual task of avoiding tyranny.

Is social conflict inevitable? The possibility of "peace." This is a pretty picture, the pessimist may argue, but what of conflict? Will not the inevitable clash of interests in society disrupt it? Suppose, for instance, that we have two leaders who are responsible to two different sets of people whose interests are opposed. A single man cannot be responsible to both groups; nobody can serve two masters. The ideal of universal responsibility, therefore, is a myth; society is a snarling pack of irreconcilable interests, and only a strong government responsible only to itself and concerned only with its own preservation can prevent society from disintegrating into anarchy. This is the view of Machiavelli and Hobbes; this is the "dismal science" of politics just as the Malthusian doctrine creates the "dismal science" of economics. Fortunately, one hopes that, as with Malthus, the "dismal theorems" can be stated in a cheerful form. *If* men are pure individuals it is true that the choice lies between anarchy and tyranny, and of these tyranny is probably preferable. The possibility of a more cheerful political science breaks through if we can deny the major premise, and suppose that men are not pure individuals, but that as they live together they grow into a sense of identification with a broader and broader community. Two movements in the history of man make this more cheerful view tenable. One is the sheer increase in his mobility and image of the world, which draws him out of his immediate environment and immediate interests and leads him to identify himself with larger and larger communities. We have seen the community grow from the family to the tribe, to the city-state, to the national state, to the sense of world community we see beginning today. The other is the growth of skill in the resolution of conflicts—that is, in substitutes for anarchy which are *not* tyranny. War slowly but surely gives place to law, and even law to mediation and conciliation, to mutual compromise and cooperation. We would be blind to suppose that this transformation has already been accomplished; we would be equally blind not to see that it is going on, and that in spite of frequent setbacks there is a growing skill in what might be called creative rather than destructive conflict, even at the level of world society. It is not too much to hope that this process might go on until *peace*—meaning *a process of continuous, creative resolution of conflict*—becomes a settled habit of mind and a secure institution of society on a world-wide scale.

Beyond Utopia: the prudential and the heroic ethic. The process of moving toward an ideal is exciting, and challenging. Suppose, however, that we arrive at our Utopia; would we not find it terribly dull, and would not this very dullness destroy it? This is not an unimportant question, and it becomes of practical importance long before Utopia is reached. The ethical systems by which men are moved fall roughly into two types, which may be called the "prudential" and the "heroic." The prudential ethic is of course that of the economist this is the ethic of Benjamin Franklin and other respectable, sensible people. In this ethic it is better to be richer than poorer, it is better to save your life than to lose it, it is better to be healthy than sick, better to be happy than miserable, better to be secure than insecure, better to get along with people than to offend them. This is the ethic of moderation, of the golden mean, of "nothing too much," of economic rationality, of calculated less or more. It does not exclude altruism, provided that it is a reasonable and moderate altruism; its hallmark however is calculation in the face of scarcity.

By contrast we have many varieties of the heroic ethic, of which the two main kinds are the religious and the military. This is the ethic of Jesus and of St. Francis—"to give and not to count the cost, to labor and ask for no reward." At another level it is the ethic of the Charge of the Light Brigade—"theirs not to reason why, theirs but to do and die." At yet another level it is the ethic of Kings College Chapel: "Tax not the Royal Saint with vain expense," says Wordsworth, because "High Heaven rejects the lore of nicely calculated less or more."

The religious, military, and romantic revolt against the prudential is something that must always be reckoned with in man's makeup: it may not move many men, but those it moves are forces to be reckoned with; they are the great disturbers of the smooth course of events. The great faiths have achieved their triumphs not by appeal to the prudential ethic, but by an appeal to the heroic in man; this is true even of secular faiths like democracy and communism. The challenge to do the impossible, to defy the niggling counsels of prudence, and to so escape man's perpetual prison of scarcity retains a perpetual appeal; indeed, were it not for this, man would lose some of his most attractive and distinctive elements.

The synthesis of the heroic and the prudential. It seems to be necessary for man to combine in some degree both these value systems, however incompatible they may seem to be. Without the heroic, man is a dull dog, a creature of the counting house, a cold, calculating, earthbound creature, incapable even of reaching his calculated ends because in fulfillment there is always a hidden frustration. Without the prudential, man is an impossible dreamer, flying to the sun and falling into the sea, ending in a nightmare of illusion and unreality, fantasy and madness. Somewhere between the dullness of the prudential and the madness of the heroic there must be an ideal human posture toward the splendid and dreadful universe in which man finds himself. Because of the basic incompatibility of these two ideals, however, it may be impossible for a single individual to attain this ideal: we cannot be prudentially heroic or heroically prudent. But perhaps in the larger framework of society these incompatibles may be resolved: the heroes break through the crust of the established order to set great dynamic processes in motion—these are the prophets, the saints, the poets, the conquerors, the revolutionaries. Then the prudent come along behind them and fit the pieces together into a new establishment; these are the priests and the popes, the professors, the politicians, and the business men. Without the heroes society soon settles down into a dull and self-perpetuating equilibrium; without the prudent society flies apart, disintegrates into chaos. Just how we will provide for this constant interaction of the heroic and the prudential in our Utopia is a question which I gladly leave to the Utopians!

Economics as a safeguard against imprudence. Economists, of course, are prudential almost by profession, and the principles of economic policy which have been outlined in this work are, in the main, prudential principles. The world which it envisages is not a world of heroes; it relies on exchange, on the great prudential principle of *quid pro quo* and not on the heroic attributes of love and self-sacrifice to make the world go round. Its model is the comfort of the thermostat rather than the adventure of the skyrocket. Obviously this does not say the last word about human aspirations. Even the skyrocket, however, must have some solid ground from which to take off. We may need to go beyond prudence: but the imprudent is not necessarily the heroic. In a sense, the task of the economist is to set up warnings against the merely imprudent—the policy which thinks it is prudent and is not. He does not point the road to heaven; he just puts up a few danger signs on the sharp curves and dead ends of earth. We might almost say that the economist's plea is to reserve heroism for those enterprises which really demand it—the great enterprises of the human spirit. In the twentieth century the world has suffered from a great excess of romantic heroism in places where prudence is more appropriate—in Communism, in Nazism, in revolution, and in war. If certain aspects of economic policy can be taken out of the heroic sphere and put firmly in the prudential, the heroic spirit will do less damage and can be liberated to more appropriate tasks.

Index